# The Descendants of Josias Cooke

## for Seven Generations

Compiled by

Thomas F. Cook

ISBN: 978-1-69-584884-9

1.1

**Introduction**

This is a genealogy in the standard NEHGS format, but it only documents a single generation of each female line — it stops when the woman married into another family and her children had a different surname. This is the only way I could keep the size manageable.

The genealogy charts seven generations of descendants of Josias Cooke. Charles Abby Cook who is the subject of a companion book is #2053. As far as numbering, there are gaps which may seem like errors (e.g., Benjamin Cooke is #20, while the next person in the list, Desire Cooke is #56.) The numbers that are missing represent descendants of the women, whose surnames were no longer Cooke but another man's. They are in my computer database, but to include them in this printed book would make it too large. In the example I've used, the missing people are surnamed Snow and Harding.

 I've tried to include notations about *Mayflower* connections, as well as anything interesting I've found and I have also included some neutral bits about American history. If there's a *Mayflower* connection I've added this little symbol. I've also added a few pointing finger ☞ symbols where something might be of interest. One example is Amaziah or Maziah Harding (on page 2.8). Maziah Harding was Josias Cooke's grandson and was mentioned in his will. There's quite a bit to read in various places about this man, as he is one of the earliest executions in America. His neighbor's testimony is very interesting, especially as it shows how differently they spoke in the early 1700s. Apparently rum was involved.

Everything has sources, but I have not marked each individual fact with a footnote which is regrettable. I hope to correct this problem in another edition. However, I have included a bibliography of all the sources I used. I have also personally gone through all the original Massachusetts vital records in microfiche form. But also, because of the *Mayflower* connection, the first five generations have been exhaustively researched by two works in particular: *The Mayflower Families for Five Generations: Stephen Hopkins*, and the article: *"Joshua Cook (Josiah, Josiah) of Eastham, Mass.,"* which appeared in the New England Historical and Genealogical Register in 1972.

Almost all of the Provincetown research is my own and based on the Provincetown Vital Records, as well as the Ferguson Manuscript which is held by the Provincetown library.

One more important note. Josias Cooke was not related to the *Mayflower* passenger Francis Cooke. But it's the most common mistake out there and has only been made worse by people using the internet to copy and paste. A lot of people will make the connection and add "this needs more research." But it doesn't. It's been proven many times over that they were not related, and the latest proof is genetic. Descendants of

Francis Cooke are not genetically related to descendants of Josias Cooke.

Generally I've tried to use the term "American Indian," rather than "Indian" or "Native American." The reason is that even though calling the inhabitants of the new world "Indian" was a mistake made by Columbus, it was never corrected and its use has persisted. In his *A People's History of the United States*, Howard Zinn used it "with reluctance." "Native American" is also a term that has sometimes been used by Caucasians about themselves, in order to discriminate against newer immigrants like the Irish, so I've chosen to stay away from it for now.

Page numbering reflects the generation and the actual page number of the book. So page 3.10 means 3rd generation and page 10 of the overall book.

# 1<sup>st</sup> Generation

1. **Josias Cooke** was born in 1610 in England. He emigrated before 1634 and lived in Plymouth, Mass. With his family and six other families he founded the town of Eastham, Mass. in 1645. He was a farmer, tavern keeper, and sometimes the constable. He signed a will on 22 Sep 1673 in Eastham, Mass. and died on 17 Oct 1673 at the age of 63. He is presumed to be buried in Eastham Cove Burying Ground, Eastham, Mass. His name also appears as Josiah. The "S" was probably silent.

He is not related to Francis Cooke, one of the passengers on *The Mayflower*. Most recently, this has been proven by genetics. Genetics also has recently shown that he was probably related to an Aaron Cooke, who was from Thorncombe, England, born in 1612 and crossed the Atlantic on the *Mary & John* in 1636. What relation they had to each other is unknown. They could have been brothers, cousins or may not have known of each other's existence at all. Any relationship could only be determined by records in England, if they exist.

Josias Cooke and **Elizabeth (Deane) Ring** were married on 16 Sep 1635 in Plymouth, Mass. Elizabeth (Deane) Ring, daughter of William Ring and Mary Durant, was baptized on 23 Feb 1600/1 in Ufford, Suffolk, England. She emigrated with her mother and siblings before 1629. She married first, Stephen Deane in September, 1629 in Plymouth, Mass. With Stephen she had Elizabeth, b. abt 1630 who married Stephen Twining; Merriam, b. about 1632, who married late in life and had no children; and Susannah, b. abt. 1634, who married Stephen Snow (brother of Anna Cooke's husband Mark). After her husband died, Elizabeth returned to Plymouth and died there in 1687 at the age of 86.

Stephen Deane arrived in Plymouth as a single man in 1623 on *The Fortune*. He became a freeman before 1633. He was given permission to operate a mill in Plymouth in 1632 and was allowed to take as payment one pottle per bushel (2 quarts). From the language of the agreement, it was clear he had previously operated a mill farther away from Plymouth. He and Elizabeth lived in a house on what is now called Billington Sea.

He died unexpectedly and a year later Josias Cooke became her husband and father to the three girls. His will shows that he believed them to be his daughters but also acknowledged that Stephen Deane was the grandfather of their children. After Elizabeth died, his adopted daughter Merriam got into a significant fight with his daughter Bethia and son Josiah. The fight was eventually settled and recorded in the court records.

Josias acquired many tracts of land either by purchase or through grants. Even this early in the formation of the U.S., some people were considered "old comers" and some were considered "new." Josias was not an "old comer," as he was almost certainly a servant for his first years in America, but he obtained a position of respect and importance during his fifteen years in Plymouth. As a result, he was granted by the Plymouth court a number of pieces of property, mostly south and southwest of Plymouth. He also purchased at least one property on the "elbow" of Cape Cod. On the following page is a copy of the deed for some land near Chatham, Mass. that Josias purchased from the American Indians Pompmo and Simon his son. I have read that Pompmo sold a lot of land to the English and sometimes more than once. The rule was that if a person like Josias purchased a piece of land from an American Indian, it had to be registered at Plymouth for it to be legal. The Nickerson genealogy states that a piece of land William Nickerson bought was also purchased by Josias. But Josias registered it, so it belonged to him until at some later date a descendant married into the Nickerson Family and it became Nickerson land again. Much of that land is now Nickerson State Park between Brewster and Orleans.

In 1645 Josias and the probably pregnant Elizabeth Cooke, with their five daughters and six other prominent Plymouth families moved from Plymouth to the middle of Cape Cod, and founded there the town of Eastham, Mass. The event was recorded by William Bradford toward the end of his history of Plymouth plantation. Shortly after they had settled in this new area, Josias's only son was born.

Josias Cooke and Elizabeth (Deane) Ring had the following children:

2    i.    **Anna Cooke**, born aft 1636; married **Capt or Lieut. Mark SNOW**, 18 Jan 1654, Eastham, Mass.; died 25 Jul 1656, Eastham, Mass.

3    ii.    **Bethia Cooke**, born aft 1638, Plymouth, Mass.; married **Joseph HARDING**, 4 Apr 1660.

4    iii.    **Josiah Cooke**, born 1645, Eastham, Mass.; married **Deborah HOPKINS**, 27 Jul 1668, Eastham, Mass.; died 31 Jan 1731/2, Eastham, Mass.

1666        Prence. Gov.

Know all men by those present that I Pompmo and Simon my son, have freely and fully bargained and sold unto Josias Cooke of Eastham to him and his heirs or assigns forever a parcel of upland commonly called Weequasett containing thereon three score acres be it more or less lying near Mannamoyet and a parcel of meadow about six acres be it more or less adjoining; This land to begin at a little slough this side the meadow called Lequansett and the upland to run by the waterside to the short cove toward Mannamoyett and so to bear up into the woods as it may hold good three score acres more or less. Also a little island that lyeth against Pottanumaquatt  toward the beach containing about ten or twelve acres be it more or less this island commonly called [B______] and further also a little piece of meadow on this side toward Pottanumaquatt  about half an acre commonly called Weesataquash; all those above said lands with every part and parcel thereof with all and several the appurtenances, privileges and ____________' today we the said Pompmo and Simon have freely and fully bargained and sold to Josias Cooke to him his heirs and assigns forever all the abovesaid parts and parcels of upland and meadow with all and singular the rights belonging thereunto, for and in consideration thereof the said Josias Cooke doth give unto the said Pompmo and Simon the sum of five pound in hand and paid until Pompmo and Simon this five and twentieth day of October, 1665. And further, the said Josias Cooke doth promise that if Mr. Thomas Prence shall at anytime come toward Pottanumaquatt, if Pompmo or Simon shall desire him to view this land and he shall judge it meet that Josias Cooke shall give the above said Pompmo or Simon more than [it] has already paid, the said Josias Cooke is willing to give accordingly, as shall be judged meet by Mr. Thomas Prence.

Signed sealed and delivered                          The mark of Simon and a seal
In the presence of                              This deed of sale of land was acknow-
Thomas Thornton                          ledged by Simon before me Thomas Prence
The mark of E. Lawrence                          Gov. the day and year above written.
The mark of F. Peter                                    The mark of Pompmo


This 7th day of November, 1665 we being
at Pottanumaquatt Simon did agree with
Josias Cooke that the land sold to him should
begin at a valley or slough, this is on the side
Ralston Tarr Pitts Toward Pottanumaquatt,
and to run as the valley runs to the Land
that to be the boundary at this end.
Joseph Freeman
Joseph Rogers

                              [I believe these scribblings are the notes of
                              registration at Plymouth.]

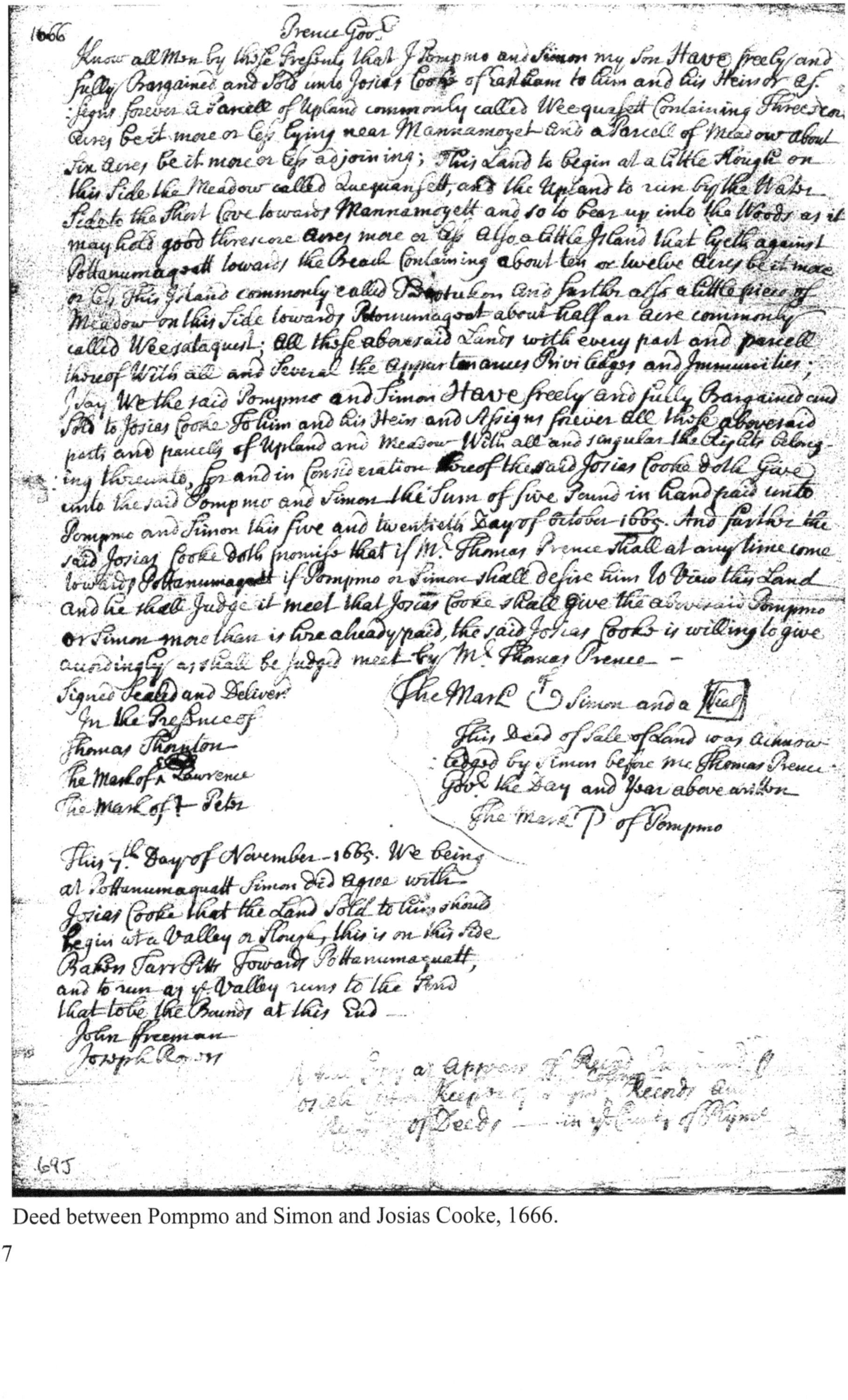

1666

Prence Goo[r]

Know all Men by these Presents that J Pompmo and Simon my Son Have freely and
fully Bargained and Sold unto Josias Cooke of Eastham to him and his Heirs or Af-
: Signs forever a Parcell of Upland commonly called Weequasset Containing Threescore
Acres be it more or Less Lying near Mannamoyet and a Parcell of Meadow about
Six Acres be it more or Less adjoining; This Land to begin at a little Rough on
this Side the Meadow called Quequanfett, and the Upland to run by the Water
Side to the Short Cove towards Mannamoyett and so to bear up into the Woods as it
may hold good threescore Acres more or Less Also a little Island that lyeth against
Pottanumaqrett towards the Beach Containing about ten or twelve Acres be it more
or Less this Island commonly called Ptootubon and farther also a little piece of
Meadow on this Side towards Potanumagoot about half an acre commonly
called Weesataquest; all these aforesaid Lands with every part and parcell
thereof With all and Several the Appurtenances Priviledges and Immunities;
J Say We the said Pompmo and Simon Have freely and fully Bargained and
Sold to Josias Cooke To him and his Heirs and Assigns forever all those abovesaid
parts and parcelly of Upland and Meadow With all and singular the Rights belong-
:ing thereunto, for and in Consideration thereof the said Josias Cooke doth Give
unto the said Pompmo and Simon the Sum of five Pound in hand paid unto
Pompmo and Simon this five and twentieth Day of October 1665. And farther the
said Josias Cooke doth promise that if Mr Thomas Prence shall at any time come
towards Pottanumaqrett if Pompmo or Simon shall desire him to View this Land
and he shall Judge it meet that Josias Cooke shall Give the aboveaid Pompmo
or Simon more than is here already paid, the said Josias Cooke is willing to give
accordingly as shall be judged meet by Mr Thomas Prence —

Signed Sealed and Deliver[ed]      The Mark [I] Simon and a [Seal]
In the Presence of
Thomas Thornton        This Deed of Sale of Land was Acknow
the Mark of Lawrence    :ledged by Simon before me Thomas Prence
the Mark of [?] Peter     Gov[r] the Day and Year above written
                      The mark P of Pompmo

This 7th Day of November 1665. We being
at Pottanumaquatt Simon did agree with
Josias Cooke that the Land Sold to him should
begin at a Valley or Slough, this is on this Side
Baken Tarr Pitts toward Pottanumaquatt,
and to run as ye Valley runs to the Pond
that tobe the Bounds at this End —
John Freeman
Joseph Ro[we]

[John Coo? as approve ... being ... ]
[... keeper ... Records ...]
[... of Deeds — in ye ...]

695

# 2<sup>nd</sup> Generation

2.  Anna Cooke (Josias-1) was born after 1636. She died on 25 Jul 1656 at the age of 20 and was buried in Eastham Cove Burying Ground, Eastham, Mass. She probably died due to complications from childbirth. She married Lieut. Mark SNOW on 18 Jan 1654 in Eastham, Mass. Lieut. Mark SNOW was the son of Nicholas SNOW and Constance HOPKINS. He was born on 9 May 1628 in Plymouth, Mass. and died before Jan. 1694 at the age of 65.

Mark Snow and Anna Cooke had the following child:

 i.   Anna SNOW, born 7 Jul 1656, Eastham, Mass.; married Eldad ATWOOD, 14 Feb 1683, Eastham, Mass.; died 7 Jul 1714, Eastham, Mass. They had eight children.  All descendants in this line are Mayflower descendants.

3.  Bethia Cooke (Josias-1) was born after 1638 in Plymouth, Mass. She married Joseph HARDING on 4 Apr 1660. Joseph Harding was the son of Joseph Harding and Martha Doane, and was born in 1629. He died after 31 May 1687 at the age of 58.

Joseph Harding and Bethia Cooke had the following children:

 i.    Martha Harding, born 13 Dec 1662; married Samuel BROWN Jr., 19 Feb 1681, Eastham, Mass. They had 4 children.
 ii.   Mary Harding was born on 19 Aug 1665.
 iii.  Capt. Joseph Harding, born 8 Jul 1667; married Dinah HEDGES, bef 1693; died 1745. There were no children.
 iv.   Josiah Harding, born 15 Aug 1669, Eastham, Mass.; married Hannah WELCH; died bef. 23 Jun 1752, Provincetown, Mass. They had 9 children.
 v.    Amaziah Harding, born 1 Nov 1671, Eastham, Mass.; married Hannah ROGERS, bef 1694; died 5 Jun 1734, Barnstable County, Mass. Amaziah (or Maziah) Harding has the distinction of being one of the earliest legally executed people in America. He killed his wife in some sort of argument, tried to pretend she died of natural causes and then tried to enlist someone's help in burying her body before she could be examined. The neighbor (Mary Freeman) refused and later testified against him. He was tried by a jury, found guilty, and hanged at the age of 62. They had 9 children.
 vi.   John Harding, born 9 Oct 1673, Eastham, Mass.; married Elizabeth Susannah RING; died 14 Jun 1697, Eastham, Mass. There were no children.
 vii.  Joshua Harding was born on 15 Feb 1675 in Eastham, Mass. He died after Mar. 1737/8 at the age of 63 in Eastham, Mass.
 viii. Nathaniel Harding, born 25 Dec 1676, Eastham, Mass.; married Hannah YOUNG, 20 Mar 1700, Eastham, Mass.; died 1 Aug 1741, Truro, Mass. They had 3 children.
 ix.   Abiah Harding, born 26 Jan 1679, Eastham, Mass.; married Rebecca YOUNG; died bef

1747, Eastham, Mass. They had 1 child.

    x.  Samuel Harding, born 1 Sep 1683, Eastham, Mass.; married Elizabeth ELDREDGE, 28 Aug 1707, Eastham, Mass.; died 29 Nov 1735, Eastham, Mass. They had 11 children.

4.  Josiah Cooke (Josias-1) was born in 1645 in Eastham, Mass. He performed "soldier service" in King Phillip's War in 1675. He signed a will on 7 Dec 1727 in Eastham, Mass. He died on 31 Jan 1731/2 at the age of 87 in Eastham, Mass. He married Deborah HOPKINS on 27 Jul 1668 in Eastham, Mass.

Deborah HOPKINS was the daughter of Giles HOPKINS and Catherine (Catone) (Katherine) WHELDON. She was born in Jun 1648 in Eastham, Mass. She died before 7 Dec 1727 at the age of 79 in Eastham, Mass.

 Giles Hopkins and his father Stephen Hopkins were passengers on the 1620 voyage of the *Mayflower*. It is through this family that all Cooks are "Mayflower descendants," though there may be other lines related to the *Mayflower*.

☞ After his father died in 1673, his mother lived another 15 years. After she died, an argument broke out between Josiah Cooke, his half sister Merriam Deane and his sister Bethia Harding. The elder Mr Cooke's will gave his property to his wife for her lifetime, and then to his son. The "moveables" were to be divided between Josiah and Bethia. (His daughter Anna had died young.) His adopted daughter Merriam, who was the only single woman at the time, was to receive a cow and 5£. There was no provision made for his other adopted daughters. This apparently did not sit well with Merriam. When the dispute was settled and filed with the court, the court noted that it was after a contest of "great varianc and strife." The net effect was that Merriam got her first choice of about an additional 5£ worth of moveables and the distinction of being part of one of the earliest American "family feuds."

As an example of how quickly people were "breeding," Josiah and Deborah had a total of 291 great grandchildren.

Josiah Cooke and Deborah HOPKINS had the following children:

    i.  Elizabeth Cooke was born on 12 Oct 1669 in Eastham, Mass. She died in Apr 1670 in Eastham, Mass.

14  ii.  Josiah Cooke, born 12 Nov 1670, Eastham, Mass.; married Mary GODFREY, bef. 1694; died aft 11 Feb 1730/1.

15  iii.  Richard Cooke, born 1 Sep 1672, Eastham, Mass.; married Hannah SMITH, 1696, Eastham, Mass.; died 25 Apr 1754, Eastham, Mass.

16  iv.  Elizabeth Cooke, born 15 Jun 1674, Eastham, Mass.; married Thomas NEWCOMB, Oct 1693; died 12 Jul 1727, Eastham, Mass.

17  v.  Caleb Cooke, born 15 Nov 1676, Yarmouth, Mass.; married Deliverance (Crow)
           CROWELL, 18 Oct 1710, Yarmouth, Mass.; died 22 Jan 1737/8, Truro, Mass.
18  vi.  Deborah Cooke, born 15 Feb 1678, Eastham, Mass.; married Moses GODFREY, abt
           1700, Eastham, Mass.; died 23 Apr 1745, Chatham, Mass.
19  vii. Joshua Cooke, born 4 Feb 1682, Eastham, Mass.; married Patience DOANE, 7 Feb
           1705/6, Eastham, Mass.; died bef 28 Sep 1746, Coventry, Conn.
20  viii.  Benjamin Cooke, born 28 Feb 1686, Eastham, Mass.; married Mercy PAINE, 23
           Nov 1710, Eastham, Mass.; died aft 7 Dec 1727, Eastham, Mass.

# 3<sup>rd</sup> Generation

14. Josiah Cooke (Josiah-2, Josias-1) was born on 12 Nov 1670 in Eastham, Mass. He moved to Truro, Mass. about 1701. He died after 11 Feb 1730/1 at the age of 60.

Josiah Cooke and Mary GODFREY were married before 1694. They moved in Middletown, Conn. in 1727. Mary Godfrey was the daughter of George David Godfrey and Hannah. She was born on 2 Jun 1672 in Truro, Mass. She died on 22 Jan 1725 at the age of 52 in Eastham, Mass.

Josiah Cooke and Mary Godfrey had the following children:

56 i. Desire Cooke, born 14 Jun 1694, Eastham, Mass.; married Beriah HIGGINS; died aft 17 May 1736, Connecticut.
57 ii. Deborah Cooke, born 12 Apr 1696, Eastham, Mass.; married Joseph HATCH, 29 May 1718, Truro, Mass.; died bef 27 Jan 1730/1.
58 iii. John Cooke, born 9 Apr 1698, Eastham, Mass.; married Desire HATCH, 15 Mar 1721/2, Truro, Mass.
59 iv. Mary Cooke, born 8 Feb 1700, Eastham, Mass.; married David VICKERY, 24 Apr 1718, Truro, Mass.; died bef 29 Apr 1720.
60 v. Joshua Cooke, born abt 1702; married Zerviah HATCH, 5 Aug 1724, Provincetown, Mass.; married Hannah Rogers, 25 Dec 1755, Truro, Mass.
61 vi. Elizabeth Cooke, born abt 1704; married Thomas DOTY, 1 Nov 1722, Truro, Mass.; died bef 23 Oct 1728.
62 vii. Hannah Cooke, born abt 1707; married Isaiah ATKINS, 12 Nov 1724, Truro, Mass.; died 21 Mar 1783, Truro, Mass.
63 viii. Jacob Cook, born abt 1708, Truro, Mass.; married Marcy (Mary) YOUNG, 18 Feb 1730, Eastham, Mass.; died 3 Sep 1800, Otis, Mass.
64 ix. Solomon Cook, born 18 Nov 1708, Truro, Mass.; married Rebekah COWELL, 4 Jun 1733, Truro, Mass.; died 21 Nov 1781, Provincetown, Mass.

15. Richard Cooke (Josiah-2, Josias-1) was born on 1 Sep 1672 in Eastham, Mass. He died on 25 Apr 1754 at the age of 81 in Eastham, Mass.

Richard Cooke and Hannah SMITH were married in 1696 in Eastham, Mass. Hannah Smith was the daughter John Smith and Hannah Williams.

Richard Cooke and Hannah Smith had the following children:

65 i. Thomas Cooke Sr, born 27 Apr 1697, Eastham, Mass.; married Dinah DOANE, 19 Sep 1719, Eastham, Mass.; died 31 May 1774, Guilford, Conn.

66 ii.  Hannah Cooke, born bet 25 Jan 1699 and 90, Eastham, Mass.; married Ebenezer
       ROGERS, 24 Mar 1719/20; died 21 Mar 1783, Truro, Mass.

67 iii.  Caleb Cook, born 11 Sep 1702, Eastham, Mass.; married Hannah BROWN, 7 Apr 1726,
       Eastham, Mass.; married Lydia WALKER, 20 Feb 1728/9, Eastham, Mass.

68 iv.  Elisabeth "Bettey" Cooke, born 30 Nov 1704, Eastham, Mass.; married Jonathan
       ROGERS, 18 Jan 1727/8, Eastham, Mass.; died 25 Jan 1778, Yarmouth, Mass.

   v.  Sarah Cooke was born on 27 Nov 1707 in Eastham, Mass.

69 vi.  Deborah Cooke, born 22 Aug 1710, Eastham, Mass.; married Sylvanus SNOW, 11 Nov
       1761, Eastham, Mass.; died 23 Mar 1772.

   vii. Anne Cooke was born on 15 Sep 1712 in Eastham, Mass.

70 viii.  Abigail Cooke, born 8 Jun 1715, Eastham, Mass.; married Simeon SMITH, 1735,
       Eastham, Mass.; died 1780, Eastham, Mass.

71 ix.  Thankful Cooke, born 12 Jun 1717, Eastham, Mass.; married Jesse NICKERSON, 25
       Feb 1736/7, Eastham, Mass.; married Nathan KENNEY, 19 Mar 1747; died 1772,
       Eastham, Mass.


16. Elizabeth Cooke (Josiah-2, Josias-1) was born on 15 Jun 1674 in Eastham, Mass. She died on 12
Jul 1727 at the age of 53 in Eastham, Mass.

Elizabeth Cooke and Thomas NEWCOMB were married in Oct 1693. Thomas Newcomb,
son of Andrew Newcomb and Sarah , was born in 1668 in Kittery, York, ME. He died in
1723 at the age of 55.

Thomas Newcomb and Elizabeth Cooke had the following children:

   i.  Edward Newcomb was born on 3 Aug 1695 in Eastham, Mass.

   ii.  Thomas Newcomb, born bet 13 Aug 1696 and 1698, Eastham, Mass.; married Hepzibah
       WOOD, 1720, Eastham, Mass.; married Merci TILTON, 31 May 1732.

   iii.  Simon "Simeon" Newcomb, born 30 Nov 1699, Eastham, Mass.; married Lydia
       BROWN, 5 Apr 1722, Eastham, Mass.; married Sarah WALKER (?), 1758; died
       1778.

   iv.  Deborah Newcomb, born 1702, Eastham, Mass.; married Thomas LAMKIN, 28 Jan
       1720; died 2 May 1749.

   v.  Mary Newcomb, born abt 1704, Eastham, Mass.; married Luke STUBBS, 11 Apr 1723,
       Eastham, Mass.

   vi.  Josiah Newcomb was born about 1706 in Eastham, Mass. He was baptized on 2 Jun 1717
       in Truro, Mass.

   vii.  Elizabeth Newcomb, born abt 1709, Eastham, Mass.; married Joshua PIERCE, 24 Jul
       1729, Eastham, Mass.; died 6 Apr 1763.

   viii.  Capt Ebenezer Newcomb, born 1712, Truro, Mass.; married Thankful FREEMAN,
       15 Jun 1738, Eastham, Mass.; married Experience BROWN, 6 Feb 1758,

Eastham, Mass.; died 11 Oct 1782, Greenwich, Mass.
  ix.  Joseph Newcomb, born abt 1715, Eastham, Mass.; married Mary ELDREDGE, 16 Mar
       1738/9, Eastham, Mass.; died 1762, Wellfleet, Mass.

17. Caleb Cooke (Josiah-2, Josias-1) was born on 15 Nov 1676 in Yarmouth, Mass. He died on 22
    Jan 1737/8 at the age of 61 in Truro, Mass.

    Caleb Cooke and Deliverance (Crow) CROWELL were married on 18 Oct 1710 in
    Yarmouth, Mass. Deliverance (Crow) Crowell, daughter of John Crowell and Hannah
    Hathaway, was born on 11 Jan 1685 in Eastham, Mass. She was admitted to the First Church
    of Truro on 23 Jul 1716 in Truro, Mass. She died after 23 Jul 1716 at the age of 31 in Truro,
    Mass. Most of their children died in childhood.

Caleb Cooke and Deliverance (Crow) Crowell had the following children:

    i.    Elizabeth Cooke was born on 2 Aug 1711 in Eastham, Mass. She died on 17 Nov 1715 at
          the age of 4 in Truro, Mass.
    ii.   Abigail Cooke was born on 22 Dec 1712 in Eastham, Mass. She died on 26 Nov 1715 at
          the age of 2 in Truro, Mass.
    iii.  Experience Cooke was born in 1714 in Truro, Mass. She was baptized on 23 Jul 1716 in
          Truro, Mass.
    iv.   Mary Cooke (Twin) was born on 2 Jun 1719 in Truro, Mass. She was baptized on 16 Jul
          1719 in Truro, Mass.
 79 v.    Cornelius Cooke (Twin), born 2 Jun 1719, Truro, Mass.; married Abigail HATCH, 26
          Mar 1751.
    vi.   Ephraim Cooke was born on 12 Jul 1722 in Truro, Mass. He was baptized on 19 Aug
          1722 in Truro, Mass. He died on 10 Apr 1729 at the age of 6 in Truro, Mass.

18. Deborah Cooke (Josiah-2, Josias-1) was born on 15 Feb 1678 in Eastham, Mass. She died on 23
    Apr 1743 at the age of 65 in Chatham, Mass. She was buried in Old Burying Ground,
    Chatham, Mass. Although there are many hundreds of gravestones to be found and there are
    older markers at Eastham Cove Burying Ground, I am including these two because they are the
    oldest of the Cooke descendants that still stand. The Chatham Old Burying Ground is found
    where George Ryder Road meets Old Queen Anne Road.

HERE RESTS Ye BODY
OF DEBORAH THE
WIFE OF Mr MOSES
GODFREY DIED APRIL
Ye 23d 1743 IN Ye
65th YEAR OF HER AGE

HERE RESTS THE
BODY OF Mr
MOSES GODFREY
DIED APRIL Ye 16th
1743 in Ye 76th
YEAR OF HIS AGE

Deborah Cooke and Moses GODFREY were married about 1700 in Eastham, Mass. Moses Godfrey, son of George David Godfrey and Hannah, was born on 27 Jan 1667 in Eastham, Mass. He died on 16 Apr 1743 at the age of 76 in Chatham, Mass. He was buried in Old Burying Ground, Chatham, Mass. I don't know why they died within a week of each other. Though this is not the largest family I've come across, (that notable fact belongs to Deborah's brother, Joshua, below), Moses Godfrey and Deborah Cooke had 12 children and 67 grandchildren.

Moses Godfrey and Deborah Cooke had the following children:

    i.   Jonathan Godfrey, born 1701, Chatham, Mass.; married Mercy NICKERSON, 21 Sep 1725, Chatham, Mass.; died 1728/9, Chatham, Mass. They had 3 children.

    ii.  Samuel Godfrey, born 1703, Chatham, Mass.; married Thankful KNOWLES, abt 1728; died 7 Jul 1760. They had 6 children.

☞  iii. Moses Godfrey Jr., born abt 1705, Chatham, Mass.; married Martha COLLINS, abt 1726, Chatham, Mass.; died aft 16 Feb 1773, Barrington, N.S. They had 9 children.

One of their many descendants was Orrin Hatch, the Republican Senator from Utah. (If you're curious, my relationship to Orrin Hatch is 9th cousin, once removed.)

iv. George Godfrey, born 1707, Chatham, Mass.; married Mercy KNOWLES, 1 Nov 1733, Chatham, Mass.; married Jane Collins, 9 Nov 1758, Chatham, Mass.; died 4 Dec 1768, Chatham, Mass. They had 10 children.

v. David Godfrey, born 1709; married Priscilla BAKER, 14 Oct 1731, Yarmouth, Mass.; died 1790, Orange County, NY. They had 1 child.

vi. Mary Godfrey, born 4 Sep 1711, Chatham, Mass.; married Caleb NICKERSON, abt 1732, Chatham, Mass.; married Seth SMITH, 18 Nov 1756, Chatham, Mass.; died 24 Apr 1782, Chatham, Mass. With her first husband she had 8 children.

vii. Desire Godfrey, born 1712; married Nathaniel RYDER, 26 Sep 1728. They had 8 children.

viii. Benjamin Godfrey, born 1715; married Elizabeth HOPKINS, 23 Aug 1738; died Nova Scotia. They had 2 children.

ix. Elizabeth Godfrey, born 15 Mar 1717/8, Chatham, Mass.; married Benjamin BEARSE Jr., 31 May 1733, Chatham, Mass.; died 1 Dec 1742, Chatham, Mass. They had 5 children.

x. Deborah Godfrey, born abt 1715; married Thomas BASSETT, 1740; died bef 1763, Chatham, Mass. They had 7 children.

xi. Joshua Godfrey, born 30 Apr 1723; married Phoebe GOULD, 27 Apr 1742, Harwich, Mass.; died 1758. They had 6 children.

xii. Richard Godfrey, born 1724; married Azubah COLLINS, bet 10 Jan 1749/50; died 6 May 1760. They had 2 children.

19. Joshua Cooke (Josiah-2, Josias-1) was born on 4 Feb 1682 in Eastham, Mass. He died before 28 Sep 1746 at the age of 64 in Coventry, Conn.

Joshua Cooke and Patience DOANE were married on 7 Feb 1705/6 in Eastham, Mass. Patience DOANE, daughter of Ephraim DOANE and Mercy (Mary) Knowles, was born on 25 Apr 1682 in Eastham, Mass. She died on 28 Sep 1746 at the age of 64 in Coventry, Conn.

☞ This is the largest 3 generation family of all Josiah Cooke's descendants. Joshua and Patience had 93 grandchildren. It also marks a decisive geographical split, with Joshua, Patience and their children moving to Connecticut, probably to follow a preacher named Isaac Smith who had led a group there, while a couple of his siblings moved farther out on the cape, to Provincetown. Joshua and his family moved to Connecticut in about 1741, just over a century after Josias Cooke originally arrived in Plymouth.

They moved to Chatham Township, which was renamed East Hampton and is named for Eastham, Mass. It is north of East Haddam on the Connecticut River. They probably ran a lumber mill, but East Hampton eventually became known for bells and there still exists there a bell manufacturer called The Bevin Brothers who have been in business since 1862.

Joshua Cooke and Patience DOANE had the following children:

    i.    Martha Cook was born on 26 Apr 1706 in Eastham, Mass.

92  ii.   Josiah Cook, born 30 Aug 1707, Eastham, Mass.; married Hannah SPARROW, 11 Feb 1730/1, Eastham, Mass.; died bef 24 Jun 1775, Chatham, Mass.

93  iii.  Joshua Cook, born 23 Mar 1708, Eastham, Mass.; married Zilpah BROWN, 8 Oct 1730, Eastham, Mass.; died 13 Mar 1801, Guilford, Conn.

    iv.  Mercy Cook was born on 2 Sep 1710 in Eastham, Mass.

94  v.   Ebenezer Cook, born 25 Nov 1711, Eastham, Mass.; married Mercy PAINE, 9 Oct 1735, Eastham, Mass.; died 1793, East Haddam, Conn.

95  vi.  Ephraim Cook, born 16 Oct 1712, Eastham, Mass.; married Mary MERRICK, 12 Feb 1734/5, Eastham, Mass.; died aft Feb 1778, Coventry, Conn.

    vii. Ruhama Cook was born on 18 Feb 1713/4 in Eastham, Mass. She died before 1721 at the age of 7.

96  viii.  Simeon Cook, born 24 Aug 1715, Eastham, Mass.; married Melatiah ROBBINS after 16 Nov 1738 in Eastham, Mass. He died bet 1762 and 1767, New Marlborough, Mass.

☞  ix.  Moses Cook was born on 11 May 1717 in Eastham, Mass. He died when he was murdered on 7 Dec 1771 at the age of 54 in Bethany, Conn. (This is not certain.) The man who killed him was an "converted Indian" named Moses Paul and there is a publication called "A Sermon Preached at the Execution of Moses Paul, an Indian," which is available online through various libraries. (The one pictured on the next page is from Amherst College.) It isn't 100% certain that the Moses Cook who was killed was this one, but there are no Moses Cook births in the Connecticut records; almost the entire Joshua Cook family had moved to areas in Connecticut that were all within a day's range and also, somewhat less significantly, is that there is no further record of Moses Cook which is unusual for this family. The sermon, although full of information about the sinner, is unfortunately void of any information about the murdered man. Waterbury, where the murdered Moses Cook was from, is about 20 miles from East Haddam and 12 miles from Bethany. Apparently, they had both been drinking and Moses Cook was attacked and killed when he left the tavern in Bethany.

97  x.   Zaccheus Cook, born abt 1719, Eastham, Mass.; married Mary HUBBARD, 13/14 May 1747, Middletown, Conn.; died 19 Apr 1812, Chatham, Conn.

98  xi.  Ruhama Cook, born abt 1721, Eastham, Mass.; married Robert SHATTUCK, 9 Sep 1742, Plymouth, Mass.; died bet 1766 and 1776, Chatham, Mass.

99  xii. Jonathan Cook, born abt 1723, Eastham, Mass.; married Deborah ROBERDS, 1751, Middle Haddam, Conn.; died bef 29 Oct 1804, Haddam, Conn.

100  xiii.  Mary Cook, born abt 1725, Eastham, Mass.; married Caleb JOHNSON, 19 Sep 1745, Haddam Neck Congregational Church, East Haddam, Conn.; died aft

1800, Burlington, Otsego, NY.

    101    xiv.    Hezekiah Cook, born abt 1728, Eastham, Mass.; married Lydia UNKNOWN bef. 1757; died 23 Apr 1793, New Marlborough, Mass.

20. Benjamin Cooke (Josiah-2, Josias-1) was born on 28 Feb 1686 in Eastham, Mass. He died after 7 Dec 1727 at the age of 41 in Eastham, Mass.

Benjamin Cooke and Mercy PAINE were married on 23 Nov 1710 in Eastham, Mass. Mercy Paine, daughter of Samuel Paine and Patience Freeman, was born on 5 Aug 1686.

Mercy Paine was a Mayflower descendant in a couple of ways. Her father, Samuel Paine, was a great grandson of Stephen Hopkins. Her mother, Patience Freeman, was the granddaughter of Governor Thomas Prence and Patience Brewster. Her great grandfather was Elder William Brewster.

Benjamin Cooke and Mercy Paine had the following children:

    i.    Shubael Cooke was born in Apr 1711 in Eastham, Mass.
    ii.    Joseph Cooke was born between 12 May 1712 and 12 May 1716 in Eastham, Mass.
  102    iii.  Nathaniel Cooke, born 6 Jul 1717, Eastham, Mass.; married Mercy REMICK, 27 Sep 1740, Eastham, Mass.

3.17

103    iv.  Richard Cooke, born 23 Nov 1718, Eastham, Mass.; married Rebecca MAYO, 23 Aug 1740, Eastham, Mass.; died aft 1769, Eastham, Mass.

# 4th Generation

56. Desire Cooke (Josiah-3, Josiah-2, Josias-1) was born on 14 Jun 1694 in Eastham, Mass. She died after 17 May 1736 at the age of 41 in Connecticut.

Desire Cooke and Beriah HIGGINS live in Truro, Mass. between 1712 and 1724. They were married. Beriah Higgins, son of Joseph Higgins and Ruth, was born about 1692 in Eastham, Mass. He died after 27 Aug 1749 at the age of 57 in Connecticut.

Beriah Higgins and Desire Cooke had the following children:

    i.   Thankful Higgins was born on 7 Aug 1717 in Truro, Mass.
    ii.  Jemima Higgins was born on 15 Jun 1719 in Truro, Mass.
    iii. Desire Higgins, born 10 Aug 1724, Truro, Mass.; married Hezekiah Sumner, 10 Feb 1744 in Connecticut. They had 7 children.
    iv. Deborah Higgins, born 26 Oct 1725, Provincetown, Mass.; married Samuel HIGGINS, 1746.
    v.  Beriah Higgins was born on 1 Apr 1727 in Provincetown, Mass
    vi. Phebe Higgins was born on 17 May 1736 in Provincetown, Mass.
    vii. ? Jethro Higgins.
    viii.  Josiah Higgins, married Sarah. There was at least 1 child.
    ix. ? Joseph Higgins.

57. Deborah Cooke (Josiah-3, Josiah-2, Josias-1) was born on 12 Apr 1696 in Eastham, Mass. She died before 27 Jan 1730/1 at the age of 34.

Deborah Cooke and Joseph HATCH were married on 29 May 1718 in Truro, Mass. Joseph Hatch, son of Thomas Hatch and Sarah Elmes, was born on 6 May 1682 in Scituate, Mass.

58. John Cooke (Josiah-3, Josiah-2, Josias-1) was born on 9 Apr 1698 in Eastham, Mass.

John Cooke and Desire HATCH were married on 15 Mar 1721/2 in Truro, Mass. They moved in Provincetown, Mass. before 1728. They moved to Middletown, Conn. before 1740. Desire Hatch, daughter of Joseph Hatch and Desire Hawes, was born on 3 Feb 1703 in Plymouth, Mass. She died in 1748 at the age of 45. The existence of the first two children is highly doubtful.

John Cooke and Desire Hatch had the following children:

    i.   ? Jacob Cooke was born.
    ii.  ? Jonathan Cooke was born.

iii. Mary Cooke was born on 27 Apr 1728 in Provincetown, Mass.
188    iv.  John Cooke, born 23 Aug 1730, Provincetown, Mass.; married Mary DOWNS.
189    v.   Jabez Cooke, born 17 Jun 1732, Provincetown, Mass.; married Abigail BLAKE, 23
           May 1754, Middletown, Conn.; died bef Nov 1764.
       vi.  George Cooke was born on 5 Sep 1740 in Middletown, Conn.
190    vii. Hannah Cooke, born 5 Sep 1742, Middletown, Conn.; married David BUTLER, 20
           Sep 1758, Middletown, Conn.
       viii.  Desire Cooke, born 8 Mar 1744, Middletown, Conn.; married Jedediah PRYOR. No
           known children.
192    ix.  Sarah Cooke, born 30 Dec 1746, Middletown, Conn.; married John UFFORD.

59. Mary Cooke (Josiah-3, Josiah-2, Josias-1) was born on 8 Feb 1700 in Eastham, Mass. She
    (possibly) died during parturition before 29 Apr 1720 at the age of 20.

    Mary Cooke and David VICKERY were married on 24 Apr 1718 in Truro, Mass.

David Vickery and Mary Cooke had the following child:

    i.   Mary Vickery was born on 17 Jan 1718/9 in Truro, Mass.

60. Joshua Cooke (Josiah-3, Josiah-2, Josias-1) was born about 1702.

    Joshua Cooke and Zerviah HATCH were married on 5 Aug 1724 in Provincetown, Mass.
    Zerviah Hatch, daughter of Joseph Hatch and Desire Hawes, was born on 10 Sep 1707 in
    Rochester, Monroe, NY. She died in 1748 at the age of 41.

Joshua Cooke and Zerviah Hatch had the following children:

    193    i.   Joshua Cooke, born 10 Jun 1725, Provincetown, Mass.; married Content COOMBS,
               17 Nov 1748, Eastham, Mass.
           ii.  Elnathan Cook was born on 15 Apr 1727 in Provincetown, Mass. He was also known as
               Jonathan Cooke.
    194    iii. Elizabeth "Betty" Cooke, born 20 Feb 1729, Provincetown, Mass.; married Benjamin
               BROWN.
           iv.  Martha Cooke was born on 1 Jun 1731 in Provincetown, Mass.

    Joshua Cooke and Hannah ROGERS were married on 25 Dec 1755 in Truro, Mass. Hannah
    Rogers, daughter of Thomas Rogers and Sarah Treat, was born on 6 Apr 1710.

61. Elizabeth Cooke (Josiah-3, Josiah-2, Josias-1) was born about 1704. She died before 23 Oct
    1728 at the age of 24.

Elizabeth Cooke and Thomas DOTY were married on 1 Nov 1722 in Truro, Mass. Thomas Doty, son of Thomas Doty and Elizabeth Harlow, was born on 26 Jan 1704 in Plymouth, Mass. He died on 23 Mar 1795 at the age of 91. He was buried in Canton Cemetery.

Thomas Doty and Elizabeth Cooke had the following child:

    i.   Elizabeth Doty, born 1726; married Perez Tillson, 20 Nov 1746, Plymouth, Mass.; died 8 Nov 1756, Plymouth, Mass. They had 1 child.

62. Hannah Cooke (Josiah-3, Josiah-2, Josias-1) was born about 1707. She died on 21 Mar 1783 at the age of 76 in Truro, Mass. She was buried in North Cem., Truro, Mass.

Hannah Cooke and Isaiah ATKINS were married on 12 Nov 1724 in Truro, Mass. Isaiah Atkins was born about 1704 in Truro, Mass. He died on 3 Apr 1782 at the age of 78 in Truro, Mass. He was buried in North Cemetery, Truro, Mass.

Isaiah Atkins and Hannah Cooke had the following children:

    i.   Hannah Atkins, born 22 Feb 1727/8, Truro, Mass.; married Elisha DYER, 21 May 1752, Truro, Mass. They had 1 child.
    ii.  John Atkins was born on 1 Apr 1730 in Truro, Mass. He died when he was lost at sea in 1754 at the age of 24.
    iii. Silas Atkins, born 15 Jan 1732/3, Truro, Mass.; married Lydia HATCH.
    iv. Nathaniel Atkins, born 6 Jul 1736, Truro, Mass.; married Mary PARKER, 7 Jun 1759, Truro, Mass. They had 7 children.
    v.  Mary Atkins, born 18 Jun 1738, Truro, Mass.; married Paul KNOWLES; died 22 Aug 1824, Truro, Mass.
    vi. Isaiah Atkins, born 25 Apr 1740, Truro, Mass.; married Elizabeth GROSS, Truro, Mass.
    vii. Henry Atkins, born 4 May 1743, Truro, Mass.; married Mary LOMBARD.
    viii.  Zaccheus Atkins, born 3 Apr 1745, Truro, Mass.; died bef 8 Mar 1782, Truro, Mass.
    ix. Benjamin Atkins was born on 1 Aug 1726 in Truro, Mass.

63. Jacob Cooke (Josiah-3, Josiah-2, Josias-1) was born about 1708 in Truro, Mass. He died on 3 Sep 1800 at the age of 92 in Otis, Mass. Jacob was buried in Norton Cemetary, Otis, Mass.

Jacob Cook and Marcy (Mary) YOUNG had marriage banns published on 3 Feb 1730 in Eastham, Mass. They were married on 18 Feb 1730 in Eastham, Mass. They moved to Provincetown, Mass. before 1731. Marcy (Mary) Young died on 31 Jul 1802 in Otis, Mass. She was born in Eastham, Mass. She was buried in Norton Cemetery, Otis, Mass.

Jacob Cooke and Marcy (Mary) Young had the following children:

4.21

203    i.  Jacob Cook, married Catherine CAMP, 4 Feb 1756.

ii.  Mercy Cook, married Samuel CLARK. No known children.

iii.  Ebenezer Cooke, born 2 Dec 1731, Provincetown, Mass.; married Mehitable ROCKWELL, 18 Nov 1764, Middletown, Conn.; died 9 Oct 1768, Middletown, Conn. There were no known children.

206    iv.  Elisabeth Cooke, born 11 Nov 1743, Middletown, Conn.; married Ichabod CRITTENDEN.

207    v.  Mary Cook (twin), born 15 Nov 1745, Middletown, Conn.; married Elijah RANNEY, 2 Mar 1763, Granville, Mass.; married Noah WARREN, 1809; died 1 Apr 1832, Waterville, NY.

208    vi.  Josiah Cook (twin), born 15 Nov 1747, Middletown, Conn.; married Miriam SHEPARD, 17 Oct 1771; died 1817.

vii.  Rebeckah Cooke was born on 26 Sep 1749 in Middletown, Conn.

viii.  Elisha Cook was born on 1 Aug 1751.

209    ix.  Lieut Elisha Cook, born 5 Dec 1756, Granville, Mass.; married Anna BALDWIN, 18 Jun 1777; married Sally LEONARD, 5 Feb 1798, Springfield, Mass.; married Lovisa WARREN, 21 Nov 1814; died 1 Oct 1829, Seville, O.

64. Solomon Cook (Josiah-3, Josiah-2, Josias-1) was born on 18 Nov 1708 in Truro, Mass. He was baptized on 18 Nov 1711 in Truro, Mass. He died on 21 Nov 1781 at the age of 73 in Provincetown, Mass. Solomon was buried in Winthrop Street Cemetery, Provincetown, Mass.

Solomon Cook and Rebekah COWELL were married 4 Jun 1733 in Truro, Mass. Rebekah Cowell, daughter of Edward Cowell and Rebekah Broughton, was born about 1713/14 in Boston, Mass. She died 19 August 1788 and is buried in Winthrop Street Cemetery, Provincetown, Mass.

## The Cooks in Provincetown

Solomon Cooke migrated to Provincetown, a short distance from Truro sometime before 1733.  Prior to its incorporation in 1727, Provincetown existed as a small collection of shacks that were built facing the sea. The only "roads" were the foot paths that went from the shacks to boats resting on the shore.

Unlike other Cape Cod towns, Provincetown wasn't a planned settlement, nor did it begin its life as a religious community. In fact, it was something of an escape from the religious utopias in other parts of Cape Cod and New England. Until 1727, the Colonial government considered the squatters settlement to be under the jurisdiction of Truro. But it was an unruly place that Truro didn't want, populated mostly by fishermen and whalers, so it was finally incorporated as a town. However, it was specifically decreed that the land of the town belonged to the Province, and the name of the town was chosen to emphasize the fact that the land belonged to the Province and not the people who lived there. The locals wanted Herrington or Herringtown, after the huge schools of Herring that were found in the bay, just as Cape Cod was named after the Cod fish that were found in the Atlantic.

It wasn't until some time in the 1800s that the land on which Solomon and his descendants and neighbors built their homes became their legal property. By then, almost a century had passed.

Solomon Cook is the progenitor of all the Provincetown Cook descendants and, because most of them didn't move from Provincetown, they became a family dynasty that thrived for about 175 years, making a living mostly from whaling and fishing.

The initial generations were lopsided in gender. Of his 11 children, only 2 were girls, and of his 32 grandchildren, only 7 were girls. For this reason, within 60 to 80 years of Solomon's first child Mary, there were or had been about 120 families named Cook in Provincetown, most of them were married with children. The number of Solomon's great grandchildren is roughly 220.

Solomon's line created at least twenty five ship Captains, as many ship owners, and scores of mariners and fisherman. There were also more than a few Cook men lost at sea in the shipwrecks around Cape Cod, leaving many widows and orphans. Child mortality was extremely high for these people, as was the death of mothers during or shortly after childbirth (parturition). There were also a number of accidental drownings and one woman was killed by lightning.

Provincetown began keeping its vital records in 1698 which is about 30 years before it was officially incorporated, and the first entry in the records is Peregrine White, the first English person born in America, who was born aboard the *Mayflower* while it was anchored in Provincetown Harbor. Provincetown is often overlooked in the stories of the *Mayflower*

4.23

because although the Mayflower Pilgrims first touched land there, they didn't stay for more than a day, and Plymouth, Mass., became the more famous town. One of the sadder stories about the *Mayflower* in the Provincetown harbor was the death or suicide of Elder William Brewster's wife, who drown when she fell overboard (or jumped) while Brewster and others were scouting the land for an appropriate place to build their town.

The first Cooke born in Provincetown (Joshua, son of Solomon's brother Joshua) is entered in 1725, but this family appears to have moved.

The people of Provincetown, especially the Cooks, profited enormously from whaling. Some of the men were fisherman, but most went after the whale and its oil, bones and ambergris. The cash from a successful trip could net $20,000, which in modern money would be about $600,000.

The earliest whaling was done from shore in rather small boats, and relied on the whales venturing near the shore. But as the whaling industry developed, the men, and sometimes their wives, would take very long journeys on large schooners that could last up to two years. Eugene O'Neill wrote a one-act play (*Ile*) about one of the Cook Captains (John A. Cook) who was, some said, an unconscionably cruel person. He drove his wife mad and kept some of his crew in chains for more than a year because of an attempted mutiny. They sued when they returned from the arctic (after four years), and won their case against him -- the only time until then a mutinous crew had won in court against their captain.

Many of the Cooks built homes beside each other on the road that led to the Cook wharf, which is now called Cook Street. Solomon's son, Jonathan Cook (#217), provided his large house on Commercial Street for King Hiram's Lodge, a temple of Freemasons which were formed in about 1775 and given their charter by Paul Revere. That still exists, although somehow the entire ground floor was demolished and the remaining two floors were lowered.

Jonathan was one of the first masters of the lodge and his portrait still hangs in that temple, along with another portrait of his son Jonathan (#667), who was also a master. King Hiram's lodge is still active.

The whaling lifestyle lasted until about the late 1800's, when Stephen Cook (born later than this geneology), another descendant of Solomon's, became the president of the Provincetown Bank, and realized from his financial perspective, that Provincetown would no longer be able to sustain itself on the fishing and whaling industries. These industries were being devastated by three things: 1) fish net trawling, 2) the discovery that oil in Pennsylvania could be turned into kerosene, and 3) the rapidly diminishing whale population.

(Starbuck's History of Whaling estimates that from 1804 to 1876 more than 193,000 Right

Whales and more than 225,000 Sperm whales were slaughtered by New England whaling industry. Fortunately, the Sperm whales have recovered and there are about 750,000 worldwide and they aren't endangered. The Right whale, unfortunately, is nearly extinct in the northern hemisphere. There are only about 400 left. They are doing better in the southern hemisphere, but the Southern Right whale is classified as separate species.)

Envisioning that the town would need a new industry to survive, Stephen Cook worked with the leaders of Provincetown to give it a new purpose: that of vacation and summer homes. Whaling and fishing collapsed, as expected, and the Cook whaling dynasty and family fortune disappeared with it. The last whaling vessel to leave Provincetown was *The Viola*, in 1909, owned by John Atkins Cook and named for his wife Viola, the woman previously mentioned who Eugene O'Neill wrote about in his one act play *Ile*.

**The Viola, 1909**

Captain Epaphras Kibby Cook was the last whaler in Provincetown, and he was flat broke. He had sold his house to a lawyer by the name of Lancy, who specialized in buying the property of destitute owners. He allowed Kibby to live in his home until he died. Lancy's wife, who was also a Cook descendant, Nabby Cook Lancy (#1558), became another "Provincetown character." Not only did she insist on having a mansion built, and had her children living in the basement, but when she died, the ground was frozen solid and she wasn't able to be buried, so they propped her up looking out of the window onto the street, combed her hair daily, trimmed her nails, until the neighbors complained about the dead woman in the window and they took her down. Later, the story goes, her son Stephen Lancy, ransacked the house looking for a

4.25

magic formula to make artificial brownstone.

In the 1890's, the tourists and vacationers began to visit Provincetown. Then, in the 1910's, artists from New York began forming communities in Provincetown, including another Cook descendant, from a different line, but related to this family. His name was George Cram Cook and Solmon Cook was his first cousin, five times removed. (This basically means a cousin separated by five generations). He had grown up in the prominent Cook Family in Davenport, Iowa. George Cook became an important, perhaps major influence in the American Theatre, because he and his wife, Susan Glaspell, started a theatre company in Provincetown and, in asking people for plays to perform, made the acquaintance of Eugene O'Neill. He brought over one of his plays to read at their home, and after that first reading, George and the Provincetown Players began producing and directing the work of America's first playwright.

George Cook and Susan Glaspell were also writers, but George Cook was not successful as a poet or novelist and is known now mainly for his role in bringing O'Neill to the world's attention. George recognized O'Neill's greatness, as did others, but he went further and basically served as his producer for the first ten years of his career, until O'Neill made a huge hit with *The Emperor Jones* and was launched in a different direction. The theatre they founded was the Provincetown Players, and it still exists on MacDougal Street in New York City. Long after George ran it, the theatre introduced Edward Albee and Bette Davis to the theatre world. Students write dissertations on The Provincetown Theatre now, in part because of George's vision for the creation and development of what he dreamed would be a completely American and organic type of theatre: something developed from the newness of America.

After George died (in Greece) and was buried at the Temple of Apollo in Parnassus, Greece, his wife Susan returned to Provincetown and become an extremely successful playwright and novelist, winning a Pulitzer Prize in 1931. There is a society called the Susan Glaspell society which meets in Provincetown every year to honor her. She wrote a biography of George called *The Road to the Temple*.

Solmon and Rebecca Cook have a 'private' plot in the first cemetery of Provincetown, called Winthrop Cemetery.  Their stones do not include an E at the end of the name, so for that reason, I've removed the E from all these descendants. It seems to have been dropped about this time.

Mary Heaton Vorse, another Provincetown writer, published a book called *Time and The Town, a Provincetown Chronicle*, which has a long chapter on the Cooks of Provincetown.

Solomon and Rebekah Cook, Winthrop Street Cemetery, Provincetown

Solomon Cook and Rebekah COWELL had the following children:

210    i.   Mary Cook, born 3 Oct 1735, Provincetown, Mass.; married Samuel DOTY, 28 Jun 1753, Plymouth, Mass.; died 20 Dec 1791.

211    ii.  Solomon Cook Sr., born 12 Sep 1737, Provincetown, Mass.; married Betsey (Elizabeth) ATKINS, bef 1760; married Catherine STAFFORD, aft 1808; died 24 Jul 1819, Provincetown, Mass.

212    iii. Rebecca Cook, born 26 Jun 1740, Provincetown, Mass.; married Thomas RIDER, 15 Nov 1759, Truro, Mass.; died 13 Dec 1793, Provincetown, Mass.

213    iv. Barnabas Cook, born abt 1745; married Phebe COOK, 1 Feb 1770, Eastham, Mass.; married Sara WHORF, abt 1792; died aft 1797, Provincetown, Mass.

214    v.   Edward Cook, born 29 Apr 1746, Provincetown, Mass.; married Experience UNKNOWN; died 11 Nov 1801, Provincetown, Mass.

215    vi. Elisha Cook, born abt 1745, Provincetown, Mass.; married Sarah Susannah ATWOOD, 29 Dec 1763, Truro, Mass.

216    vii. John Cook, born abt 1752, Provincetown, Mass.; married Mary C. NEWCOMB, 12 Apr 1770, Truro, Mass.; died 27 Apr 1823, Provincetown, Mass.

217    viii.Jonathan Cook Sr., born 22 Jul 1753, Provincetown, Mass.; married Mercy TILTON, abt 1770; married Mary, 27 Oct 1831; died 2 Aug 1835, Provincetown, Mass.

218    ix. Capt. Samuel Cook, born 29 Aug 1756, Provincetown, Mass.; married Jane Jenny NICKERSON, 25 Jul 1777, Provincetown, Mass.; died 18 Feb 1825, Provincetown, Mass.

4.27

x. Lemuel Cook was born about 1760 in Provincetown, Mass. He died before 1765 at the age of 5.

65. Thomas Cooke Sr (Richard-3, Josiah-2, Josias-1) was born on 27 Apr 1697 in Eastham, Mass. He signed a will on 25 Mar 1774 in Durham, Conn. He died on 31 May 1774 at the age of 77 in Guilford, Conn.

Thomas Cooke Sr and Dinah DOANE were married on 19 Sep 1719 in Eastham, Mass. Dinah Doane, daughter of Samuel Doane and Martha Hamblen, was born on 30 Dec 1700 in Eastham, Mass.

Thomas Cooke and Dinah Doane had the following children:

219 i. Rebecca Cook, born 3 Oct 1720, Eastham, Mass.; married Abner SNOW, 29 Jul 1741; died bef Mar 1774.

 ii. Gideon Cook was born on 23 Jul 1722 in Eastham, Mass.

220 iii. Sarah Cook, born 23 Jul 1724, Eastham, Mass.; married Unknown AUSTIN.

221 iv. Asenath Cook, born 3 May 1726, Eastham, Mass.; married Moses LUCAS, 22 May 1746, Middletown, Conn.; died 25 Dec 1778, Middletown, Conn.

222 v. Dinah Cook, born 22 Feb 1732/3, Eastham, Mass.; married NORTON; died 25 Mar 1774.

223 vi. Thomas Cook Jr., born 1728, Durham, Middlesex, Conn; married Hannah TRYON, bef 13 Jul 1755, Middlesex, Hartford, Conn.; died aft 1800, New Durham, Schoharie, NY.

224 vii. Jesse Cook, born 1738; married Ruth FAIRCHILD, 21 Oct 1760, Durham, Middlesex, Conn; married Rhoda TALCOT, 27 Oct 1766, Durham, Middlesex, Conn; married Anne (Smithson) GRISWOLD, 20 Oct 1771, Durham, Conn.

225 viii. Samuel Doane Cook, born bef 1743; married Rebecca PICKET, 4 Dec 1766, Durham, Middlesex, Conn; died 26 Mar 1780, Greenfield, Mass.

66. Hannah Cooke (Richard-3, Josiah-2, Josias-1) was born 25 Jan 1699/70 in Eastham, Mass. She died on 21 Mar 1783 at the age of 84 in Truro, Mass.

Hannah Cooke and Ebenezer ROGERS were married on 24 Mar 1719/20. Ebenezer Rogers, son of John Rogers and Priscilla Hamblen, was born on 17 Feb 1679 in Harwich, Mass. He died before 25 Jun 1769 at the age of 90 in Lyme, Conn.

Ebenezer Rogers and Hannah Cooke had the following children:

 i. Zaccheus Rogers, born 30 Dec 1720; married Elizabeth KING.

 ii. Joshua Rogers, born 30 Oct 1722, Harwich, Mass.; married Elizabeth COLE, 17 Mar

1743, Harwich, Mass.; died 12 Feb 1761, Chatham, Mass. They had 2 children.

iii. Ebenezer Rogers was born on 20 Sep 1724 in Harwich, Mass. He died on 13 Oct 1789 at the age of 65 in Lyme, Conn.

iv. Thankful Rogers, born 16 Jul 1726, Harwich, Mass.; married Ezekiel ANDREWS, 28 Feb 1749/50, Harwich, Mass. They had 1 child.

v. Richard Rogers, born 17 May 1728, Harwich, Mass.; married Sarah HIGGINS. They had 6 children.

vi. Samuel Rogers was born on 9 Apr 1730 in Harwich, Mass.

vii. Caleb Rogers, born 19 Apr 1732, Harwich, Mass.; married Marcy KING, 24 Jan 1754, Harwich, Mass.

viii.    Lemuel Rogers, born 10 Jul 1734, Harwich, Mass.; married Hannah ST. JOHN.

ix. Benjamin Rogers, born 1 Aug 1736, Harwich, Mass.; married Temperence PHINNEY, 5 Apr 1763, Harwick, Worchester, Mass.   They had 3 children.

x. Hannah Rogers was born on 24 Jun 1739 in Harwich, Mass.

xi. Patience Rogers, born 9 Sep 1741, Harwich, Mass.; married Zaccheus COVELL.

67. Caleb Cook (Richard-3, Josiah-2, Josias-1) was born on 11 Sep 1702 in Eastham, Mass.

Caleb Cook and Hannah BROWN were married on 7 Apr 1726 in Eastham, Mass. Hannah Brown was born on 1 May 1694 in Eastham, Mass. She died on 17 Mar 1726/7 at the age of 32.

Caleb Cook and Lydia WALKER were married on 20 Feb 1728/9 in Eastham, Mass. Lydia Walker was born about 1705.

Caleb Cook and Lydia Walker had the following children:

233    i.    Samuel Cook, born 31 Jan 1732, Eastham, Mass.; married Deborah ATWOOD, 17 Apr 1753, Eastham, Mass.

234    ii.  Lydia Cook, born 2 Apr 1736, Eastham, Mass.

235    iii.  Caleb Cooke Jr., born 2 Jun 1742, Eastham, Mass.; married Jane SMITH.

iv.  Susanna Cooke was born on 5 Aug 1744 in Eastham, Mass.

68. Elisabeth "Bettey" Cooke (Richard-3, Josiah-2, Josias-1) was born on 30 Nov 1704 in Eastham, Mass. She died on 25 Jan 1778 at the age of 73 in Yarmouth, Mass.

Elisabeth "Bettey" Cooke and Jonathan ROGERS were married on 18 Jan 1727/8 in Eastham, Mass. Jonathan Rogers, son of John Rogers and Priscilla Hamblen, was born on 20 Mar 1703 in Harwich, Mass. He died on 13 Feb 1781 at the age of 77 in Yarmouth, Mass.

Jonathan Rogers and Elisabeth Cooke had the following children:

    i.   Caleb Rogers was born on 19 Oct 1728 in Yarmouth, Mass. He died on 13 Dec 1731 at the age of 3 in Yarmouth, Mass.

    ii.  Precilah Rogers was born on 15 Nov 1730 in Yarmouth, Mass. She died of drowning with four others in an accident on 30 Aug 1751 at the age of 20 in Yarmouth, Mass.

    iii. Abigail Rogers, born 11 Sep 1732, Yarmouth, Mass.; married John ROBBINS, 4 Feb 1758.

    iv. Caleb Rogers, born 1 Mar 1734/5, Yarmouth, Mass.; married Hannah HAMILTON, 1 Aug 1761, Yarmouth, Mass.

69. Deborah Cooke (Richard-3, Josiah-2, Josias-1) was born on 22 Aug 1710 in Eastham, Mass. She died on 23 Mar 1772 at the age of 61.

Deborah Cooke and Sylvanus SNOW were married on 11 Nov 1761 in Eastham, Mass. Sylvanus Snow, son of Jabez Snow and Elizabeth Treat, was born on 16 Feb 1705 in Eastham, Mass. He died on 23 Mar 1772 at the age of 67 in Eastham, Mass.

70. Abigail Cooke (Richard-3, Josiah-2, Josias-1) was born on 8 Jun 1715 in Eastham, Mass. She died in 1780 at the age of 65 in Eastham, Mass.

Abigail Cooke and Simeon SMITH were married in 1735 in Eastham, Mass. Simeon Smith, son of Jeremiah Smith and Abigail Smith, was born on 10 May 1712 in Eastham, Mass.

Simeon Smith and Abigail Cooke had the following children:

    i.   Simeon Smith, born 26 Feb 1739, Eastham, Mass.; married Susannah STUBS, 29 Dec 1757, Eastham, Mass.; married Elizabeth SWEET, 13 Dec 1764, Wellfleet, Mass. They had 2 children.

    ii.  Thomas Smith was born on 6 Feb 1741/2 in Eastham, Mass.

    iii. Jesse Smith was born abt 28 Feb 1742 in Eastham, Mass.

    iv. George Smith was born on 16 Aug 1746 in Eastham, Mass.

    v.  Nehemiah Smith, born 14 Dec 1751, Eastham, Mass.; married Jedidah AREY; died 1773.

    vi. Jeremiah Smith, born 8 Apr 1758, Eastham, Mass.; married Abigail (poss. DEMONT). They had at least 1 child.

    vii. Richard Smith was born on 14 Dec 1760 in Eastham, Mass.

71. Thankful Cooke (Richard-3, Josiah-2, Josias-1) was born on 12 Jun 1717 in Eastham, Mass. She died in 1772 at the age of 55 in Eastham, Mass.

Thankful Cooke and Jesse NICKERSON were married on 25 Feb 1736/7 in Eastham, Mass. Jesse Nickerson, son of John Nickerson and Sarah Bassett, was born about 1716 in Harwich, Mass. He died when he was lost as sea about 1745 at the age of 29.

Thankful Cooke and Nathan KENNEY were married on 19 Mar 1747. Nathan Kenney was born on 5 May 1709 in Boston, Suffolk, Mass. He died on 4 Feb 1754 at the age of 44.

79. Cornelius Cooke (Twin) (Caleb-3, Josiah-2, Josias-1) was born on 2 Jun 1719 in Truro, Mass. He was baptized on 16 Jul 1719 in Truro, Mass.

Cornelius Cooke (Twin) and Abigail HATCH were married on 26 Mar 1751. Abigail Hatch was born in Mansfield.

Cornelius Cooke and Abigail Hatch had the following children:

    i.   Prince Cooke was born in 1752 in Marshfield, Mass.
    ii.  Deliverance Cooke was born in 1753 in Marshfield, Mass.

92. Josiah Cook (Joshua-3, Josiah-2, Josias-1) was born on 30 Aug 1707 in Eastham, Mass. He signed a will on 30 May 1775 in Chatham, Mass. He died before 24 Jun 1775 at the age of 67 in Chatham, Mass. Josiah had his estate probated on 24 Jun 1775 in Chatham, Mass.

Josiah Cook and Hannah SPARROW had marriage banns published on 16 Jan 1730/1 in Eastham, Mass. and they were married there on 11 Feb 1730/1. They moved in Haddam, Conn. in 1740. Hannah Sparrow, daughter of Richard Sparrow and Mercy Cobb, was born on 12 Oct 1711 in Eastham, Mass. She died on 20 Sep 1784 at the age of 72 in Chatham, Conn.

Josiah Cook and Hannah Sparrow had the following children:

        i.   Elijah Cook was born on 26 Jan 1731 in Eastham, Mass. He died before 1737 at the age of 6.
322   ii.  Elizabeth Cook, born 23 Feb 1733/4, Eastham, Mass.; married Ebenezer SEARS Jr., 25 Jan 1753, Middletown, Conn.; died 4 Jul 1797, Middletown, Conn.
323   iii. Josiah Cook, born 3 Dec 1735, Eastham, Mass.; married Mary RIDER, 2 Mar 1767, Chatham, Conn.; died 1813, Chatham, Conn.
324   iv. Capt. Elijah Cook, born 8 Jun 1737, Eastham, Mass.; married Hannah HALE, 27 Feb 1760, Middletown, Conn.; died aft 1796, Canajoharie, NY.
325   v.  Joshua Cook, born 12 Apr 1740, Eastham, Mass.; married Mary, Chatham, Conn.; later married Elizabeth CARY, 4 Dec 1783, East Hampton Congregational Church, Middlesex, Conn.; died 21 Mar 1790, Middle Haddam, Conn.
326   vi. Deacon Moses Cook, born 23 Oct 1742, Middletown, Conn.; married Elizabeth CONE, 18 Dec 1765, East Hampton Congregational Church, Middlesex, Conn.; married second, Ede (Clark) NORTON, 11 Apr 1809, East Hampton Congregational Church, Middlesex, Conn.; died 15 May 1818, East Hampton, Conn.

327    vii. Mercy Cook, born 15 Feb 1745, Middletown, Conn.; married Lieut. Titus CARRIER, 19 Dec 1765, East Hampton Congregational Church, Middlesex, Conn.

328    viii.    Hannah Cook, born bef 22 Mar 1748, East Hampton, Conn.; married Isaac KNEELAND, 23 May 1764, East Hampton Congregational Church, Middlesex, Conn.

329    ix. Roda Cook, married Simeon WRIGHT, 22 Nov 1769, East Hampton Congregational Church, Middlesex, Conn.

330    x. Richard Cook, born 17 Mar 1753, Middletown, Conn.; married Mary ROWLEY, 11 Aug 1779, East Hampton Congregational Church, Middlesex, Conn.; died 13 Aug 1833, Plainfield, Otsego, NY.


93. Joshua Cook (Joshua-3, Josiah-2, Josias-1) was born on 23 Mar 1708 in Eastham, Mass. He appeared in the census in 1790 in Guilford, Conn. He died on 13 Mar 1801 at the age of 92 in Guilford, Conn.

Joshua Cook and Zilpah BROWN were married on 8 Oct 1730 in Eastham, Mass. They moved to Mansfield, Conn. on 31 Jul 1737. They moved to Guilford, Conn. before 1751. Zilpah Brown, daughter of James Brown and Ruth Snow, was born on 18 Oct 1708 in Eastham, Mass. She died on 14 Apr 1783 at the age of 74 in Eastham, Mass.

Joshua Cook and Zilpah Brown had the following children:

331    i.    James Cook, born 7 Jun 1731, Eastham, Mass.; married Martha HILL; died 7 Dec 1759.

332    ii.    Mercy Cook, born 30 Jun 1733, Eastham, Mass.; married Thomas ADKINS, 23 Mar 1758; died 1828, Leroy, Jefferson, NY.

       iii. Isayah Cook was born on 3 Jun 1735 in Eastham, Mass.

       iv. Isaiah Cook was born on 13 Jul 1737 in Chatham, Mass. He served and died in the French and Indian War on 6 Sep 1758 at the age of 21.

333    v.    Joshua Cook, born bef 1745; married Mary COOK, 5 Nov 1767, Chatham, Conn.; died aft 1819, Silver Creek, O.


94. Ebenezer Cook (Joshua-3, Josiah-2, Josias-1) was born on 25 Nov 1711 in Eastham, Mass. He died in 1793 at the age of 82 in East Haddam, Conn. He served in the military in the American Revolution as a private in Captain Long's company.

Ebenezer Cook and Mercy PAINE were married on 9 Oct 1735 in Eastham, Mass. They moved in East Haddam, Conn. between 1737 and 1741 Mercy PAINE, daughter of John PAINE and Bennett FREEMAN, was born on 3 Apr 1712 in Eastham, Mass. She died in Jun 1774 at the age of 62 in Connecticut.

 Mercy Paine was a descendant of two *Mayflower* passengers. Through her father, she was a descendant of Stephen Hopkins and through her mother, a descendant of William Brewster. She and her husband were 3rd cousins.

Ebenezer Cook and Mercy PAINE had the following children:

      i.   Ruth Cook was born on 23 Jan 1736/7 in Eastham, Mass.

      ii.  John Cook was baptized on 14 Jun 1741 in East Haddam First Congregational Church, Middlesex, Conn. He served in the military in the 9th Company under Windham officers. in 1762. He died on 25 Dec 1762 in East Haddam, Conn.

334    iii.  Rebecca Cook, married Samuel Mitchell, 10 Nov 1762, East Haddam, Conn.

335    iv.  Ebenezer Cook Jr., born bef 12 Oct 1746; married Mary WEST, 1770; married Abigail Weeks, 14 Nov 1782, Stockbridge, Mass.; died 28 Mar 1813, New Hartford, Oneida, NY.

336    v.  Gideon Cook, born 10 Jan 1750, East Haddam, Conn.; married Huldah Lisk, 20 Mar 1776, East Haddam, Conn.; died 12 Apr 1806, East Haddam, Conn.

      vi.  Mary Cook was baptized on 21 Sep 1755 in Second Church, Colchester, Conn.

95. Ephraim Cook (Joshua-3, Josiah-2, Josias-1) was born on 16 Oct 1712 in Eastham, Mass. He died after Feb 1778 at the age of 65 in Coventry, Conn.

Ephraim Cook and Mary MERRICK were married on 12 Feb 1734/5 in Eastham, Mass. They moved to Mansfield or Coventry, Connecticut abt 1742. Mary Merrick, daughter of Joseph Merrick and Elizabeth Twining, was born on 31 Jul 1717 in Eastham, Mass. She died in Feb 1778 at the age of 60 in Coventry, Conn. She was also known as Mary Myrick.

Ephraim Cook and Mary Merrick had the following children:

337    i.  Shubael Cook, born 6 Jun 1736, Eastham, Mass.; married Catherine EDWARDS, 2 Feb 1758, Coventry, Conn.; died Aug 1795, Coventry, Conn.

338    ii.  Moses Cook, born 1738, Coventry, Conn.; married Eunice ALLIN, 17 Jan 1760, Coventry, Conn.; died aft 1810, Locke, Cayuga, NY.

339    iii.  Reuben Cook, born 20 Aug 1741, Eastham, Mass.; married Maria TURNER; married Elizabeth EDWARDS, 1763, Coventry, Conn.; died 12 Feb 1814, Orwell, Vt.

340    iv.  Ephraim Cook, born abt 1743, Mansfield or Coventry, Connecticut; married Huldah LOOMIS; married Unknown ; died aft 1800, Canaan, Conn.

      v.  Mary Cook was born between 1743 and 1750. She was unmarried, living with her sister Abigail, in 1796 in Lebanon, CT.

341    vi.  Joseph Cook, born abt 1750, Connecticut; married Jerusha TURNER, 19 Mar 1772, Coventry, Conn.; married Mehitable BADCOCK, 30 Nov 1785, Coventry, Conn.; died bef 1808, New York.

4.33

342    vii. Nathan Cook, born abt 1754, Coventry, Conn.; married Mary YOUNG, 3 Feb 1779, Windham, NY.; died Feb 1793, Coventry, Conn.

343    viii.   John Cook, born abt 1756, Coventry, Conn.; married Sarah REYNOLDS; died 6 Jan 1806, Hebron, Conn.

344    ix. Abigail Cook, born abt 1758, Coventry, Conn.; married Samuel PERKINS.

345    x. Elizabeth Cook, born abt 1759, Coventry, Conn.; married Samuel SPRAGUE.

96. Simeon Cook (Joshua-3, Josiah-2, Josias-1) was born on 24 Aug 1715 in Eastham, Mass. Simeon died between 1762 and 1767 at the age of 47 in New Marlborough, Mass.

Simeon Cook and Melatiah ROBBINS had marriage banns published on 16 Nov 1738 in Eastham, Mass.

Simeon Cook and Melatiah Robbins had the following children:

346    i. Ruhammah Cook, born abt 1739, Lee, Mass.; married Nathan BALL, abt 1767; died 21 Sep 1838, Lee, Mass.

347    ii. Moses Cook, born abt 1740; married Hannah HOWE; died aft 1820, Amenia, NY.

348    iii. Martha Cook, married Abraham BENTON, 14 May 1759, Sandisfield, Mass.; died 7 Sep 1824, Sandisfield, Mass.

iv. Abigail Cook died on 23 Feb 1829 in New Marlborough, Mass.

v. Priscilla "Dolly" Cook died on 30 Oct 1834 in New Marlborough, Mass.

vi. Mary Cook died on 18 Jan 1833 in New Marlborough, Mass.

vii. Thankful Cook died on 17 Apr 1829 in New Marlborough, Mass.

349    viii.   Joseph Cook, born 27 Sep 1751, New Marlborough, Mass.; married Abigail PECK, 24 Nov 1775, New Haven, New Haven, Conn.; married Olive UNKNOWN, bef 3 Aug 1811; died bet 18 Mar 1845 and 13 Jan 1852, Townshend, Huron, O.

ix. Simeon Cook died before 29 Nov 1775 in Canaan, Conn.

97. Zaccheus Cook (Joshua-3, Josiah-2, Josias-1) was born about 1719 in Eastham, Mass. He bought land with Josiah Cook several times in 1742 in Middletown, Conn. He died on 19 Apr 1812 at the age of 93 in Chatham, Conn.

Zaccheus Cook and Mary HUBBARD were married 13/14 May 1747 in Middletown, Conn. Mary Hubbard, daughter of George Hubbard and Mary Roberts, was born on 20 Mar 1727/8 in Middletown, Conn. She died after 11 Jun 1785 at the age of 57.

Zaccheus Cook and Mary Hubbard had the following children:

350    i. Mary Cook, born 26 Jul 1748, Middletown, Conn.; married Joshua COOK, 5 Nov

1767, Chatham, Conn.

351     ii.  Zaccheus Cook, born 5 Apr 1751, Middletown, Conn.; married Mercy GOFFE, 18 Jan 1776.

352     iii. Martha Cook, born 3 Mar 1755, Middletown, Conn.; married Josiah PURPLE, 4 Jan 1776; died 1829, Chatham, Conn.

353     iv.  Huldah Cook, born 20 Mar 1758, Haddam, Conn.; married William THOMAS, 11 Oct 1785, East Hampton Congregational Church, Middlesex, Conn.

354     v.   Nathaniel Cook, born abt 1760, Middletown, Conn.; married Olive ROWLEY, 2 Mar 1786, Middle Haddam, Conn.; died 8 Apr 1786.

355     vi.  Zuba Cook, born abt 1765, Middletown, Conn.; married John HAILING, 30 Dec 1784, East Hampton Congregational Church, Middlesex, Conn.

        vii. Asa Cook was born on 12 May 1766 in Chatham, Conn. He was baptized on 18 May 1766 in East Hampton, Conn.

356     viii.    Mehitable Cook, born abt Jul 1769, Chatham, Conn.; married Roswell HUBBARD, 5 Feb 1788, East Hampton Congregational Church, Middlesex, Conn.

98. Ruhama Cook (Joshua-3, Josiah-2, Josias-1) was born about 1721 in Eastham, Mass. She died between 1766 and 1776 at the age of 45 in Chatham, Mass.

Ruhama Cook and Robert SHATTUCK were married on 9 Sep 1742 in Plymouth, Mass. Robert Shattuck, son of Robert Shattuck and Mary Pratt, was born on 3 Jun 1721 in Plymouth, Mass. He died on 12 Feb 1802 at the age of 80 in Middletown, Conn.

Robert Shattuck and Ruhama Cook had the following children:

   i.   Randall Shattuck, born 11 Jun 1748, Middletown, Conn.; married Comfort TYLER, 4 Jan 1770, East Hampton Congregational Church, Middlesex, Conn.; died 1804, Torrington, Conn. They had 9 children.
   ii.  William Shattuck, born 13 Aug 1750, Middletown, Conn.; married Hannah SPENCER, 22 Mar 1780, East Hampton Congregational Church, Middlesex, Conn. They had 6 children.
   iii. Thomas Shattuck, born 1 Jul 1752, Middletown, Conn.; married Olive PHELPS; married Ruth Wells. They had 5 children.
   iv.  Patience Shattuck was born on 12 Jun 1754 in Middletown, Conn.
   v.   Robert Shattuck, born 1 Oct 1756, Middletown, Conn.; married Anna LOOMIS. They had 9 children
   vi.  David Shattuck, born 12 Sep 1758, Middletown, Conn.; married Dorothy ALCOTT. They had 6 children.
   vii. Maria Patience Shattuck, born 19 Jul 1761, Middletown, Conn.; married Lemuel MITCHELL. They had at least 1 child.

4.35

viii.   Moses Shattuck, born 29 Dec 1763, Middletown, Conn.; married Betsey VAUGHN. They had 4 children.

ix.   Polly Shattuck, born 17 Nov 1766, Middletown, Conn.; married Ozias SPENCER. They had 4 children.


99. Jonathan Cook (Joshua-3, Josiah-2, Josias-1) was born about 1723 in Eastham, Mass. He died before 29 Oct 1804 at the age of 81 in Haddam, Conn. His estate was insolvent, and his son Nathaniel Cook filed bond to cover the debts.

Jonathan Cook and Deborah ROBERDS were married in 1751 in Middle Haddam, Conn. Deborah Roberds, daughter of Nathaniel Roberds and Mehitable Brainerd, was born on 13 Mar 1731/2 in Middletown, Conn.

Jonathan Cook and Deborah Roberds had the following children:

☞ i.   Jonathan Cook was born in Apr 1752 in Haddam, Conn. He was baptized on 16 Apr 1752 in Haddam Neck Congregational Church, East Haddam, Conn. He died as a prisoner of war in Aug 1777 at the age of 25 in New York, NY. (What is today the Brooklyn Navy Yards was, during the revolution, the place where the British kept their prison ships anchored. Prisoners were not given much thought and many were poisoned simply to get rid of them. Jonathan Cook was probably one of those who was poisoned.)

365   ii.   Deborah Cook, born abt May 1754, Haddam, Conn.; married Seymour HURLBURT, 19 Feb 1778, Chatham, Conn.; died 28 Apr 1840, Chatham, Conn.

366   iii.   Sgt. Nathaniel Cook, born abt Feb 1756, Haddam, Conn.; married Anna SEARS, 7 Dec 1780; died 18 Oct 1816, Haddam, Conn.

367   iv.   Hannah Cook, born bef 8 Mar 1758, Haddam, Conn.; married Jesse BRAINERD, 28 Jun 1781, Middle Haddam, Conn.; died 25 Jun 1837, Haddam, Conn.

v.   Ichabod Cook was born on 14 Nov 1759 in Chatham, Conn. He was baptized on 14 Nov 1759 in Chatham, Mass. He died after 1800 at the age of 41 in Chatham, Mass.

368   vi.   Amos Cook, born bef 11 Jul 1762, Haddam, Conn.; married Jane BAILEY, 1787, Haddam Neck Congregational Church, East Haddam, Conn.

369   vii.   Jemimah Cook, born bef 27 Mar 1768, Haddam, Conn.; married Elihu SMITH, 24 Mar 1788, Haddam Neck Congregational Church, East Haddam, Conn.

370   viii.   Patience Cook, born 6 Jan 1771; married Edward BRINES, 3 Jun 1793, Chatham, Conn.; died 25 Jul 1855, Wabash County, Ill.

ix.   Ruhama Cook was born before 12 Nov 1775. She was baptized on 12 Nov 1775 in Haddam Neck Congregational Church, East Haddam, Conn.


100. Mary Cook (Joshua-3, Josiah-2, Josias-1) was born about 1725 in Eastham, Mass. She died after 1800 at the age of 75 in Burlington, Otsego, NY.

Mary Cook and Caleb JOHNSON were married on 19 Sep 1745 in Haddam Neck Congregational Church, East Haddam, Conn. Caleb Johnson, son of James Johnson and Ann Cooke, was born about 1724 in Middletown, Conn. He died after 1800 at the age of 76 in Burlington, Otsego, NY.

Caleb Johnson and Mary Cook had the following children:

i. John Johnson, born 1748, Chatham, Conn.; married Lois BRAINERD, 31 Oct 1771, East Hampton, Conn.; married Mary (Cole) BAILEY; died 28 Jun 1842, East Hampton, Conn. With his first wife they had 9 children.
ii. Joseph Johnson, born 1750; married Jerusha KILBOURN. They had 3 children.
iii. Mary Johnson, born abt 1753, East Haddam, Conn.; married Jedediah CONE, 1 Jul 1779.
iv. Elizabeth Johnson, born abt 1756, East Hampton, Conn.; married Aaron GATES, 9 May 1776, East Haddam, Conn.; she died 2 Aug 1816 of dropsy, Hartland, Middlesex, Ct. They had 8 children. (Dropsy (swelling) was a symptom of heart disease.)
v. Ruhama Johnson, born abt 1758, East Haddam, Conn.; married Abner MOSES, 15 May 1787, East Hampton, Conn.; died 1800, Ohio. They had 3 children.
vi. Mercy Johnson, born 1 Oct 1760; married Jabez GIDDINGS, 20 Sep 1784, East Hampton Congregational Church, Middlesex, Conn.; married Dr. Amherst COLT, 28 Sep 1806, East Hartland, Hartford, Conn. With her first husband she had 2 children. With her second husband she had 4 children.
vii. Elisha Johnson, born 13 Dec 1764, East Hampton, Conn.; married Olive HUBBARD. They had 8 children.
viii. Isaac Johnson, born 9 Apr 1767, East Hampton, Conn.; married Mary ROLLO; died 20 Feb 1859, Burlington, Otsego, NY. They had 5 children.
ix. Harris Johnson, born 12 Jun 1769; married Martha PERKINS, 20 Nov 1794; died 30 Jan 1818, Burlington, Otsego, NY. They had 11 children.

101. Hezekiah Cook (Joshua-3, Josiah-2, Josias-1) was born about 1728 in Eastham, Mass. He served in the military in the French and Indian war about 1762. He later served in the American Revolution in Berkshire County, Mass. He died on 23 Apr 1793 at the age of 65 in New Marlborough, Mass. He was buried in New Marlborough Cemetery, New Marlborough, Mass.

Hezekiah Cook and Lydia lived in Middletown, Conn. on 1 Jan 1749/50. They moved to Bolton, Conn. between 1757 and 1760. They were living in New Marlborough, Mass. in 1762. Lydia was born about 1734. She died on 2 Jan 1821 at the age of 87 in New Marlborough, Mass. She was buried in New Marlborough Cemetery, New Marlborough, Mass.

Hezekiah Cook and Lydia had the following children:

4.37

       i.   Eunice Cook was born about 1757 in Bolton, Conn. She died on 23 Apr 1774 at the age of 17 in New Marlborough, Mass. She was buried in New Marlborough Cemetery, New Marlborough, Mass.

      ii.  Azuba Cook was born about 1759 in prob. Bolton, CT. She died on 10 Nov 1836 at the age of 77 in New Marlborough, Mass. She was buried in New Marlborough Cemetery, New Marlborough, Mass.

380    iii. Solomon Cook, born 21 Dec 1761, New Marlborough, Mass.; married Elizabeth PECK, 4 Nov 1782, New Haven, New Haven, Conn.; died 21 Feb 1823, German, Chenango, NY.

      iv. Benjamin Cook was born on 14 Feb 1764 in New Marlborough, Mass. He died on 18 Aug 1773 at the age of 9 in New Marlborough, Mass. He was buried in New Marlborough Cemetery, New Marlborough, Mass.

381    v.  Russell Cook, born 12 Aug 1766, New Marlborough, Mass.; married Martha KEYES, 25 Apr 1792; married Rebecca ; died 22 May 1832, New Marlborough, Mass.

382    vi. Eli Cook, born 16 Nov 1768, New Marlborough, Mass.; married Rachel CHURCH, 5 Oct 1791.

     vii. Patience Cook was born on 21 Sep 1771 in New Marlborough, Mass. She died on 16 Aug 1773 at the age of 1 in New Marlborough, Mass. She was buried in New Marlborough Cemetery, New Marlborough, Mass.

383   viii. Levi N. Cook, born 26 Feb 1774, New Marlborough, Mass.; married Elizabeth (Betsey) BROWN, 24 Jul 1794, New Marlborough, Mass.

384    ix. Benjamin Warren Cook, born 19 Aug 1777, New Marlborough, Mass.; married Louisa KASSON, bef 1807; died bef 3 Nov 1840, Lenox, Mass.

**102.** Nathaniel Cooke (Benjamin-3, Josiah-2, Josias-1) was born on 6 Jul 1717 in Eastham, Mass.

Nathaniel Cooke and Mercy REMICK were married on 27 Sep 1740 in Eastham, Mass. Mercy Remick, daughter of Christian Remick and Hannah Freeman, was born on 30 Nov 1718 in Eastham, Mass. She died after 1783 at the age of 65.

Nathaniel Cooke and Mercy Remick had the following children:

      i.   Nathaniel Cook was born on 25 Jan 1741/2 in Eastham, Mass.

385    ii.  Shubal Cook, born 23 Jan 1743/4, Eastham, Mass.; married Jenne THACHER, 19 Feb 1776, Harwich, Mass.

386    iii. John Cooke, married Mary NEWCOMB.

**103.** Richard Cooke (Benjamin-3, Josiah-2, Josias-1) was born on 23 Nov 1718 in Eastham, Mass. He died after 1769 at the age of 51 in Eastham, Mass.

Richard Cooke and Rebecca MAYO were married on 23 Aug 1740 in Eastham, Mass. Rebecca Mayo, daughter of Joseph Mayo and Apphia Atwood, died after 18 Jul 1769. She was born in Eastham, Mass.

Richard Cooke and Rebecca Mayo had the following children:

|     | i. | Bethiah Cook was born on 17 Dec 1740 in Eastham, Mass. |
| 387 | ii. | Sarah Cook, born 31 Oct 1742, Eastham, Mass.; married Simeon MAYO, 4 Dec 1766. |
| 388 | iii. | Phebe Cook, born 27 Mar 1745; married Barnabas COOK, 1 Feb 1770, Eastham, Mass. |
| 389 | iv. | Joanna Cook, born 25 Mar 1747; married Benjamin PENFIELD. |
| 390 | v. | Elisha Cook, born 4 Jul 1750, Eastham, Mass.; married Hannah DOANE. |
|     | vi. | Nathan Cook was born on 26 Oct 1751 in Eastham, Mass. |
|     | vii. | Rebecca Cook was born on 13 Nov 1753 in Eastham, Mass. |
| 391 | viii. | Hannah Cook, born 22 Dec 1756, Eastham, Mass.; married Hezekiah SMITH; died 13 Dec 1792, Gorham, Me. |
|     | ix. | Richard Cook was born on 14 Mar 1759 in Eastham, Mass. He died on 17 Oct 1759 at the age of 0 in Eastham, Mass. |
|     | x. | Abigail Cook was born on 22 Nov 1760 in Eastham, Mass. |
|     | xi. | Lydia Cook was born on 21 Mar 1763 in Eastham, Mass. |
| 392 | xii. | Apphia Cook, born 16 Sep 1765, Eastham, Mass.; married Captain John ATWOOD, 16 Nov 1788, Wellfleet, Mass.; died 22 Mar 1810, Wellfleet, Mass. |
| 393 | xiii. | Zenas Cook, born 18 Jul 1769, Eastham, Mass.; married Experience PARKER. |

# 5<sup>th</sup> Generation

188. John Cooke (John-4, Josiah-3, Josiah-2, Josias-1) was born on 23 Aug 1730 in Provincetown, Mass. He was a seaman.

John Cooke and Mary DOWNS were married.

John Cooke and Mary Downs had the following child:

    i.    James Cook was born on 15 Sep 1770 in Provincetown, Mass.

189. Jabez Cooke (John-4, Josiah-3, Josiah-2, Josias-1) was born on 17 Jun 1732 in Provincetown, Mass. He died before Nov 1764 at the age of 32.

Jabez Cooke and Abigail BLAKE were married on 23 May 1754 in Middletown, Conn.

Jabez Cooke and Abigail Blake had the following child:

    i.    Mary Cooke was born on 7 Mar 1755 in Middletown, Conn.

190. Hannah Cooke (John-4, Josiah-3, Josiah-2, Josias-1) was born on 5 Sep 1742 in Middletown, Conn.

Hannah Cooke and David BUTLER were married on 20 Sep 1758 in Middletown, Conn.

David Butler and Hannah Cooke had the following child:

    i.    David Butler was born on 5 Feb 1759 in Middletown, Conn.

192. Sarah Cooke (John-4, Josiah-3, Josiah-2, Josias-1) was born on 30 Dec 1746 in Middletown, Conn.

Sarah Cooke and John UFFORD were married. John Ufford, son of John Ufford and Abigail Shore, was born on 29 Apr 1739 in Portland, Conn.

John Ufford and Sarah Cooke had the following children:

    i.    Molly Ufford was born on 11 Oct 1766.
    ii.   John Ufford was born on 5 Apr 1767.
    iii.  Ephraim Ufford was born on 26 Mar 1769.
    iv.  Charles Ufford, born 25 Aug 1771; married Elizabeth HAZEN; died 19 Apr 1861. No

known children.

- v.  Rosannah Ufford was born on 3 Jul 1774.
- vi.  Michael Ufford, born 5 May 1776, Middletown, Conn.; married Marsha NELSON; died 1 Jan 1865. No known children.
- vii. Lucy Ufford was born in Dec 1778.

193. Joshua Cooke (Joshua-4, Josiah-3, Josiah-2, Josias-1) was born on 10 Jun 1725 in Provincetown, Mass.

Joshua Cooke and Content COOMBS were married on 17 Nov 1748 in Eastham, Mass. Content Coombs was the daughter of Solomon Coombs and Content Mayo.

194. Elizabeth "Betty" Cooke (Joshua-4, Josiah-3, Josiah-2, Josias-1) was born on 20 Feb 1729 in Provincetown, Mass.

Elizabeth "Betty" Cooke and Benjamin BROWN were married.

Benjamin Brown and Elizabeth Cooke had the following children:

- i.  Abijah Brown.
- ii.  Benjamin Brown.
- iii. Joseph Brown.
- iv. Betty Brown.

203. Jacob Cook (Jacob-4, Josiah-3, Josiah-2, Josias-1) lived in Loudon, Mass. in 1790.

Jacob Cook and Catherine CAMP were married on 4 Feb 1756.

Jacob Cook and Catherine Camp had the following children:

- i.  Asher Cook was born on 18 Mar 1757 in Granville, Mass.
- ii.  Benjamin Cook was born on 19 Aug 1762 in Granville, Mass.
- iii. Joseph Cook was born on 15 Sep 1759 in Granville, Mass.

206. Elisabeth Cooke (Jacob-4, Josiah-3, Josiah-2, Josias-1) was born on 11 Nov 1743 in Middletown, Conn.

Elisabeth Cooke and Ichabod CRITTENDEN were married. Ichabod Crittenden, son of Ichabod Crittenden and Sarah Sumner, was born on 25 Oct 1751 in Middletown, Conn.

Ichabod Crittenden and Elisabeth Cooke had the following children (all born Sandisfield, Mass.):

i.   Ichabod Crittenden III, born 16 Feb 1775; married Eliza LORING, 2 Jul 1801, Otis, Mass.; died abt 1850. They had 5 children.
ii.  Hiram Crittenden was born on 12 May 1777. He died about 1830 at the age of 53.
iii. William Crittenden, born 2 Aug 1782; married Thankful UNKNOWN; died 12 Feb 1859, Sandisfield, Mass. They had 2 children.
iv.  Sally Crittenden was born on 16 Jul 1785.
v.   Elizabeth Crittenden was born on 3 Aug 1787. She died about 1850 at the age of 63.
vi.  Huldah Crittenden was born on 5 Dec 1788. She died about 1860 at the age of 72.
vii. Alva Crittenden was born on 3 Jan 1792.
viii.   Lewis Crittenden was born on 7 Nov 1794. He died about 1860 at the age of 66.
ix.  Eunice Crittenden was born on 3 Apr 1797. She died about 1860 at the age of 63.

207. Mary Cook (Jacob-4, Josiah-3, Josiah-2, Josias-1) was born on 15 Nov 1745 in Middletown, Conn. She died on 1 Apr 1832 at the age of 86 in Waterville, NY. She was buried in Waterville, NY.

Mary Cook and Elijah RANNEY were married on 2 Mar 1763 in Granville, Mass. They moved to Blandford, Hampshire, Mass. in 1773. Elijah Ranney was born on 6 Oct 1735 in East Middletown, Conn. He died before 7 Oct 1789 at the age of 54.

Elijah Ranney and Mary Cook had the following children:

i.   Mary Ranney, born 1 Aug 1763; married Jonathan NORTON, 11 Dec 1780, Otis, Mass. They had 7 children.
ii.  Sybil Ranney, born 29 Jul 1765; married CRANE.
iii. Deacon Jeremiah Ranney, born 5 May 1769; married Alice UNKNOWN; died 23 Sep 1835. They had 4 children.
iv.  Elijah Ranney was born. He moved in Watervliet, NY. He was a merchant and a goldsmith.
v.   Ebenezer Ranney, born 25 May 1776; married Almeda BARTHOLOMEW, 23 Feb 1800, Watertown, NY.; died 12 Apr 1860, Valley Mills, NY. They had 7 children.
vi.  Rufus Ranney, born 1779, Blandford, Hampshire, Mass.; married Dolly D. BLAIR; died 29 Oct 1849, Freedom, Portage, O. They had 8 children.
629   vii. Roxana Ranney, born bet 1770 and 1780; married John Lloyd, 1791, Blandford, Hampshire, Mass.; died 11 Nov 1875, Wickliffe, Lake, O. They had 5 children.
viii.   Eunice Ranney, married Darius STEPHENS. They had 7 children.

Mary Cook and Noah WARREN were married in 1809.

208. Josiah Cook (Jacob-4, Josiah-3, Josiah-2, Josias-1) was born on 15 Nov 1747 in Middletown, Conn. He appeared in the census in 1790 in Loudon, Mass. He died in 1817 at the age of 70.

Josiah Cook and Miriam "Betsy" SHEPARD were married on 17 Oct 1771. They moved to Otis, Mass. in 1799. Miriam "Betsy" Shepard, daughter of Jonathan Shepard and Miriam Strong, was born on 4 Jul 1755 in Westfield, Mass. She died on 6 Jun 1834 at the age of 78 in Augusta, NY.

Josiah Cook and Miriam Shepard had the following children:

631     i.    Miriam Cook, born 1772; married Russel DEWOLF, 27 Aug 1792, Otis, Mass.

632    ii.    Mercy Cook, born 10 Jul 1774; married William STEADMAN, 1809.

633   iii.    Elizabeth Cook, born 1776; married Randall WOODWORTH.

      iv.   Dan Cook was born in 1778.

       v.   Josiah Cook was born in 1779. He died in 1821 at the age of 42.

     vi.   Joseph Cook was born in 1781. He died in 1821 at the age of 40.

634   vii.    Ebenezer Cook, born 29 Dec 1783; married Leonora COOMBS, Jan 1807; died 1820.

    viii.    Barnabas Cook was born in 1785.

635    ix.    Jonathan Cook, born 1788; married Polly GRAVES.

       x.   Paul Cook was born in 1790.

636    xi.    Sally Cook, born 1792; married Murray BROWN; died 1863.

     xii.   Silas Cook was born in 1794. He died in 1898 at the age of 104.

    xiii.    Orange Russell Cook was born in 1797. He appeared in the census in 1820 in Augusta, NY. He appeared in the census in 1830 in Smithfield, NY. Orange died on 30 May 1844 at the age of 47 in Morrisville, NY. He was a physician.

637    xiv.    Philander Cook, born 1799; married Ester GRAVES.

209. Lieut. Elisha Cook (Jacob-4, Josiah-3, Josiah-2, Josias-1) was born on 5 Dec 1756 in Granville, Mass. He died on 1 Oct 1829 at the age of 72 in Seville, Oh.

Lieut Elisha Cook and Anna BALDWIN were married on 18 Jun 1777. Anna Baldwin, daughter of Benjamin Baldwin and Ruth Porter, was born on 9 Jul 1756. She died on 27 Sep 1797 at the age of 41.

Elisha Cook and Anna Baldwin had the following children:

       i.   Elisha Cook Jr. was born on 8 Nov 1779. He died on 14 Apr 1787 at the age of 7.

638    ii.    John Cook, born 23 Apr 1781; married Dorcas CASE, 2 Apr 1804, Otis, Mass.; died 1826.

639   iii.    Anna Cook, born 7 Dec 1782; married Edmon KIMBALL, 6 Aug 1801, Otis, Mass.

640    iv.    Theophilus Cook, born 17 Aug 1784, Otis, Mass.; married Esther TYLER.

641     v.    Abigail Cook, born 9 Dec 1785; married Quinsey JOHNSON.

642    vi.    Polly Cook, born 8 Aug 1787; married Lyman WOODWORTH.

5.43

643     vii. Elisha Cook Jr., born 28 Apr 1789; married Esther WOODBRIDGE.

644     viii.    Solomon Cook, born 21 Feb 1791; married Lorinda SCOTT.

645     ix.  Alva Cook, born 7 Sep 1793; married Lydia COOPER, 14 Feb 1814, West
            Springfield, Mass.

Lieut Elisha Cook and Sally LEONARD were married on 5 Feb 1798 in Springfield, Mass. Sally Leonard was born on 18 Aug 1755. She died on 8 Jun 1814 at the age of 58.

Elisha Cook and Sally Leonard had the following child:

  i.   Leonard Cook was born on 8 Sep 1799. He died on 28 Jun 1803 at the age of 3 in Otis, Mass.

Lieut. Elisha Cook and Lovisa WARREN were married on 21 Nov 1814. Lovisa Warren was born on 21 Feb 1767 in Springfield, Mass. She died on 11 Nov 1844 at the age of 77 in Seville, Oh.

210. Mary Cook (Solomon-4, Josiah-3, Josiah-2, Josias-1) was born on 3 Oct 1735 in Provincetown, Mass. She died on 20 Dec 1791 at the age of 56.

Mary Cook and Samuel DOTY were married on 28 Jun 1753 in Plymouth, Mass. Samuel Doty, son of Samuel Doty and Mercy Cobb, was born on 15 Aug 1729 in Plymouth, Mass.

 Samuel Doty was a *Mayflower* descendant in three ways. First, his grandfather was Edward Doty, who was a *Mayflower* passenger and known as one of the most belligerent people in Plymouth. Josias Cooke's first appearance in the Plymouth records is for an altercation he had with Edward Doty in which Edward drew blood. Edward Doty also fought the first duel in America. Second, Samuel Doty's mother was Elizabeth Cooke. Her grandfather was Francis Cooke, who was a *Mayflower* passenger and also one of the signers of the Mayflower Compact, the document which is often cited as the foundation of American self government and democracy. There are many error-filled genealogies which try to link Josias Cooke to Francis Cooke, but they are not related, and genetics has proven this. Finally, Elizabeth Cooke's mother was Damaris Hopkins who was Stephen Hopkins daughter.

Mary Cook and her husband were 3rd cousins, once removed, through Stephen Hopkins.

Samuel Doty and Mary Cook had the following children (note that the surname started to change):

  i.   Rebecca Doten was born on 30 Nov 1753 in Plymouth, Mass. She died on 14 Dec 1753 in Plymouth, Mass.

ii.  Samuel Doten, born 15 Jul 1758, Plymouth, Mass.; married Eunice ROBBINS, 8 Jun 1781; died 2 Nov 1847, North Yarmouth, Cumberland, Me. They had 10 children.

iii.  Mary Doty, born 19 Sep 1762, Plymouth, Mass.

iv.  Hannah Doty, born abt 1765, Plymouth, Mass.; married William HOLMES, 21 Jan 1787, Plymouth, Mass. They had 8 children.

v.  Rebecca Doten, born 27 Dec 1770, Plymouth, Mass.; married John TUELL, 10 May 1796, Paris, Oxford, Me.; died 3 Oct 1857, Plymouth, Mass. They had 6 children.

211. Solomon Cook Sr. (Solomon-4, Josiah-3, Josiah-2, Josias-1) was born on 12 Sep 1737 in Provincetown, Mass. He served in the military in the American Revolution about 1776 in State of Massachusetts. He appeared in the census in 1810 in Provincetown, Mass. Solomon died on 24 Jul 1819 at the age of 81 in Provincetown, Mass. He was buried in Winthrop Street Cemetery, Provincetown, Mass.

Solomon Cook Sr. and Betsey (Elizabeth) ATKINS were married before 1760. They appeared in the census in 1790 in Provincetown, Mass. They appeared in the census in 1800 in Provincetown, Mass. Betsey (Elizabeth) Atkins was born in 1738. She died on 13 Oct 1808 at the age of 70 in Provincetown, Mass. She was buried after 13 Oct 1808 in Winthrop Street Cemetery, Provincetown, Mass.

Solomon Cook and Betsey (Elizabeth) Atkins had the following children:

650     i.  Capt Paron Cowell Cook (Twin), born 4 Jan 1760, Provincetown, Mass.; married Hannah S. GOODSPEED, bef 1781; married Mary , bef 1780, Provincetown, Mass.; died 18 Oct 1834, Provincetown, Mass.

ii.  Frank Lowell Cook (Twin) was born on 4 Jan 1760 in Provincetown, Mass.

651     iii.  Rebecca Cowell Cook, born 1 Aug 1762, Provincetown, Mass.; married David KILBURN; married Joshua NICKERSON, 1783, Provincetown, Mass.

652     iv.  Capt. Solomon Cook Jr., born 12 Aug 1764, Provincetown, Mass.; married Susanna BATES, bef 1788; died 21 Mar 1840, Provincetown, Mass.

v.  Barnabas Cook was born before 14 Apr 1771 in Provincetown, Mass. He was baptized on 14 Apr 1771 in Provincetown, Mass.

653     vi.  Mary "Betty" Cook, born 1770; married James NICKERSON; died 15 Sep 1789, Provincetown, Mass.

vii.  Isaac Cook was born in 1772 in Provincetown, Mass. He was baptized on 18 Jul 1772 in Truro, Mass.

654     viii.  Capt. Joshua Cook, born 17 Oct 1774, Provincetown, Mass.; married Elizabeth ATKINS, bef 1797; died 20 Sep 1852, Provincetown, Mass.

Solomon Cook Sr. and Catherine STAFFORD were married after 1808. Catherine Stafford was born in 1768. She died on 14 May 1822 at the age of 54 in Provincetown, Mass. She was buried in Winthrop Street Cemetery, Provincetown, Mass.

212. Rebecca Cook (Solomon-4, Josiah-3, Josiah-2, Josias-1) was born on 26 Jun 1740 in
Provincetown, Mass. She appeared in the census in 1790 in Provincetown, Mass. She died on
13 Dec 1793 at the age of 53 in Provincetown, Mass. Rebecca was buried in Winthrop Street
Cemetery, Provincetown, Mass.

Rebecca Cook and Thomas RIDER were married on 15 Nov 1759 in Truro, Mass. Thomas
Rider, son of Gershom and Bathsheba Rider, was born in 1737. He died on 8 Oct 1786 at the
age of 49 in Provincetown, Mass.

Thomas Rider and Rebecca Cook had the following children:

   655    i.   Rebecca Rider, born 5 Jun 1765; died 24 Mar 1826.
   656    ii.  Nathaniel Rider, born 12 May 1775; married Martha Ridley; died 1850.

213. Barnabas Cook (Solomon-4, Josiah-3, Josiah-2, Josias-1) was born about 1745. He died after
1797 at the age of 52 in Provincetown, Mass.

Barnabas Cook and Phebe COOK were married on 1 Feb 1770 in Eastham, Mass. They
appeared in the census in 1790 in Provincetown, Mass. Phebe Cook, daughter of Richard
Cooke and Rebecca Mayo, was born on 27 Mar 1745. Barnabas and Phebe were second
cousins.

Barnabas Cook and Phebe Cook had the following child:

     i.   Marcy Cook was born on 12 Aug 1770 in Eastham, Mass. She appeared in the census in
1790 in Provincetown, Mass.

Barnabas Cook and Sara WHORF were married about 1792. Sara Whorf, daughter of John
Whorf and Rebecca Wilbert (?), was born on 16 Sep 1758 in Provincetown, Mass.

Barnabas Cook and Sara Whorf had the following child:

   657    i.   Barnabas Cook, born 25 Dec 1793, Provincetown, Mass.; married Dorcas Hinckley
BANGS, 24 Nov 1818, Truro, Mass.; died 3 Oct 1841, at sea.

214. Edward Cook (Solomon-4, Josiah-3, Josiah-2, Josias-1) was born on 29 Apr 1746 in
Provincetown, Mass. He died of smallpox on 11 Nov 1801 at the age of 55 in Provincetown,
Mass. He was buried in the Provincetown Smallpox Cemetery.

Edward Cook and Experience UNKNOWN  were married. She died of smallpox on 19 Dec 1801 in Provincetown, Mass. She was buried in Provincetown Smallpox Cemetery.

Edward Cook and Experience Unknown had the following children:

 i. Hannah Cook was born on 24 Oct 1767 in Provincetown, Mass. She was baptized on 1 May 1768 in Truro, Mass.
 ii. Jacob Cook was born before 29 Oct 1769. He was baptized on 29 Oct 1769 in Truro, Mass.
 iii. Mercy Cook was born before 1772. She was baptized on 19 Jan 1772 in Truro, Mass.

215. Elisha Cook (Solomon-4, Josiah-3, Josiah-2, Josias-1) was born about 1745 in Provincetown, Mass. He was baptized on 15 Apr 1770 in Truro, Mass.

Elisha Cook and Sarah Susannah ATWOOD were married on 29 Dec 1763 in Truro, Mass. Sarah Susannah Atwood was the daughter of Stephen Atwood and Sarah Collins.

Elisha Cook and Sarah Susannah Atwood had the following children:

 i. Lemuel Cook was born on 5 Aug 1766 in Provincetown, Mass. He was baptized on 27 May 1770 in Truro, Mass.
 ii. Sarah Cook was born on 16 Aug 1768 in Provincetown, Mass.
658 iii. Elisha Cook, born 11 Oct 1770, Provincetown, Mass.; married Abigail UNKNOWN, bef 1794, Provincetown, Mass.; married Ruth HOPKINS, 1801, Provincetown, Mass.; married Polly YOUNG, 19 Jan 1812, Provincetown, Mass.
659 iv. David A. Cook, born 20 Dec 1774, Provincetown, Mass.; married Huldah UNKNOWN, 1794; married Lydia SMITH, 3 Dec 1804, Truro, Mass.; married Susannah MAYO, 1814, Provincetown, Mass.; died 18 May 1857, Provincetown, Mass.

216. John Cook (Solomon-4, Josiah-3, Josiah-2, Josias-1) was born about 1752 in Provincetown, Mass. He was baptized on 26 Jan 1772. He died on 27 Apr 1823 at the age of 71 in Provincetown, Mass.

John Cook and Mary C. NEWCOMB were married on 12 Apr 1770 in Truro, Mass. Mary C. Newcomb, daughter of Thomas Newcomb and Merci Tilton, was born about 1752 in Provincetown, Mass. She died on 24 Feb 1825 at the age of 73 in Provincetown, Mass.

John Cook and Mary C. Newcomb had the following children:

660 i. James Cook, born 15 Sep 1771, Provincetown, Mass.; married Polly Sweetser

SPARKS.

661   ii.  Capt. Isaac Cook, born 24 Dec 1775, Provincetown, Mass.; married Tabitha SMITH, 1798, Provincetown, Mass.; died 13 Jun 1860, Provincetown, Mass.

662   iii.  Abigail Cook, born 4 Feb 1777, Provincetown, Mass.; married James SPARKS, abt 1795, Provincetown, Mass.; died 16 Jun 1854, Provincetown, Mass.

663   iv.  John Cook Jr., born 30 May 1783, Provincetown, Mass.; married Martha BUSH, 1802, Provincetown, Mass.; died bef 1820, Provincetown, Mass.

664   v.  Josiah Cook, born 23 Jan 1791, Provincetown, Mass.; married Sara E. BOWLEY, 18 Jan 1832, Provincetown, Mass.; married Betsey STUDLY, 13 Aug 1816, Provincetown, Mass.

**217.** Jonathan Cook Sr. (Solomon-4, Josiah-3, Josiah-2, Josias-1) was born on 22 Jul 1753 in Provincetown, Mass. He served in the military in the American Revolution about 1776 in State of Massachusetts. Jonathan lived at 292 Commercial Street in Provincetown, Mass. He died on 2 Aug 1835 at the age of 82 in Provincetown, Mass. He was buried in Hamilton Cemetery, Provincetown, Mass.

Jonathan Cook Sr. and Mercy TILTON were married about 1770. Mercy Tilton, daughter of Philip and Desire Tilton, was born on 23 Oct 1750. She died in 1831 at the age of 81 in Provincetown, Mass.

Jonathan was one of the earliest masters of King Hiram's Lodge. This portrait still hangs there. His son Jonathan (#667) was also a master, about thirty years later.

Jonathan Cook and Mercy Tilton had the following children:

665   i.  Patty Martha Cook, born 27 Aug 1773, Provincetown, Mass.; married Joshua Freeman GROZIER, 24 Mar 1793, Truro, Mass.; died 26 Sep 1826, Provincetown, Mass.

666   ii.  David Newcomb Cook, born 29 Aug 1776, Provincetown, Mass.; married Salome LOMBARD, 23 Nov 1800, Provincetown, Mass.; died 16 Jun 1849, Provincetown, Mass.

667   iii.  Capt. Jonathan Cook Jr., born 23 Feb 1780, Provincetown, Mass.; married Sabra BROWN, 23 Apr 1802, Provincetown, Mass.; died 26 Apr 1862, Provincetown, Mass.

668   iv.  Capt. Philip Cook, born 15 Oct 1781, Provincetown, Mass.; married Hannah SMITH, 1 Feb 1806, Provincetown, Mass.; died 9 Apr 1849, Provincetown, Mass.

     v.  Sabra Cook was born on 15 Mar 1783 in Provincetown, Mass.

669   vi.  Bethia Cook, born 14 Oct 1784, Provincetown, Mass.; married Thomas Smith SPARKS, 1802, Provincetown, Mass.

670     vii. Capt. Lemuel Cook, born 13 Sep 1786, Provincetown, Mass.; married Rebecca
WHORF, 29 Dec 1807, Provincetown, Mass.; died 25 Jan 1828, St. Gago De
Cuba.

671     viii.    Edward Cook (Twin), born 16 Mar 1789, Provincetown, Mass.; married Survina
LEWIS, 14 Jul 1825, Provincetown, Mass.

       ix. Sally Cook (Twin) was born on 16 Mar 1789 in Provincetown, Mass. She died in 1789.

Jonathan Cook Sr. and Mary UNKNOWN were married on 27 Oct 1831.

218. Capt. Samuel Cook (Solomon-4, Josiah-3, Josiah-2, Josias-1) was born on 29 Aug 1756 in
Provincetown, Mass. He died when he perished on the wreck of the "Only Son" on their
passage from Boston, off Wood End, on 18 Feb 1825 at the age of 68 in Provincetown, Mass.
He was buried in Hamilton Cemetery, Provincetown, Mass.

Capt. Samuel Cook and Jane Jenny NICKERSON were married on 25 Jul 1777 in
Provincetown, Mass. Jane Jenny Nickerson, daughter of Phinneas Nickerson and Susannah
Smith, was born on 12 Dec 1757 in Provincetown, Mass. She died on 27 Apr 1829 at the age
of 71 in Provincetown, Mass. She was buried in Hamilton Cemetery, Provincetown, Mass.

Samuel Cook and Jane Jenny Nickerson had the following children:

672     i.   Eleanor Cook, born 19 Jan 1778, Provincetown, Mass.; married Cyrenus BROWN,
25 Apr 1793, Provincetown, Mass.

673     ii.   Ephraim Cook, born 4 Feb 1779, Provincetown, Mass.; married Rebecca
LOMBARD, 22 Apr 1802, Provincetown, Mass.; died 27 Aug 1833,
Provincetown, Mass.

674     iii. Capt. Samuel Cook, born 17 Oct 1781, Provincetown, Mass.; married Tamsey
(Tamsin) BROWN; married Eunice F. GROSS, 15 May 1853, Provincetown,
Mass.; died 11 Jan 1867, Provincetown, Mass.

675     iv. Capt. Jesse Cook, born 13 Jun 1783, Provincetown, Mass.; married Thankful Hopkins
SMITH, 27 Nov 1806, Truro, Mass.; died 9 Jul 1871, Provincetown, Mass.

676     v. Capt. Stephen Cook, born 29 Oct 1786, Provincetown, Mass.; married Delliah
CROWELL, 1807, Provincetown, Mass.; died 8 Jan 1859, Provincetown, Mass.

       vi. Ebenezer Cook was born on 21 Oct 1788 in Provincetown, Mass. He died on 30 Aug
1810 at the age of 21 in Provincetown, Mass.

       vii. Jane "Jenne" Cook was born on 24 Jun 1791 in Provincetown, Mass. She died on 28 Feb
1796 at the age of 4.

677     viii.    Betsey Cook, born 12 Oct 1794, Provincetown, Mass.; married Rev. Epaphras
KIBBY, 24 Apr 1815, Provincetown, Mass.

678     ix. Capt. James Tilton Cook, born 10 Apr 1796, Provincetown, Mass.; married Phebe
NICKERSON, 3 Feb 1818, Provincetown, Mass.; married Louisa SPARKS,

1835, Provincetown, Mass.; married Bethia GROZIER, 16 Jun 1850, Provincetown, Mass.; died 8 Mar 1871, Provincetown, Mass.

679    x.   Jane "Jenne" Cook, born 21 Jul 1799, Provincetown, Mass.; married Abraham SMALLEY Jr., 7 Feb 1820, Provincetown, Mass.; died 14 Feb 1872, Provincetown, Mass.

219. Rebecca Cook (Thomas-4, Richard-3, Josiah-2, Josias-1) was born on 3 Oct 1720 in Eastham, Mass. She died before Mar 1774 at the age of 53.

Rebecca Cook and Abner SNOW were married on 29 Jul 1741. Abner Snow, son of Nathaniel Snow and Hannah Parslow, was born in Jan 1715 in Eastham, Mass.

Abner Snow and Rebecca Cook had the following children:

    i.   Joseph Snow was born before 30 Jun 1751 in Durham, Conn.
   ii.   Hannah Snow, born 6 Jan 1754, Durham, Middlesex, Conn; married Benjamin PELTON, 9 Dec 1775, Haddam, Conn. They had 7 children.

220. Sarah Cook (Thomas-4, Richard-3, Josiah-2, Josias-1) was born on 23 Jul 1724 in Eastham, Mass.

Sarah Cook and Unknown AUSTIN were married.

221. Asenath Cook (Thomas-4, Richard-3, Josiah-2, Josias-1) was born on 3 May 1726 in Eastham, Mass. She died on 25 Dec 1778 at the age of 52 in Middletown, Conn.

Asenath Cook and Moses LUCAS were married on 22 May 1746 in Middletown, Conn. They appeared in the census in 1790 in Middletown, Conn. Moses Lucas, son of Thomas Lucas and Susan Unknown, was born on 17 Jul 1719 in Middletown, Conn. He died in Long Hill, Conn.

Moses Lucas and Asenath Cook had the following children:

    i.   Elnathan Lucas, born 16 Dec 1747, Middletown, Conn.; married Mary Margaret WARD, 17 Jun 1773, Middletown, Conn.; died 10 Jul 1777, Middletown, Conn. They had 2 children.
   ii.   Rhoda Lucas, born 10 May 1750, Middletown, Conn.; married John Tryon, 29 Apr 1769, Eastham, Mass.; died Aug 1814, Berlin, Rensselaer, NY.
  iii.   Moses Lucas Jr., born 16 Dec 1753, Long Hill, Middlesex, Conn.; married Abiah Barnes, 27 Jan 1780, Middlesex County, Conn.; died Nov 1829, Arcadia, Wayne, NY. They had 1 child.

iv. Asenath Lucas was born on 5 Sep 1755 in Middletown, Conn. She died on 2 Dec 1756 at the age of 1 in Middletown, Conn.

v. Thomas Lucas was born on 12 Sep 1757 in Middletown, Conn. He died on 11 Oct 1824 at the age of 67 in Middletown, Conn.

vi. Noah Lucas was born on 13 Mar 1760 in Middletown, Conn.

vii. Asenath Lucas was born on 1 Jan 1763 in Middletown, Conn. She died on 24 Jul 1851 at the age of 88 in Middletown, Conn.

viii. Abigail Lucas was born on 31 Oct 1765 in Middletown, Conn.


222. Dinah Cook (Thomas-4, Richard-3, Josiah-2, Josias-1) was born on 22 Feb 1732/3 in Eastham, Mass. She was baptized on 30 Jul 1769 in Durham, Conn. She died on 25 Mar 1774 at the age of 41.

Dinah Cook and Unknown NORTON were married.

223. Thomas Cook Jr. (Thomas-4, Richard-3, Josiah-2, Josias-1) was born in 1728 in Durham, Conn. He died after 1800 at the age of 72 in New Durham, Schoharie, NY. He lived in Durham, Greene, NY. Thomas served in the military in the American Revolution.

[The connection to this genealogy seems somewhat uncertain now, as there is a photograph of the transcription of his bible by his grandson Benjamin Cook (son of Miles) which states that he was born near Boston and was of Welsh descent. As this was Miles's record of his mother and father, it seems possible that Miles had heard a different story about his father's background.

The photographs can be seen in the "Find a grave," web site. The site has more information about his military service and it acknowledges that he is the son of Thomas Cooke and Dinah Doane.]

Thomas Cook Jr. and Hannah TRYON were married before 13 Jul 1755 in Middlesex, Hartford, Conn. Hannah Tryon was born in 1733 in Middletown, Conn. She died after 1790 at the age of 57 in New Durham, Schoharie, NY.

Thomas Cook and Hannah Tryon had the following children:

i. Hannah Cook was born before 24 Aug 1755 in Durham, Conn. She was baptized on 24 Aug 1755 in Durham, Conn.

ii. Hulda Cook was born before 1763. She was baptized on 21 Aug 1763 in Durham, Conn.

684 iii. Miles Cook, born bef 16 Jun 1765, Durham, Middlesex, Conn; married Sarah GRIFFIN, 1790, Durham, Conn; died 10 Jul 1846, Russell, St. Lawrence County, NY.

685 iv. Elisha Cook, born 17 May 1767, New Durham, Schoharie, NY.; married Wealthy

5.51

BISHOP, 7 Mar 1795, Middletown, Conn.; died 1841, Rodman, Jefferson, NY.

686    v.  Dinah Cook, born 1769; married Unknown NORTON.

687    vi.  Tryon Cook, born bef 27 Oct 1771, Durham, Middlesex, Conn; married Mary GRIFFIN, 23 Jan 1795, Middletown, Conn.

vii. Benjamin Cook was born on 17 Feb 1774. He died on 30 Aug 1774.

viii.   Content Cook was born on 10 Dec 1775 in Durham, Conn.

**224.** Jesse Cook (Thomas-4, Richard-3, Josiah-2, Josias-1) was born in 1738.

Jesse Cook and Ruth FAIRCHILD were married on 21 Oct 1760 in Durham, Conn. Ruth Fairchild died on 5 Apr 1766 in Durham, Conn. She was born in Haddam, Conn.

Jesse Cook and Ruth Fairchild had the following children:

i.  Millicent Cook was born on 19 Nov 1761 in Durham, Conn. She was baptized on 23 Jan 1763 in Durham, Conn.

ii.  Robert Cook was born on 11 Mar 1763 in Durham, Conn. He was baptized on 20 Mar 1763 in Durham, Conn.

iii.  Sarah Cook was born on 17 Jan 1765 in Durham, Conn. She was baptized on 27 Jan 1765 in Durham, Greene, NY.

Jesse Cook and Rhoda TALCOT were married on 27 Oct 1766 in Durham, Conn. Rhoda Talcot, daughter of Hezekiah Talcot and Jemima Parsons, was born on 6 Feb 1731 in Connecticut. She died on 29 Jul 1771 at the age of 40.

Jesse Cook and Rhoda Talcot had the following children:

i.  Edmund Cook was born on 17 Nov 1767 in Durham, Conn. He was baptized on 29 Nov 1767 in Durham, Conn. He died on 17 Feb 1768 in Durham, Conn.

ii.  Ruth Cook was born on 27 Jul 1769. She was baptized on 10 Sep 1769 in Durham, Conn.

Jesse Cook and Anne (Smithson) GRISWOLD were married on 20 Oct 1771 in Durham, Conn. Anne (Smithson).

Jesse Cook and Anne (Smithson) Griswold had the following children:

688    i.  Delight Cook, born bef 13 Mar 1774, Durham, Middlesex, Conn; married Oliver EASTON, 31 Dec 1794; died 5 Jan 1860, Afton, NY.

ii.  Rhoda Cook was born on 15 Jul 1772 in Durham, Conn. She was baptized on 16 Aug 1772 in Durham, Conn.

iii.  Joyie Cook was born before 15 Oct 1775. She was baptized on 15 Oct 1775 in Durham,

Conn.

689    iv.  Bela Cook, born abt 1779, Durham, Middlesex, Conn; died 23 Nov 1854, Union Parish, Louisiana.

690    v.  Talcott Fairchild Smithson Cook, born 31 Dec 1784, Wilmington, Windham, Vt.; married Rachel UNKNOWN; died 26 Oct 1876.

225. Samuel Doane Cook (Thomas-4, Richard-3, Josiah-2, Josias-1) was born before 1743. He was baptized on 19 Jun 1743 in Durham, Conn. He died on 26 Mar 1780 at the age of 37 in Greenfield, Mass.

Samuel Doane Cook and Rebecca PICKET were married on 4 Dec 1766 in Durham, Conn. Rebecca Picket was born in 1747 in Haddam, Conn. She died on 26 May 1782 at the age of 35 in Greenfield, Mass.

Samuel Doane Cook and Rebecca Picket had the following children:

    i.  Noah Cook was born on 11 Dec 1767 in Durham, Conn. He was baptized on 15 Jan 1769 in Durham, Conn.
    ii.  Phebe Doane Cook was born on 6 May 1769 in Durham, Conn. She was baptized on 7 May 1769 in Durham, Conn.
    iii.  Samuel Cook was born before 28 Jul 1771 in Durham, Conn. He was baptized on 28 Jul 1771 in Durham, Conn.
    iv.  Katherine Cook was born before 18 Jul 1773 in Durham, Conn. She was baptized on 18 Jul 1773 in Durham, Conn.
    v.  Content Cook was born on 15 Mar 1778 in Greenfield, Mass.

233. Samuel Cook (Caleb-4, Richard-3, Josiah-2, Josias-1) was born on 31 Jan 1732 in Eastham, Mass.

Samuel Cook and Deborah ATWOOD were married on 17 Apr 1753 in Eastham, Mass. Deborah Atwood died on 11 Apr 1772 in Eastham, Mass.

Samuel Cook and Deborah Atwood had the following children:

    i.  Gideon Cook was born on 27 Jan 1754 in Eastham, Mass.
    ii.  Joseph Cook was born on 14 Jul 1756 in Eastham, Mass.
    iii.  Dorcas Cook was born on 21 Apr 1758 in Eastham, Mass.
    iv.  Samuell Cook was born on 16 Jun 1760 in Eastham, Mass.

693    v.  Deborah Cook, born 13 Oct 1762, Eastham, Mass.; married Uriah NICKERSON, 14 Feb 1788, Eastham, Mass.
    vi.  Hannah Cook was born on 17 Jul 1765 in Eastham, Mass. She died before 1770 at the

age of 5 in Eastham, Mass.

694 vii. John Cook, born 4 Jan 1768, Eastham, Mass.; married Rachel UNKNOWN.

 viii. Hannah Cook was born on 29 May 1770 in Eastham, Mass. She died in Jul 1772 at the age of 2 in Eastham, Mass.

234. Lydia Cook (Caleb-4, Richard-3, Josiah-2, Josias-1) was born on 2 Apr 1736 in Eastham, Mass.

Lydia Cook and John MAYO had marriage banns published on 25 Feb 1760 in Eastham, Mass. John Mayo, son of John Mayo and Tabitha Snow, was born on 19 Apr 1733 in Eastham, Mass. He served in the military in the American Revolution about 1776 in State of Massachusetts. He died on 11 Feb 1816 at the age of 82 in Eastham, Mass.

John Mayo and Lydia Cook had the following children:

i. Abijah Mayo was born on 24 May 1761 in Eastham, Mass.
ii. Josiah Mayo was born on 18 Feb 1763 in Eastham, Mass.
iii. Abijah Mayo was born on 4 Jun 1765 in Eastham, Mass.
iv. Susannah Mayo was born on 27 Apr 1768 in Eastham, Mass.
v. John Mayo was born on 23 Aug 1771 in Eastham, Mass.

235. Caleb Cooke Jr. (Caleb-4, Richard-3, Josiah-2, Josias-1) was born on 2 Jun 1742 in Eastham, Mass.

Caleb Cooke Jr. and Jane Smith were married.

Caleb Cooke and Jane Smith had the following children:

i. Thomas Cook was born on 20 Mar 1766 in Eastham, Mass.
ii. David Cook was born on 15 Apr 1768 in Eastham, Mass.
iii. Sarah Cook was born on 7 Oct 1770 in Eastham, Mass.
iv. Jane Cook was born on 6 Mar 1773 in Eastham, Mass.
v. Hannah Cook was born on 6 Dec 1775 in Eastham, Mass.
vi. Nathan Cook was born on 7 May 1778 in Eastham, Mass.
vii. William Cook was born on 13 Nov 1780 in Eastham, Mass.
viii. Susannah Cook was born on 29 Jun 1783 in Eastham, Mass.
ix. Ruth Smith Cook was born on 21 Aug 1785 in Eastham, Mass.
x. Lydia Cook was born on 28 Jan 1788 in Eastham, Mass.

244. Mary C. Newcomb (Thomas-4, Elizabeth Cooke-3, Josiah-2, Josias-1) was born about 1752 in Provincetown, Mass. She died on 24 Feb 1825 at the age of 73 in Provincetown, Mass. (See

322. Elizabeth Cook (Josiah-4, Joshua-3, Josiah-2, Josias-1) was born on 23 Feb 1733/4 in Eastham, Mass. She was baptized on 4 Oct 1741 in Haddam Neck Congregational Church, East Haddam, Conn. She died on 4 Jul 1797 at the age of 63 in Middletown, Conn.

Elizabeth Cook and Ebenezer SEARS Jr. were married on 25 Jan 1753 in Middletown, Conn. Ebenezer Sears Jr., son of Ebenezer Sears and Sarah Gorham Howes, was born on 13 Jun 1723 in Yarmouth, Mass. He died on 29 Dec 1814 at the age of 91 in Chatham, Conn.

Ebenezer Sears and Elizabeth Cook had the following children:

i. Anna Sears, born 17 Feb 1755, Chatham, Conn.; married Amos CLARKE, 12 Jul 1781; died 8 Jul 1835. They had 6 children.
ii. Lieut. David Sears, born 27 Nov 1752, Chatham, Conn.; married Lucy HALL; died 29 Apr 1842. They had 2 children.
iii. Sarah Sears, born 1759, Chatham, Conn.; married Seth ALVORD Jr., 5 Sep 1793, East Hampton Congregational Church, Middlesex, Conn.; died 2 Feb 1819. They had 4 children.
iv. Hannah Sears, born 3 Jun 1760, Chatham, Conn.; married Capt Timothy RUGGLES. They had 1 child.
v. Betsy Sears, born 4 Oct 1768, Chatham, Conn.; married John WILLEY Jr., 5 Aug 1794, Granby, Hartford, Conn.

323. Josiah Cook (Josiah-4, Joshua-3, Josiah-2, Josias-1) was born on 3 Dec 1735 in Eastham, Mass. He was baptized on 4 Oct 1741 in Haddam Neck Congregational Church, East Haddam, Conn. He served in the military in the French and Indian war under Captain Eleazor Fitch, 4th Regiment, 3rd Company in 1759. He died in 1813 at the age of 78 in Chatham, Conn.

Josiah Cook and Mary RIDER were married on 2 Mar 1767 in Chatham, Conn.

Josiah Cook and Mary Rider had the following children:

i. Elizabeth Cook, born 27 Jan 1768, Chatham, Conn.; married Jesse GRAHAM, 16 Aug 1792, Haddam Neck Congregational Church, East Haddam, Conn.
ii. Mary Cook was born on 27 Jun 1777 in Chatham, Conn.
iii. Hannah Cook was born about 1786 in Chatham, Conn. She was baptized on 16 Jul 1786 in East Hampton Congregational Church, Middlesex, Conn.

324. Capt. Elijah Cook (Josiah-4, Joshua-3, Josiah-2, Josias-1) was born on 8 Jun 1737 in Eastham,

Mass. He was baptized on 4 Oct 1741 in Haddam Neck Congregational Church, East Haddam, Conn. He served in the military French and Indian war in 1758. He died after 1796 at the age of 59 in Canajoharie, NY.

Capt. Elijah Cook and Hannah HALE were married on 27 Feb 1760 in Middletown, Conn. Hannah Hale, daughter of John Hale, was born on 4 Jul 1736 in Middletown, Conn.

Elijah Cook and Hannah Hale had the following children:

    i.   A son Cook was born about 1761.
    ii.  Nathaniel Cook was born on 18 Apr 1764 in East Hampton, Conn. He was baptized on 22 Apr 1764 in East Hampton Congregational Church, Middlesex, Conn. He died on 8 Apr 1786 at the age of 21.
    iii. Mary Cook was born on 8 Oct 1766. She was baptized in Oct 1766.
    iv. Hannah Cook was born on 22 Dec 1768. She was baptized on 15 Jan 1769.
    v.  Eunice Cook was born on 13 Apr 1771. She was baptized on 28 Apr 1771.
881    vi. John Cook, born 1774; married Caty SHAFT, 1 Jun 1796.
    vii. Josiah Cook was born before 3 Aug 1783. He was baptized on 3 Aug 1783.

325. Joshua Cook (Josiah-4, Joshua-3, Josiah-2, Josias-1) was born on 12 Apr 1740 in Eastham, Mass. He was baptized on 4 Oct 1741 in Haddam Neck Congregational Church, East Haddam, Conn. He served in the military in the French and Indian war in 1758. He served in the military as an Ensign in the American Revolution for the Connecticut.  Joshua died on 21 Mar 1790 at the age of 49 in Middle Haddam, Conn.

Joshua Cook and Mary UNKNOWN were married in Chatham, Conn. Mary died on 11 Jun 1783 in East Haddam, Conn. She was also known as Marita Cook.

Joshua Cook and Mary  had the following children:

    i.   Elihu Cook was born in Mar 1765 in East Haddam, Conn. He was baptized on 31 Mar 1765 in Haddam Neck Congregational Church, East Haddam, Conn. He died on 4 Jun 1782 at the age of 17 in New York. Elihu served in the military in the American Revolution from Connecticut under Col. Butler.
    ii.  Sarah Cook was born before 15 Nov 1767 in East Haddam, Conn. She was baptized on 15 Nov 1767 in Haddam Neck Congregational Church, East Haddam, Conn.
    iii. Ansel Cook was born about Mar 1770 in East Haddam, Conn. He was baptized on 18 Mar 1770 in Haddam Neck Congregational Church, East Haddam, Conn.
    iv. Esther Cook was baptized on 4 Jul 1773 in Haddam Neck Congregational Church, East Haddam, Conn. She was born about Jul 1773 in East Haddam, Conn.
882    v.   Josiah Sparrow Cook, born 7 Nov 1775, West Springfield, Conn.; married Abiah

SIKES; died 29 Dec 1861, Agawam, Mass.

   vi. (Stillborn) Cook was born on 11 Jun 1777.

Joshua Cook and Elizabeth CARY were married on 4 Dec 1783 in East Hampton Congregational Church, Middlesex, Conn. Elizabeth Cary died on 31 Aug 1796. She was born in Middle Haddam, Conn.

326. Deacon Moses Cook (Josiah-4, Joshua-3, Josiah-2, Josias-1) was born on 23 Oct 1742 in Middletown, Conn. He was baptized after 23 Oct 1742 in Haddam Neck Congregational Church, East Haddam, Conn. He served in the military doing public service for the American Revolution in 1776 in Connecticut. He died on 15 May 1818 at the age of 75 in East Hampton, Conn.

Deacon Moses Cook and Elizabeth CONE were married on 18 Dec 1765 in East Hampton Congregational Church, Middlesex, Conn. Elizabeth Cone, daughter of Noah Cone and Hannah Unknown, was born in 1744. She was born on 24 Sep 1744 in Haddam, Conn. She died in 1808 at the age of 64. Elizabeth died on 8 Oct 1808 at the age of 64.

Moses Cook and Elizabeth Cone had the following children:

     i. Daughter Cook was born on 23 Sep 1766.

     ii. Selden Cook was born on 7 Mar 1768 in East Hampton, Conn. He was baptized on 14 May 1769 in East Hampton Congregational Church, Middlesex, Conn. He died on 16 Nov 1769 at the age of 1.

883   iii. Lydia Cook, born bef 14 May 1769; married Comfort BEEBE, 4 Jan 1787.

884   iv. Moses Cook, born 7 Jan 1772, East Hampton, Conn.; married Dorothy PERCIVAL, Jan 1797, Berlin, Hartford, Conn.

885   v. Elizabeth Cook, born 1774; married Adonijah STRONG, 11 Sep 1794, East Hampton Congregational Church, Middlesex, Conn.; died 14 Aug 1851.

     vi. Susannah Cook was born in 1776. She died on 8 May 1778 at the age of 2.

     vii. Josiah Cook was born about 1777. He died on 4 Jun 1778 at the age of 1.

     viii. Josiah Cook was born before 9 May 1779. He was baptized on 9 May 1779.

886   ix. Susannah Cook, born abt 5 Sep 1779; married Daniel Butler NEWTON, 25 Apr 1798, East Hampton Congregational Church, Middlesex, Conn.; married Henry Strong, 17 Sep 1801; died 15 Apr 1820.

     x. Hannah Cook was born before 16 Jun 1782. She was baptized on 16 Jun 1782.

887   xi. Livia Cook, born bef 18 Jul 1784; married Wix WATROUS, 3 Nov 1803, East Hampton Congregational Church, Middlesex, Conn.

888   xii. Selden Cook, born bef 25 Jun 1786; married Sally BRAINERD.

889   xiii. Owen Cook, born abt Nov 1788, East Hampton, Conn.; married Mary PARMELEE, 22 Jun 1813.

5.57

xiv.    Daniel Butler was born before 3 Feb 1802. He was baptized on 3 Feb 1802 in East Hampton Congregational Church, Middlesex, Conn. He was adopted.

Deacon Moses Cook and Ede (Clark) NORTON were married on 11 Apr 1809 in East Hampton Congregational Church, Middlesex, Conn. Ede (Clark) Norton, daughter of Jabez Clark and Sarah Judd, was born on 29 Aug 1745 in Middletown, Conn. She died in Mar 1828 at the age of 82 in Middle Haddam, Conn.

327. Mercy Cook (Josiah-4, Joshua-3, Josiah-2, Josias-1) was born on 15 Feb 1745 in Middletown, Conn. She was baptized on 24 Mar 1745 in Haddam Neck Congregational Church, East Haddam, Conn.

Mercy Cook and Lieut. Titus CARRIER were married on 19 Dec 1765 in East Hampton Congregational Church, Middlesex, Conn. Lieut. Titus Carrier, son of John Carrier and Mary Brown, was born on 23 Aug 1733. He served in the military as an ensign in the American Revolution. Titus died on 26 Jul 1796 at the age of 62.

☞ Titus Carrier was the great grandson of Martha Carrier, who had been hanged as a witch in 1692 during the famous witch hunts. His father John was born about 5 years after his grandmother had been killed. There are many books and plays written about or based on this awful event. One of the best non-fictional accounts is "The Salem Witch Trials: a day-by-day Chronicle of a Community Under Siege" by Marilynne K. Roach. The 1953 play, "The Crucible," by Arthur Miller was based on some aspects of the event. A fictional work which focuses exclusively on Martha Carrier was written by one of her descendants, entitled "The Heretic's Daughter," by Kathleen Kent. It was based, in part, on some of the stories that had been passed down through the family. The transcript of the trial shows that Martha was a very strong woman, and stood up to the accusations which were designed to find her guilty of this imaginary crime.

Martha Carrier memorial.

Titus Carrier and Mercy Cook had the following children:

    i.   Mary Carrier, born 4 Oct 1766, Chatham, Conn.; married James GOFF, 30 Mar 1786, East Hampton Congregational Church, Middlesex, Conn.; died 1 Apr 1851. They had 3 children.

    ii.  Mercy Carrier was baptized on 14 May 1769 in Chatham, Mass.

    iii.  John Carrier, born 11 Dec 1769, Chatham, Conn.; married Lucy DAILEY, 26 Feb 1795, East Hampton Congregational Church, Middlesex, Conn.; married Harriet SAGE, 1807; died 1809, Canton, Conn. With Lucy they had 7 children.

    iv.  Richard Carrier, born 23 Feb 1774, Chatham, Conn.; married Livia JOHNSON, Mar 1801, East Hampton Congregational Church, Middlesex, Conn. They had 10 children.

    v.  Mercy Carrier, born 15 May 1776, Chatham, Conn.; married Capt. Joseph BUELL, 4 Nov 1795, Colchester, New London, Conn.; died 28 Aug 1858. They had 10 children.

    vi.  Titus Carrier, born 24 Jul 1781, Chatham, Conn.; married Mehitable WATROUS, 24 May 1804, East Hampton Congregational Church, Middlesex, Conn.; died Nov 1848. They had 8 children.

328. Hannah Cook (Josiah-4, Joshua-3, Josiah-2, Josias-1) was born before 22 Mar 1748 in East Hampton, Conn. She was baptized on 22 Mar 1748 in Haddam Neck Congregational Church, East Haddam, Conn.

Hannah Cook and Isaac KNEELAND were married on 23 May 1764 in East Hampton

Congregational Church, Middlesex, Conn. They moved to East Hampton, Conn. about 1771
Isaac Kneeland, son of Isaac Kneeland and Sarah Beach, was born on 13 Oct 1741 in
Hebron, Conn.

Isaac Kneeland and Hannah Cook had the following children:

    i.   Hannah Kneeland was born on 26 Apr 1765 in Hebron, Conn.
    ii.  Isaac Kneeland was born on 28 Jan 1767 in Hebron, Conn.
    iii. Dudlee Kneeland was born on 8 Aug 1768 in Hebron, Conn.
    iv. Sarah Beach Kneeland was born on 28 Jan 1772 in Chatham, Mass. She was baptized on
        2 Mar 1772 in East Hampton, Conn.
    v.  Lucy Kneeland was born on 9 May 1779 in East Hampton, Conn.
    vi. Deborah Kneeland was born before 30 Jul 1780. She was baptized on 30 Jul 1780 in East
        Hampton, Conn.
    vii. Russell Kneeland was born before 28 Nov 1784. He was baptized on 28 Nov 1784 in
        East Hampton Congregational Church, Middlesex, Conn.

329. Roda Cook (Josiah-4, Joshua-3, Josiah-2, Josias-1) was baptized on 15 Apr 1750 in Haddam
    Neck Congregational Church, East Haddam, Conn.

    Roda Cook and Simeon WRIGHT were married on 22 Nov 1769 in East Hampton
    Congregational Church, Middlesex, Conn. Simeon Wright was born about 1736. He served in
    the military as a private in the American Revolution in 1776 in Connecticut. He died on 22 May
    1832 at the age of 96.

Simeon Wright and Roda Cook had the following child:

    i.   A daughter was born on 27 Oct 1770 in East Hampton, Conn.

330. Richard Cook (Josiah-4, Joshua-3, Josiah-2, Josias-1) was born on 17 Mar 1753 in
    Middletown, Conn. He served in the military in the American Revolution in 1776 in
    Connecticut. He died on 13 Aug 1833 at the age of 80 in Plainfield, Otsego County, NY.

    Richard Cook and Mary ROWLEY were married on 11 Aug 1779 in East Hampton
    Congregational Church, Middlesex, Conn. Mary Rowley, daughter of Ebenezer Rowley and
    Susannah Annibal, was born on 4 Aug 1758 in Chatham, Conn. She died on 13 Apr 1808 at
    the age of 49.

Richard Cook and Mary Rowley had the following children:

    895    i.   Lucy Cook, born 7 Aug 1784, Chatham, Conn.; married James Hall ALVORD, 11

Oct 1804, East Hampton Congregational Church, Middlesex, Conn.; died 11 Sep
1850, Winchester, Conn.

896    ii. Alvan Cook, born 1786, Connecticut; married Lucretia SMITH, 12 Aug 1811, East
Hampton Congregational Church, Middlesex, Conn.; died 1856.

    iii. Richard Cook died before 7 Sep 1833.

    iv. Percy Cook.

897    v. Floras Cook, born 26 Apr 1793; died 12 Apr 1819.

898    vi. Nathaniel Cook, married Betsy FULLER.

    vii. Allen Cook.


**331.** James Cook (Joshua-4, Joshua-3, Josiah-2, Josias-1) was born on 7 Jun 1731 in Eastham, Mass.
He served in the military in the French and Indian war in 1759. He died in that war on 7 Dec
1759 at the age of 28.

James Cook and Martha HILL were married. Martha Hill was born in Guilford, Conn.

James Cook and Martha Hill had the following child:

    i. James Cook was born before 1755 in Guilford, Conn. James died on 23 Nov 1811 at the
age of 56. He was buried in Alderbrook Cemetery, Guilford, Conn.


**332.** Mercy Cook (Joshua-4, Joshua-3, Josiah-2, Josias-1) was born on 30 Jun 1733 in Eastham,
Mass. She died in 1828 at the age of 95 in Leroy, Jefferson, NY. Her name is sometimes
spelled Marcy Cook.

Mercy Cook and Thomas ADKINS were married on 23 Mar 1758. Thomas Adkins was born
about 1737 in North Guilford, Conn.

Thomas Adkins and Mercy Cook had the following children:

    i. John Adkins was born on 4 Jan 1759 in Guilford, Conn.

    ii. Isaiah Adkins, born 6 Jan 1761, Guilford, Conn.; married Jemimah UNKNOWN. They
had 4 children.

    iii. Mercy Adkins was born in 1764 in Guilford, Conn.

    iv. Mary (or Mercy) Adkins was baptized on 1 Sep 1776 in Guilford, Conn.


**333.** Joshua Cook (Joshua-4, Joshua-3, Josiah-2, Josias-1) was born before 1745. He was baptized
on 30 Jun 1745 in Mansfield, Conn. He served in the military as an Ensign in the American
Revolution about 1776 in onnecticut. Joshua died after 1819 at the age of 74 in Silver Creek,
Greene, O.

Joshua Cook and Mary COOK [#350] were married on 5 Nov 1767 in Chatham, Conn. They moved in Canajoharie, NY. before 1790. Mary Cook, daughter of Zaccheus Cook and Mary Hubbard, was born on 26 Jul 1748 in Middletown, Conn. Joshua and his wife were first cousins.

Joshua Cook and Mary Cook had the following children:

900    i.   Isaiah Cook, born 18 Jul 1768, Chatham, Conn.; married Clarissa GROSVENER, 6 Jun 1796, Lawyersville, NY.

901    ii.   Levina Cook, born 10 Oct 1770, Haddam, Conn.; married Henry HAUGHTON, abt 1793; died 1836.

902    iii.   Jedida Cook, born 3 Apr 1773, Chatham, Mass.; married Earl WRIGHT, 1791; died 14 May 1843, New York.

334. Rebecca Cook (Ebenezer-4, Joshua-3, Josiah-2, Josias-1) was baptized on 22 May 1743 in East Haddam First Congregational Church, Middlesex, Conn.

Rebecca Cook and Samuel MITCHELL were married on 10 Nov 1762 in East Haddam, Conn. Samuel Mitchell was born in 1738 in Colchester, Essex, England. He served in the military as a private in the 3rd Connecticut regiment about 1776 in Connecticut.

Samuel Mitchell and Rebecca Cook had the following children:

i.   James Mitchell, born 15 Mar 1764, East Haddam, Conn.; married Abigail SPENCER, 5 Dec 1791, East Haddam, Conn.

ii.   Anna Mitchell was born on 17 Apr 1766 in East Haddam, Conn.

iii.   Ruth Mitchell was born on 4 Mar 1768.

iv.   Lydia Mitchell was born on 11 Mar 1770.

v.   Rebecca Mitchell was born on 26 Jan 1772.

vi.   Samuel Mitchell, born 24 Jan 1774, East Haddam, Conn.; married Speneth Lucinda COOK, 2 Jan 1806, Windsor, Hartford, Conn. They had 10 children.

vii.   Selden Mitchell was born on 3 Nov 1776.

viii.   Joseph Mitchell, born 8 Mar 1782; married Clarissa CONE, abt 1830, East Haddam, Conn. They had at least 1 child.

ix.   Abigail Mitchell was born on 20 Dec 1784.

x.   Mary Mitchell was born on 3 Mar 1786.

xi.   Gelston Mitchell was born on 7 Apr 1788.

335. Ebenezer Cook Jr. (Ebenezer-4, Joshua-3, Josiah-2, Josias-1) was born before 12 Oct 1746. He was baptized on 12 Oct 1746 in East Haddam First Congregational Church, Middlesex, Conn. He served in the military in the American Revolution under Col. John Brown as a Minute Man

Captain in Massachusetts. Ebenezer signed a will on 29 Jan 1812 in Berkshire, Tioga, NY. He might be recorded in the New Hartford Presbyterian Church Deaths list in 1812 in New Hartford, Oneida, NY. He died on 28 Mar 1813 at the age of 66 in New Hartford, Oneida, NY.

Ebenezer Cook Jr. and Mary WEST were married in 1770. Mary WEST was born in 1747. She died in 1781 at the age of 34 in Stockbridge, Mass.

Ebenezer Cook and Mary WEST had the following children:

906 i. Col William Walker Cook, born 31 Aug 1773, Stockbridge, Mass.; married Roxanna WHITTELSEY, 26 Feb 1795, Stockbridge, Mass.; died 23 Feb 1830, Killawog, NY.

907 ii. Ebenezer Cook Jr., born abt 1771; married Elizabeth CHURCHILL, 3 Apr 1793, Stockbridge, Mass.; died 17 Mar 1812, Lisle, Broome, New York.

908 iii. Lydia Cook, born 1775; married Stephen BRADLEY, 7 Jan 1795, Stockbridge, Mass.

909 iv. Ira Cook, born 4 Apr 1780, Berkshire County, Mass.; married Patience T. EELS, 14 Sep 1803; married Rachel Davis FAXON, 16 Mar 1809, Whitestown, NY.; died 16 Apr 1845, Davenport, Ia.

910 v. Mary West Cook, born bef Aug 1784; married William CURTIS, 14 Apr 1804, Stockbridge, Mass.

Ebenezer Cook Jr. and Abigail WEEKS were married on 14 Nov 1782 in Stockbridge, Mass. They moved to Berkshire, Tioga County, NY. in 1797. Abigail Weeks was born about 1740 in Norwalk, CT. She died on 14 Jan 1814 at the age of 74 in New Hartford, Oneida, NY. Abigail might be recorded in the New Hartford Presbyterian Church Deaths in 1814 in New Hartford, Oneida, NY.

His 4th child, Ira Cook wrote in a letter to one of his descendants many years later that his father was a huge and very athletic man: about 6' tall, heavy, but that he could jump over a rope held at the height of a person's head.

**The Boston Purchase**

When America was being explored and turned into the property of Europe it wasn't known (by the Europeans) what existed to the west. As colonies like Massachusetts and Connecticut were organized after 1620, they were granted all the land from sea to sea between certain lines of latitude. In the case of Massachusetts, this meant the state claim continued through New York, Lake Erie, Canada, Michigan, Wisconsin, Iowa, South Dakota, Wyoming, Idaho and Oregon.

The Province of New York was created when the Peter Stuyvesant the last director-general of New Amsterdam ceded it to England, along with all the territory in 1664. King Charles renamed it New York in honor his brother James, the Duke of York. As a colony, it was governed by England but declared itself a self governing state in 1775, about a year before the Declaration of Independence was signed.

The federal government went through many incarnations in the years between the signing of the declaration and when the constitution was created and went into effect in 1789. Much of the governing was necessary simply to conduct the war with England. But there were other accomplishments besides the war. The Congress of the Confederation ruled from 1781 to 1789 and in 1787 it abolished all claims to the land west of Pennsylvania and north of the Ohio River with what was called the Northwest Ordinance. This piece of legislation dealt with land that had mostly been unexplored and did not deal with the land that was part of both New York and Massachusetts. A lawsuit was launched the same year by Massachusetts against New York, and a commission of ten men was formed by the Congress to determined who owned the land. The commission, in a complicated decision, decided that New York should cede to Massachusetts the "right of preemption of the soil from the native Indians and all other estate, except government, sovereignty, and jurisdiction."

What this meant is that Massachusetts (or more specifically, her citizens) was allowed to take possession of the land in that area by bargaining and paying the American Indians who had settled that area, but that Massachusetts would not have any legal jurisdiction over it and that the land would become part of New York.

This land became known as The Boston Purchase. It comprised 230,400 acres and it was granted to a single person: Samuel Brown, of Stockbridge, Massachusetts, and his associates. Ebenezer Cook lived in Stockbridge and was one of his associates. His name is #58 on the list of 60 original purchasers of The Boston Purchase.

The land in question abuts the top border of Pennsylvania on its eastern side. It was purchased by Samuel Brown, Orringh (Orange) Stoddard, and Joseph Raymond, of Stockbridge, from the American Indians for 3,333 Spanish Milled Dollars on the 22nd of June, 1787.

In Chenango, there were two men who already claimed ownership of the land. They had lived there from a time before the revolution. Joshua Whitney (whose name would eventually be given to that area which is now known as Whitney Point) and Thomas Richards (Reichardt). Joshua accepted 400 acres and Thomas 200 acres. They probably didn't have much choice.

The rest of the land was divided up and given to Brown and his associates. This is how and why Ebenezer Cook took his family from Stockbridge to Berkshire, New York, and how the area around Whitney's Point and Lisle, New York became so central to this branch of descendants. He probably moved around 1797 and then later, in 1808, he moved to New Hartford.

336. Gideon Cook (Ebenezer-4, Joshua-3, Josiah-2, Josias-1) was born on 10 Jan 1750 in East Haddam, Conn. He was baptized on 26 Jan 1751/2 in East Haddam First Congregational Church, Middlesex, Conn. He died on 12 Apr 1806 at the age of 56 in East Haddam, Conn. Gideon served in the military in the American Revolution in Connecticut. He was buried in Higganum Cemetery.

Gideon Cook and Huldah LISK were married on 20 Mar 1776 in East Haddam, Conn. Huldah Lisk, daughter of Andrew Lisk and Elizabeth Bradford, was born on 18 Aug 1754 in Lebanon, Conn. She died on 10 May 1841 at the age of 86 in East Haddam, Conn. She was buried in Higganum Cemetery.

Gideon Cook and Huldah Lisk had the following children:

911    i.    Anna Cook, born 14 Mar 1777, East Haddam, Conn.; married Henry SNOW, 9 Oct 1800, East Haddam, Conn.; died 30 May 1848, East Haddam, Conn.

912    ii.    John Cook, born 11 Dec 1778, East Haddam, Conn.; married Phebe REDINGTON, 1 Dec 1809, Richmond, Mass.; died 2 Sep 1824, East Haddam, Conn.

iii.    Gideon Cook was born on 28 Nov 1780. He died on 1 May 1813 at the age of 32.

iv.    David Cook was born on 25 Nov 1782. He died on 2 Nov 1828 at the age of 45.

913    v.    William Cook, born 10 Jul 1785, East Haddam, Conn.; married Jerusha SPENCER, 1 Oct 1807, East Haddam, Conn.

914    vi.    Andrew Cook, born 19 May 1787; married Elizabeth MCWHORTEN; died 24 Jun 1858, Stayner, Ontario, Canada.

vii.    Huldah Cook was born on 11 Sep 1789.

viii.    A Child Cook was born in 1790. He/she died in 1790 at the age of 0.

915    ix.    Azel Cook, born 17 Oct 1791; died 20 Oct 1871, Wolfe Island, Ontario, Canada.

916    x.    Fanny Cook, born 22 Dec 1793; married Matthew Smith FULLER; died 11 Aug 1816.

917    xi.    Ebenezer Cook, born 23 Feb 1796; married Louisa P. EMMONS, 13 Dec 1832, East Haddam, Conn.; died bef 1880.

337. Shubael Cook (Ephraim-4, Joshua-3, Josiah-2, Josias-1) was born on 6 Jun 1736 in Eastham, Mass. He died in Aug 1795 at the age of 59 in Coventry, Conn.

Shubael Cook and Catherine EDWARDS were married on 2 Feb 1758 in Coventry, Conn. Catherine Edwards, daughter of Thomas Edwards and Mary C., was born on 17 Apr 1738 in Coventry, Conn. She signed a will on 9 Mar 1801. She died on 7 Feb 1806 at the age of 67 in Coventry, Conn. Her estate was probated on 4 Mar 1806.

338. Moses Cook (Ephraim-4, Joshua-3, Josiah-2, Josias-1) was born in 1738 in Coventry, Conn. He
served in the military in the French and Indian War in the 8th Company in 1757 in Connecticut.
He served in the military Revolutionary War with sons Moses Jr., James and Aaron between
1776 and 1784 in Dutchess County, NY. He was living in Locke, Cayuga, NY. in 1810. He
died in 1810 at the age of 72 in Locke, NY.

Moses Cook and Eunice Allin were married on 17 Jan 1760 in Coventry, Conn. Eunice
ALLIN, daughter of George Allin and Naomi Grover, was born on 26 Oct 1738 in Coventry,
Conn.

Moses Cook and Eunice Allin had the following children:

      i.   Jemima Cook was born on 10 Oct 1760 in Coventry, Conn.
918   ii.   Moses Bassett Cook, born 6 Apr 1762, New Marlborough, Mass.; married Phebe
        PERKINS, 14 Dec 1788, Nine Partners, Dutchess County, NY.; died 9 Aug
        1839.
919   iii.   James Cook, born 1763, New Marlborough, Mass.; married Eunice LOOMIS, 14
        Dec 1788, Nine Partners, Dutchess County, NY.; married Diana BROWN, aft
        1820; died 19 Apr 1851, Mecca, Oh.
     iv.   Aaron Cook was born between 1765 and 1770. He served in the revolutionary war from
        Freehold, Cayuga, NY.
920   v.   John B. Cook, born abt 1775; married Catherine UNKNOWN.

339. Reuben Cook (Ephraim-4, Joshua-3, Josiah-2, Josias-1) was born on 20 Aug 1741 in Eastham,
Mass. He served in the military in the French and Indian War as a private in the 12th Co. under
Hebron, CT officers between 25 May 1759 and 14 Dec 1759. He served in the military in the
French and Indian War as a Sergeant in the 11th Co. under a Plainfield Captain between 16
Mar 1763 and 3 Dec 1763. He died on 12 Feb 1814 at the age of 72 in Orwell, Vt.

Reuben Cook and Maria TURNER were married.

Reuben Cook and Maria Turner had the following children:

921   i.   Ivory Cook, born bet 1765 and 1770, Coventry, Conn.; married Charlotte BUSH, abt
        1791; died in Vermont.
922   ii.   Capt. David Cook, born 15 Dec 1767, Coventry, Conn.; married Elizabeth
        HUMPHREY, bef 1793; died 15 Aug 1827, Orwell, Vt.
    iii.   Benajah Cook was born between 1765 and 1784 in Shoreham, Vt.
    iv.   John Cook.
    v.   A daughter.

Reuben Cook and Elizabeth EDWARDS were married in 1763 in Coventry, Conn. Elizabeth Edwards was born on 2 Nov 1742 in Coventry, Conn. She died in Coventry, Conn.

Reuben Cook and Elizabeth Edwards had the following child:

923    i.   Oliver Cook, born bef 16 Oct 1763, Coventry, Conn.; married Mercy HARRIS; married Esther BROWN; died aft 1850, West Haven, Rutland, Vt.

340. Ephraim Cook (Ephraim-4, Joshua-3, Josiah-2, Josias-1) was born about 1743 in Mansfield or Coventry, Connecticut. He served in the military served in the 10 Company, Connecticut's First Regiment between 18 Mar 1762 and 3 Dec 1762. He died after 1800 at the age of 57 in Canaan, Conn.

Ephraim Cook and Huldah LOOMIS were married. Huldah Loomis, daughter of Zachariah Loomis and Huldah Jones, was born on 1 Jan 1756 in Andover, Tolland, Conn.

Ephraim Cook and Huldah Loomis had the following children:

924    i.   John Cook, born 13 Apr 1791, Canaan, Conn.; married Sally Bronson; died 6 Nov 1862, Cornwall, Conn.
    ii.  Huldah Cook was born in 1800. She died on 14 May 1856 at the age of 56 in Cornwall, Conn.

Ephraim Cook married a second time and had the following children:

    i.   Jason Cook was born before 1765.
    ii.  A son Cook was born between 1775 and 1790.
925   iii.  Silas Cook, born 1 Jan 1772; married Abiah Hewitt, 8 Jul 1792, Canaan, Conn.
    iv.  A daughter Cook was born before 1790.

341. Joseph Cook (Ephraim-4, Joshua-3, Josiah-2, Josias-1) was born about 1750 in Connecticut. He died before 1808 in New York.

Joseph Cook and Jerusha TURNER were married on 19 Mar 1772 in Coventry, Conn. Jerusha Turner was born on 28 Dec 1744 in Coventry, Conn.

Joseph Cook and Mehitable BADCOCK were married on 30 Nov 1785 in Coventry, Conn. Mehitable Badcock, daughter of Robert Badcock and Jededah Turner, was born on 5 Jul 1762 in Coventry, Conn. She died in 1842 at the age of 80.

Joseph Cook and Mehitable Badcock had the following children:

5.67

i. Hannah Cook was born on 14 Nov 1772 in Coventry, Conn.

ii. Asenath Cook was born on 8 Sep 1786 in Coventry, Conn.

iii. Luther Cook was born on 24 Apr 1788 in Coventry, Conn.

926 iv. Daniel Cook, born 24 Apr 1788, Coventry, Conn.; married Betsey UNKNOWN.

v. Narcissus Cook was born on 27 Feb 1790 in Coventry, Conn.

vi. Anna Cook was born on 21 Feb 1792 in Coventry, Conn.

vii. Robert Cook was born on 14 Jul 1794 in Coventry, Conn.

viii. Mehitable Cook was born on 1 Mar 1797 in Coventry, Conn.

ix. Jerusha Cook was born on 1 Mar 1797 in Coventry, Conn.


342. Nathan Cook (Ephraim-4, Joshua-3, Josiah-2, Josias-1) was born about 1754 in Coventry, Conn. He died in Feb 1793 at the age of 39 in Coventry, Conn.

Nathan Cook and Mary YOUNG were married on 3 Feb 1779 in Windham, NY. Mary Young, daughter of John Young and Zerviah Huntington, was born on 15 Mar 1755 in Windham, NY.

Nathan Cook and Mary Young had the following children:

i. Nancy Cook was born about 1782 in Coventry, Conn. She was baptized in Aug 1782 in Coventry First Church, Coventry, Conn.

927 ii. John Young Cook, born 1783, Coventry, Conn.; married Hannah UNKNOWN.

iii. Hannah Cook was born in 1783 in Coventry, Conn. She was baptized in May 1786 in Coventry First Church, Coventry, Conn. She lived.

928 iv. Fanny Cook, born bef May 1786, Coventry, Conn.; married Calvin EDWARDS.

v. Phebe Cook was born before May 1786 in Coventry, Conn. She was baptized in May 1786 in Coventry First Church, Coventry, Conn.

929 vi. David Cook, born bef Feb 1787, Coventry, Conn.; married Sabina Chloe MOORE; died 1859, Suffield, Oh.

vii. Philena Cook was born before Oct 1793 in Coventry, Conn. She was baptized in Oct 1793 in Coventry First Church, Coventry, Conn.

930 viii. Bela Reynolds Cook, born bef Oct 1793, Coventry, Conn.; married Electa PARKER, Apr 1815; died 25 Oct 1866, Andover, Tolland, Conn.

931 ix. Nathan Cook, born bef Oct 1793, Coventry, Conn.; married Lucy A. AVERY.


343. John Cook (Ephraim-4, Joshua-3, Josiah-2, Josias-1) was born about 1756 in Coventry, Conn. He died on 6 Jan 1806 at the age of 50 in Hebron, Conn. He was buried in Andover Cemetery, Andover, Conn.

John Cook and Sarah REYNOLDS were married. Sarah Reynolds was the daughter of Thomas Reynolds and Mary Wentworth.

344. Abigail Cook (Ephraim-4, Joshua-3, Josiah-2, Josias-1) was born about 1758 in Coventry, Conn.

Abigail Cook and Samuel PERKINS were married. Samuel Perkins, son of Thomas Perkins and Elizabeth Loomis, was born on 4 Sep 1751 in Lebanon, Conn.

345. Elizabeth Cook (Ephraim-4, Joshua-3, Josiah-2, Josias-1) was born about 1759 in Coventry, Conn.

Elizabeth Cook and Samuel SPRAGUE were married. Samuel Sprague, son of Samuel Sprague and Jerusha Unknown, was born on 24 Dec 1758 in Coventry, Conn. He died on 6 Feb 1816 at the age of 57 in Coventry, Conn.

Samuel Sprague and Elizabeth Cook had the following children:

    i.    Ethalinda Sprague, married Abel JOSLYN.
    ii.    Roxena Sprague, married Unknown NORTON.
    iii.    Phebe Sprague.
    iv.    Cynthia Sprague.
    v.    Sally Sprague, born 1783; married Harry DOW, 24 Sep 1807.
    vi.    Elias Sprague, born 1794; married Lucinda WHALEY, May 1825, Coventry, Conn.; married Clarinda MAINE.
    vii.    Achsah Sprague was born in 1800.
    viii.    Eliza Sprague, born 5 Jan 1804, East Hampton, Conn.; married Nathaniel Porter METCALF, 23 Nov 1825.

346. Ruhammah Cook (Simeon-4, Joshua-3, Josiah-2, Josias-1) was born about 1739 in Lee, Mass. She died on 21 Sep 1838 at the age of 99 in Lee, Mass. She was buried in Center Cemetery, Lee, Mass.

Ruhammah Cook and Nathan BALL were married about 1767. Nathan BALL was born on 27 Apr 1737 in Waltham, Mass. He died on 29 Dec 1797 at the age of 60 in Lee, Mass. He was buried in Lee, Mass.

Nathan BALL and Ruhammah Cook had the following children:

    i.    Captain Nathan BALL Jr., born 23 Feb 1768, Stockbridge, Mass.; married Fear CHADWICK, 29 Jun 1797, Lee, Mass.; died 30 Oct 1856, Ogden Town, Monroe, NY. They had 11 children.
    ii.    Lydia BALL, born 6 Jun 1769, Stockbridge, Mass.; married Daniel WILCOX, 19 Oct 1794; died 20 Aug 1846. They had at least 2 children.

iii. Polly BALL was born on 16 Mar 1772 in Stockbridge, Mass.

iv. Sarah BALL was born on 25 Apr 1773 in Stockbridge, Mass. She died on 1 Aug 1784 at the age of 11 in Lee, Mass.

939 v. Elizabeth BALL, born 21 Jan 1775, Stockbridge, Mass.; married Zenas HINCKLEY, 29 Jun 1797.

940 vi. Martha Ball, born 13 May 1776, Lee, Mass.; married Asahel Stanton; died 10 Mar 1855.

941 vii. John BALL, born 25 Jul 1777, Lee, Mass.; married Anne PERCIVAL, 13 Feb 1806, Lee, Mass.; married Eunice CHADWICK, 13 Feb 1827, Lee, Mass.; died 27 Apr 1860, Lee, Mass.

viii. Anna BALL was born on 14 Dec 1778 in Lee, Mass.

942 ix. James BALL, born 18 Oct 1781, Lee, Mass.; married Lucretia THATCHER, 30 May 1810, Lee, Mass.

943 x. Samuel BALL, born 20 Aug 1783, Lee, Mass.; married Sally BENTON, Nov 1807, Lee, Mass.; married Experience HOWLAND, 15 Oct 1826, Lee, Mass.; died 12 May 1841, Lee, Mass. They had 6 children.

944 xi. Isaac BALL, born 1 Jul 1785, Lee, Mass.; married Lydia BASSET, 25 Mar 1819, Lee, Mass.; married Sylvania WILKINS, 3 Dec 1863, Lee, Mass.; died 23 Dec 1866. They had 3 children.

945 xii. Capt Joseph BALL, born 30 Apr 1787, Lee, Mass.; married Esther NYE, 28 Nov 1811, Lee, Mass.; died 2 Mar 1888, Spencerport, Monroe, NY. They had 9 children.

946 xiii. Sarah "Sally" BALL, born 31 Oct 1788, Lee, Mass.; married John NYE, 11 May 1809, Lee, Mass.; died Lee, Mass. They had at least 1 child.


347. Moses Cook (Simeon-4, Joshua-3, Josiah-2, Josias-1) was born about 1740. He served in the American Revolution, enlisting both in Vermont and West Point, NY between 10 Apr 1776 and 12 Jun 1783. Moses moved to Amenia, NY. between 1790 and 1800, where he lived one door away from his brother Joseph. He died after 1820 at the age of 80 in Amenia, NY.

Moses Cook and Hannah HOWE were married. They moved to Townshend, Vt and later Amenia, NY. Hannah Howe, daughter of John Howe, was born in 1745. She was baptized in 1753 in Hopkinton, Mass.

Moses Cook and Hannah Howe had the following children:

i. Mary Cook was born on 18 Nov 1769 in Townshend, Vt.

ii. Hannah Cook was born on 13 Mar 1772 in Townshend, Vt.

iii. Anna Cook was born on 7 Apr 1775 in Townshend, Vt.

947 iv. Lemuel Cook, born 9 Oct 1778, Townshend, Vt.; married Phebe SHAW.

v. Lydia Cook was born on 4 Nov 1780 in Townshend, Vt.

vi. Elizabeth Cook was born about 1785. She was living with her parents, a "consumptive", in 1820.

348. Martha Cook (Simeon-4, Joshua-3, Josiah-2, Josias-1) died on 7 Sep 1824 in Sandisfield, Mass.

Martha Cook and Abraham BENTON were married on 14 May 1759 in Sandisfield, Mass. Abraham Benton was born about 1725. He died on 24 Oct 1806 at the age of 81 in Sandisfield, Mass.

Abraham Benton and Martha Cook had the following children, all born Sandisfield, Mass.:

i. Abraham Benton was born on 10 Jun 1760. He died before 25 Feb 1766 at the age of 5 in Sandisfield, Mass.
ii. Martha Benton was born on 15 Apr 1763. She died before 18 Oct 1782 at the age of 19 in Sandisfield, Mass.
iii. Joseph Benton was born on 12 Dec 1764. He died before 12 Apr 1767 at the age of 2 in Sandisfield, Mass.
iv. Abraham Benton was born on 25 Feb 1766.
v. Joseph Benton was born on 12 Apr 1767.
vi. Elijah Benton was born on 13 Jun 1769.
vii. Isaac Benton was born on 6 Jan 1773.
viii. Meltiah Benton was born on 5 Jan 1775.
ix. Stephen Benton was born in Dec 1777.
x. Samuel Benton was born on 13 Jun 1779. He died before 1 Mar 1785 at the age of 5 in Sandisfield, Mass.
xi. Martha Benton was born on 18 Oct 1782.
xii. Samuel Benton was born on 1 Mar 1785.

349. Joseph Cook (Simeon-4, Joshua-3, Josiah-2, Josias-1) was born on 27 Sep 1751 in New Marlborough, Mass. He served in the military in the American Revolution about 1776 in New Marlborough, Mass. He moved in Amenia, NY. between 1790 and 1800. Joseph moved to Sherburne, NY in 1810. He moved to Norwich, NY between 1820 and 1830. He moved to Townshend, O. in 1845. Joseph died between 18 Mar 1845 and 13 Jan 1852 at the age of 93 in Townshend, O.

Joseph Cook and Abigail PECK were married on 24 Nov 1775 in New Haven, New Haven, Conn.

Joseph Cook and Abigail Peck had the following children:

i. Hannah (Roby) Cook).

5.71

948    ii.  Sarah Cook, born bet 1775 and 1780, Connecticut; married William THOMPSON,
                bef spring of 1802, Stonington, Conn.; died in Wisconsin.
949    iii.  Abigail Cook, married Abner PURDY.
950    iv.  Spencer Cook, married Harriet ARNOLD.
951    v.   Simeon Cook, born bet 1775 and 1780; married Sarah CRANDALL, 1 Jul 1800;
                married Elizabeth CRANDALL; died aft 1820.
        vi.  Zena Cook was born before 6 Feb 1780. She was baptized on 6 Feb 1780 in First
                Congregational Church of New Haven, Conn.
952    vii. William Cook, born bet 1780 and 1790; married Anna PURDY.
953    viii.    Aaron Cook, born abt 1787; married Lydia CULVER.
954    ix.  Lyman Cook, born bet 1790 and 1800; married Polly FISHER.

       Joseph Cook and Olive UNKNOWN were married before 3 Aug 1811.


350.    Mary Cook (Zaccheus-4, Joshua-3, Josiah-2, Josias-1) was born on 26 Jul 1748 in
           Middletown, Conn.

        Mary Cook and Joshua COOK [#333] were married on 5 Nov 1767 in Chatham, Conn. Their
        children are listed under Joshua's entry.


351.  Zaccheus Cook (Zaccheus-4, Joshua-3, Josiah-2, Josias-1) was born on 5 Apr 1751 in
Middletown, Conn.

        Zaccheus Cook and Mercy GOFFE were married on 18 Jan 1776.


352. Martha Cook (Zaccheus-4, Joshua-3, Josiah-2, Josias-1) was born on 3 Mar 1755 in
           Middletown, Conn. She died in 1829 at the age of 74 in Chatham, Conn.

        Martha Cook and Josiah PURPLE were married on 4 Jan 1776. Josiah Purple was born in
        1752. He died on 17 Nov 1836 at the age of 84 in Chatham, Conn.

Josiah Purple and Martha Cook had the following children:

955    i.   Ruth Purple, born 10 Jul 1777, Chatham, Mass.; married Jeremiah House, 30 Oct
                1796; died 11 Feb 1863, Glastonbury, Conn.
       ii.  Martha Purple was born on 22 Sep 1779.
956    iii. Josiah Purple, born 13 Dec 1781; married Hannah Higgins, 19 Jan 1804.
       iv.  James Purple was born on 17 Nov 1783.
       v.   Lydia Purple was born on 16 Sep 1785.
       vi.  Mehitable Purple was born on 16 Oct 1787.
957    vii. Nathaniel Purple, born 4 Mar 1790; married Electa Smith; married Dorothy Percival;

died 18 Jun 1870.

     viii.   Liva Purple was born on 14 Mar 1792.

     ix.  Julia Purple was born on 19 Mar 1794.

     x.  Polly Purple was born on 26 May 1796.

958    xi.  Phila Amanda PURPLE, born 7 May 1798, Exeter, Otsego, NY.; married Smith BRAINARD, 24 Nov 1840, Burlington, Otsego, NY.; died 9 Mar 1873.

**353.** Huldah Cook (Zaccheus-4, Joshua-3, Josiah-2, Josias-1) was born on 20 Mar 1758 in Haddam, Conn. She was baptized on 16 Apr 1758.

Huldah Cook and William THOMAS were married on 11 Oct 1785 in East Hampton Congregational Church, Middlesex, Conn. William Thomas served in the military as a marine in the American Revolution. in 1776 in Connecticut.

**354.** Nathaniel Cook (Zaccheus-4, Joshua-3, Josiah-2, Josias-1) was born about 1760 in Middletown, Conn. He died on 8 Apr 1786 at the age of 26.

Nathaniel Cook and Olive ROWLEY were married on 2 Mar 1786 in Middle Haddam, Conn. Olive Rowley, daughter of Ebenezer Rowley and Susannah Annibal, was born on 10 Aug 1760 in Chatham, Conn. She died in Chatham, Conn.

**355.** Zuba Cook (Zaccheus-4, Joshua-3, Josiah-2, Josias-1) was born about 1765 in Middletown, Conn.

Zuba Cook and John HAILING were married on 30 Dec 1784 in East Hampton Congregational Church, Middlesex, Conn.

**356.** Mehitable Cook (Zaccheus-4, Joshua-3, Josiah-2, Josias-1) was born about Jul 1769 in Chatham, Conn. She was baptized on 23 Jul 1769 in East Hampton, Conn.

Mehitable Cook and Roswell HUBBARD were married on 5 Feb 1788 in East Hampton Congregational Church, Middlesex, Conn. Roswell Hubbard was born about 1768 in Chatham, Conn. He died on 17 Sep 1812 at the age of 44 in New York.

**365.** Deborah Cook (Jonathan-4, Joshua-3, Josiah-2, Josias-1) was born about May 1754 in Haddam, Conn. She died on 28 Apr 1840 at the age of 85 in Chatham, Conn.

Deborah Cook and Seymour HURLBURT were married on 19 Feb 1778 in Chatham, Conn. Seymour Hurlburt, son of David Hurlburt and Ruth Belden, was born on 13 Jun 1756 in Haddam, Conn. He died on 29 Nov 1840 at the age of 84 in Chatham, Conn.

Seymour Hurlburt and Deborah Cook had the following children:

    i.   A child Hurlburt. Died 14 Oct 1778.
    ii.  Jonathan Hurlburt, born bef 15 Apr 1780, Middle Haddam, Conn.; married Louisa ACKLEY, 3 Jun 1804. They had 7 children.
    iii. Clarissa Hurlburt, born bef 15 Apr 1780, Chatham, Mass.; married Walter WEIR, 9 Jul 1799, Congregational Church, Glastonbury, Conn. They had 5 children.
    iv. Ruth Hurlburt, born bef 23 Feb 1783, Middle Haddam, Conn.; married Asa WEIR, 16 Jan 1803. They had 8 children.
    v.  Belinda Hurlburt, born bef 10 May 1788, Chatham, Conn.; married Chester CHURCHILL. They had 6 children.
    vi. Seymour Hurlburt, born bef 22 Dec 1790, Chatham, Mass.; married Asenath PENFIELD, abt 1812. They had 9 children.
    vii. Deborah Hurlburt, born 22 Dec 1790; married Elijah SPARKS; died 1824. They had 5 children.
    viii. Mary Hurlburt, born abt 1791; married Chester CALDWELL, 26 Aug 1809, Wilbraham, Hampden, Mass. They had 11 children.
    ix. Job Hurlburt, born bef 3 Jul 1796, Chatham, Mass.; married Cordelia STOCKING, 1818. They had 7 children.
    x.  Alanson Ames Hurlburt, born 26 Jul 1799, Middle Haddam, Conn.; married Charlotte Selina WELCH, 4 Jul 1836. They had 7 children. He and his wife were related through Joshua Cooke (#19). They were second cousins, twice removed.
    xi. David Hurlburt, born 22 Apr 1802, Chatham, Mass.; married Ann E. JONES, 26 Apr 1835, Glastonbury, Conn. They had 4 children.
    xii. Hannah Hurlburt, born bef 6 o t 1853, Chatham, Mass.; married Walter WEIR. They had 3 children.

366. Sgt. Nathaniel Cook (Jonathan-4, Joshua-3, Josiah-2, Josias-1) was born about Feb 1756 in Haddam, Conn. He served in the military as a Corporal and then Sergeant in the American Revolution in Connecticut. Nathaniel died on 18 Oct 1816 at the age of 60 in Haddam, Conn. He was buried in Old Rock Landing Cemetery. He was a shoemaker.

Sgt. Nathaniel Cook and Annice SEARS were married on 7 Dec 1780. Annice Sears, daughter of Hezekiah Sears and Deborah Spencer, was born on 3 Jun 1758 in Middletown, Conn. She died on 8 Sep 1850 at the age of 92.

Nathaniel Cook and Annice Sears had the following children:

    i.   A child was born in 1781 in Chatham, Mass.
    ii.  A child was born between 1782 and 4.
1008   iii. Sally Cook, born 1785; married Jabez ARNOLD.

iv. A son was born between 1785 and 94.
1009   v.   Hezekiah Sears Cook, born 14 Nov 1789; married Roxana ARNOLD; married Sally UNKNOWN; died 15 Nov 1826, Middlefield, Conn.
vi. A son was born between 1795 and 1800.
1010   vii. Willard Cook, born 18 Sep 1799, New York; married Abigail BRAINERD, 8 Jan 1823, Haddam Neck Congregational Church, East Haddam, Conn.; died 9 Aug 1873, Chicago, Cook, Ill.
viii.   A son was born between 1800 and 1810.
ix.  A daughter was born between 1800 and 1810.

367. Hannah Cook (Jonathan-4, Joshua-3, Josiah-2, Josias-1) was born before 8 Mar 1758 in Haddam, Conn. She died on 25 Jun 1837 at the age of 79 in Haddam, Conn.

Hannah Cook and Jesse BRAINERD were married on 28 Jun 1781 in Middle Haddam, Conn. Jesse Brainerd, son of Nathan Brainerd and Sarah Gates, was born on 29 Sep 1756 in Middle Haddam, Conn. He died on 18 Sep 1839 at the age of 82 in Haddam, Conn.

Jesse Brainerd and Hannah Cook had the following children:

i.   Sally Brainerd, born 29 Feb 1786, Haddam, Conn.; married Warren BRAINERD, 9 May 1802, Middlesex, Conn.; died 1 Jan 1880, Fairfield, Shiawassee, Mich. They had 5 children.
ii.  Betsey Brainerd was born in 1786. She was christened on 15 Oct 1786 in Haddam, Conn. She died in Feb 1826 at the age of 40.
iii. Selinda Brainerd was christened on 6 May 1788 in Haddam, Conn. She died about 1789 at the age of 1.
iv.  Polly Brainerd was christened on 6 May 1788 in Haddam, Conn.
v.   Sylvester Brainerd was born on 5 Jun 1789 in Haddam, Conn.
vi.  Bella Brainerd was christened on 8 Apr 1792 in Haddam, Conn.
vii. Lyman Brainerd was born on 8 Mar 1794 in Haddam, Conn.
viii.   Polly Brainerd was born on 7 Sep 1796 in Haddam, Conn.
ix.  Russell Brainerd was christened on 4 Aug 1801 in Haddam, Conn. He died about Feb 1803 at the age of 2.
x.   William Brainerd was born about 1803 in Haddam, Conn.
xi.  Russell Brainerd was born about 1805 in Haddam, Conn.

368. Amos Cook (Jonathan-4, Joshua-3, Josiah-2, Josias-1) was born before 11 Jul 1762 in Haddam, Conn. He was baptized on 11 Jul 1762 in Haddam Neck Congregational Church, East Haddam, Conn.

Amos Cook and Jane BAILEY were married in 1787 in Haddam Neck Congregational Church, East Haddam, Conn. They moved in Windham, NY. in 1795 Jane Bailey was born about 1770.

Amos Cook and Jane Bailey had the following children:

1012  i.   Ichabod Cook, born 3 Jun 1792, Connecticut; married Hannah UNKNOWN, bef
              1815; married Elizabeth BRANDOW, aft 1815; died 23 Oct 1866, Ashland, NY.
      ii.  Ashbel Cook.
1013  iii. Amos Cook.
      iv.  Ruth Cook.
      v.   Julia Cook.
      vi.  Jesse Cook was born before 1800.

369. Jemimah Cook (Jonathan-4, Joshua-3, Josiah-2, Josias-1) was born before 27 Mar 1768 in
      Haddam, Conn. She was baptized on 27 Mar 1768 in Haddam Neck Congregational Church,
      East Haddam, Conn.

      Jemimah Cook and Elihu SMITH were married on 24 Mar 1788 in Haddam Neck
      Congregational Church, East Haddam, Conn.

370. Patience Cook (Jonathan-4, Joshua-3, Josiah-2, Josias-1) was born on 6 Jan 1771. She died on
      25 Jul 1855 at the age of 84 in Wabash County, Ill.

      Patience Cook and Edward BRINES were married on 3 Jun 1793 in Chatham, Conn. Edward
      BRINES was born about 1765.

Edward BRINES and Patience Cook had the following children:

      i.    Levi Brines died about 1834.
      ii.   ??? Brines was born in 1794.
      iii.  Edward (2) Brines was born about 1795.
      iv.   Martha Brines was born in Oct 1797.
      v.    Lyman Brines was born on 15 Sep 1802.
      vi.   Asahel Brines was born in 1803. He married Susan HULL. They had 3 children.
      vii.  Russell Brines was born on 13 Jun 1804. He died on 28 Jan 1881 at the age of 76.
      viii.    Roswell Brines was born on 13 May 1806 in New York. He died on 23 Jul 1896 at
              the age of 90 in Schuyler County, Ill.
      ix.   Charlotta Brines was born on 11 Apr 1807 in Alleghany, NY. She died on 15 Oct 1887 at
              the age of 80 in Schuyler County, Ill.
      x.    Jefferson Brines was born about 1810. He died about 1849 at the age of 39.
      xi.   Henry P Brines was born on 16 Nov 1811 in New York. He died on 13 Feb 1854 at the
              age of 42.

xii. A boy was born about 1814. He died about 1820 at the age of 6.

380. Solomon Cook (Hezekiah-4, Joshua-3, Josiah-2, Josias-1) was born on 21 Dec 1761 in New
Marlborough, Mass. He served in the military in the American Revolution, including a period as
a substitute for his father about 1778 in State of Massachusetts. Solomon died on 21 Feb 1823
at the age of 61 in German, Chenango, NY.

Solomon Cook and Elizabeth PECK were married on 4 Nov 1782 in New Haven, New
Haven, Conn. Elizabeth Peck was born (date unknown).

Solomon Cook and Elizabeth Peck had the following children:

      i.   Patience Almira Cook was born on 21 Oct 1783. She died on 9 Mar 1784.
1051  ii.  Capt Lewis Cook, born 18 Apr 1785, New Marlborough, Mass.; married Abigail
         Rhodes, 1804, New Marlborough, Mass.; died 24 Jan 1861, New Marlborough,
         Mass.
      iii. Lydia Cook was born on 29 Apr 1787. She died on 6 Aug 1787.
      iv. Lydia Cook was born on 8 Jun 1788.
      v.  Julea Cook was born on 24 Dec 1790 in New Marlborough, Mass.
      vi. Pattey (Martha?) Cook was born on 3 Mar 1793 in New Marlborough, Mass. She died
         on 9 Jan 1797 at the age of 3.
1052  vii. Lorrin Cook, born 14 Sep 1797, New Marlborough, Mass.; married Hannah Warner;
         died 30 Apr 1878, South Oteselic, Chenango, NY.

381. Russell Cook (Hezekiah-4, Joshua-3, Josiah-2, Josias-1) was born on 12 Aug 1766 in New
Marlborough, Mass. He died on 22 May 1832 at the age of 65 in New Marlborough, Mass.

Russell Cook and Martha KEYES were married on 25 Apr 1792. Martha Keyes was born
about 1756. She died on 2 Jun 1828 at the age of 72.

Russell Cook and Rebecca UNKNOWN were married.

Russell Cook and Rebecca had the following child:

      i.   Lorin Cook was born on 14 Oct 1794. He died on 11 Mar 1797 at the age of 2.

382. Eli Cook (Hezekiah-4, Joshua-3, Josiah-2, Josias-1) was born on 16 Nov 1768 in New
Marlborough, Mass.

Eli Cook and Rachel CHURCH were married on 5 Oct 1791. They lived in New York in
1832. They moved to Canajoharie, NY.

5.77

383. Levi N. Cook (Hezekiah-4, Joshua-3, Josiah-2, Josias-1) was born on 26 Feb 1774 in New Marlborough, Mass. He appeared in the census in 1800 in New Marlborough, Mass.

Levi N. Cook and Elizabeth (Betsey) BROWN were married on 24 Jul 1794 in New Marlborough, Mass. They moved to New York after 1800.

Levi N. Cook and Elizabeth (Betsey) Brown had the following children:

    i.   Lyman Cook was born on 18 Feb 1796 in New Marlborough, Mass.
    ii.  Patience Almira Cook was born on 6 Jun 1798 in New Marlborough, Mass.

384. Benjamin Warren Cook (Hezekiah-4, Joshua-3, Josiah-2, Josias-1) was born on 19 Aug 1777 in New Marlborough, Mass. He died before 3 Nov 1840 at the age of 63 in Lenox, Mass.

Benjamin Warren Cook and Louisa KASSON were married before 1807. Louisa Kasson was born on 3 May 1778 in Voluntown, New London, Conn. She appeared in the census in 1850 in Lenox, Mass.

Benjamin Warren Cook and Louisa Kasson had the following children:

    i.   Volney Cook lived in Syracuse, NY. in 1840.
1053   ii.  Luna Cook, born abt 1807, Lenox, Mass.; married Thomas SEDGWICK.
    iii. Russell S. Cook lived in New York, NY. in 1840. He appeared in the census in 1850 in New York, NY. He was a Congregational Church clergyman.
1054   iv. Laura S. Cook, born 1811, State of Massachusetts; married George S. FITCH.

385. Shubal Cook (Nathaniel-4, Benjamin-3, Josiah-2, Josias-1) was born on 23 Jan 1743/4 in Eastham, Mass.

Shubal Cook and Jenne THACHER were married on 19 Feb 1776 in Harwich, Mass. Jenne Thacher, daughter of Benjamin Thacher and Hannah Lumbart, was born on 19 Feb 1776 in Harwich, Mass.

Shubal Cook and Jenne Thacher had the following children:

    i.   Jane Cook was born in 1777 in Harwich, Mass.
    ii.  Shubael Cook was born about 1778 in Harwich, Mass.
    iii. Elizabeth Cook was born on 27 Aug 1784 in Harwich, Mass.
    iv. Jonathan Cook was born about 1787 in Harwich, Mass.

386. John Cooke (Nathaniel-4, Benjamin-3, Josiah-2, Josias-1) was christened on 29 Oct 1749 in

Eastham, Mass.

John Cooke and Mary NEWCOMB were married. They lived in Provincetown, Mass.

387. Sarah Cook (Richard-4, Benjamin-3, Josiah-2, Josias-1) was born on 31 Oct 1742 in Eastham, Mass.

Sarah Cook and Simeon MAYO were married on 4 Dec 1766. Simeon Mayo, son of John Mayo and Tabitha Snow, was born in Mar 1745 in Eastham, Mass.

Simeon Mayo and Sarah Cook had the following children:

    i.   Phebe Mayo was born in 1767.
    ii.  Joseph Mayo was born in 1769. He died in 1789 at the age of 20.
    iii. Tamsen Mayo, born 24 Dec 1771, Eastham, Mass.; married John GOULD, 15 Dec 1791, Eastham, Mass. They had 8 children.
    iv. Sarah Mayo was born in 1774.

388. Phebe Cook (Richard-4, Benjamin-3, Josiah-2, Josias-1) was born on 27 Mar 1745.

Phebe Cook and Barnabas COOK were married on 1 Feb 1770 in Eastham, Mass. Barnabas Cook, son of Solomon Cook and Rebekah COWELL, was born about 1745. He died after 1797 at the age of 52 in Provincetown, Mass. Phebe and Barnabas were second cousins. The record is very uncertain regarding Barnabas.

Barnabas Cook and Phebe Cook had the following child:

    i.   Marcy Cook was born on 12 Aug 1770 in Eastham, Mass.

389. Joanna Cook (Richard-4, Benjamin-3, Josiah-2, Josias-1) was born on 25 Mar 1747.

Joanna Cook and Benjamin PENFIELD were married. Benjamin Penfield was born on 2 Sep 1744 in Middletown, Conn. He died in 1780 at the age of 36.

Benjamin Penfield and Joanna Cook had the following children:

1056  i.   Sally Penfield, born abt 1770; married Ezra FICKETT.
1057  ii.  Nathan Cook Penfield, born 1776, Gorham, Me.; married Mary GREEN, 11 Dec 1800, Gorham, Me.; died 14 Oct 1850.

390. Elisha Cook (Richard-4, Benjamin-3, Josiah-2, Josias-1) was born on 4 Jul 1750 in Eastham, Mass.

Elisha Cook and Hannah DOANE were married.

391. Hannah Cook (Richard-4, Benjamin-3, Josiah-2, Josias-1) was born on 22 Dec 1756 in Eastham, Mass. She died on 13 Dec 1792 at the age of 35 in Gorham, Me.

Hannah Cook and Hezekiah SMITH were married. Hezekiah Smith, son of Samuel Smith and Mary Hatch, was born about 1754 in Wellfleet, Mass. He died on 15 Jul 1824 at the age of 70 in Windham, Me.

Hezekiah Smith and Hannah Cook had the following child:

  1058   i.   Bethia Smith, born 1776; married James LOMBARD, 13 Dec 1792, Gorham, Me. They had 7 children; married Robert WEEKS, 13 Dec 1808, Gorham, Me.; died 11 Apr 1842, Gorham, Me.

392. Apphia Cook (Richard-4, Benjamin-3, Josiah-2, Josias-1) was born on 16 Sep 1765 in Eastham, Mass. She died on 22 Mar 1810 at the age of 44 in Wellfleet, Mass.

Apphia Cook and Captain John ATWOOD were married on 16 Nov 1788 in Wellfleet, Mass. Captain John Atwood, son of Timothy Atwood and Susanna Harding, was born on 11 Oct 1765 in Wellfleet, Mass. He died on 25 Sep 1860 at the age of 94 in Wellfleet, Mass. There may have been too much family blood as Apphia and her husband were related in five different ways: they were third cousins, fourth cousins, third cousins once removed (twice) and fourth cousins once removed. In total, they had 8 common ancestors.

John Atwood and Apphia Cook had the following children:

    i.   Hitte Mayo Atwood was born on 7 Oct 1789 in Wellfleet, Mass. She died on 20 Nov 1793 at the age of 4 in Wellfleet, Mass.
   ii.   Nathan Atwood was born on 26 Jul 1792 in Wellfleet, Mass. He died on 4 Aug 1817 at the age of 25 in Wellfleet, Mass.
  iii.   Zenas Cook Atwood was born on 2 Sep 1794 in Wellfleet, Mass.
   iv.   Hitte Mayo Atwood was born on 19 Oct 1796 in Wellfleet, Mass. She died on 12 Aug 1798 in Wellfleet, Mass.
    v.   Apphia Atwood was born on 15 Jan 1799 in Wellfleet, Mass. She died on 13 Sep 1800.
   vi.   John Atwood, born 24 Dec 1801, Wellfleet, Mass.; married Hannah NEWCOMB, 8 Jun 1823, Wellfleet, Mass. They had 1 child.
  vii.  Moses Lewis Atwood was born on 25 Apr 1804 in Wellfleet, Mass.

viii.    Timothy Atwood, born 22 Feb 1808, Wellfleet, Mass.; married Sarah Snow
        Newcomb, 15 Oct 1837, Wellfleet, Mass.; died 11 Aug 1865, Wrentham, Mass.
        They had 5 children.

393. Zenas Cook (Richard-4, Benjamin-3, Josiah-2, Josias-1) was born on 18 Jul 1769 in Eastham,
    Mass.

    Zenas Cook and Experience PARKER were married. Experience Parker was born (date
    unknown).

# 6<sup>th</sup> Generation

631. Miriam Cook (Josiah-5, Jacob-4, Josiah-3, Josiah-2, Josias-1) was born in 1772.

Miriam Cook and Russel DEWOLF were married on 27 Aug 1792 in Otis, Mass.

632. Mercy Cook (Josiah-5, Jacob-4, Josiah-3, Josiah-2, Josias-1) was born on 10 Jul 1774.

Mercy Cook and William STEADMAN were married in 1809. William Steadman was born on 6 Aug 1769 in South Kingston, R.I.

William Steadman and Mercy Cook had the following children:

    i.   Josiah Cook Steadman, born est 1810, New York; married Narcissa CHORN, 5 Feb 1837, Green County, Ill.; married Sarah FRENCH, 18 Aug 1848, Eaton Rapids, Mich.; died bet 1860 and 1870. They had 8 children.

    ii.  Miriam Steadman, born 28 Apr 1812, Genesee County, NY.; married Edward Eugene LATSON, 20 Apr 1833, Wyoming County, NY.; died 1 Jun 1889, Howell, Mich. They had 7 children.

    iii. George Russell Steadman, born abt 1815; married Elizabeth UNKNOWN; married Emma MARSH. They had 4 children.

    iv. Ebenezer Steadman was born about 1817 in New York.

633. Elizabeth Cook (Josiah-5, Jacob-4, Josiah-3, Josiah-2, Josias-1) was born in 1776.

Elizabeth Cook and Randall WOODWORTH were married.

Randall Woodworth and Elizabeth Cook had the following children:

    i.   Lyman Woodworth.

    ii.  Elizabeth Cook Woodworth.

    iii. Fanny Woodworth.

    iv. Josiah Woodworth.

634. Ebenezer Cook (Josiah-5, Jacob-4, Josiah-3, Josiah-2, Josias-1) was born on 29 Dec 1783. He died in 1820 at the age of 37.

Ebenezer Cook and Leonora COOMBS were married in Jan 1807. Leonora Coombs was born on 24 Jul 1784.

Ebenezer Cook and Leonora Coombs had the following children:

i. Melinda Cook was born on 3 Oct 1807. She died on 25 Feb 1808.

1440 ii. Washington Ebenezer Cook, born 29 Dec 1808; married Eunice Allen KELLOGG, 30 May 1832.

iii. Harriett Leonora Cook was born on 21 Oct 1810. She died on 28 Oct 1831 at the age of 21.

iv. Joseph Addison Cook was born on 24 Jul 1812. He died on 10 Sep 1813.

1441 v. Watson Cook, born 11 Jul 1814; married Harriet M. MINOR, 21 Jan 1846; died 30 Jun 1859.

1442 vi. Mary Cook, born 7 Feb 1816; married Eugene Franklin SKINNER, 28 Nov 1839.

1443 vii. Clarissa Emily Cook, born 21 Jan 1818; married Thomas MORGAN, 30 Nov 1836.

635. Jonathan Cook (Josiah-5, Jacob-4, Josiah-3, Josiah-2, Josias-1) was born in 1788.

Jonathan Cook and Polly GRAVES were married.

636. Sally Cook (Josiah-5, Jacob-4, Josiah-3, Josiah-2, Josias-1) was born in 1792. She died in 1863 at the age of 71.

Sally Cook and Murray BROWN were married.

637. Philander Cook (Josiah-5, Jacob-4, Josiah-3, Josiah-2, Josias-1) was born in 1799.

Philander Cook and Ester GRAVES were married.

Philander Cook and Ester Graves had the following children:

i. Eben Cook.
ii. Ann Jeanette Cook.
iii. Paul Cook.
iv. Caroline Cook.
v. Azelia Cook.
vi. Oscar Cook.
vii. Clinton Cook.

1444 viii. Orrin Philander Cook, born 17 Jun 1819; married Anne Caroline WEATHERLOW, 10 Aug 1842, Arcade, NY.

638. John Cook (Elisha-5, Jacob-4, Josiah-3, Josiah-2, Josias-1) was born on 23 Apr 1781. He died in 1826 at the age of 45.

John Cook and Dorcas CASE were married on 2 Apr 1804 in Otis, Mass. Dorcas Case was born in 1783. She died in 1838 at the age of 55.

6.83

John Cook and Dorcas Case had the following children:

> i.   John Milton Cook was born on 22 May 1804 in Otis, Mass.
> ii.  George W. Cook was born on 13 Jan 1808 in Otis, Mass.
> iii. Sally L. Cook was born on 24 Dec 1809 in Otis, Mass.
> iv.  Elisha Cook was born on 31 Mar 1812 in Hartford, Hartford, Conn. He died in 1850 at the age of 38.
> v.   Laury A. Cook was born on 2 Jan 1815 in Otis, Mass.
> vi.  Mary Ann Cook was born on 2 Dec 1816 in Otis, Mass.
> vii. Eliza Ann Cook was born on 21 Jan 1818 in Otis, Mass.
> viii.   Esther Celestia Cook was born on 13 Apr 1819 in Otis, Mass.
> ix.  Jane Cook was born on 10 Apr 1821 in Otis, Mass.
> x.   Adeline Cook was born on 7 Jun 1822 in Otis, Mass.
> xi.  Ophelia Cook was born on 9 Oct 1824 in Otis, Mass.

639. Anna Cook (Elisha-5, Jacob-4, Josiah-3, Josiah-2, Josias-1) was born on 7 Dec 1782.

Anna Cook and Edmon KIMBALL were married on 6 Aug 1801 in Otis, Mass.

640.  Theophilus Cook (Elisha-5, Jacob-4, Josiah-3, Josiah-2, Josias-1) was born on 17 Aug 1784 in Otis, Mass.

Theophilus Cook and Esther TYLER were married.

641. Abigail Cook (Elisha-5, Jacob-4, Josiah-3, Josiah-2, Josias-1) was born on 9 Dec 1785.

Abigail Cook and Quinsey JOHNSON were married.

642. Polly Cook (Elisha-5, Jacob-4, Josiah-3, Josiah-2, Josias-1) was born on 8 Aug 1787.

Polly Cook and Lyman WOODWORTH were married.

643. Elisha Cook Jr. (Elisha-5, Jacob-4, Josiah-3, Josiah-2, Josias-1) was born on 28 Apr 1789.

Elisha Cook Jr. and Esther WOODBRIDGE were married.

644. Solomon Cook (Elisha-5, Jacob-4, Josiah-3, Josiah-2, Josias-1) was born on 21 Feb 1791.

Solomon Cook and Lorinda SCOTT were married.

645. Alva Cook (Elisha-5, Jacob-4, Josiah-3, Josiah-2, Josias-1) was born on 7 Sep 1793.

Alva Cook and Lydia COOPER were married on 14 Feb 1814 in West Springfield, Mass. Lydia Cooper, daughter of Enoch Cooper and Mary Leonard, was born on 21 Jul 1792. She died on 5 Feb 1880 at the age of 87.

Alva Cook and Lydia Cooper had the following children:

1445   i.   Albert Leonard Cook, born 1 Nov 1814, Otis, Mass.; married Catharine MCDONALD; died 9 Mar 1880.

1446   ii.   Harriet Eliza Cook, born 5 Jun 1818, Otis, Mass.; married James ELDER; died 10 Sep 1839.

1447   iii.   Julia Ann Cook, born 15 Jul 1820, Otis, Mass.; married James WHITESIDE; died 12 Oct 1865.

1448   iv.   Mary Elizabeth Cook, born 8 Sep 1822, Otis, Mass.; married Henry M. BRADLEY, 1 Jan 1846; died 28 Aug 1905.

1449   v.   Francis Edwin Cook, born 13 Dec 1824, Otis, Mass.; married Frances M. DIX; died 1 Oct 1904.

       vi.   John Milton Cook was born on 29 Dec 1826 in Seville, Oh. He appeared in the census in 1850 in Guilford, Medina, O. He died "in the goldrush" in 1851 at the age of 25 in California.

1450   vii.   Lucy Maria Cook, born 4 Jul 1829, Seville, Oh.; married James STOAKS after 1850.

1451   viii.   Elisha Baldwin Cook, born 11 Nov 1831, Seville, Oh.; married Mary Elizabeth HOWE, 1875, Sparta, O.; married Christine WILKIN, 6 Jun 1882, Bloomfield, Trumbull, O.

1452   ix.   Charles E. Cook, born 25 May 1834, Seville, Oh.; married Priscilla UNKNOWN.

1453   x.   Adaline Elmira Cook, born 29 Nov 1838, Seville, Oh.; married Richard V. STREETER, 4 May 1861, Medina, O.; died 17 May 1909, Hartford, Licking, O.


650. Capt Paron Cowell Cook (Twin) (Solomon-5, Solomon-4, Josiah-3, Josiah-2, Josias-1) was born on 4 Jan 1760 in Provincetown, Mass. He was baptized on 4 Apr 1762 in Truro, Mass. He died on 18 Oct 1834 at the age of 74 in Provincetown, Mass. Paron was buried in Hamilton Cemetery, Provincetown, Mass.

Capt Paron Cowell Cook (Twin) and Hannah S. GOODSPEED were married before 1781. Hannah S. Goodspeed was born in Mar 1756. She died on 28 Aug 1836 at the age of 80 in Provincetown, Mass. She was buried in Hamilton Cemetery, Provincetown, Mass.

Paron Cowell Cook and Hannah S. Goodspeed had the following children:

1474   i.   Hannah Cook, born 17 Dec 1781, Provincetown, Mass.; married Capt. Elisha (Isaiah) YOUNG, 1798, Provincetown, Mass.; died 19 Aug 1836, Provincetown, Mass.

1475   ii.   Newcomb Cook, born 3 Aug 1783, Provincetown, Mass.; married Nancy WELLS,

24 Dec 1807, Provincetown, Mass.; married Betsey YOUNG, 1 Oct 1816, Provincetown, Mass.

1476   iii.  Salome Cook, born 7 Aug 1785, Provincetown, Mass.; married Benjamin DYER, 24 Nov 1802, Provincetown, Mass.; died 8 Jan 1867, Provincetown, Mass.

1477   iv.  Zerviah Cook, born 7 Jul 1787, Provincetown, Mass.; married Elisha HOLMES.

       v.  Paron Cook was born on 11 Jan 1789 in Provincetown, Mass. He died on 2 Nov 1808 at the age of 19 in Provincetown, Mass. He was buried after 2 Nov 1808 in Winthrop Street Cemetery, Provincetown, Mass.

1478   vi.  Thomas Cook, born 1 Aug 1792, Provincetown, Mass.; married Caroline UNKNOWN; died 30 Oct 1852, Provincetown, Mass.

1479   vii.  Betsey Cook, born 28 Jun 1795, Provincetown, Mass.; married Capt. Samuel SOPER, 18 Nov 1813, Provincetown, Mass.; died 15 Apr 1826, Provincetown, Mass.

     viii.  Rebecca Cook was born on 25 Sep 1798 in Provincetown, Mass. She died on 19 Apr 1832 at the age of 33 in Provincetown, Mass. She was buried in Hamilton Cemetery, Provincetown, Mass.

Capt Paron Cowell Cook (Twin) and Mary UNKNOWN were married before 1780 in Provincetown, Mass.

651. Rebecca Cowell Cook (Solomon-5, Solomon-4, Josiah-3, Josiah-2, Josias-1) was born on 1 Aug 1762 in Provincetown, Mass. She was baptized on 29 Aug 1762 in Provincetown, Mass.

Rebecca Cowell Cook and David KILBURN were married. David Kilburn was the son of Thomas Kilburn and Mehitable Rider.

Rebecca Cowell Cook and Joshua NICKERSON were married in 1783 in Provincetown, Mass. Joshua Nickerson, son of Seth Nickerson and Martha Atwood, was born on 7 Dec 1761 in Provincetown, Mass. He was baptized on 4 Apr 1762 in Truro, Mass. He died on 22 Oct 1794 at the age of 32 in North Bucksport, Me.

Joshua Nickerson and Rebecca Cowell Cook had the following children:

1480   i.  Isaac "Isaiah" Nickerson, born 28 Aug 1784; married Bethia RYDER; died Jan 1819.

1481   ii.  Joshua Nickerson, born 10 Sep 1786; married Hannah HINKS.

1482   iii.  Rebecca Nickerson, born 9 Nov 1788, Provincetown, Mass.; married Rev. Charles ATKINS.

1483   iv.  Abraham Nickerson, born 25 Jul 1791; married Tamsin HINKS; died Apr 1811, At sea.

1484   v.  Mary "Polly" Nickerson, born 28 Jul 1793, Provincetown, Mass.; married Thomas KILBURN.

652. Capt. Solomon Cook Jr. (Solomon-5, Solomon-4, Josiah-3, Josiah-2, Josias-1) was born on 12
Aug 1764 in Provincetown, Mass. He died on 21 Mar 1840 at the age of 75 in Provincetown,
Mass. He was buried in Provincetown, Mass.

Capt. Solomon Cook Jr. and Susanna BATES were married before 1788. Susanna Bates,
daughter of Reuben and Molly Bates, was born in 1767 in Scituate, Mass. Susanna died of
breast cancer which she had for 1 year on 6 Sep 1860 at the age of 93 in Provincetown, Mass.

Solomon Cook and Susanna Bates had the following children:

1485   i.   Capt. Reuben Cook, born 3 Oct 1788, Provincetown, Mass.; married Elizabeth
KILBURN, bef 1811; died 3 Sep 1862, Provincetown, Mass.
1486   ii.  Solomon D. Cook III, born 10 Sep 1790, Provincetown, Mass.; married Sally
COOK, 12 Dec 1813, Provincetown, Mass.; married Mary FREEMAN, 18 Oct
1840, Provincetown, Mass.; died 24 Jul 1868, Provincetown, Mass.
1487   iii. Polly Cook, born 4 Sep 1792, Provincetown, Mass.; married George BRYANT, 10
Mar 1812, Provincetown, Mass.; died 1 Aug 1821, Provincetown, Mass.
1488   iv. Joshua Cook II, born 23 Feb 1794, Provincetown, Mass.; married Rebecca
ATKINS, 1817; married Mercy P. KNOWLES, 15 Jun 1862; died 26 Jan 1881,
Provincetown, Mass.
1489   v.  James Cook, born 1 Sep 1797, Provincetown, Mass.; married Sally PAINE, 26 Dec
1819, Provincetown, Mass.; married Anna HINKS, 29 Jan 1828, Provincetown,
Mass.; died 26 Dec 1881, Provincetown, Mass.
1490   vi. Elisha Cook II, born 11 Jul 1799, Provincetown, Mass.; married Almira JONES, 23
Nov 1820, Provincetown, Mass.; married Ann UNKNOWN, aft 1838,
Provincetown, Mass.; died 23 Mar 1874, Provincetown, Mass.
1491   vii. Hannah Cook, born 30 Jul 1801, Provincetown, Mass.; married John ATKINS, 12
Mar 1819, Provincetown, Mass.
1492   viii.  Coleman Cook, born 1803, Provincetown, Mass.; married Susan ELDRIDGE,
1825.
1493   ix. Susanna Cook, born 6 Jun 1805, Provincetown, Mass.; married James WHORF, 19
Sep 1825, Provincetown, Mass.

653. Mary "Betty" Cook (Solomon-5, Solomon-4, Josiah-3, Josiah-2, Josias-1) was born in 1770.
She was christened on 14 Apr 1771 in Truro, Mass. She died on 15 Sep 1789 at the age of 19
in Provincetown, Mass. Betty was buried in Winthrop Street Cemetery, Provincetown, Mass.

Mary "Betty" Cook and James NICKERSON were married. James Nickerson, son of
Phinneas Nickerson and Susannah Smith, was born before 8 Oct 1769 in Provincetown, Mass.
He was christened on 8 Oct 1769 in Truro, Mass. He died on 14 Sep 1840 at the age of 70 in

Wellfleet, Mass.

James Nickerson and Mary Cook had the following child:

    i.   A son Nickerson was born in 1789 in Provincetown, Mass. He died in 1789.

654. Capt. Joshua Cook (Solomon-5, Solomon-4, Josiah-3, Josiah-2, Josias-1) was born on 17 Oct 1774 in Provincetown, Mass. He died of palsy on 20 Sep 1852 at the age of 77 in Provincetown, Mass. (This was probably Parkinson's.) He was buried in Hamilton Cemetery, Provincetown, Mass.

Capt. Joshua Cook and Elizabeth ATKINS were married before 1797. Elizabeth Atkins was born in 1776. She died of palsy on 13 Jul 1845 at the age of 69 in Provincetown, Mass. She was buried in Cemetery Number Two, Old Section, Provincetown, Mass.

Joshua Cook and Elizabeth Atkins had the following children:

1494   i.   Capt. Jacob Cook, born 9 Sep 1797, Provincetown, Mass.; married Mary ATKINS, 12 Feb 1820, Truro, Mass.; died 25 Dec 1871, Provincetown, Mass.

1495   ii.   Joshua Cook II, born 25 Aug 1799, Provincetown, Mass.; married Joanna HIGGINS, 2 Jan 1823, Provincetown, Mass.; died 10 Mar 1867, Provincetown, Mass.

1496   iii.   Elizabeth Cook, born 15 Sep 1801, Provincetown, Mass.; married Lemuel PAINE, 9 Mar 1820, Provincetown, Mass.; died 17 Sep 1828, Provincetown, Mass.

1497   iv.   Richard Atkins Cook, born 30 Jun 1804, Provincetown, Mass.; married Martha ATKINS, 10 Jan 1828, Provincetown, Mass.; married Betsy (Collins) LOMBARD, 13 Sep 1846; died 25 Jun 1862, Provincetown, Mass.

1498   v.   Harvey Cook, born 11 Sep 1806, Provincetown, Mass.; married Jedediah A. SMITH, 13 Jul 1839, Provincetown, Mass.; married Hannah G. ELLINGOOD; married Susan P. UNKNOWN.

1499   vi.   Roxana Cook, born 12 Dec 1808, Provincetown, Mass.; married Reuben ATKINS, 18 Dec 1826, Provincetown, Mass.; died 20 Sep 1888, Provincetown, Mass.

1500   vii.   Maria Cook, born 13 Apr 1812 or 30 Apr 1812, Provincetown, Mass.; married Samuel COOK Jr., 19 Jan 1832, Provincetown, Mass.; died 23 Dec 1888, Provincetown, Mass.

       viii.   Michael Cook was born on 17 Nov 1815 in Provincetown, Mass.

657. Barnabas Cook (Barnabas-5, Solomon-4, Josiah-3, Josiah-2, Josias-1) was born on 25 Dec 1793 in Provincetown, Mass. He died at sea when his ship foundered on 3 Oct 1841 at the age of 47.

Barnabas Cook and Dorcas Hinckley BANGS had marriage banns published on 18 Mar 1818

in and were married on 24 Nov 1818 in Truro, Mass. Dorcas Hinckley BANGS, daughter of
Perez Bangs, was born on 5 May 1796 in Truro, Mass.

Barnabas Cook and Dorcas Hinckley Bangs had the following children:

1509   i.   Sally A. Cook, born 14 Jun 1820, Truro, Mass.; married Isaac R. AYDELOT, 29
            Nov 1837, Truro, Mass.; died bef 1850.
1510   ii.  Dorcas B. Cook, born 21 Nov 1823, Truro, Mass.; married John DOROTHY, 5 Jan
            1841, Truro, Mass.
1511   iii. Anna Cook, born 6 Apr 1825, Truro, Mass.; married Joshua RICH, 26 Oct 1844,
            Truro, Mass.
1512   iv.  Harriet G. Cook, born 22 Oct 1828, Truro, Mass.; married Daniel LOMBARD, 6 Jun
            1847, Truro, Mass.
1513   v.   Barnabas Cook, born 31 Dec 1830, Truro, Mass.; married Rebecca (Pierce) COOK,
            2 Dec 1851, Wellfleet, Mass.
       vi.  Alexander Cook was born on 26 Oct 1834 in Truro, Mass. He died on 6 Nov 1834.
       vii. Alexander Cook was born in 1837 in Truro, Mass. He died on 14 Dec 1859 at the age
            of 22 in Truro, Mass.
       viii.   Jonathan Rider "Jerusha" Cook was born on 18 Dec 1839 in Truro, Mass.

658. Elisha Cook (Elisha-5, Solomon-4, Josiah-3, Josiah-2, Josias-1) was born on 11 Oct 1770 in
Provincetown, Mass. He was baptized on 14 Apr 1771 in Truro, Mass.

Elisha Cook and Abigail UNKNOWN were married before 1794 in Provincetown, Mass.
Abigail died on 18 Apr 1800 at the age of 31 in Provincetown, Mass. She was buried in
Winthrop Street Cemetery, Provincetown, Mass.

Elisha Cook and Abigail Unknown had the following children:

1514   i.   Sally Cook, born 4 May 1794, Provincetown, Mass.; married Solomon D. COOK III,
            12 Dec 1813, Provincetown, Mass.; died 12 Oct 1871, Provincetown, Mass.
1515   ii.  Elisha Cook 2nd, born 1 Aug 1797, Provincetown, Mass.; married Sally HILLYARD,
            30 Dec 1824, Provincetown, Mass.; married Rebecca COOK, 24 Mar 1850,
            Provincetown, Mass.
       iii. Lemuel Cook was born about 15 Dec 1799 in Provincetown, Mass. He died on 25 Apr
            1800.

Elisha Cook and Ruth HOPKINS were married in 1801 in Provincetown, Mass. They
appeared in the census in 1810 in Provincetown, Mass. Ruth Hopkins, daughter of Jonathan
Hopkins and Mary Paine, was born in 1778. She died on 3 Jun 1810 at the age of 32 in
Provincetown, Mass. She was buried in Winthrop Street Cemetery, Provincetown, Mass.

6.89

Elisha Cook and Ruth Hopkins had the following child:

1516   i.   Abigail Cook, born 2 Jul 1806, Provincetown, Mass.; married Taylor SMALL.

Elisha Cook and Polly YOUNG were married on 19 Jan 1812 in Provincetown, Mass. Polly Young, daughter of Eleazor Young and Rebecca Smalley, was born in Jul 1787 in Provincetown, Mass. She died of consumption on 17 May 1856 at the age of 68 in Provincetown, Mass.

Elisha Cook and Polly Young had the following child:

1517   i.   Polly Cook, born 8 Jun 1815, Provincetown, Mass.; married Hon. Joseph Proper JOHNSON; died 14 Jun 1842, Provincetown, Mass.

659. David A. Cook (Elisha-5, Solomon-4, Josiah-3, Josiah-2, Josias-1) was born on 20 Dec 1774 in Provincetown, Mass. He died when his clothes caught fire on 18 May 1857 at the age of 82 in Provincetown, Mass. He was buried in Winthrop Street Cemetery, Provincetown, Mass.

David A. Cook and Huldah UNKNOWN were married in 1794. She was born in May 1778 in Provincetown, Mass. She died on 28 Dec 1802 at the age of 24 in Provincetown, Mass. She was buried in Winthrop Street Cemetery, Provincetown, Mass.

David A. Cook and Lydia SMITH were married on 3 Dec 1804 in Truro, Mass. Lydia Smith, daughter of Barzillai Smith, was born in 1780. She died on 9 Apr 1812 at the age of 32 in Provincetown, Mass. She was buried in Winthrop Street Cemetery, Provincetown, Mass.

David A. Cook and Lydia Smith had the following children:

1518   i.   Capt. Lemuel "Captain Lem" Cook, born 21 Sep 1804, Provincetown, Mass.; married Belinda NICKERSON, 11 Apr 1827, Provincetown, Mass.; died 7 May 1869, Provincetown, Mass.
1519   ii.  David Cook Jr., born 15 Nov 1808, Provincetown, Mass.; married Louisa ATKINS, 4 Apr 1831, Provincetown, Mass.; died 1839 at sea.
1520   iii. Elizabeth Paine Cook, born 27 Nov 1806, Provincetown, Mass.; married Enoch NICKERSON, 19 Dec 1827, Provincetown, Mass.; died 8 Mar 1893.
       iv.  Barzilla S. Cook was born about Nov 1810 in Provincetown, Mass. He died on 9 Apr 1812 at the age of 1 in Provincetown, Mass. He was buried in Winthrop Street Cemetery, Provincetown, Mass.

David A. Cook and Susannah MAYO were married in 1814 in Provincetown, Mass. Susannah Mayo was born on 28 Sep 1769 in Provincetown, Mass. She died on 9 Aug 1839 at the age of 69. She was buried in Winthrop Street Cemetery, Provincetown, Mass.

660. James Cook (John-5, Solomon-4, Josiah-3, Josiah-2, Josias-1) was born on 15 Sep 1771 in Provincetown, Mass. He was baptized on 24 May 1772 in Truro, Mass.

James Cook and Polly Sweetser SPARKS were married. Polly Sweetser Sparks, daughter of Thomas Sparks and Sarah Smith, was born (date unknown).

James Cook and Polly Sweetser Sparks had the following child:

    1521   i.   Mary "Polly" Cook, born 1801, Provincetown, Mass.; married Henry PARTRIDGE, abt 1817; died 1880, Maine.

661. Capt. Isaac Cook (John-5, Solomon-4, Josiah-3, Josiah-2, Josias-1) was born on 24 Dec 1775 in Provincetown, Mass. He died of paralysis on one side (4 weeks, mortification dry) ["mortification" is gangrene] on 13 Jun 1860 at the age of 84 in Provincetown, Mass. Isaac was buried in Hamilton Cemetery, Provincetown, Mass.

Capt. Isaac Cook and Tabitha SMITH were married in 1798 in Provincetown, Mass. Tabitha Smith was born in Eastham, Mass.

Isaac Cook and Tabitha Smith had the following children:

    1522   i.   Rebecca Cook, born 29 Aug 1805, Provincetown, Mass.; married Samuel Parker BROOKS; married Charles REED, 15 Mar 1836, Provincetown, Mass.; married Elisha COOK 2nd, 24 Mar 1850, Provincetown, Mass.; died 5 Sep 1896, Provincetown, Mass.

    1523   ii.  Capt. Isaac Cook Jr., born 7 Oct 1809, Provincetown, Mass.; married Phebe NICKERSON, 10 Oct 1831, Provincetown, Mass.; died 30 Apr 1851, Provincetown, Mass.

    1524   iii. Myrick S. Cook, born 15 Dec 1813, Provincetown, Mass.; married Elizabeth E. BURT, 26 Apr 1840, Provincetown, Mass.; died 11 Jun 1877, Provincetown, Mass.

662. Abigail Cook (John-5, Solomon-4, Josiah-3, Josiah-2, Josias-1) was born on 4 Feb 1777 in Provincetown, Mass. She died of "stomach disease" on 16 Jun 1854 at the age of 77 in Provincetown, Mass.

Abigail Cook and James Sparks were married about 1795 in Provincetown, Mass. James SPARKS was the son of Thomas Sparks and Sarah Smith.

6.91

James Sparks and Abigail Cook had the following children:

    i.   Hannah Sparks, born 1796, Provincetown, Mass.; married Samuel White ATKINS.

    ii.  James Sparks Jr., born 1798, Provincetown, Mass.; married Sally GOODSPEED; died 1853, Provincetown, Mass.

    iii. Abigail "Nabby" Sparks, born 1801, Provincetown, Mass.; married Barzilla HIGGINS. They had 2 children.

    iv. Thomas Sparks, born 2 Jul 1804, Provincetown, Mass.; married Hannah YOUNG, 30 Dec 1828, Provincetown, Mass.; married Ann ATWOOD; married Lurania GROSS; died 1895.

    v.   Mary Sparks, born 1807, Provincetown, Mass.; married Isaiah YOUNG.

    vi. Louisa Sparks, born 7 Aug 1809, Provincetown, Mass.; married Capt. James Tilton COOK, 1835, Provincetown, Mass.; died 15 Sep 1846, Provincetown, Mass. They had 5 children.

    vii. Heman C. Sparks, born 1811, Provincetown, Mass.; married Betsey RYDER; married Elizabeth RYDER.

    viii. David Sparks, born 1814, Provincetown, Mass.; married Rebecca DYER; married Martha Dyer SMALL; died 1897.

    ix. Harvey Sparks, born 1817, Provincetown, Mass.; married Clarissa Macomber GALAACAR; married Chloe B. HOLWAY; died 1886.

**663.** John Cook Jr. (John-5, Solomon-4, Josiah-3, Josiah-2, Josias-1) was born on 30 May 1783 in Provincetown, Mass. He died before 1820 at the age of 37 in Provincetown, Mass.

John Cook Jr. and Martha BUSH were married in 1802 in Provincetown, Mass. Martha Bush, daughter of William and Desire Bush, was born in Feb 1784 in Provincetown, Mass. She died of old age on 10 Nov 1868 at the age of 84 in Provincetown, Mass.

John Cook and Martha Bush had the following children:

    i.   James Cook was born on 10 Jan 1803 in Provincetown, Mass.

    ii.  John Cook was born on 21 Dec 1804 in Provincetown, Mass. He died before 1818 at the age of 14.

    iii. Patty Cook was born on 18 Feb 1806 in Provincetown, Mass. She died on 14 Aug 1808 at the age of 2 in Provincetown, Mass.

1534  iv. Josiah Cook, born 31 Jul 1809, Provincetown, Mass.; married Caroline KENT, 10 Jul 1842, Provincetown, Mass.; died 6 Apr 1874, Provincetown, Mass.

1535  v.  Desire B. Cook, born 1 Dec 1811, Provincetown, Mass.; married John YOUNG Jacobs.

1536  vi. Capt. John J. Cook, born 22 Mar 1818, Provincetown, Mass.; married Elizabeth S. TAYLOR, bef 1849; died 1907, Provincetown, Mass.

664. Josiah Cook (John-5, Solomon-4, Josiah-3, Josiah-2, Josias-1) was born on 23 Jan 1791 in
Provincetown, Mass.

Josiah Cook and Sara E. BOWLEY were married on 18 Jan 1832 in Provincetown, Mass.

Josiah Cook and Sara E. Bowley had the following children:

    1537   i.   James E. Cook, born 27 Jul 1839, Provincetown, Mass.; married Abigail C. CASE,
Provincetown, Mass.

          ii.  A daughter was born in 1843 in Provincetown, Mass.

Josiah Cook and Betsey STUDLY were married on 13 Aug 1816 in Provincetown, Mass.

665. Patty Martha Cook (Jonathan-5, Solomon-4, Josiah-3, Josiah-2, Josias-1) was born on 27 Aug
1773 in Provincetown, Mass. She died on 26 Sep 1826 at the age of 53 in Provincetown,
Mass.

Patty Martha Cook and Joshua Freeman Grozier were married on 24 Mar 1793 in Truro,
Mass. Joshua Freeman Grozier, son of John Grozier and Mercy Hopkins, was born on 2 Apr
1769 in Truro, Mass. He died on 29 Apr 1829 at the age of 60.

Joshua Freeman Grozier and Patty Martha Cook had the following children:

      i.   William Grozier, born 17 Apr 1794, Provincetown, Mass.; married Martha WRIGHT;
married Rebekah PERRY, 4 Dec 1817, Provincetown, Mass.; died 11 Sep 1844.
With his second wife they had 6 children.

     ii.  Joshua Grozier was born on 7 Jul 1796 in Provincetown, Mass. He died from drowning on
25 Dec 1824 at the age of 28. He was buried in Winthrop Street Cemetery,
Provincetown, Mass.

   iii. Freeman Grozier was born on 7 Jul 1796 in Provincetown, Mass. He died on 27 Sep 1797
in Provincetown, Mass.

   iv. Freeman Grozier was born on 17 Nov 1798 in Provincetown, Mass. He died on 17 Nov
1798 in Provincetown, Mass.

     v.  Mercy Grozier was born on 22 Jul 1800 in Provincetown, Mass.

    vi.  Patty Grozier was born on 20 Feb 1802 in Provincetown, Mass. She died on 4 Mar 1803
at the age of 1 in Provincetown, Mass.

   vii. Sally (Sarah) E. Grozier, born 28 Aug 1803, Provincetown, Mass.; married Nathaniel
Holmes, 25 Nov 1824, Provincetown, Mass.; died 29 Jan 1892, Provincetown, Mass.
They had 3 children.

  viii.   Saloma Grozier, born 14 Oct 1805, Provincetown, Mass.; married Isaiah Atkins, 27
Feb 1827, Provincetown, Mass.; died 24 Feb 1838, Truro, Mass. They had 3

children.

    ix.  Caleb Upham Grozier was born on 7 Jan 1808 in Provincetown, Mass. He died in May 1853 at the age of 45 in Calcutta, India.

    x.  Rebecca Atkins Grozier, born 4 Oct 1810, Provincetown, Mass.; married Henry Willard M.D., 18 Jan 1831, Provincetown, Mass. They had 2 children.

666. David Newcomb Cook (Jonathan-5, Solomon-4, Josiah-3, Josiah-2, Josias-1) was born on 29 Aug 1776 in Provincetown, Mass. He died on 16 Jun 1849 at the age of 72 in Provincetown, Mass.

David Newcomb Cook and Salome LOMBARD were married on 23 Nov 1800 in Provincetown, Mass. Salome Lombard was born about 1780 in Truro, Mass. She died of consumption on 20 Mar 1845 at the age of 65 in Provincetown, Mass. She was buried in Hamilton Cemetery, Provincetown, Mass.

David Newcomb Cook and Salome Lombard had the following children:

       i.  Rebecca Cook was born on 7 Sep 1801 in Provincetown, Mass. She died on 15 Mar 1803 in Provincetown, Mass.

1542   ii.  Martha "Patty" Cook, born 9 Jan 1804, Provincetown, Mass.; married James STANFORD, 15 Jun 1823, Provincetown, Mass.; died 12 May 1857, Provincetown, Mass.

1543   iii. Rebecca Cook, born 9 Jul 1806, Provincetown, Mass.; married Thomas LOTHROP, 30 Apr 1826, Provincetown, Mass.; died 3 Nov 1892, Provincetown, Mass.

     iv. Salome Cook was born on 31 Dec 1808 in Provincetown, Mass. She died on 2 Oct 1823 at the age of 14 in Provincetown, Mass.

1544   v.  Lemuel Cook 2nd, born 2 Nov 1811, Provincetown, Mass.; married Mary Jones WEEKS, 4 Feb 1841, Provincetown, Mass.; married Ann (Atwood) LEWIS, 17 Apr 1861, Provincetown, Mass.; died 15 Jan 1888, Provincetown, Mass.

1545   vi. Rosetta Cook, born 31 May 1814, Provincetown, Mass.; married Capt. Enoch HALL, 29 Dec 1840, Provincetown, Mass.; died 29 Mar 1849, Provincetown, Mass.

   vii. Thomas Dunlop Cook was born on 15 Jan 1817 in Provincetown, Mass. He died on 6 Sep 1823 at the age of 6 in Provincetown, Mass.

1546  viii.  Benjamin Lombard Cook, born 5 Oct 1819, Provincetown, Mass.; married Anne E. HAMMERSLEY, 23 Mar 1845, Provincetown, Mass.

1547  ix. Eliza Bryant Cook, born 26 Feb 1822, Provincetown, Mass.; married Peter E. DOLLIVER, 24 Jan 1841, Provincetown, Mass.

667. Capt. Jonathan Cook Jr. (Jonathan-5, Solomon-4, Josiah-3, Josiah-2, Josias-1) was born on 23
Feb 1780 in Provincetown, Mass. He died of "Old Age" on 26 Apr 1862 at the age of 82 in

Provincetown, Mass.   He was buried in Provincetown Cemetery Number Two.

Capt. Jonathan Cook Jr. and Sabra BROWN were married on 23 Apr 1802 in Provincetown, Mass. Sabra Brown, daughter of William Brown and Temperance , was born on 15 Mar 1783. She died on 20 Aug 1872 at the age of 89 in Provincetown, Mass. She was buried in Hamilton Cemetery, Provincetown, Mass.

Jonathan was a master of King Hiram's Lodge in 1829-1830. The Provincetown museum has a portrait of both him and his wife (above), as well as many of their belongings, including a family tree that Sabra had sewn on a pillow.

Jonathan Cook and Sabra Brown had the following children:

1548   i.   Edward Cook, born 30 Nov 1804, Provincetown, Mass.; married Servina LEWIS, 14 Jul 1826, Provincetown, Mass.; died 2 Oct 1825, Provincetown, Mass.

      ii.  Jonathan Cook was born on 1 Oct 1806 in Provincetown, Mass. He died on 7 Oct 1825 at the age of 19 in Provincetown, Mass.   He was buried in Hamilton Cemetery, Provincetown, Mass.

1549  iii. Capt. William Cook, born 1 Oct 1808, Provincetown, Mass.; married Rebecca RYDER, bef 1832, Provincetown, Mass.; married Joanna R. Higgins, 24 Feb 1841, Provincetown, Mass.; died 5 Jul 1868, Provincetown, Mass.

1550  iv.  Philip Cook II, born 28 Apr 1810, Provincetown, Mass.; married Eliza A. WHORF, 9 Feb 1832, Provincetown, Mass.; married Betsy N. FREEMAN, 18 Nov 1838, Provincetown, Mass.; died 9 Mar 1893, Provincetown, Mass.

1551   v.  Sally Cook, born 23 Feb 1812, Provincetown, Mass.; married Stephen HILLIARD, 4 Mar 1830, Provincetown, Mass.; died 11 Oct 1892.

1552  vi.  Cordelia Cook, born 25 Feb 1814, Provincetown, Mass.; married Paron C.

6.95

HOLMES, 9 Nov 1829, Provincetown, Mass.; married John BELCHER, 23 Jun 1839, Provincetown, Mass.

1553   vii. Olive Wadsworth Cook, born 15 Apr 1818, Provincetown, Mass.; married Capt. Russell Knox ELLIOT, 18 Nov 1838, Provincetown, Mass.; died 1907, Provincetown, Mass.

1554   viii. James Munroe Cook, born 9 Apr 1820, Provincetown, Mass.; married Levina HOWES, 5 Mar 1843, Provincetown, Mass.; married Louisa ; died 1898, Provincetown, Mass.

1555   ix. Capt. Charles Augustus Cook, born 14 Jul 1822, Provincetown, Mass.; married Sarah Higgins DUNHAM, 8 Nov 1843, Provincetown, Mass.; married Olive ATKINS, 19 Dec 1848, Provincetown, Mass.; died 8 Oct 1891, Provincetown, Mass.

1556   x. Salome Cook, born 27 Sep 1824, Provincetown, Mass.; married Jonathan N. YOUNG, 1 Dec 1844, Provincetown, Mass.

668. Capt. Philip Cook (Jonathan-5, Solomon-4, Josiah-3, Josiah-2, Josias-1) was born on 15 Oct 1781 in Provincetown, Mass. He died of consumption on 9 Apr 1849 at the age of 67 in Provincetown, Mass. He was buried in Hamilton Cemetery, Provincetown, Mass.

Capt. Philip Cook and Hannah SMITH were married on 1 Feb 1806 in Provincetown, Mass. Hannah Smith, daughter of Nehemiah Smith and Jedidah Arey, was born on 18 Oct 1779. She died on 2 Feb 1869 at the age of 89 in Provincetown, Mass. She was buried in Hamilton Cemetery, Provincetown, Mass. Philip and Hannah were third cousins.

Philip Cook and Hannah Smith had the following children:

1557   i. Almira Cook, born 1809, Provincetown, Mass.; married Anthony BROWN, 17 May 1829, Provincetown, Mass.; died 20 Mar 1851, Provincetown, Mass.

1558   ii. Abigail "Nabby" Cook, born 3 Jul 1812, Provincetown, Mass.; married Benjamin LANCY; died 27 Feb 1896, Provincetown, Mass.

669. Bethia Cook (Jonathan-5, Solomon-4, Josiah-3, Josiah-2, Josias-1) was born on 14 Oct 1784 in Provincetown, Mass.

Bethia Cook and Thomas Smith Sparks were married in 1802 in Provincetown, Mass. Thomas Smith Sparks was the son of Thomas Sparks and Sarah Smith.

Thomas Smith Sparks and Bethia Cook had the following children:

i. Rebecca Cook Sparks, born 14 Aug 1803, Provincetown, Mass.; married Oliver BOWLEY.

ii. Bethiah Sparks, born 9 Oct 1805, Provincetown, Mass.; married John ATKINS.

iii. Betsy Sparks, born 18 Nov 1807, Provincetown, Mass.; married Elisha YOUNG Jr., 9 Feb 1827; died 14 Apr 1873, Provincetown, Mass.

iv. Freeman Grozier Sparks was born on 25 Jan 1810 in Provincetown, Mass.

v.  Maria Sparks was born on 30 Nov 1812 in Provincetown, Mass.

vi. Polly Sparks was born on 17 Mar 1815 in Provincetown, Mass.

vii. Thomas Smith Sparks, born 11 Nov 1817, Provincetown, Mass.; married Laurana GROSS.

viii.   Francis Fluker Sparks was born on 28 Aug 1820 in Provincetown, Mass.

ix. William Tilton Sparks was born on 20 Oct 1823 in Provincetown, Mass.


670. Capt. Lemuel Cook (Jonathan-5, Solomon-4, Josiah-3, Josiah-2, Josias-1) was born on 13 Sep 1786 in Provincetown, Mass. He died on 25 Jan 1828 at the age of 41 in St. Gago De Cuba. He was buried in Gifford Cemetery, Provincetown, Mass.

Capt. Lemuel Cook and Rebecca WHORF were married on 29 Dec 1807 in Provincetown, Mass.  Rebecca Whorf, daughter of John Whorf and Rebecca Rider, was born on 20 Jul 1790 in Provincetown, Mass. Rebecca died on 27 Sep 1849 at the age of 59 in Provincetown, Mass.

Lemuel Cook and Rebecca Whorf had the following children:

1563   i.   David Cook, born 15 Oct 1808, Provincetown, Mass.; married Sally WATKINS, 24 Oct 1830, Provincetown, Mass.; died 7 Dec 1849, At sea.

1564   ii.  Capt. Tilton Cook, born 10 Jul 1810, Provincetown, Mass.; married Clarinda COOK, 15 Dec 1835, Provincetown, Mass.; died 1893, Provincetown, Mass.

1565   iii. Charles Dyer Cook, born 12 Jun 1813, Provincetown, Mass.; married Ellen B. UNKNOWN, bef 1846, Provincetown, Mass.; died 13 Feb 1888, Provincetown, Mass.

1566   iv. Emily Cook, born 12 Oct 1815, Provincetown, Mass.; married Jarius H. HILLIARD, 20 Feb 1833, Provincetown, Mass.; died 29 Mar 1886, Provincetown, Mass.

1567   v.  Ephraim Ryder Cook, born 16 Jul 1818, Provincetown, Mass.; married Abbie H. CONNANT, 29 Oct 1847, Provincetown, Mass.

vi. Sally Cook was born on 5 Apr 1825 in Provincetown, Mass. She died on 29 Jul in Provincetown, Mass. She was buried in Provincetown, Mass.

1568   vii. Lemuel Cook 3rd, born 30 Mar 1828, Provincetown, Mass.; married Rebecca A. MORGAN, 15 Nov 1852, Provincetown, Mass.; died 11 Nov 1885, Provincetown, Mass.


671. Edward Cook (Twin) (Jonathan-5, Solomon-4, Josiah-3, Josiah-2, Josias-1) was born on 16 Mar 1789 in Provincetown, Mass.

Edward Cook (Twin) and Survina LEWIS were married on 14 Jul 1825 in Provincetown, Mass. Survina Lewis was born in Provincetown, Mass.

Edward Cook and Survina Lewis had the following child:

> i.   Servina Edward Cook was born on 21 May 1826 in Provincetown, Mass.

672. Eleanor Cook (Samuel-5, Solomon-4, Josiah-3, Josiah-2, Josias-1) was born on 19 Jan 1778 in Provincetown, Mass.

Eleanor Cook and Cyrenus BROWN were married on 25 Apr 1793 in Provincetown, Mass. Cyrenus Brown, son of David Brown, was born between 1775 and 1785 in Provincetown, Mass.

Cyrenus Brown and Eleanor Cook had the following children:

> i.    Jonathan Brown was born on 24 Jan 1795 in Provincetown, Mass.
> ii.   John Brown was born on 19 Jan 1778 in Provincetown, Mass.
> iii.  Ephraim Brown was born on 10 Jan 1799 in Provincetown, Mass.
> iv.   Phineas Brown was born on 3 Dec 1800 in Provincetown, Mass.
> v.    Alamira Brown was born on 22 Aug 1804 in Provincetown, Mass.
> vi.   Cyrenus Brown.
> vii.  Samuel Brown.
> viii.    Reuben Brown.

673. Ephraim Cook (Samuel-5, Solomon-4, Josiah-3, Josiah-2, Josias-1) was born on 4 Feb 1779 in Provincetown, Mass. He died on 27 Aug 1833 at the age of 54 in Provincetown, Mass. Ephraim was buried in Hamilton Cemetery, Provincetown, Mass.

Ephraim Cook and Rebecca LOMBARD had marriage banns published on 3 Apr 1802 in Truro, Mass. They were married on 22 Apr 1802 in Provincetown, Mass. Rebecca Lombard, daughter of Cornelius Lombard, was born on 4 Jan 1784. She died of heart disease on 13 Jul 1858 at the age of 74 in Provincetown, Mass. Rebecca was buried in Hamilton Cemetery, Provincetown, Mass.

Ephraim Cook and Rebecca Lombard had the following children:

> i.   Daniel Cross was born on 1 Jun 1795 in Provincetown, Mass. Daniel Cross is listed in the Provincetown birth records as Daniel Cross Cook, p. 162, son of Ephraim and Rebecca.  He is also listed in the Family Record sheet, as their servant. They named another child Daniel Cross Cook 27 years later so they probably considered him to be

their adopted son. He couldn't have been a servant at the age of 7, when Ephraim and Rebecca were married. He was possibly taken in from a Cross Family.

1569   ii.   Parker Cook, born 18 Aug 1804, Provincetown, Mass.; married Hannah HINKS, 14 Sep 1834, Provincetown, Mass.; died 12 Sep 1849, Provincetown, Mass.

1570   iii.  Capt. Ephraim Cook, born 3 Nov 1806, Provincetown, Mass.; married Rebecca E. WILEY, abt 1834; married Hannah CHENEY, bef 1860, Provincetown, Mass.; married Betsy L. COOK, 25 Oct 1870, Provincetown, Mass.; died 22 Feb 1891, Provincetown, Mass.

1571   iv.   Anna Cook, born 23 Dec 1808, Provincetown, Mass.; married Harvey NICKERSON, 11 Jan 1831, Provincetown, Mass.; died 17 Nov 1887, Provincetown, Mass.

1572   v.    Ebenezer Cook, born 2 Feb 1811, Provincetown, Mass.; married Sarah R. NICKERSON, 9 Oct 1839, Provincetown, Mass.; died 10 Oct 1898, Provincetown, Mass.

1573   vi.   Rebecca (Nickerson) Cook, born 29 Aug 1813, Provincetown, Mass.; married Thomas HILLIARD, 4 Aug 1850, Provincetown, Mass.; married Nathaniel Lewis NICKERSON, 27 Feb 1834, Provincetown, Mass.; died 1901.

       vii.  Cornelius Cook was born in Mar 1815 in Provincetown, Mass. He died on 19 Feb 1816. He was buried in Winthrop Street Cemetery, Provincetown, Mass.

       viii. Aphia Cook was born on 27 Mar 1817 in Provincetown, Mass. She died on 22 Aug 1833 at the age of 16 in Provincetown, Mass. She was buried in Provincetown Cemetery Number Two.

1574   ix.   Cornelius Cook, born 15 Nov 1819, Provincetown, Mass.; married Mary Brown HILLIARD, 24 Nov 1846, Provincetown, Mass.; died 16 Nov 1849, Provincetown, Mass.

1575   x.    Capt. Daniel Cross Cook, born 30 Jan 1822, Provincetown, Mass.; married Mary Brown HILLIARD, 22 Jan 1851, Provincetown, Mass.; died 18 Dec 1888, Provincetown, Mass.

1576   xi.   Capt. Epephras Kibby Cook, born 14 Jun 1824, Provincetown, Mass.; married Sarah UNKNOWN. ; died 25 Jul 1905, Provincetown, Mass.

       xii.  Sally E. Cook was born on 5 Jan 1828 in Provincetown, Mass. She died on 24 Jul 1844 at the age of 16 in Provincetown, Mass. She was buried in Hamilton Cemetery, Provincetown, Mass.


674. Capt. Samuel Cook (Samuel-5, Solomon-4, Josiah-3, Josiah-2, Josias-1) was born on 17 Oct 1781 in Provincetown, Mass. In 1845 he was a ship owner in Provincetown, Mass. He died on 11 Jan 1867 at the age of 85 in Provincetown, Mass. Samuel was buried in Hamilton Cemetery, Provincetown, Mass.

Capt. Samuel Cook and Tamsey (Tamsin) BROWN were married in 1803 in Provincetown, Mass. Tamsey (Tamsin) Brown, daughter of William Brown, was born on 16 Apr 1785 in

Provincetown, Mass. She died of liver failure on 7 Oct 1851 at the age of 66 in Provincetown, Mass. She was buried in Hamilton Cemetery, Provincetown, Mass.

Samuel Cook and Tamsey (Tamsin) Brown had the following children:

1577   i.   Betsy Cook, born 8 Jul 1804, Provincetown, Mass.; married James SMALLEY, 4 Jan 1825, Provincetown, Mass.; died 15 Apr 1847, Provincetown, Mass.

1578   ii.   Samuel Cook Jr., born 21 Aug 1806, Provincetown, Mass.; married Maria COOK, 19 Jan 1832, Provincetown, Mass.; died 14 Feb 1841, Provincetown, Mass.

      iii.   Nathan Cook was born on 3 Oct 1808 in Provincetown, Mass. He died of cancer on 24 Jul 1874 at the age of 65 in Provincetown, Mass. He was buried in Hamilton Cemetery, Provincetown, Mass.

1579   iv.   Tamsin "Tamsey" Cook, born 22 Jun 1810, Provincetown, Mass.; married Elisha TILLSON, 21 Dec 1831, Provincetown, Mass.

1580   v.   Sylvanus Cook, born 19 Apr 1812, Provincetown, Mass.; married Louisa YOUNG, 17 Nov 1844, Provincetown, Mass.; died 1892, Provincetown, Mass.

1581   vi.   Capt. Henry Cook, born 29 Nov 1813, Provincetown, Mass.; married Abigail Rich DYER, 14 Dec 1837, Provincetown, Mass.; died 26 May 1893, Provincetown, Mass.

1582   vii.   Capt. Alfred Cook, born 12 Aug 1816, Provincetown, Mass.; married Rebecca Macomber BOWLEY, 27 Sep 1842, Provincetown, Mass.; married Caroline E. (Howard) SMITH, 16 Mar 1871, Provincetown, Mass.; married Emily S. CHAPEL, 21 Nov 1888, Provincetown, Mass.; died 16 May 1897, Provincetown, Mass.

1583   viii.   Mary A. Cook, born 19 Aug 1819, Provincetown, Mass.; married John ADAMS; married Solomon N. ADAMS, 24 Jul 1867, Provincetown, Mass.

1584   ix.   Dorinda Cook, born 30 Aug 1820, Provincetown, Mass.; married Silas Small YOUNG, 31 Dec 1837, Provincetown, Mass.; died 2 Oct 1851, Provincetown, Mass.

1585   x.   Louisa Cook, born 20 Sep 1823, Provincetown, Mass.; married Nathaniel N. COOK, 8 Oct 1843, Provincetown, Mass.; died 18 Dec 1890, Provincetown, Mass.

      xi.   Jonathan Cook was born on 29 Oct 1825 in Provincetown, Mass. He died of unknown causes on 7 Dec 1884 at the age of 59 in Provincetown, Mass. Jonathan was buried in Hamilton Cemetery, Provincetown, Mass.

1586   xii.   Phebe A. Cook, born 23 Sep 1828, Provincetown, Mass.; married Eleazor YOUNG, 1 Nov 1846, Provincetown, Mass.; died 1914, Provincetown, Mass.


Capt. Samuel Cook and Eunice F. GROSS were married on 15 May 1853 in Provincetown, Mass. Eunice F. Gross, daughter of Gross and Eunice Unknown, was born in 1812 in Provincetown, Mass.

675. Capt. Jesse Cook (Samuel-5, Solomon-4, Josiah-3, Josiah-2, Josias-1) was born on 13 Jun
1783 in Provincetown, Mass. He died of old age on 9 Jul 1871 at the age of 88 in
Provincetown, Mass. He was buried in Hamilton Cemetery, Provincetown, Mass.

Capt. Jesse Cook and Thankful Hopkins SMITH were married on 27 Nov 1806 in Truro,
Mass. Thankful Hopkins Smith, daughter of Archilaus Smith, was born in 1786. She died
"Liver complaint" on 10 Mar 1863 at the age of 77 in Provincetown, Mass. She was buried in
Hamilton Cemetery, Provincetown, Mass.

Jesse Cook and Thankful Hopkins Smith had the following children:

    i.   Ephraim S. Cook was born on 6 Sep 1807 in Provincetown, Mass. He died of
hypochondria, seven years, on 15 Jun 1867 at the age of 59 in Provincetown, Mass.
Ephraim was buried in Hamilton Cemetery, Provincetown, Mass. (Note that it's not
possible to die of hypochondria, but this is what is recorded..)

1587  ii.  Eleanor Cook, born 23 Aug 1809, Provincetown, Mass.; married Charles
NICKERSON, 8 Jan 1835, Provincetown, Mass.; died 30 Mar 1893,
Provincetown, Mass.

    iii.  Emeline Cook was born on 23 Mar 1811 in Provincetown, Mass. She died on 14 Mar
1812 in Provincetown, Mass. She was buried after 14 Mar 1812 in Winthrop Street
Cemetery, Provincetown, Mass.

    iv.  Emeline Cook was born on 8 Dec 1812 in Provincetown, Mass. She appeared in the
census in 1850 in Provincetown, Mass. She died of an enlarged heart on 12 Jan 1870
at the age of 57 in Provincetown, Mass. Emeline was buried in Hamilton Cemetery,
Provincetown, Mass.

1588  v.  Jesse Cook Jr., born 16 Oct 1814, Provincetown, Mass.; married Adeline ADAMS,
14 Jan 1838, Provincetown, Mass.; died 2 Nov 1876, Provincetown, Mass.

    vi.  Harriet Cook was born on 29 Jul 1817 in Provincetown, Mass. Harriet was buried in
Hamilton Cemetery, Provincetown, Mass.

    vii. Sarah Cook was born on 31 Jul 1825 in Provincetown, Mass. She died of dropsy on 4
Oct 1886 at the age of 61 in Provincetown, Mass. Sarah was buried in Hamilton
Cemetery, Provincetown, Mass.

676. Capt. Stephen Cook (Samuel-5, Solomon-4, Josiah-3, Josiah-2, Josias-1) was born on 29 Oct
1786 in Provincetown, Mass. In 1845 he was a ship owner in Provincetown, Mass. He died of
apoplexy on 8 Jan 1859 at the age of 72 in Provincetown, Mass.

Capt. Stephen Cook and Delliah CROWELL were married in 1807 in Provincetown, Mass.
Delliah Crowell, daughter of Robert Crowell and Ellen Unknown, was born on 22 Dec 1788 in
Provincetown, Mass. She died of old age on 24 Sep 1872 at the age of 83 in Provincetown,
Mass.

6.101

Stephen Cook and Delliah Crowell had the following children:

    1589   i.   Capt. Leonard Cook, born 5 Sep 1809, Provincetown, Mass.; married Calista NICKERSON, 2 May 1836, Provincetown, Mass.; died 25 Dec 1882, Provincetown, Mass.

           ii.  Sally Cook was born on 14 Jan 1812 in Provincetown, Mass. She died on 31 Aug 1825 at the age of 13 in Provincetown, Mass.

    1590  iii.  Jane C. Cook, born 22 Nov 1814, Provincetown, Mass.; married Joshua Elsbery BOWLEY, 21 Feb 1837, Provincetown, Mass.; died 14 Apr 1883, Provincetown, Mass.

    1591   iv.  Stephen Cook Jr., born 20 May 1817, Provincetown, Mass.; married Lucy Ann WILEY, bef 1847; married Mary A. HIGGINS, aft 1848; married Julia F. HIGGINS, 26 Jan 1865, Provincetown, Mass.; married Jane Eliza CHURCHILL, 17 Oct 1871, Provincetown, Mass.; died 3 Sep 1888, Provincetown, Mass.

    1592   v.  Dilliah "Dilley" Cook, born 1 Aug 1822, Provincetown, Mass.; married Joseph P. KNOWLES, 25 Nov 1841, Provincetown, Mass.; died 9 Jul 1899, Provincetown, Mass.

          vi.  Sally Cook was born on 25 Jun 1825 in Provincetown, Mass.

    1593  vii.  Sarah Cook, born 25 Apr 1826, Provincetown, Mass.; married Silas Small YOUNG, aft 1851; died 5 Jun 1872, Provincetown, Mass.

        viii.  Betsey Kibby Cook was born on 26 May 1828 in Provincetown, Mass. She died on 28 Jul 1832 at the age of 4 in Provincetown, Mass.

**677.** Betsey Cook (Samuel-5, Solomon-4, Josiah-3, Josiah-2, Josias-1) was born on 12 Oct 1794 in Provincetown, Mass. She was buried in Winthrop Street Cemetery, Provincetown, Mass.

Betsey Cook and Reverend Epaphras Kibby were married on 24 Apr 1815 in Provincetown, Mass. Epaphras Kibby was a beloved pastor, and his name was adopted into the Cook families until the last whaler (Epaphras Kibbe Cook) died in the early 20th century. .

**678.** Capt. James Tilton Cook (Samuel-5, Solomon-4, Josiah-3, Josiah-2, Josias-1) was born on 10 Apr 1796 in Provincetown, Mass. James died of a bowel hemorrhage on 8 Mar 1871 at the age of 74 in Provincetown, Mass. He was buried in Hamilton Cemetery, Provincetown, Mass.

Capt. James Tilton Cook and Phebe NICKERSON were married on 3 Feb 1818 in Provincetown, Mass. Phebe Nickerson, daughter of Seth Nickerson and Phebe Hopkins, was born on 18 Sep 1798 in Provincetown, Mass. She died on 24 Jul 1834 at the age of 35 in Provincetown, Mass. She was buried in Hamilton Cemetery, Provincetown, Mass.

James Tilton Cook and Phebe Nickerson had the following children:

i. Clarinda Cook was born on 17 Oct 1825 in Provincetown, Mass. She died in 1889 at the age of 64 in Provincetown, Mass.

1594 ii. James Tilton Cook, born 17 Oct 1820, Provincetown, Mass.; married Emily ATKINS, 13 Dec 1846, Provincetown, Mass.; died 7 Dec 1889, Provincetown, Mass.

Capt. James Tilton Cook and Louisa SPARKS were married in 1835 in Provincetown, Mass. They appeared in the census in 1840 in Provincetown, Mass. Louisa Sparks, daughter of James Sparks and Abigail Cook, was born on 7 Aug 1809 in Provincetown, Mass. She died of dysentery on 15 Sep 1846 at the age of 37 in Provincetown, Mass.

James Tilton Cook and Louisa Sparks had the following children:

1595 i. Harvey S. Cook, born 9 Dec 1835, Provincetown, Mass.; married Charlotte HOOTON, 20 Nov 1856; died 22 Feb 1905, Provincetown, Mass.

1596 ii. Phebe A. Cook, born 13 Apr 1836, Provincetown, Mass.; married James Collins Nickerson PAINE, 16 Nov 1857, Provincetown, Mass.; died 11 Feb 1923, Provincetown, Mass.

1597 iii. Heman S. Cook, born 26 May 1840, Provincetown, Mass.; married Hannah C. FREEMAN, 26 May 1840; died 4 Nov 1927, Provincetown, Mass.

iv. Horace Porter Stevens Cook was born on 21 Nov 1842 in Provincetown, Mass. He died of a rupture of the bowels on 2 Aug 1865 at the age of 22 in Provincetown, Mass. He was buried in Provincetown Cemetery Number Two.

v. A son was born on 7 Aug 1846 in Provincetown, Mass. He was stillborn.

Capt. James Tilton Cook and Bethia GROZIER were married on 16 Jun 1850 in Provincetown, Mass. Bethia Grozier, daughter of John Grozier and Bethia Unknown, was born in 1819 in Provincetown, Mass.

James Tilton Cook and Bethia Grozier had the following children:

i. Sylvestus "Sylvester" Cook was born on 2 May 1852 in Provincetown, Mass. He died aboard the Etta G. Fogg in 1867 at the age of 15. He was also known as Norman Cook. Sylvester was buried in Provincetown Cemetery Number Two.

ii. A son Cook was born on 1 Aug 1853 in Provincetown, Mass.

iii. Samuel Tilton Cook was born on 7 Nov 1854 in Provincetown, Mass. He died on 26 Oct 1855. He was buried in Provincetown Cemetery Number Two.

iv. A son Cook was born on 8 Apr 1855 in Provincetown, Mass.

v. S.F. Cook (Twin) was born on 8 Feb 1856 in Provincetown, Mass. She died on 6 Oct 1856 at the age of 0 in Provincetown, Mass.

vi. Bethia T. Cook (Twin) was born on 8 Apr 1856 in Provincetown, Mass. She died of dysentery on 8 Sep 1857 in Provincetown, Mass. She was buried in Provincetown

Cemetery Number Two.

vii. A son Cook was born on 17 Jul 1859 in Provincetown, Mass. He died of infantile death on 18 Jul 1859 in Provincetown, Mass.

679. Jane "Jenne" Cook (Samuel-5, Solomon-4, Josiah-3, Josiah-2, Josias-1) was born on 21 Jul 1799 in Provincetown, Mass. She died on 14 Feb 1872 at the age of 72 in Provincetown, Mass.

Jane "Jenne" Cook and Abraham SMALLEY Jr. were married on 7 Feb 1820 in Provincetown, Mass. Abraham Smalley Jr., son of Abraham Smalley and Polly , was born on 14 Sep 1794 in Provincetown, Mass.

Abraham Smalley and Jane Cook had the following children:

i.   Norman S.K. Smalley was born in 1820 in Provincetown, Mass. He died in 1844 at the age of 24 in Provincetown, Mass.
ii.  Jane C. Smalley was born in 1827 in Provincetown, Mass. She died in 1843 at the age of 16.
iii. Mary E. Smalley was born in 1829 in Provincetown, Mass. She died in 1832 at the age of 3 in Provincetown, Mass.
iv.  Abraham Smalley was born in 1832 in Provincetown, Mass. He died in 1832.
v.   Abraham Smalley was born in 1833 in Provincetown, Mass. He died in 1875 at the age of 42 in Provincetown, Mass.

684. Miles Cook (Thomas-5, Thomas-4, Richard-3, Josiah-2, Josias-1) was born before 16 Jun 1765 in Durham, Conn. He was baptized on 16 Jun 1765 in Durham, Conn. He died on 10 Jul 1846 at the age of 81 in Russell, St. Lawrence County, NY. Miles was buried in Foster-Kinne Cemetery, Antwerp, Jefferson, NY. He served in the military as a drummer in the American Revolution.

Miles Cook and Sarah GRIFFIN were married in 1790 in Durham, Conn. They appeared in the census in 1800 in Bristol, Schoharie, NY. Sarah Griffin was born in 1768 in Durham, Conn. She died on 14 Mar 1837 at the age of 69 in Wilma, Jefferson, NY. She was buried in Foster-Kinne Cemetery, Antwerp, Jefferson, NY.

Miles Cook and Sarah Griffin had the following children:

1607  i.   Benjamin Cook, born 1791; married Lucinda Foster, bef 1832; died 13 Jun 1880, Jefferson County, NY.
      ii.  Jesse Cook was born in 1793. He appeared in the census in 1820 in Antwerp, Jefferson, NY.

1608   iii. Samuel Cook, born 1795, NY; died 27 Jun 1874, Wilma, Jefferson, NY.

1609   iv. Miles Cook Jr., born 1797; married Hannah Unknown.

1610   v. Mary Griffin Cook, born 1800, New York; married John Raven, 1825, Antwerp, Jefferson, NY. (poss.); died bet 20 Jul 1845 and 18 Jun 1847, Lawrence, Van Buren, Mich.

1611   vi. Gideon Cook, born 1803, New York; married Ruth Nelson, bef 1836.

       vii. Ruth Cook was born in 1806 in New York.

1612   viii. Rhoda Cook, born 1810; married Horace Graves.

**685.** Elisha Cook (Thomas-5, Thomas-4, Richard-3, Josiah-2, Josias-1) was born on 17 May 1767 in New Durham, Schoharie, NY. He appeared in the census in 1800 in Bristol, Schoharie, NY. He died in 1841 at the age of 74 in Rodman, Jefferson, NY. Elisha was buried in Fairview Cemetery, Rodham, NY.

Elisha Cook and Wealthy Bishop were married on 7 Mar 1795 in Middletown, Conn. They appeared in the census in 1810 in Rodman, Jefferson, NY. They appeared in the census in 1820 in Rodman, Jefferson, NY. Wealthy Bishop was born on 16 Feb 1772 in Durham, Conn. She died on 21 Jun 1839 at the age of 67.

Elisha Cook and Wealthy Bishop had the following children:

1613   i. Thomas Bishop Cook, born 31 Jul 1796, Schoharie County, NY.; married Leah JOHNSON, 1835.

1614   ii. Seth Cook, born 22 Feb 1798, Schoharie County, NY.; married Lucy , 1 Jan 1824; married Nancy Ann MILAM, 1844; died 21 Jul 1873, Chilicothe, Ia.

       iii. Curtis Cook was born in 1799.

       iv. James Cook was born in 1801.

       v. Phoebe Cook was born in 1802.

       vi. Joseph Benjamin Cook was born in 1802 in Schoharie County, NY.

       vii. Anna Cook was born in 1805.

1615   viii. Wealthy Cook, born 5 Aug 1806, Schoharie County, NY.; married Enoch Major TERRILL, 1824.

       ix. Content Cook was born in 1808.

1616   x. Elisha Cook, born 18 Mar 1811, Schoharie County, NY.; married Charlotte M. UNKNOWN, 5 Sep 1833; died 15 Dec 1880, Ottumwa, Ia.

1617   xi. David Cook, born 3 Sep 1813, Schoharie County, NY.; died 16 Jan 1891, Ottumwa, Ia.

1618   xii. Hannah Ann Cook, born 28 Mar 1816; married David P. FERRIS.

       xiii. Rebecca Cook was born on 26 Apr 1819. She died on 5 May 1819.

**686.** Dinah Cook (Thomas-5, Thomas-4, Richard-3, Josiah-2, Josias-1) was born in 1769.

Dinah Cook and Unknown Norton were married.

687. Tryon Cook (Thomas-5, Thomas-4, Richard-3, Josiah-2, Josias-1) was born before 27 Oct
1771 in Durham, Conn. He was baptized on 27 Oct 1771 in Durham, Conn.

Tryon Cook and Mary GRIFFIN were married on 23 Jan 1795 in Middletown, Conn. They
appeared in the census in 1800 in Bristol, Schoharie, NY.

Tryon Cook and Mary Griffin had the following child:

    i.   A son Cook was born about 1794. He died before 1800 at the age of 6.

688. Delight Cook (Jesse-5, Thomas-4, Richard-3, Josiah-2, Josias-1) was born before 13 Mar 1774
in Durham, Conn. She was baptized on 13 Mar 1774 in Durham, Conn. She died on 5 Jan
1860 at the age of 85 in Afton, NY.

Delight Cook and Oliver EASTON were married on 31 Dec 1794. They appeared in the
census in 1830 in Bainbridge, NY. Oliver Easton, son of Elijah Easton, was born on 20 Nov
1765 in Suffield, Conn. He died on 11 Dec 1839 at the age of 74 in Bainbridge, NY

Oliver Easton and Delight Cook had the following children:

1619   i.   Chauncy G. Easton, born 17 Jan 1796, Wilmington, Vt.; died 24 Sep 1825.
      ii.  Ebenezer Noble Easton was born on 25 Sep 1797 in Wilmington, Vt.
1620   iii. Jesse Cook Easton, born 13 Jul 1799, Wilmington, Vt.; married Irene STONE, 12 Oct
           1825; married Elizabeth EASTON, May 1835; died 2 Dec 1881, Wellsville, NY.
1621   iv. Louisa Easton, born 4 Oct 1801, Wilmington, Vt.; married Stephen WILLIAMS, 25
           Oct 1827; died 13 Feb 1848, Coventry, NY.
1622   v.  Leicester Easton, born 24 Nov 1803, Wilmington, Vt.; married Asenath NICHOLS,
           11 May 1826, Bainbridge, NY; died 12 May 1876, Afton, NY.
1623   vi. Lucretia Easton, born 9 Dec 1805; married Heman SMITH, 7 Oct 1827; died 22 Sep
           1884, Afton, NY.
1624   vii. Rufus Easton, born 2 Feb 1808; married Prudence De Wolf, 31 Dec 1835; died 10
           Sep 1845, South Bainbridge, NY.
1625   viii.  Riley Easton, born 13 Sep 1809, Bainbridge, NY; married Betsey BATEMAN, 1
           Sep 1836; died 27 Mar 1887, Afton, NY.
1626   ix. Abbey Ann Easton, born 11 Oct 1811, Bainbridge, NY; married Samuel Carpenter
           BUMP, 9 Feb 1837; died 27 Mar 1854, Bainbridge, NY
1627   x.  Elijah Easton, born 18 May 1815, Afton, NY.; married Jerusha E. JONES, 22 Feb
           1839.
      xi. Cynthia Easton was born on 11 Jan 1818.

689. Bela Cook (Jesse-5, Thomas-4, Richard-3, Josiah-2, Josias-1) was born about 1779 in Durham, Conn. Bela appeared in the census in 1850 in Union, La. He died on 23 Nov 1854 at the age of 75 in Union Parish, Louisiana.

Bela Cook and Abigail F. PARKER appeared in the census in 1830 in State of Mississippi.

Bela Cook and Abigail F. Parker had the following children:

    1628   i.   Don Pedro Aquilla Cook, born 16 Sep 1803, Hancock County, Ga.; married Mary Jane TURNER, 18 Aug 1826, Mississippi, U.S.; married Susan Amanda BEATY, 19 Jul 1842, Union Parish, Louisiana; died 18 Jul 1873, Union Parish, Louisiana.

           ii.  Caroline Cook was born in 1823.

          iii.  William Cook was born in 1825.

          iv.  Ann Cook was born in 1832.

690. Talcott Fairchild Smithson Cook (Jesse-5, Thomas-4, Richard-3, Josiah-2, Josias-1) was born on 31 Dec 1784 in Wilmington, Vt. He died on 26 Oct 1876 at the age of 91.

Talcott Fairchild Smithson Cook and Rachel UNKNOWN appeared in the census in 1860 in Payson, Ill. Rachel Unknown was born in 1785. She died in 1861 at the age of 76.

Talcott Fairchild Smithson Cook and Rachel Unknown had the following child:

    1629   i.   Alonzo Talcott Cook, born 11 Dec 1821, Afton, Chenango, NY.; married Susan WELLS, 18 Feb 1847, Adams, Ill.; died 6 Sep 1893.

693. Deborah Cook (Samuel-5, Caleb-4, Richard-3, Josiah-2, Josias-1) was born on 13 Oct 1762 in Eastham, Mass.

Deborah Cook and Uriah NICKERSON were married on 14 Feb 1788 in Eastham, Mass. Uriah Nickerson, son of Hatsel Nickerson and Hannah Myrick, was born in 1763 in Eastham, Mass. He served in the military in the American Revolution under Capt. Joseph Brown on 18 Jul 1780. He died on 4 Apr 1849 at the age of 86 in Eastham, Mass.

Uriah Nickerson and Deborah Cook had the following children:

    1282   i.   Dorcas Cook Nickerson, born 3 Nov 1789; married Nathan H. BURGESS, 24 Sep 1814, Brewster, Barnstable, Mass.; died 7 Feb 1877.

          ii.  Deborah Atwood Nickerson was born on 16 Dec 1791. She died on 4 May 1816 at the age of 24.

    1283  iii.  Capt. Uriah Nickerson, born 13 Jan 1794; married Rebecca COVEL, 5 Feb 1824,

Dennis, Mass.; died 15 Aug 1824, Eastham, Mass.

1284    iv.  Samuel Nickerson (Twin), born 6 Jun 1796; married Rowena MAYO, Dec 1818, Eastham, Mass.; died 26 May 1875, Eastham, Mass.

1285    v.  Hatsel Nickerson (Twin), born 7 Jun 1796, Eastham, Mass.; married Sally PAINE, Dec 1819, Eastham, Mass.; married Sylvia Tripp HALL, 10 Nov 1859, Eastham, Mass.; died Oct 1881/2, Eastham, Mass.

        vi.  Nehemiah Nickerson was born on 22 Aug 1798 in Eastham, Mass. He died on 10 Mar 1822 at the age of 23 in Eastham, Mass.

1286    vii. Capt. Joshua Walker Nickerson, born 12 Aug 1805, Eastham, Mass.; married Mercy WALKER, 1830, Eastham, Mass.; died 24 Mar 1868, Eastham, Mass.


694. John Cook (Samuel-5, Caleb-4, Richard-3, Josiah-2, Josias-1) was born on 4 Jan 1768 in Eastham, Mass.

John Cook and Rachel UNKNOWN were married.

John Cook and Rachel Unknown had the following children:

    i.   Phebe Cook was born on 17 Sep 1788 in Eastham, Mass.
    ii.  John Cook was born on 14 Aug 1792 in Eastham, Mass.


695. Hannah Smith (Nehemiah-5, Abigail Cooke-4, Richard-3, Josiah-2, Josias-1) was born on 18 Oct 1779. She died on 2 Feb 1869 at the age of 89 in Provincetown, Mass. She was buried in Hamilton Cemetery, Provincetown, Mass.

Hannah Smith and Capt. Philip Cook (#668) were married on 1 Feb 1806 in Provincetown, Mass. For children see Philip Cook's entry (#668)

880. Elizabeth Cook (Josiah-5, Josiah-4, Joshua-3, Josiah-2, Josias-1) was born on 27 Jan 1768 in Chatham, Conn. She was baptized on 3 Aug 1773.

Elizabeth Cook and Jesse GRAHAM were married on 16 Aug 1792 in Haddam Neck Congregational Church, East Haddam, Conn.

881. John Cook (Elijah-5, Josiah-4, Joshua-3, Josiah-2, Josias-1) was born in 1774.

John Cook and Caty SHAFT were married on 1 Jun 1796. Caty Shaft was the daughter of John Shaft.

883. Lydia Cook (Moses-5, Josiah-4, Joshua-3, Josiah-2, Josias-1) was born before 14 May 1769. She was baptized on 14 May 1769 in East Hampton Congregational Church, Middlesex,

Conn.

Lydia Cook and Comfort BEEBE were married on 4 Jan 1787.

884. Moses Cook (Moses-5, Josiah-4, Joshua-3, Josiah-2, Josias-1) was born on 7 Jan 1772 in East
Hampton, Conn. He was baptized on 3 Apr 1772 in East Hampton Congregational Church,
Middlesex, Conn.

Moses Cook and Dorothy PERCIVAL were married in Jan 1797 in Berlin, Hartford, Conn.
They appeared in the census in 1800 in Waterbury First Society, Conn. They appeared in the
census in 1820 in Waterbury, Conn. Moses and Dorothy appeared in the census in 1830 in
Madison, Miss. They appeared in the census in 1840 in Hancock, Miss. They appeared in the
census in 1850 in Hancock, Miss. Dorothy Percival was born on 24 Mar 1779 in Farmington,
CT.

Moses Cook and Dorothy Percival had the following child:

   i.   A child Cook was born in 1799 in East Hampton, Conn. He/she died on 23 Feb 1802 at
        the age of 3 in East Hampton, Conn.

885. Elizabeth Cook (Moses-5, Josiah-4, Joshua-3, Josiah-2, Josias-1) was born in 1774. She died
     on 14 Aug 1851 at the age of 77.

Elizabeth Cook and Adonijah STRONG were married on 11 Sep 1794 in East Hampton
Congregational Church, Middlesex, Conn. Adonijah Strong, son of Adonijah Strong and Mary
Polly Kellogg, was born in May 1773 in Connecticut. He died when he drowned on 17 Apr
1809 at the age of 35 in East Hampton, Conn.

Adonijah Strong and Elizabeth Cook had the following children:

   i.    Elizabeth Strong, born 1795; married Bliss WELCH, 25 Jul 1811, East Hampton
         Congregational Church, Middlesex, Conn. They had 12 children.
   ii.   Charlotte Strong, born 18 Jan 1797; married Nathaniel Clark SMITH, 23 May 1816, East
         Hampton Congregational Church, Middlesex, Conn. They had 11 children.
   iii.  Lydia Strong, born 15 Dec 1798; married Henry BUSH, 4 Feb 1816, East Hampton
         Congregational Church, Middlesex, Conn.; died 16 Oct 1844. They had 10 children.
   iv.   Lucy Strong, born bet 1799 and 1801; married Henry STRONG Jr., 28 Feb 1822,
         Chatham, Conn.
   v.    Hannah Strong, born 8 Oct 1802; married Gilbert HILLS, 29 Jan 1823, Chatham, Conn.
         He had 11 children.
   vi.   Charles Adonijah Strong, born 6 Jul 1804; married Lucy HURLBURT, 21 Nov 1827,

Chatham, Conn.; married Sally HURLBURT, 1 May 1836, Chatham, Conn. He had 3 children.

vii. Julia Ann Strong, born 1806; married Harvey (Henry) HARDING, 7 May 1823, East Hampton Congregational Church, Middlesex, Conn. They had 8 children.

viii. Polly Strong, born 3 Nov 1808, East Hampton, Conn.; married George Kilbourne WHITE, 4 Jul 1827, Chatham, Conn.; died 18 Aug 1848, Annsville, Oneida, NY. They had 7 children.

886. Susannah Cook (Moses-5, Josiah-4, Joshua-3, Josiah-2, Josias-1) was born about 5 Sep 1779. She was baptized on 6 Sep 1779 in East Hampton Congregational Church, Middlesex, Conn. She died on 15 Apr 1820 at the age of 40.

Susannah Cook and Daniel Butler NEWTON were married on 25 Apr 1798 in East Hampton Congregational Church, Middlesex, Conn.

Susannah Cook and Henry STRONG were married on 17 Sep 1801. Henry Strong, son of , was born (date unknown).

Henry Strong and Susannah Cook had the following children:

i. Henry Strong Jr., born 27 Aug 1802; married Lucy STRONG, 28 Feb 1822, Chatham, Conn.

ii. Susan Strong, married Julius GATES, 28 Nov 1822, East Hampton Congregational Church, Middlesex, Conn.

iii. Elizabeth Mary Strong, married Nehemiah GATES, 22 Dec 1825, East Hampton Congregational Church, Middlesex, Conn.

iv. Butler Newton Strong, born 1808; married Julia A. UNKNOWN. They had at least 4 children.

v. Deidana Strong.

vi. Adeline Strong.

vii. Daniel Strong.

viii. Philanda Strong.

ix. Samuel Leverett Strong.

887. Livia Cook (Moses-5, Josiah-4, Joshua-3, Josiah-2, Josias-1) was born before 18 Jul 1784. She was baptized on 18 Jul 1784.

Livia Cook and Wix WATROUS were married on 3 Nov 1803 in East Hampton Congregational Church, Middlesex, Conn. Wix Watrous was born in Colchester, New London, Conn.

888. Selden Cook (Moses-5, Josiah-4, Joshua-3, Josiah-2, Josias-1) was born before 25 Jun 1786.
He was baptized on 25 Jun 1786.

Selden Cook and Sally BRAINERD appeared in the census in 1850 in Portland, Conn. They
were married. Sally Brainerd was born on 30 Jan 1776.

889. Owen Cook (Moses-5, Josiah-4, Joshua-3, Josiah-2, Josias-1) was born about Nov 1788 in
East Hampton, Conn. He was baptized on 16 Nov 1788 in East Hampton Congregational
Church, Middlesex, Conn.

Owen Cook and Mary PARMELEE were married on 22 Jun 1813.

895. Lucy Cook (Richard-5, Josiah-4, Joshua-3, Josiah-2, Josias-1) was born on 7 Aug 1784 in
Chatham, Conn. She died on 11 Sep 1850 at the age of 66 in Winchester, Conn.

Lucy Cook and James Hall ALVORD were married on 11 Oct 1804 in East Hampton
Congregational Church, Middlesex, Conn. They moved in Winsted, Conn. in 1809 James Hall
Alvord, son of Ruel Alvord and Hannah Hall, was born on 8 Aug 1781 in East Hampton,
Conn. He died on 29 Jul 1868 at the age of 86 in Winsted, Conn. James was a saddler.

James Hall Alvord and Lucy Cook had the following children:

     i.  Clarissa Penfield Alvord was born on 7 Aug 1805 in East Hampton, Conn. She died on 4
Dec 1877 at the age of 72 in Winsted, Conn.

2035  ii.  Rev. John Watson Alvord, born 18 Apr 1807, East Hampton, Conn.; married Mytilla
Mead PECK, 3 Jun 1845, Stamford, Conn.; died 14 Jan 1880, Denver, Col. They
had 8 children.

     iii.  Mary Cook Alvord was born on 26 Feb 1809 in Winchester, Conn. She died on 12 Feb
1830 at the age of 20.

2036  iv.  Susan Brown Alvord, born 12 Feb 1811, Winchester, Conn.; married Asahel Munson
RICE, 30 May 1838, Winsted, Conn. They had 1 child.

     v.  Richard Alvord was born on 8 Mar 1813 in Winchester, Conn. He died on 1 Dec 1818 at
the age of 5 in Winchester, Conn.

     vi.  Catharine Alvord was born on 12 Feb 1815 in Winchester, Conn. She died on 12 Oct
1895 at the age of 80 in Winchster, Conn.

     vii. James Alvord (Twin) was born on 16 Aug 1819 in Winchester, Conn. He died on 17 Mar
1820 in Winchester, Conn.

2037  viii.  Charles Alvord (Twin), born 16 Aug 1819, Winchester, Conn.; married Melissa
WATSON, 5 Jun 1844, Hartford, Hartford, Conn.; died 17 Mar 1889,
Winsted, Conn. They had 4 children.

2038  ix.  Amanda Malvina Alvord, born 30 Aug 1821, Winchester, Conn.; married John

6.111

HINSDALE, 31 Aug 1841, Winsted, Conn.; died 19 Mar 1897, Winsted, Conn. They had 2 children.

2039   x.  James Richard Alvord, born 7 Oct 1823, Winchester, Conn.; married Mary Eliza LANDON, 3 Dec 1849, Winsted, Conn.; died 17 Feb 1890, Winsted, Conn. They had 6 children.

2040   xi.  George Alvord, born 23 Oct 1825, Winchester, Conn.; married Elizabeth Peck HUBBARD, 1 Jun 1863, Sunderland, Mass.; died 10 Dec 1882, Hartford, Hartford, Conn.

xii. Jabez Alvord was born on 3 Feb 1828 in Winchester, Conn. He was a machinist.

**896. Alvan Cook** (Richard-5, Josiah-4, Joshua-3, Josiah-2, Josias-1) was born in 1786 in Connecticut. He died in 1856 at the age of 70.

Alvan Cook and Lucretia SMITH were married on 12 Aug 1811 in East Hampton Congregational Church, Middlesex, Conn. They appeared in the census in 1850 in Plainfield, Otsego, NY. Lucretia Smith was born in 1786 in Connecticut.

**897. Floras Cook** (Richard-5, Josiah-4, Joshua-3, Josiah-2, Josias-1) was born on 26 Apr 1793. He died on 12 Apr 1819 at the age of 25.

Floras Cook and Mary Couch were married.

**898. Nathaniel Cook** (Richard-5, Josiah-4, Joshua-3, Josiah-2, Josias-1) appeared in the census in 1850 in Plainfield, Otsego, NY.

Nathaniel Cook and Betsy FULLER were married.

**900. Isaiah Cook** (Joshua-5, Joshua-4, Joshua-3, Josiah-2, Josias-1) was born on 18 Jul 1768 in Chatham, Conn. He was baptized on 28 Aug 1768 in East Hampton Congregational Church, Middlesex, Conn.

Isaiah Cook and Clarissa GROSVENER were married on 6 Jun 1796 in Lawyersville, NY. Clarissa Grosvener, daughter of Moses Grosvener and Dorcas Sharp, was born on 4 Dec 1767 in Pomfret, Windham, Mass. She died in Ondoga County, NY.

Isaiah Cook and Clarissa Grosvener had the following children:

2041   i.  Jacob Cook, born abt 1800, Ondoga County, NY.; married Candice UNKNOWN.

ii. James Cook was born in Ondoga County, NY.

iii. Charles Cook was born in Ondoga County, NY.

iv. Walter Cook was born in Ondoga County, NY.

901. Levina Cook (Joshua-5, Joshua-4, Joshua-3, Josiah-2, Josias-1) was born on 10 Oct 1770 in
Haddam, Conn. She was baptized on 15 Oct 1770 in East Hampton Congregational Church,
Middlesex, Conn. She died in 1836 at the age of 66.

Levina Cook and Henry HAUGHTON were married about 1793. Henry Haughton, son of
Samuel and Lois Haughton , was born in Dec 1766 in Haddam, Conn. He died in 1845 at the
age of 79. Henry served in the military in the War of 1812. He was also known as Henry
Horton.

Henry Haughton and Levina Cook had the following children:

   i.   Lois Haughton, born 1794; married Gilbert OSBORN in Connecticut; died 1871. They
        had 2 children.
   ii.  Samuel Haughton, born 31 Oct 1794, Marcellus, NY.; married Amanda OSBORN, 1 Jan
        1821, Trumbull Co., Ohio; died 9 Dec 1857. They had 6 children.
   iii. Aretus Haughton was born in 1796 in Marcellus, NY. He died on 11 Dec 1845 at the age
        of 49 in Southington, Trumbull, Oh.
   iv.  Chauncey B. Haughton, born 1800, New York; married Abigail GILBERT, 6 Apr 1836,
        Geauga County, Oh. They had 1 child.
   v.   Louisa Haughton, born 6 Apr 1805, Marcellus, NY.; married Sterling OSBORN, 25 Jan
        1827, Trumbull Co., Ohio; died 12 Jun 1876, Southington, Trumbull, Oh. They had 1
        child.
   vi.  Mary Ann Haughton, born 21 May 1808, Marcellus, NY.; married Nelson CURTIS, 17
        Feb 1831, Trumbull County, O.; died 1 Nov 1896, Spring Brook, Dunn, Wi. They had
        10 children.
   vii. Alonzo Haughton, born 25 Sep 1812, New York; married Abigail ENSIGN, 19 Oct
        1838, Hartford, Hartford, Conn.; died 18 Feb 1898, New Lothrop, Michigan. They
        had 6 children.

902. Jedida Cook (Joshua-5, Joshua-4, Joshua-3, Josiah-2, Josias-1) was born on 3 Apr 1773 in
Chatham, Mass. She died on 14 May 1843 at the age of 70 in New York. She was buried in
Ogden, NY.

Jedida Cook and Earl WRIGHT were married in 1791. Earl Wright was born in 1766. He died
on 4 Jan 1849 at the age of 83 in NY. He was buried in Ogden, NY.

Earl Wright and Jedida Cook had the following child:

   2048   i.   Locena Wright, born 9 Sep 1806, Maryland, Otsego, NY.; married Gideon
              COMSTOCK, bef 1850; died 20 Mar 1902, Akron, Erie, NY.

906. Col William Walker Cook (Ebenezer-5, Ebenezer-4, Joshua-3, Josiah-2, Josias-1) was born on
31 Aug 1773 in Stockbridge, Mass. He appeared in the census on 2 Aug 1790 in Stockbridge,
Mass. He served in the military in the war of 1812. William signed a will on 22 Feb 1830 in
Lisle, Broome, NY. He died on 23 Feb 1830 at the age of 56 in Killawog, NY and is buried in
Killawog Cemetery. Cook Hill and Cook Hill Road in Killawog are named after him.

Col William Walker Cook and Roxanna "Roxy" WHITTELSEY were married on 26 Feb
1795 in Stockbridge, Mass. They moved in Broome County, NY. in 1798 They appeared in
the census in 1800 in Tioga County, NY. They appeared in the census in 1810 in Owasco,
Cayuga, NY. Roxanna "Roxy" WHITTELSEY, daughter of Ezra WHITTELSEY and Ann
Pixley, was born in 1775 in Stockbridge, Mass. She died on 15 Sep 1855 at the age of 80 in
Killawog, NY.

William Walker Cook and Roxanna WHITTELSEY had the following children:

     i.   Ira Cook was born on 22 Mar 1799. He died on 20 Dec 1820 at the age of 21. He was
buried on 22 Dec 1820 at Killawog Cemetery in Killawog, New York.

2052   ii.   William W. Cook, born 22 Oct 1803, Broome County, NY.; married Frances Maria
WHITNEY (Twin), 2 Mar 1825, Whitney Point, NY.; died 7 Mar 1889, Whitney
Point, NY.

2053   iii.   Charles Abby Cook, born 11 Dec 1805, Killawog, NY; married Phebe Odell FORD,
3 Feb 1831, Lisle, NY; married Hannah OSBORNE, 3 Feb 1871; died 23 Jan
1881, Whitney Point, NY.

2054   iv.   Mary West Cook, born 17 Jul 1808; married George O. WILLS, 31 Aug 1829.

     v.   Mason Wattles Cook was born on 21 Jul 1811.

    vi.   Lyman Root Cook was born on 6 Jun 1814. He died when he was probably murdered, on

Ira Cook,
Killawog Cemetery

William Walker Cook,
Killawog Cemetery

21 Dec 1847 at the age of 33 in LaGrange, Tex. (SEE letter dated: Feb. 19 1848 to
William Cook from J.H. Arnold, Esq.)

907. Ebenezer Cook Jr. (Ebenezer-5, Ebenezer-4, Joshua-3, Josiah-2, Josias-1) was born about
1771. He appeared in the census on 2 Aug 1790 in Stockbridge, Mass. He signed a will on 29
Jan 1812 in Berkshire, Tioga, NY. Ebenezer died on 17 Mar 1812 at the age of 41 in Lisle,
Broome, New York.

Ebenezer Cook Jr. and Elizabeth CHURCHILL were married on 3 Apr 1793 in Stockbridge,
Mass. They appeared in the census in 1800 in Berkshire, Tioga, NY. They appeared in the
census in 1810 in Berkshire, Tioga, NY. Elizabeth Churchill, daughter of Samuel Churchill and
Elizabeth Curtis, was born on 18 Sep 1774. She died on 23 Jun 1845 at the age of 70.

Ebenezer Cook and Elizabeth Churchill had the following children:

2055　i.　Harriet Cook, born 22 Oct 1793; married William BALL, 1818; died 1870.
2056　ii.　Aurilla Cook, born Oct 1795; married Dennis CORSAW, 1813; died 1817.
　　　iii.　Clarissa Cook was born in Jun 1798 in Lisle, Broome, New York. Clarissa died in 1814 at
　　　　　the age of 16.
2057　iv.　Charles West Cook, born 1 Feb 1800; married Amy ROYCE, 1823; married Amanda
　　　　　NEWTON, 1836; died 19 May 1845.
　　　v.　Mary West Cook was born before 1800.
　　　vi.　Abigail West Cook was born in 1802. She died in 1804 at the age of 2.
2058　vii.　Abigail West Cook, born 26 Apr 1804; married James Hobart FORD, 29 Apr 1835;
　　　　　died 24 Nov 1874.
　　　viii.　Henry William Cook was born in 1806. He died on 3 Aug 1825 at the age of 19.
　　　ix.　George West Cook was born on 9 Dec 1808. He died by dorwning on 15 Jun 1810 at the
　　　　　age of 1.
2059　x.　George Churchill Cook, born 10 Mar 1811; married Lucy Maria MCWILLIAMS, 10
　　　　　Nov 1834.

908. Lydia Cook (Ebenezer-5, Ebenezer-4, Joshua-3, Josiah-2, Josias-1) was born in 1775.

Lydia Cook and Stephen BRADLEY were married on 7 Jan 1795 in Stockbridge, Mass. They
appeared in the census in 1850 in Lee, Mass. Stephen Bradley, son of Elisha Bradley and
Mary Ives, was born on 19 Jul 1774 in Stockbridge, Mass. He died on 1 Apr 1857 at the age
of 82 in Lee, Mass.

Stephen Bradley and Lydia Cook had the following children:

2060　i.　Ebenezer Cook Bradley, born 18 Jun 1796, Stockbridge, Mass.; married Abigail
　　　　　STURGIS, 25 Feb 1819, Stockbridge, Mass.
　　　ii.　Elisha Bradley was born in May 1798. He died on 11 Mar 1854 at the age of 55.
2061　iii.　Stephen Bradley Jr., born 11 Aug 1808; married Hannah AUSTIN, 20 Sep 1824,

Lee, Mass.

2062   iv.  William Bradley, born 27 Dec 1803; married Betsey A. UNKNOWN.
2063   v.   Mary West Bradley, born 29 Dec 1805; married Joseph Warren BARLOW, 20 Sep
                1824, Lee Township, Berkshire, Mass.; died 12 Sep 1864.
2064   vi.  Lydia Bradley, born 26 Sep 1809; married William PECK, 10 Apr 1828, Lee, Mass.
2065   vii. Charles Bradley, born 12 Oct 1812; married Emily CROSBY, 15 Mar 1834, Lee,
                Mass.
        viii.    George Bradley was born on 20 Feb 1850.


909. Ira Cook (Ebenezer-5, Ebenezer-4, Joshua-3, Josiah-2, Josias-1) was born on 4 Apr 1780 in
        Berkshire County, Mass. He appeared in the census on 2 Aug 1790 in Stockbridge, Mass. He
        moved in New Hartford, Oneida, NY in 1807. Ira moved in Stephenson, Ill. on 8 Nov 1835.
        Stephenson was the town which is now called Rock Island, Illinois. He moved to Davenport,
        Ia. in 1836. Between 1837 and 1845 he was a farmer in Davenport, Ia. Ira died of cancer on
        16 Apr 1845 at the age of 65 in Davenport, Ia.


### The Cooks in Iowa

Although much more could be said, with his children and their families, Ira Cook was one
of the first settlers of Davenport, Ia. and was its mayor, very briefly, in 1861. He is featured in
the State Historical Museum of Des Moines. Appendix A is an account, written by his son Ira,
of the family's move from NY to the new territory of Iowa. His son also wrote [Appendix B]
about being a government surveyor of the new Iowa territory.) Ira's other sons (John and
Edward) became prominent leaders in Davenport. John Parsons Cook became was a
representative in the House of Representatives, though he later lost re-election due to his pro-
slavery stance. George Cram Cook, who has an important place in the history of the American
theatre, was another of Ira's descendants. He was a Greenwich Village bohemian, writer,
producer, several times divorced, socialist, who had a knack for nuturing great talent, including
that of his wife and, most famously, Eugene O'Neill.  George was also interested in family
history, and in his papers at the New York Public Library's Berg Collection are notes and
letters which tell stories of "Old Ebenezer" and "Old Stockbridge."

Ira Cook and Patience T. "Priscilla" EELS were married on 14 Sep 1803. Patience T.
"Priscilla" Eels was born on 14 Feb 1782 in Marlborough, Conn. She died on 26 Feb 1807 at
the age of 25 in Stockbridge, Mass.

Ira Cook and Patience T. Eels had the following children:

   i.   William Lord Cook was born before 19 Aug 1804 in Stockbridge, Mass. He was baptized
            on 19 Aug 1804 in Stockbridge, Mass.
   ii.  Frederic Cook was born on 12 Dec 1805. He was baptized on 13 Jul 1806 in

Stockbridge, Mass.

Ira Cook and Rachel Davis FAXON were married on 16 Mar 1809 in Whitestown, NY. They appeared in the census in 1830 in Lisle, Broome, NY. Rachel Davis Faxon, daughter of Thomas Faxon and Rachel Davis, was born on 25 Jun 1783 in Conway, Mass. She moved to Davenport, Ia. in 1836. She died on 18 Oct 1837 at the age of 54 in Davenport, Ia.

Ira Cook and Rachel Davis Faxon had the following children:

2066   i.   Ebenezer Cook, born 14 Feb 1810, Whitestown, NY.; married Clarissa Bryan UNKNOWN, 6 Feb 1833; died 7 Oct 1871, Davenport, Ia.

2067   ii.   Patience Ells Cook, born 18 Oct 1811, Whitestown, NY.; married William Van TUYL, 7 Oct 1835.

       iii.   Abby Maria Cook was born on 10 Sep 1813 in Whitestown, NY. She died on 13 Dec 1848 at the age of 35.

2068   iv.   Mary Curtis Cook, born 17 Nov 1815, Whitestown, NY.; married John Wright BROWN, 11 Sep 1833.

2069   v.   John Parsons Cook, born 31 Aug 1817, Whitestown, NY.; married Eliza Ann ROWE, 26 Oct 1842; died 16 Apr 1872, Davenport, Ia.

2070   vi.   Ira S. Cook, born 26 Oct 1821, Whitestown, NY.; married Mary Crane OWENS, 26 Apr 1854, Center Lisle, Broome, NY.

910. Mary West Cook (Ebenezer-5, Ebenezer-4, Joshua-3, Josiah-2, Josias-1) was born before Aug 1784. She was baptized on 15 Aug 1784 in Stockbridge, Mass.

Mary West Cook and William CURTIS were married on 14 Apr 1804 in Stockbridge, Mass.

William Curtis and Mary West Cook had the following children:

     i.   Abigail Ann Curtis was born in 1808.
     ii.   William Curtis.
     iii.   Harriet Curtis.
     iv.   James Curtis.

911. Anna Cook (Gideon-5, Ebenezer-4, Joshua-3, Josiah-2, Josias-1) was born on 14 Mar 1777 in East Haddam, Conn. She died on 30 May 1848 at the age of 71 in East Haddam, Conn.

Anna Cook and Henry SNOW were married on 9 Oct 1800 in East Haddam, Conn.

912. John Cook (Gideon-5, Ebenezer-4, Joshua-3, Josiah-2, Josias-1) was born on 11 Dec 1778 in East Haddam, Conn. He died on 2 Sep 1824 at the age of 45 in East Haddam, Conn.

6.117

John Cook and Phebe REDINGTON were married on 1 Dec 1809 in Richmond, Mass.
Phebe Redington was born between 1782 and 1792. She died on 15 Aug 1832 at the age of
50.

John Cook and Phebe Redington had the following children:

    i.   George Cook was born in 1810 in East Haddam, Conn. He died by drowning on 11 Jun 1826 at the age of 16.

    ii.  Mary Cook was born before 3 Jul 1812. She was baptized on 3 Jul 1812 in East Haddam First Congregational Church, Middlesex, Conn.

    iii. John Cook was born before Jul 1815. He was baptized in Jul 1815 in East Haddam First Congregational Church, Middlesex, Conn.

2071   iv. Olive Martha Cook, born bef Jul 1816; married Charles CRUTTENDEN, 8 Apr 1840.

    v.   Phebe Ann Cook was born before Dec 1817. She was baptized on 28 Jun 1818. She died on 14 Dec 1821 at the age of 4.

    vi.  Azel Cook was born between 1818 and 1823. He was baptized on 25 Sep 1825 in East Haddam First Congregational Church, Middlesex, Conn.

    vii. David Cook was born between 1819 and 1824. He was baptized on 25 Sep 1825 in East Haddam First Congregational Church, Middlesex, Conn.

913. William Cook (Gideon-5, Ebenezer-4, Joshua-3, Josiah-2, Josias-1) was born on 10 Jul 1785 in East Haddam, Conn.

William Cook and Jerusha SPENCER were married on 1 Oct 1807 in East Haddam, Conn. Jerusha Spencer, daughter of David Spencer and Huldah Brainerd, was born on 13 Feb 1789 in Millington Parish, East Haddam, Conn.

William Cook and Jerusha Spencer had the following children:

2072  i.   David Brainerd Cook, born 23 Jul 1808, East Haddam, Conn.; married Esther Ann AUGER.

    ii.  William Henry Cook was born on 5 Dec 1809 in East Haddam, Conn.

    iii. Jerusha Ann Cook was born on 23 Jun 1811 in East Haddam, Conn.

    iv. Ora Agnesia Cook was born on 21 Apr 1814 in East Haddam, Conn.

914. Andrew Cook (Gideon-5, Ebenezer-4, Joshua-3, Josiah-2, Josias-1) was born on 19 May 1787. He died on 24 Jun 1858 at the age of 71 in Stayner, Ontario, Canada.

Andrew Cook and Elizabeth MCWHORTEN were married.

915. Azel Cook (Gideon-5, Ebenezer-4, Joshua-3, Josiah-2, Josias-1) was born on 17 Oct 1791. He died on 20 Oct 1871 at the age of 80 in Wolfe Island, Ontario, Canada. He was buried in Wolfe Island, Ontario, Canada.

Elizabeth LOBDELL was born on 23 Jul 1796 in Kingston, Ont., Canada. She died on 28 Feb 1888 at the age of 91 in Wolfe Island, Ontario, Canada.

Azel Cook and Elizabeth Lobdell had the following child:

    2073   i.   Lucinda Cook, born 19 Sep 1829, Kingston, Ont., Canada; died 31 Dec 1912, Wolfe Island, Ontario, Canada.

916. Fanny Cook (Gideon-5, Ebenezer-4, Joshua-3, Josiah-2, Josias-1) was born on 22 Dec 1793. She died on 11 Aug 1816 at the age of 22. She was buried on 12 Aug 1816 in Vernon, Tolland, Conn.

Fanny Cook and Matthew Smith FULLER were married. Matthew Smith Fuller was born (date unknown).

917. Ebenezer Cook (Gideon-5, Ebenezer-4, Joshua-3, Josiah-2, Josias-1) was born on 23 Feb 1796. He died before 1880 at the age of 84. He was buried at Higganum Cemetery.

Ebenezer Cook and Louisa P. EMMONS were married on 13 Dec 1832 in East Haddam, Conn. Louisa P. Emmons, daughter of Gilbert Emmons and Dolly Chapman, was born on 20 Jul 1800. She died on 4 Jun 1888 at the age of 87. She was buried at Higganum Cemetery.

Ebenezer Cook and Louisa P. Emmons had the following children:

    2074   i.   James Cook, born 24 Apr 1834; married Emma L. FAY, 10 Jun 1903; died 10 Jun 1903, Meriden, New Haven, Conn.
    2075   ii.   Henry Cook, born 4 Dec 1835; married Alice GLADWIN, 25 Mar 1870, Episcopal Church, Middletown, Mass; died 17 Feb 1909.
    2076   iii.   Susan Louisa Cook, born 1838; married Joseph HUBBARD; died 4 Oct 1916.

918. Moses Bassett Cook (Moses-5, Ephraim-4, Joshua-3, Josiah-2, Josias-1) was born on 6 Apr 1762 in New Marlborough, Mass. He served in the military for three years in the American Revolution about 1779 in Fishkill, NY. He died on 9 Aug 1839 at the age of 77. Moses was buried in Adrian, Mich.

Moses Bassett Cook and Phebe PERKINS were married on 14 Dec 1788 in Nine Partners, Dutchess County, NY. They moved to Lenawee County, Mich. in 1831. Phebe Perkins, daughter of Thomas Perkins and Elizabeth Loomis, was born on 12 Mar 1748/9 in Lebanon, CT. She died on 11 Aug 1837 at the age of 88 in Lenawee County, Mich.

Moses Bassett Cook and Phebe Perkins had the following children:

2077   i.   Elizabeth Cook, born 25 Nov 1794, Connecticut; married John Hawthorne CARPENTER, 2 Nov 1815, Elmira, NY.; died 18 Jun 1866, Lenawee County, Mich.
2078   ii.  Lydia Cook, born abt 1798; married William C. LOWE.

919. James Cook (Moses-5, Ephraim-4, Joshua-3, Josiah-2, Josias-1) was born in 1763 in New Marlborough, Mass. He served in the military in the American Revolution for three months in 1780. He served in the military for an additional 3 months in the American Revolution in 1781. James was one of the first four settlers in Cuyuga County, NY. in 1790. In 1810 he was a the first Innkeeper in Locke, Cayuga, NY. He served in the military in the War of 1812. James moved to Mecca, Trumbull, Oh. in 1832. He appeared in the census in 1840 in Trumbull County, O. He signed a will in Aug 1847 in Trumbull County, O. He died on 19 Apr 1851 at the age of 88 in Mecca, Oh. He was buried in Apr 1851 in East Mecca Cemetery, Mecca, Oh.

James Cook and Eunice LOOMIS were married on 14 Dec 1788 in Nine Partners, Dutchess County, NY. Eunice Loomis, daughter of Zachariah Loomis and Huldah Jones, was born on 13 Feb 1761 in Coventry, Conn. She died in 1820 at the age of 59 in Locke, Cayuga, NY.

James Cook and Eunice Loomis had the following children:

2079   i.   Zachariah Cook, born 10 Sep 1786; married Polly LOOMIS; died 23 Feb 1827, Locke, Cayuga, NY.
2080   ii.  Deacon John Cook, born 10 Sep 1786, Freehold, Cayuga, NY.; married Ruth CURTIS, bef 1820; married Elizabeth GRAY, 1 Apr 1851, Concord, Erie, NY.; died 5 Aug 1857, Mecca, Oh.
2081   iii. Nathan Cook, born abt 1800, Locke, Cayuga, NY.; married Permilia Hadlock, 1819; died 24 Nov 1887, Mecca, Oh.
2082   iv.  Samuel Cook, born bef 1791; married Philinda ; died 4 Mar 1825, Groton, NY.
       v.   Lois Cook was born between 1784 and 1790 in New Paltz, Ulster, NY.
       vi.  Amos Cook was born between 1780 and 1794 in New York.

James Cook and Diana Brown were married after 1820. Diana Brown was born before 23 Nov 1785 in New York. She died on 23 Nov 1850 at the age of 65 in Mecca, Oh.

James Cook and Diana Brown had the following children:

i.    Eunice Cook was born in 1822 in Locke, Cayuga, NY. She lived with her parents James and Diana in 1850.

2083   ii.   Lovina Cook, born abt 1827, Locke, Cayuga, NY.; married Silas N. Jones.

iii.  A child "(Unconfirmed)" Cook was born (date unknown).

920. John B. Cook (Moses-5, Ephraim-4, Joshua-3, Josiah-2, Josias-1) was born about 1775. He was the male over 45 in 1820 in Elmira, NY.

John B. Cook and Catherine Unknown were married. Catherine Unknown was born on 2 Aug 1769. She died on 12 Feb 1842 at the age of 72 in Elmira, NY.

921. Ivory Cook (Reuben-5, Ephraim-4, Joshua-3, Josiah-2, Josias-1) was born between 1765 and 1770 in Coventry, Conn. He appeared in the census in 1810 in Orwell, Vt. He died in State of Vermont.

Ivory Cook and Charlotte Bush were married about 1791. Charlotte Bush was born about 1772. She died on 7 Dec 1849 at the age of 77 in Shoreham, Vt. She was buried in Jenison cemetery, Shoreham, VT.

Ivory Cook and Charlotte Bush had the following children:

2084   i.    Reuben C. Cook, born Aug 1792, Orwell, Vt.; married Roxalana Wilson, 9 Oct 1817; died 3 Feb 1885, Shoreham, Vt.

2085   ii.   Ivory Cook Jr., born 11 Oct 1793, Orwell, Vt.; married Calista Cook; died 22 Oct 1879, West Haven, Rutland, Vt.

2086   iii.  Phebe Cook, married Harry Culver.

2087   iv.   Truman Cook, married Dolly Unknown, 1790, Orwell, Vt.

2088   v.    Omira Cook, born 11 Sep 1798, Orwell, Vt.; married James Wilson, 19 Oct 1821; died 8 Jun 1875, Shoreham, Vt.

2089   vi.   Oliver Cook, married Unknown .

2090   vii.  Marie Cook, married Ezra Goodenow.

2091   viii.   Melista Cook, married Atwood Marsh.

2092   ix.   Chauncey Cook, born 1808, Orwell, Vt.; married Salina Converse.

2093   x.    Emily Cook, married William Spooner.

922. Capt. David Cook (Reuben-5, Ephraim-4, Joshua-3, Josiah-2, Josias-1) was born on 15 Dec 1767 in Coventry, Conn. He appeared in the census in 1810 in Orwell, Vt. He died on 15 Aug 1827 at the age of 59 in Orwell, Vt.

Capt. David Cook and Elizabeth Humphrey were married before 1793. They moved in Orwell, Vt. in 1793 They appeared in the census in 1800 in Orwell, Vt. Elizabeth Humphrey, daughter of Thomas Humphrey and Elizabeth Hopkins, was born on 22 Nov 1768 in Cornwall, Conn. She died on 15 Apr 1813 at the age of 44 in Orwell, Vt.

David Cook and Elizabeth Humphrey had the following children:

2094   i.    Daniel Mason Cook, born 9 Dec 1790, Canaan, NY.; married Elizabeth Brewer, 30 Nov 1814, Orwell, Vt.; died 22 Dec 1873, Orwell, Vt.

2095   ii.   Cynthia Cook, born 5 Apr 1792, Orwell, Vt.; married William Fuller, 1810; married William Fisher, 1821; married John Brown; died 9 Apr 1853, Orwell, Vt.

2096   iii.  Nancy Cook, born 23 Apr 1795, Orwell, Vt.; married Levi Wilkinson, abt 1816, State of Vermont.

        iv.  David Manning Cook was born on 5 Feb 1797 in Orwell, Vt. He died on 17 Dec 1815 at the age of 18.

2097   v.   Henry Gordon Cook (Twin), born 9 Dec 1798, Orwell, Vt.; married Marina Doane; died 6 Jan 1879, Malone, Franklin, NY.

2098   vi.  Harriet Cook (Twin), born 9 Dec 1798, Orwell, Vt.; married Dr. Russell Humphrey, 1816, Bainbridge, Chenango, NY; died 1832.

2099   vii. Maria Cook, born 29 Apr 1801; married Unknown Brooks.

2100   viii.  Russell Humphrey Cook, born 5 Jul 1803, Benson, Vt.; married Peninnah Baker, Feb 1832, Little Sandusky, Ohio; died 21 Oct 1837, Salt Lick, O.

2101   ix.  Elizabeth Cook, born 30 May 1805, Orwell, Vt.; married Zuriel Fowler; died Cedar Rapids, Linn, Ia.

        x.   Ruel Plum Cook was born on 24 Feb 1808 in Orwell, Vt. She died on 7 Jan 1877 at the age of 68 in Clymer, Chautauqua, NY.

2102   xi.  Lorenzo Hopkins Cook, born 2 Apr 1810, Orwell, Vt.; married Eliza Cudwith; married Sabina Adams; died 10 Apr 1874, Ohio.

923. Oliver Cook (Reuben-5, Ephraim-4, Joshua-3, Josiah-2, Josias-1) was born before 16 Oct 1763 in Coventry, Conn. He died after 1850 at the age of 87 in West Haven, Rutland, Vt.

Oliver Cook and Mercy Harris were married. Mercy Harris was born on 2 Oct 1763 in Mansfield, Tolland, Conn. She died about 1825 at the age of 62 in State of Vermont.

Oliver Cook and Mercy Harris had the following children:

2103   i.    Clarissa Cook, born abt 1788, Coventry, Conn.; married Elisha Adams, 16 Mar 1806, Coventry First Church, Coventry, Conn.; died 1 Mar 1846, Benson, Vt.

2104   ii.   Millie Cook, married Samuel Swetland, 31 Aug 1806, Coventry, Conn.

        iii. A son Cook died in Mar 1794 in Coventry, Conn.

2105   iv.  Benajah Cook, born abt 1794, Connecticut; married Nancy Coleman, abt 1824; married Ruth Jennison, 17 Mar 1819, Shoreham, Vt.; married Eliza Perry, 27 Mar

1857, Middletown, Conn.; died 26 Oct 1865, Middletown, Vt.

2106   v.  Calista Cook, born abt 1799, Coventry, Conn.; married Ivory Cook Jr.; died 3 Jan 1872, West Haven, Rutland, Vt.

2107   vi.  Gordon Cook, born abt 1804, Coventry, Conn.; married Adeline Warren, 9 Jan 1827, Orwell, Vt.

Oliver Cook and Esther Brown moved in Orwell, Vt. before 1820 They moved in West Haven, Rutland, Vt. before 1830 They appeared in the census in 1850 in West Haven, Rutland, Vt. Oliver and Esther were married. Esther Brown died on 23 Nov 1863 in West Haven, Rutland, Vt.

924. John Cook (Ephraim-5, Ephraim-4, Joshua-3, Josiah-2, Josias-1) was born on 13 Apr 1791 in Canaan, Conn. He died on 6 Nov 1862 at the age of 71 in Cornwall, Conn.

John Cook and Sally Bronson were married. Sally Bronson was born in 1791. She died on 29 Nov 1852 at the age of 61 in Cornwall, Conn.

John Cook and Sally Bronson had the following children:

     i.  Solomon Cook.

     ii.  Betsey Cook.

2108   iii.  Herman S. Cook, married Philena M. Wedge, 24 Jul 1846.

     iv.  Cynthia Cook was born in 1815. She died on 7 Apr 1833 at the age of 18.

2109   v.  Melissa Cook, married Sheldon Clark.

925. Silas Cook (Ephraim-5, Ephraim-4, Joshua-3, Josiah-2, Josias-1) was born on 1 Jan 1772. He appeared in the census in 1800 in Canaan, Conn.

Silas Cook and Abiah Hewitt were married on 8 Jul 1792 in Canaan, Conn.

Silas Cook and Abiah Hewitt had the following children:

     i.  Abiah Cook.

     ii.  Arabella Cook.

     iii.  A child was born on 23 Nov 1794 in Canaan, Conn. He/she died on 25 Nov 1794 in Canaan, Conn.

     iv.  Pollyphene Cook was born on 13 Dec 1795 in Canaan, Conn.

     v.  Rozina Cook was born on 30 Mar 1798 in Canaan, Conn.

2110   vi.  Ephraim Cook, born 23 Apr 1804, Canaan, Conn.; married Eliza CURTIS, 13 Nov 1830, Portage, Oh.; died 9 Dec 1861, Bedford, Oh.

6.123

926. Daniel Cook (Joseph-5, Ephraim-4, Joshua-3, Josiah-2, Josias-1) was born on 24 Apr 1788 in
        Coventry, Conn.

        Daniel Cook and Betsey UNKNOWN were married. Betsey Unknown was born in 1798 in
        New York.

927. John Young Cook (Nathan-5, Ephraim-4, Joshua-3, Josiah-2, Josias-1) was born in 1783 in
        Coventry, Conn. He was associated with  in 1783 in Coventry First Church, Coventry, Conn.
        He lived in Columbia, Conn. in 1836.

        John Young Cook and Hannah UNKNOWN were married.

John Young Cook and Hannah Unknown had the following children:

   2111   i.   Sidney R. Cook, born 1 Feb 1807, Coventry, Conn.; married Pamelia R. PORTER,
                    16 Nov 1829, Coventry, Conn.; died 12 May 1869, Springfield, Mass.
          ii.  Fanny Cook was born in 1814.

928. Fanny Cook (Nathan-5, Ephraim-4, Joshua-3, Josiah-2, Josias-1) was born before May 1786 in
        Coventry, Conn. She was baptized in May 1786 in Coventry First Church, Coventry, Conn.

        Fanny Cook and Calvin EDWARDS were married.

929. David Cook (Nathan-5, Ephraim-4, Joshua-3, Josiah-2, Josias-1) was born before Feb 1787 in
        Coventry, Conn. He served in the military served in the War of 1812 in 1812. David died in
        1859 at the age of 72 in Suffield, Oh.

        David Cook and Sabina Chloe MOORE moved to Suffield, Oh. after 1812. Sabina Chloe
        Moore, daughter of Nathan Moore and Julia Lee, was born on 24 Oct 1788 in New
        Hampshire. She died in 1879 at the age of 91 in Ohio.

David Cook and Sabina Chloe Moore had the following children:

   2112   i.   Mary Cook, married Unknown Potzer; died bef 1885.
   2113   ii.  Nathan Moore Cook, born 9 Apr 1816, Suffield, Oh.; married Clarinda HULBERT,
                    14 Jan 1842; died 2 Feb 1875, Suffield, Oh.
          iii. John Cook died before 1885.
   2114   iv.  Lee Cook, born 11 Nov 1821; married Phebe BUCKMAN; married Margaret EBEL.
   2115   v.   Galvin Cook, born abt 1827, Suffield, Oh.; married Mary Ann STOUT; died aft 1885.
          vi.  Orange Cook was born about 1830 in Suffield, Oh. He died after 1885 at the age of 55.
   2116   vii. Rachel Cook, married Stahl SMITH; died aft 1885.

930. Bela Reynolds Cook (Nathan-5, Ephraim-4, Joshua-3, Josiah-2, Josias-1) was born before Oct
1793 in Coventry, Conn. He was baptized in Oct 1793 in Coventry First Church, Coventry,
Conn. He died on 25 Oct 1866 at the age of 73 in Andover, Conn.

Bela Reynolds Cook and Electa PARKER were married in Apr 1815. Electa Parker was born
on 29 Dec 1793 in Hatfield, Mass. She died in 1884 at the age of 91 in Andover, Conn.

Bela Reynolds Cook and Electa Parker had the following children:

2117   i.   William P Cook, born 1821, Andover, Tolland, Conn.; married Martha E. A.
            HENDEE, 26 Dec 1852, Andover, Tolland, Conn.; died 16 Jun 1867, Andover,
            Tolland, Conn.
2118   ii.  DeLance Cook, born Jul 1827, Andover, Tolland, Conn.; married Mary Lucinda LEE,
            28 Mar 1852, Hebron, Tolland, Conn.; died 1902, Hampton, Rock Island, Ill.
2119   iii. Oliver Cook, born 1829, Connecticut, U.S.; married Sarah Elizabeth LEE, 12 Sep
            1852, Hebron, Tolland, Conn.; died 13 May 1906, Hampton, Rock Island, Ill.

931. Nathan Cook (Nathan-5, Ephraim-4, Joshua-3, Josiah-2, Josias-1) was born before Oct 1793 in
Coventry, Conn. He was baptized in Oct 1793 in Coventry First Church, Coventry, Conn.

Nathan Cook and Lucy A. AVERY were married.

947. Lemuel Cook (Moses-5, Simeon-4, Joshua-3, Josiah-2, Josias-1) was born on 9 Oct 1778 in
Townshend, Vt.

Lemuel Cook and Phebe SHAW were married.

Lemuel Cook and Phebe Shaw had the following child:

2140   i.   Noah Cook, born 1804, Dutchess County, NY.; married Annie WARES; died Jun
            1896, Chattaraugus County, NY.

948. Sarah Cook (Joseph-5, Simeon-4, Joshua-3, Josiah-2, Josias-1) was born between 1775 and
1780 in Connecticut. She died in Wisconsin.

Sarah Cook and William THOMPSON were married bef spring of 1802 in Stonington, New
London, Conn. William Thompson, was born on 22 Mar 1776 in Rhode Island. He died after
1860 at the age of 84 in Wisconsin.

William THOMPSON and Sarah Cook had the following children:

6.125

2141   i.  Hannah Thompson, born bef 1800.
      ii.  Claracy Thompson was born before 1800. She was also known as Sally.
2142   iii. Reuben Thompson, born 1802, Pharsalia, NY.; married Esther HOFFMAN, bef 1825.
2143   iv. George Washington Thompson, born abt 1803, New York; married Lucy UNKNOWN, bef 1830.
      v.  William Thompson Jr. was born before 1806.
2144   vi. Rial T. Thompson, born 1806, Plymouth, NY.
2145   vii. Lewis Thompson, born abt 1810, New York.
2146   viii.   Luman Thompson, born 1812, Genesee, NY.; married Lauretta BUTTON, 5 Dec 1833, Dunkirk, NY.; died 16 Jun 1898, Waupaca, Wisc.
2147   ix. Johial Thompson, born abt 1816, New York; died aft 1880, Scotch Ridge, Oh.
2148   x.  Phoebe Thompson, born bef 1820.
2149   xi. Wealthy Thompson, born bef 1820.
2150   xii. Lorin Thompson, born 30 Mar 1821, New York; married Alvira WRIGHT, 1848, Northeast Township, Erie, Pennsylvania; died 22 Apr 1904, Dunbridge, Oh.

949. Abigail Cook (Joseph-5, Simeon-4, Joshua-3, Josiah-2, Josias-1) was born (date unknown).

Abigail Cook and Abner Purdy were married.

950. Spencer Cook (Joseph-5, Simeon-4, Joshua-3, Josiah-2, Josias-1) was born (date unknown).

Spencer Cook and Harriet ARNOLD were married.

951. Simeon Cook (Joseph-5, Simeon-4, Joshua-3, Josiah-2, Josias-1) was born between 1775 and 1780. He lived in Amenia, NY. in 1800. He moved in Sherburne, NY. in 1813. Simeon moved to Norwich, NY in 1820. He died after 1820 at the age of 45.

Simeon Cook and Sarah CRANDALL were married on 1 Jul 1800. Sarah Crandall was the daughter of Laban Crandall.

Simeon Cook and Elizabeth CRANDALL were married. Elizabeth Crandall, the daughter of Samuel Crandall, was born on 7 Jan 1789.

Simeon Cook and Elizabeth Crandall had the following child:

      i.  Sally Cook.

952. William Cook (Joseph-5, Simeon-4, Joshua-3, Josiah-2, Josias-1) was born between 1780 and 1790. He bought land with Aaron Cook on 6 Jan 1812 in Norwich, NY. In 1865 he was a the

director of the Sherburne National Bank (and again in 1869).

William Cook and Anna PURDY were married..

953. Aaron Cook (Joseph-5, Simeon-4, Joshua-3, Josiah-2, Josias-1) was born about 1787.

Aaron Cook and Lydia CULVER were married.

954. Lyman Cook (Joseph-5, Simeon-4, Joshua-3, Josiah-2, Josias-1) was born between 1790 and
1800.

Lyman Cook and Polly FISHER were married.

1008.Sally Cook (Nathaniel-5, Jonathan-4, Joshua-3, Josiah-2, Josias-1) was born in 1785.

Sally Cook and Jabez ARNOLD appeared in the census in 1850 in Rocky Hill, Hartford,
Conn. Jabez Arnold was born in 1786 in Connecticut.

1009.Hezekiah Sears Cook (Nathaniel-5, Jonathan-4, Joshua-3, Josiah-2, Josias-1) was born on 14
Nov 1789. He died on 15 Nov 1826 at the age of 37 in Middlefield, Conn.

Hezekiah Sears Cook and Roxana ARNOLD were married. Roxana Arnold was born on 1
Apr 1789 in Haddam, Conn. She died on 18 Feb 1821 at the age of 31.

Hezekiah Sears Cook and Sally UNKNOWN were married. Sally was born about 1788. She
died on 11 Nov 1862 at the age of 74 in Middlefield, Conn.

1010.Willard Cook (Nathaniel-5, Jonathan-4, Joshua-3, Josiah-2, Josias-1) was born on 18 Sep 1799
in New York. He died on 9 Aug 1873 at the age of 73 in Chicago, Ill.

Willard Cook and Abigail BRAINERD were married on 8 Jan 1823 in Haddam Neck
Congregational Church, East Haddam, Conn. They appeared in the census in 1850 in Fremont,
Ill. Abigail Brainerd, daughter of Ansel Brainerd and Hannah Dart, was born in 1801 in
Connecticut. She died on 26 Dec 1854 at the age of 53 in Chicago, Ill.

Willard Cook and Abigail Brainerd had the following children:

    2256   i.   Ansel Cook, born 18 Aug 1823, Haddam, Conn.; married Helen M. FOSTER, 2 Dec
                1849; married Annie B. BARROWS, 2 Feb 1882.
    2257   ii.  Abby Florilla Cook, born 27 Nov 1827, Haddam, Conn.; married John F.
                MENDSEN, 21 Nov 1859.

6.127

iii. Helen M. Cook was born in 1828. She appeared in the census in 1850 in Fremont, Lake, Ill.

2258 iv. Charles Willard Cook, born 13 Jul 1832, Haddam, Conn.; married Sarah A. COONLEY, 1857; married Jennie W. (Sterges) WADE, 18 Jun 1874.

2259 v. Ellen Sophia Cook, born 6 Aug 1840, Haddam, Conn.; married Rev Edwin Luther JAGGER, 29 Apr 1861.

1012.Ichabod Cook (Amos-5, Jonathan-4, Joshua-3, Josiah-2, Josias-1) was born on 3 Jun 1792 in Connecticut. He served in the military as a private under Capt. Van Dalsen in 1812 in New York. He died on 23 Oct 1866 at the age of 74 in Ashland, NY. Ichabod signed a will on 8 Jan 1867 in Ashland, NY. He was buried in Mountain Valley Cemetery, Ashland, Green, NY.

Ichabod Cook and Hannah UNKNOWN were married before 1815.

Ichabod Cook and Hannah Unknown had the following children:

2261 i. Jerusha "Rue" Cook, born 1815, Greene County, NY.; married Charles Peter BEAUJEAN; died 3 Mar 1877, Mayville, NY.

ii. Betsy Cook was born in 1815. She died in 1827 at the age of 12. She was buried in Mountain Valley Cemetery, Ashland, NY.

Ichabod Cook and Elizabeth "Betsy" BRANDOW were married after 1815. They appeared in the census in 1850 in Ashland, NY. Elizabeth "Betsy" Brandow, daughter of Henrick I. Brandow and Elizabeth Austin, was born on 29 Jun 1798 in Greene County, NY. She died on 13 Mar 1876 at the age of 77 in Ashland, NY. She was buried in Mountain Valley Cemetery, Ashland, NY.

Ichabod Cook and Elizabeth Brandow had the following children:

i. Anna "Anny" Cook was born about 1818 in Ashland, NY. She died on 17 Nov 1897 at the age of 79. She was buried in Mountain Valley Cemetery, Ashland, NY.

2262 ii. Henry S. Cook, born 8 Jun 1820, Windham, NY.; married Elizabeth BEERS, 10 May 1843, West Settlement, Ashland,NY.; died 19 Mar 1887.

iii. Sally Cook was born in May 1822 in Ashland, NY. She died on 8 Feb 1832 at the age of 9 in Ashland, NY. She was buried in Mountain Valley Cemetery, Ashland, NY.

iv. Fletcher Cook was born about Oct 1824 in Ashland, NY. He died on 20 Feb 1825 in Ashland, NY. He was buried in Mountain Valley Cemetery, Ashland, NY.

2263 v. Margaret B. Cook (Twin), born 16 Jan 1827, Ashland, NY.; married Calvin Luther SUTTON, 4 Jun 1846, Windham, NY.; died 5 Feb 1903, Ashland, NY.

2264 vi. Clarissa B. "Clarry" Cook (Twin), born 16 Jan 1827, Ashland, NY.; married Stephen W. TRUESDELL; died 28 Mar 1906.

2265 vii. Elizabeth "Betsy" Cook, born 14 Jul 1830, Ashland, NY.; married Addison SUTTON, bef 1855; died 14 Jan 1863, Windham, NY.

2266 viii. Terressa H. Cook, born abt Mar 1834; married Addison SUTTON, aft 1863; died 25 Jan 1871.

2267 ix. Polly S. Cook, born abt 1836, Ashland, NY.; married Rev. George W. FERRIS, 1861; died 1903, Ashland, NY.

2268 x. Thomas Bradley Cook, born 1839, New York; married Mary SUTTON; died 1903, Ashland, NY.

2269 xi. Ichabod Cook Jr., born 13 Sep 1842, Ashland, NY.; married Electa CHRISTIAN, 30 Oct 1865, Ashland, NY.; died 9 Jul 1894, Ashland, NY.

1013.Amos Cook (Amos-5, Jonathan-4, Joshua-3, Josiah-2, Josias-1) was born (date unknown).

Amos Cook had the following child:

2270 i. Ashbel Cook, born 1794, Connecticut; married Julia A. UNKNOWN.

1051.Capt Lewis Cook (Solomon-5, Hezekiah-4, Joshua-3, Josiah-2, Josias-1) was born on 18 Apr 1785 in New Marlborough, Mass. He served in the military as a captain in the State Militia of Massachusetts in about 1810. He appeared in the census in 1810 in New Marlborough, Mass. He died on 24 Jan 1861 at the age of 75 in New Marlborough, Mass. He was buried in Old Southfield Cemetery, New Marlboro, Mass.

Capt Lewis Cook and Abigail RHODES were married in 1804 in New Marlborough, Mass. They moved to South Oteselic, NY. in 1810 They moved in New Marlborough, Mass. in 1827. Abigail Rhodes was born about 1789. She died on 1 Jul 1872 at the age of 83 in New Marlborough, Mass.

Lewis Cook and Abigail Rhodes had the following children:

2280 i. Alanson Cook, born 17 Dec 1804, New Marlborough, Mass.; married Emily PALMER, 29 Sep 1830, New Marlborough, Mass.

2281 ii. Levi Cook, born 7 Jun 1807, New Marlborough, Mass.; married Amelia TODD, 21 Sep 1829, Sandisfield, Mass.; died May 1871, Colebrook, Conn.

2282 iii. Isaac Rhodes Cook, born 10 Oct 1809, New Marlborough, Mass.; married Eliza UNKNOWN, 15 Oct 1836, Charlestown, Mass.

2283 iv. Lydia Perna Cook, born 29 Jul 1812, New Marlborough, Mass.; married Reuben FREEMAN, 16 Oct 1829, New Marlborough, Mass.

v. Zena Cook was born on 25 Jan 1815 in New Marlborough, Mass.

1052.Lorrin Cook (Solomon-5, Hezekiah-4, Joshua-3, Josiah-2, Josias-1) was born on 14 Sep 1797 in New Marlborough, Mass. He died on 30 Apr 1878 at the age of 80 in South Oteselic, NY.

Lorrin Cook and Hannah Warner were married. Hannah Warner was born in 1800 in Sandisfield, Mass. She died in 1889 at the age of 89 in New York.

Lorrin Cook and Hannah Warner had the following children:

    2284   i.   Alvin Cook, born 1820, New York; married Adeline UNKNOWN.
    2285   ii.  Ledyard Cook, born abt 1823, New York; married Esther UNKNOWN.
            iii. Alanson Cook was born in 1827 in New York.
            iv. Ellen Cook was born about 1833 in New York.
            v.  Mary Ann Cook was born in 1838 in New York.
            vi. Harriet Cook was born about 1840 in New York.

1053.Luna Cook (Benjamin Warren-5, Hezekiah-4, Joshua-3, Josiah-2, Josias-1) was born about 1807 in Lenox, Mass.

Luna Cook and Thomas SEDGWICK appeared in the census in 1850 in Lenox, Mass. Thomas Sedgwick, son of Unknown Sedgwick and Temperence Unknown, was born on 11 Jul 1803 in Washington, Berkshire, Mass. In 1850 he was a farmer in Lenox, Mass. In 1860 he was a president of a bank in Lenox, Mass.

Thomas Sedgwick and Luna Cook had the following child:

       i.   Henry Sedgwick, born 1830; married Mary J. UNKNOWN. They had 5 children.

1054.Laura S. Cook (Benjamin Warren-5, Hezekiah-4, Joshua-3, Josiah-2, Josias-1) was born in 1811 in State of Massachusetts.

Laura S. Cook and George S. FITCH appeared in the census in 1850 in New York, NY. George S. Fitch was born in 1805 in Connecticut. He was a merchant of dry goods.

George S. Fitch and Laura S. Cook had the following children:

       i.   George Fitch was born in 1836.
       ii.  Elizabeth Fitch, born 1844; married Franklin FIELD. They had 1 child.
       iii. Mary Fitch was born in 1846.

# 7<sup>TH</sup> Generation

1440.Washington Ebenezer Cook (Ebenezer-6, Josiah-5, Jacob-4, Josiah-3, Josiah-2, Josias-1) was
born on 29 Dec 1808.

Washington Ebenezer Cook and Eunice Allen KELLOGG were married on 30 May 1832.
Eunice Allen Kellogg, daughter of Eliphalet and Elizabeth Kellogg, was born on 4 Aug 1818 in
Bethany, Pa.

Washington Ebenezer Cook and Eunice Allen Kellogg had the following children:

    i.  George Washington Ebenezer Cook was born on 23 Jun 1834 in Pennsylvania.

3015  ii.  Helen Josephine Cook, born 20 May 1837, State of Pennsylvania; married Dorie
Gillespie WARNER, 4 Sep 1856.

3016  iii.  Isabel Virginia Cook, born 23 Mar 1839, Pennsylvania; married Smith Monroe
GARRETT, 14 Apr 1862, Matamora, Ill.

3017  iv.  Martin Kellogg Cook, born 20 Sep 1840, Pennsylvania; married Margaret
BUCHANAN, 14 Apr 1864; died 31 Mar 1869.

1441Watson Cook (Ebenezer-6, Josiah-5, Jacob-4, Josiah-3, Josiah-2, Josias-1) was born on 11 Jul
1814. He died on 30 Jun 1859 at the age of 44.

Watson Cook and Harriet M. MINOR were married on 21 Jan 1846. Harriet M. Minor was
born in Princeton, Ill.

Watson Cook and Harriet M. Minor had the following children:

    i.  Harriet Leonora Cook was born on 20 Aug 1846 in Lacon, Ill. She died Mar 1847.

3018  ii.  Mary Emily Cook, born 11 Feb 1847, Lacon, Ill; married John Henry SPENCER, 18
Dec 1865.

    iii.  Frances Catharine Cook was born on 25 Oct 1849 in Lacon, Ill.

    iv.  Clara Augusta Cook was born on 9 Sep 1850 in Lacon, Ill.

    v.  John Miner Cook was born on 20 Sep 1852 in Lacon, Ill. He died on 30 Nov 1853.

    vi.  Charles Watson Cook was born on 10 Oct 1855 in Lacon, Ill.

    vii. Nora Cook was born on 5 Sep 1856 in Lacon, Ill.

1442.Mary Cook (Ebenezer-6, Josiah-5, Jacob-4, Josiah-3, Josiah-2, Josias-1) was born on 7 Feb
1816.

Mary Cook and Eugene Franklin SKINNER were married on 28 Nov 1839. Eugene Franklin
Skinner was born in Nov 1807. He died on 15 Dec 1864 at the age of 57 in Eugene, Ore.

Eugene Franklin Skinner and Mary Cook had the following children:

    i.   Amelia Skinner was born on 10 Jul 1842 in Eugene, Lane, Ore. She died on 10 Sep 1844 in Eugene, Lane, Ore.

    ii.   Mary Elizabeth Skinner was born on 2 Dec 1846 in Eugene, Lane, Ore. She died on 3 Nov 1860 at the age of 13 in Eugene, Ore.

    iii.   Lenora Combs Skinner was born on 9 Sep 1848 in Eugene, Lane, Ore. She died on 2 Oct 1868 at the age of 20 in Eugene, Ore.

3019   iv.   Phebe Ball Skinner, born 20 Mar 1850, Eugene, Lane, Ore.; married John KINSEY, 30 Aug 1868.

1443.Clarissa Emily Cook (Ebenezer-6, Josiah-5, Jacob-4, Josiah-3, Josiah-2, Josias-1) was born on 21 Jan 1818.

Clarissa Emily Cook and Thomas MORGAN were married on 30 Nov 1836. Thomas Morgan was born on 6 Feb 1806 in Lansing, Tompkins, NY. He died on 30 Apr 1868 at the age of 62.

Thomas Morgan and Clarissa Emily Cook had the following children:

    i.   John Watson Morgan was born on 24 Jan 1838. He died on 22 Oct 1838.

    ii.   Helen Josephine Morgan was born on 15 Mar 1840.

    iii.   James Thomas Morgan was born on 17 Jun 1843. He died on 15 Dec 1844.

    iv.   Dwight Elston Morgan was born on 9 Jun 1846.

    v.   Algenia Knox Morgan was born on 9 May 1848. She died on 10 Sep 1850.

    vi.   Mary Jones Morgan was born on 23 May 1852. She died on 23 Sep 1852.

    vii.   Greeley Tefft Morgan was born on 22 Jun 1854. He died on 23 Sep 1854.

1444.Orrin Philander Cook (Philander-6, Josiah-5, Jacob-4, Josiah-3, Josiah-2, Josias-1) was born on 17 Jun 1819.

Orrin Philander Cook and Anne Caroline WEATHERLOW were married on 10 Aug 1842 in Arcade, NY. Anne Caroline Weatherlow was born on 26 Aug 1820. She died on 19 Jul 1893 at the age of 72.

Orrin Philander Cook and Anne Caroline Weatherlow had the following children:

    i.   Esther Ann Cook was born on 12 Apr 1844.

    ii.   Viola Cook was born in 1846.

    iii.   Ramira Cook was born in 1848.

3020   iv.   Frank Philander Cook, born 30 Jun 1853; married Adelaide E. FREEBORN.

v.   Ray W. Cook was born on 15 Apr 1848.
vi.   Romeo Cook was born on 2 Jun 1851.

1445. Albert Leonard Cook (Alva-6, Elisha-5, Jacob-4, Josiah-3, Josiah-2, Josias-1) was born on 1
Nov 1814 in Otis, Mass. He died on 9 Mar 1880 at the age of 65. He was a farmer.

Albert Leonard Cook and Catharine MCDONALD appeared in the census in 1850 in
Guilford, Oh.

Albert Leonard Cook and Catharine McDonald had the following children:

3021   i.   Lydia Cook, born 1843; married William MCCABE.
3022   ii.   Eliza Cook Cook, born 1846; married Leavitt K. HOSMER.
iii.   Elisha Baldwin Cook was born in 1846.
3023   iv.   Adelaide "Addie" Cook, born 1848; married Charles COOK.
3024   v.   Imerta "Myrtie" Cook, born 1856; married a VANDERBILT.
3025   vi.   Elmer Cook, born 1862; married KRITZ.

1446. Harriet Eliza Cook (Alva-6, Elisha-5, Jacob-4, Josiah-3, Josiah-2, Josias-1) was born on 5 Jun
1818 in Otis, Mass. She died of childbirth on 10 Sep 1839 at the age of 21.

Harriet Eliza Cook and James ELDER were married.

James Elder and Harriet Eliza Cook had the following child:

i.   Leonard Elder was born in Sep 1839. He died in the civil war about 1863 at the age of 24.

1447. Julia Ann Cook (Alva-6, Elisha-5, Jacob-4, Josiah-3, Josiah-2, Josias-1) was born on 15 Jul
1820 in Otis, Mass. She died on 12 Oct 1865 at the age of 45.

Julia Ann Cook and James WHITESIDE were married.

James Whiteside and Julia Ann Cook had the following child:

3026   i.   Amanda Whiteside, married BRINSTNALL. They had 1 child.

1448. Mary Elizabeth Cook (Alva-6, Elisha-5, Jacob-4, Josiah-3, Josiah-2, Josias-1) was born on 8
Sep 1822 in Otis, Mass. She died on 28 Aug 1905 at the age of 82.

Mary Elizabeth Cook and Henry M. BRADLEY were married on 1 Jan 1846. Henry M.
Bradley was born on 7 May 1824 in Lee, Mass. He died on 28 Aug 1905 at the age of 81 in

7.133

Duluth, Minn.

Henry M. Bradley and Mary Elizabeth Cook had the following children:

i.   Alice Almira Bradley, born 8 Jun 1847, Litchfield, OH; married Guardis D. EDWARDS, Bay City, Mich.; died 22 May 1918, Duluth, Minn. They had 2 children.
ii.  Alva William Bradley, born 4 Apr 1849, Litchfield, OH; married Orlena TENNEY, 10 Dec 1878, Newark, Oh. They had 2 children.
iii. Elisha L. Bradley was born on 21 Sep 1851.
iv.  George M. Bradley was born on 12 Oct 1855 in Bay City, Mich.
v.   Frank E. Bradley was born on 31 Jan 1858 in Bay City, Mich.
vi.  Charles Henry Bradley, born 4 Nov 1858, Sparta, Oh.; married Magdalina Ten EYCK, 1 Dec 1875, Bay City, Mich. They had 1 child.
vii. Edward L. Bradley, born 22 Jan 1860; married Lucretia Ann PRINGLE. They had 1 child.
viii.    Adelaide May Bradley, born 14 Oct 1863, Bay City, Mich.; married Carl NORPELL, 16 Jun 1885, Bay City, Mich.; died 13 Mar 1946, Northington, Oh. They had 5 children.

1449.Francis Edwin Cook (Alva-6, Elisha-5, Jacob-4, Josiah-3, Josiah-2, Josias-1) was born on 13 Dec 1824 in Otis, Mass. He appeared in the census in 1850 in Guilford, Oh. He died on 1 Oct 1904 at the age of 79.

Francis Edwin Cook and Frances M. DIX appeared in the census in 1880 in Gilman, Ia. Frances M. Dix was born in Ohio.

Francis Edwin Cook and Frances M. Dix had the following children:

i.   Ada Cook.
ii.  Katie A. Cook was born in 1862. She appeared in the census in 1880 in Gilman, Ia.

1450.Lucy Maria Cook (Alva-6, Elisha-5, Jacob-4, Josiah-3, Josiah-2, Josias-1) was born on 4 Jul 1829 in Seville, Oh.

Lucy Maria Cook and James Stoaks were married after 1850.

James Stoaks and Lucy Maria Cook had the following children:

i.   Hattie Stoaks, married CUNNINGHAM. They had 2 children.
ii.  Mary Stoaks, married DUNLAP.
iii. Sarah Stoaks, married NOTESTEIN.

1451.Elisha Baldwin Cook (Alva-6, Elisha-5, Jacob-4, Josiah-3, Josiah-2, Josias-1) was born on 11 Nov 1831 in Seville, Oh. He appeared in the census in 1880 in Centerburgh, Oh. In 1880 he was a lumber dealer.

Elisha Baldwin Cook and Mary Elizabeth HOWE were married in 1875 in Sparta, Oh. Mary Elizabeth Howe was born on 12 May 1842. She died on 28 Jul 1879 at the age of 37.

Elisha Baldwin Cook and Mary Elizabeth Howe had the following children:

3035　i.　Hattie Madge Cook, born 29 Jan 1876, Centerburgh, Oh.; married S. Robert BEST, 11 Oct 1897, Centerburgh, Oh.

　　　ii.　Maggie Vida Cook was born after 1877. She died before 1880 at the age of 3.

Elisha Baldwin Cook and Christine WILKIN were married on 6 Jun 1882 in Bloomfield, Oh. They appeared in the census in 1900 in Hilliard, Oh. Christine Wilkin was born on 6 Mar 1854 in Germany.

Elisha Baldwin Cook and Christine Wilkin had the following children:

　　　i.　Adelaide Cook was born on 11 Sep 1884. She appeared in the census in 1900 in Hilliard, Oh.

3036　ii.　Altje Wilken Cook, born 21 Jun 1886, Centerburgh, O.; married Chester CLELAND, 26 Oct 1915, Granville, Oh.

1452.Charles E. Cook (Alva-6, Elisha-5, Jacob-4, Josiah-3, Josiah-2, Josias-1) was born on 25 May 1834 in Seville, Oh. He appeared in the census in 1850.

Charles E. Cook and Priscilla were married.

1453.Adaline Elmira Cook (Alva-6, Elisha-5, Jacob-4, Josiah-3, Josiah-2, Josias-1) was born on 29 Nov 1838 in Seville, Oh. She appeared in the census in 1850. She died on 17 May 1909 at the age of 70 in Hartford, Oh.

Adaline Elmira Cook and Richard V. STREETER were married on 4 May 1861 in Medina, Oh. They moved in Hartford, Oh. in 1872. Richard V. Streeter was born on 26 Mar 1838 in Boardmen, Oh. He was a carriage maker.

Richard V. Streeter and Adaline Elmira Cook had the following children:

　　　i.　Alice Edith Streeter, born 13 Feb 1863, Sparta, O.; married Carl Schurz Hoover, 21 Aug 1883, Hartford, Licking, O.; died 19 Apr 1938, Croton, O. They had 1 child.

ii.   Frank Elisha Streeter, born 3 Sep 1865, Sparta, O.; married Leota Jenkins, Jun 1923, Columbus, O.
iii.  Addie May Streeter, born 13 Dec 1869, Marengo, O.; married Grant C. Green, 29 Jul 1891, Hartford, O.; died 13 Feb 1915, Dallas, Dallas, Tex. They had 1 child.
iv.   Maude Nina Streeter, born 29 Jul 1873, Hartford, Licking, O.; married Warner W. Stockberger, 6 Jul 1896, Hartford, O. They had 3 children.
v.    Lydia Blanche Streeter, born 11 Mar 1876, Hartford, O.; married Alva M. Leach, 5 Aug 1900, Hartford, O. They had 3 children.
vi.   Ralph Eugene Streeter, born 7 Oct 1882, Hartford, O.; married Caroline Mellis, 1906, St. Louis, Mo.; married Minnie Salter, 1909, Beaumont, Tex.

1474. Hannah Cook (Paron Cowell-6, Solomon-5, Solomon-4, Josiah-3, Josiah-2, Josias-1) was born on 17 Dec 1781 in Provincetown, Mass. She was baptized on 25 Aug 1782 in Truro, Mass. She died on 19 Aug 1836 at the age of 54 in Provincetown, Mass. Hannah was buried in Provincetown Cemetery Number Two.

Hannah Cook and Capt. Elisha (Isaiah) YOUNG were married in 1798 in Provincetown, Mass. Capt. Elisha (Isaiah) Young was born in 1775. He died on 5 Dec 1848 at the age of 73 in Provincetown, Mass. He was a sea captain.

Elisha (Isaiah) Young and Hannah Cook had the following children:

i.     ?Sarah H. Young.
ii.    ?Elisha Young was born in Jan 1800.
iii.   Isaiah Young, born 1803, Provincetown, Mass.; married Hannah E. N. SAWTELL.
iv.    Elisha Young Jr., born 31 May 1805, Provincetown, Mass.; married Betsy SPARKS, 9 Feb 1827; died 20 Mar 1873, Provincetown, Mass. They had 6 children.
v.     Hannah Young, born 31 Aug 1808, Provincetown, Mass.; married Thomas SPARKS, 30 Dec 1828, Provincetown, Mass.
vi.    John Young, born 2 Mar 1811, Provincetown, Mass.; married Maria NICKERSON.
vii.   ?Reuben Young was born on 26 Sep 1813 in Provincetown, Mass.
viii.  Henry Young, born 16 Feb 1815, Provincetown, Mass.; married Emily DOANE.
ix.    Newcomb C. Young was born on 13 Oct 1818 in Provincetown, Mass. He died in 1832 at the age of 14.
x.     Zerviah Holmes Young, born 21 May 1821, Provincetown, Mass.; married Jesse Small; died 1852.

1475. Newcomb Cook (Paron Cowell-6, Solomon-5, Solomon-4, Josiah-3, Josiah-2, Josias-1) was born on 3 Aug 1783 in Provincetown, Mass. He appeared in the census in 1830 in Provincetown, Mass.

Newcomb Cook and Nancy WELLS were married on 24 Dec 1807 in Provincetown, Mass. They appeared in the census in 1810 in Provincetown, Mass. Nancy Wells was born in 1787. She died on 17 Feb 1815 at the age of 28 in Provincetown, Mass. She was buried in Winthrop Street Cemetery, Provincetown, Mass.

Newcomb Cook and Nancy Wells had the following children:

      i.   Hannah Cook was born on 5 Jul 1809 in Provincetown, Mass.

3066  ii.  Paron Cook, born 7 Oct 1811, Provincetown, Mass.; married Hannah S. BOWLEY, 7 Jan 1836, Provincetown, Mass.

3067  iii.  Francis Wells Cook, born 19 Jan 1815, Provincetown, Mass.; married Elizabeth B. HOLWAY, 19 Nov 1843, Provincetown, Mass.; died 9 May 1889, Provincetown, Mass.

Newcomb Cook and Betsey YOUNG were married on 1 Oct 1816 in Provincetown, Mass. They appeared in the census in 1820 in Provincetown, Mass. Betsey Young was born on 11 Dec 1784 in Provincetown, Mass. She died of consumption on 3 Apr 1847 at the age of 62 in Provincetown, Mass.

Newcomb Cook and Betsey Young had the following children:

      i.   Nancy Wells Cook was born on 17 Sep 1817 in Provincetown, Mass.

      ii.  Betsy S. Cook was born in 1829 in Provincetown, Mass. She died on 15 Mar 1838 at the age of 9 in Provincetown, Mass.

1476. Salome Cook (Paron Cowell-6, Solomon-5, Solomon-4, Josiah-3, Josiah-2, Josias-1) was born on 7 Aug 1785 in Provincetown, Mass. She died on 8 Jan 1867 at the age of 81 in Provincetown, Mass.

Salome Cook and Benjamin DYER were married on 24 Nov 1802 in Provincetown, Mass. They appeared in the census in 1810 in Provincetown, Mass. They appeared in the census in 1820 in Provincetown, Mass. Benjamin Dyer was born about 1780 in Provincetown, Mass.

Benjamin Dyer and Salome Cook had the following children:

      i.   Atkins Dyer was born on 23 Jun 1808 in Provincetown, Mass.

      ii.  Joshua Dyer, born 13 Jun 1818, Provincetown, Mass.; married Laura Ann COOK, 10 Mar 1840, Provincetown, Mass.; married Betsey DYER, 16 Dec 1849, Provincetown, Mass. With Laura, he had 1 child.

1477. Zerviah Cook (Paron Cowell-6, Solomon-5, Solomon-4, Josiah-3, Josiah-2, Josias-1) was born on 7 Jul 1787 in Provincetown, Mass.

Zerviah Cook and Elisha HOLMES were married.

1478. Thomas Cook (Paron Cowell-6, Solomon-5, Solomon-4, Josiah-3, Josiah-2, Josias-1) was born on 1 Aug 1792 in Provincetown, Mass. He appeared in the census in 1830 in Provincetown, Mass. He appeared in the census in 1840 in Provincetown, Mass. Thomas died of dysentery on 30 Oct 1852 at the age of 60 in Provincetown, Mass.

Thomas Cook and Caroline UNKNOWN were married.

Thomas Cook and Caroline had the following child:

    i.   Sarah E. Cook was born on 5 May 1826 in Provincetown, Mass.

1479. Betsey Cook (Paron Cowell-6, Solomon-5, Solomon-4, Josiah-3, Josiah-2, Josias-1) was born on 28 Jun 1795 in Provincetown, Mass. She died probably of childbirth on 15 Apr 1826 at the age of 30 in Provincetown, Mass.  She was buried in Winthrop Street Cemetery, Provincetown, Mass.

Betsey Cook and Capt. Samuel SOPER were married on 18 Nov 1813 in Provincetown, Mass. Capt. Samuel Soper, son of Robert Soper and Isabel Smalley, was born on 21 Jul 1791 in Provincetown, Mass. He died on 8 Dec 1860 at the age of 69.

Samuel Soper and Betsey Cook had the following children:

    i.   Robert Soper, born 10 Oct 1814, Provincetown, Mass.; married Mary Bryant COOK, 30 Nov 1837, Provincetown, Mass. They had 2 children.
    ii.  Betsey Cook Soper, born 3 Oct 1816, Provincetown, Mass.; married John SWIFT; died 5 May 1888, Provincetown, Mass. They had 2 children.
    iii. A child Soper was born on 3 Nov 1818 in Provincetown, Mass. He/she was buried in Winthrop Street Cemetery, Provincetown, Mass.
    iv. Lucy Holmes Soper, born 16 Nov 1820, Provincetown, Mass.; married Richard W. HILLARD, 25 Oct 1841; died 18 Oct 1849.
    v.  Samuel Thomas Soper, born 23 Nov 1823; married Abbie W. CHAMPNEY, 16 Nov 1849, Provincetown, Mass.; died 4 Feb 1898, Provincetown, Mass.
    vi. Elisha Holmes Soper was born on 29 Mar 1826 in Provincetown, Mass. He died on 10 Sep 1826. He was buried in Winthrop Street Cemetery, Provincetown, Mass.

1485. Capt. Reuben Cook (Solomon-6, Solomon-5, Solomon-4, Josiah-3, Josiah-2, Josias-1) was born on 3 Oct 1788 in Provincetown, Mass. Reuben died of Cholera on 3 Sep 1862 at the age of 73 in Provincetown, Mass.

Capt. Reuben Cook and Elizabeth KILBURN were married before 1811. Elizabeth Kilburn, daughter of Samuel Kilburn and Hannah Unknown, was born in Aug 1787 in Provincetown, Mass. She died of consumption on 17 Sep 1856 at the age of 69 in Provincetown, Mass. Elizabeth was buried in Hamilton Cemetery, Provincetown, Mass.

Reuben Cook and Elizabeth Kilburn had the following children:

3074   i.   Lydia Brown Cook, born 24 Sep 1811, Provincetown, Mass.; married Francis SMALL, 11 Apr 1832, Provincetown, Mass.; died 15 Feb 1882, Provincetown, Mass.

       ii.   Reuben Cook was born on 2 Jun 1814 in Provincetown, Mass. He died by drowning on 19 Oct 1832 at the age of 18 in Provincetown, Mass.

       iii.  George B. Cook was born about 1816 in Provincetown, Mass.He died on 27 Jul 1825 at the age of 9 in Provincetown, Mass. George was buried in Hamilton Cemetery, Provincetown, Mass.

       iv.   Polly B. Cook was born in Aug 1822 in Provincetown, Mass. She died on 31 Oct 1838 at the age of 16 in Provincetown, Mass. She was buried in Hamilton Cemetery, Provincetown, Mass.

1486.Solomon D. Cook III (Solomon-6, Solomon-5, Solomon-4, Josiah-3, Josiah-2, Josias-1) was born on 10 Sep 1790 in Provincetown, Mass. He died of typhoid fever on 24 Jul 1868 at the age of 77 in Provincetown, Mass.

Solomon D. Cook III and Sally COOK were married on 12 Dec 1813 in Provincetown, Mass. Sally Cook, daughter of Elisha Cook and Abigail Unknown, was born on 4 May 1794 in Provincetown, Mass. She died on 12 Oct 1871 at the age of 77 in Provincetown, Mass. Slomon and Sally were second cousins.

Solomon D. Cook and Sally Cook had the following children:

3075   i.   Abigail E. "Abby or Nabby" Cook, born 17 Oct 1813, Provincetown, Mass.; married Ephraim Nickerson, 4 Dec 1833, Provincetown, Mass.; married Thomas Jacobs, 21 Aug 1859, Provincetown, Mass.; died 1896.

3076   ii.  Sally Cook, born 6 Mar 1815, Provincetown, Mass.; married Edward Cook Parker, 6 Dec 1837, Provincetown, Mass.; died 22 Aug 1869, Provincetown, Mass.

3077   iii. Mary Bryant Cook, born 4 Sep 1817, Provincetown, Mass.; married Robert Soper, 30 Nov 1837, Provincetown, Mass.

3078   iv.  Elisha Cook, born 15 Dec 1818, Provincetown, Mass.; married Sarah H. Fish, 27 Oct 1846, Provincetown, Mass.; died 1907, Provincetown, Mass.

3079    v.   Almira Cook, born 18 Sep 1820, Provincetown, Mass.; married Joshua Nickerson
             2nd, 5 Mar 1843, Provincetown, Mass.
3080    vi.  Jane Bates Cook, born 20 Nov 1822, Provincetown, Mass.; married Elisha
             Nickerson, 30 Jun 1841, Provincetown, Mass.; died 28 Jun 1843, Provincetown,
             Mass.
3081    vii. George Bryant Cook, born 23 Dec 1824, Provincetown, Mass.; married Bessie
             Unknown; died 16 Sep 1846, At sea.
3082    viii.    Rachel Willis Cook, born 1 Aug 1827, Provincetown, Mass.; married Nathaniel
             Covell Jr., 1848, Provincetown, Mass.; died 5 Mar 1889.
        ix.  Thomas Coleman Cook was born on 12 Dec 1829 in Provincetown, Mass. He died on 2
             Mar 1832 at the age of 2 in Provincetown, Mass.
3083    x.   Melissa Coleman Cook, born 7 May 1832, Provincetown, Mass.; married Robert H.
             Patton, 12 Nov 1854, Provincetown, Mass.; died 1917, Provincetown, Mass.
        xi.  Thomas Coleman Cook was born on 18 Mar 1835 in Provincetown, Mass. He died on 28
             May 1836 at the age of 1 in Provincetown, Mass.
3084    xii. David P. Cook, born 31 Mar 1837, Provincetown, Mass.; married Mary M. E. Rich,
             29 Nov 1860, Provincetown, Mass.; died 9 May 1907, Provincetown, Mass.


Solomon D. Cook III and Mary FREEMAN were married on 18 Oct 1840 in Provincetown,
Mass.


1487.Polly Cook (Solomon-6, Solomon-5, Solomon-4, Josiah-3, Josiah-2, Josias-1) was born on 4
      Sep 1792 in Provincetown, Mass. She died on 1 Aug 1821 at the age of 28 in Provincetown,
      Mass.


Polly Cook and George BRYANT were married on 10 Mar 1812 in Provincetown, Mass.


1488.Joshua Cook II (Solomon-6, Solomon-5, Solomon-4, Josiah-3, Josiah-2, Josias-1) was born on
      23 Feb 1794 in Provincetown, Mass. He died of heart disease on 26 Jan 1881 at the age of 86
      in Provincetown, Mass. He was buried in Cemetery Number Two, Old Section, Provincetown,
      Mass.


Joshua Cook II and Rebecca ATKINS were married in 1817. Rebecca Atkins, daughter of
Joseph Atkins and Ruth Nickerson, was born on 28 Sep 1797 in Provincetown, Mass. She
died on 29 Apr 1861 at the age of 63 in Provincetown, Mass. She was buried in Hamilton
Cemetery, Provincetown, Mass.


Joshua Cook and Rebecca Atkins had the following children:

2960    i.   Melvina Cook, born 12 Oct 1817, Provincetown, Mass.; married Francis
             NICKERSON, 10 Nov 1836, Provincetown, Mass.; died 11 Nov 1904, Pittsfield,

Mass.

2961  ii.  Nathaniel N. Cook, born 17 Nov 1821, Provincetown, Mass.; married Louisa COOK, 8 Oct 1843, Provincetown, Mass.; died 12 Jul 1888, Provincetown, Mass. They were 3rd cousins.

2962  iii.  Martha W. Cook, born 31 Dec 1826, Provincetown, Mass.; married Moses YOUNG, 22 Oct 1843, Provincetown, Mass.

iv.  Ann G. Cook was born on 23 Mar 1834 in Provincetown, Mass. She appeared in the census in 1850 in Provincetown, Mass.

Joshua Cook II and Mercy P. KNOWLES were married on 15 Jun 1862. Mercy P. Knowles, daughter of Samuel and Hanna Knowles, was born on 18 Mar 1814 in Eastham, Mass. She died on 6 Oct 1891 at the age of 77 in Provincetown, Mass. She was buried in Hamilton Cemetery, Provincetown, Mass.

1489. James Cook (Solomon-6, Solomon-5, Solomon-4, Josiah-3, Josiah-2, Josias-1) was born on 1 Sep 1797 in Provincetown, Mass. He died of cystitis and prostate cancer on 26 Dec 1881 at the age of 84 in Provincetown, Mass. He was buried in Hamilton Cemetery, Provincetown, Mass.

James Cook and Sally PAINE were married on 26 Dec 1819 in Provincetown, Mass. Sally Paine was born in 1799 in Provincetown, Mass. She died on 8 Apr 1827 at the age of 28 in Provincetown, Mass. She was buried in Hamilton Cemetery, Provincetown, Mass.

James Cook and Sally Paine had the following children:

3085  i.  Lucy F. Cook, born 17 Oct 1820, Orleans, Barnstable, Mass.; married Abija GILL Jr., 1 Sep 1845, Provincetown, Mass.

ii.  Rachel W. Cook was born on 25 Jul 1821 in Provincetown, Mass. She died on 11 Jul 1823 in Provincetown, Mass. She was buried in Hamilton Cemetery, Provincetown, Mass.

3086  iii.  Coleman Cook, born 25 Aug 1822, Provincetown, Mass.; married Bethia R. MORGAN; married Margery (Wiley) HINKS, 28 Aug 1862, Provincetown, Mass.

iv.  Rachel W. Cook was born in 1826 in Provincetown, Mass. She died in 1826.

James Cook and Anna HINKS were married on 29 Jan 1828 in Provincetown, Mass. Anna Hinks, daughter of Elisha and Temperance Hinks, was born on 20 Jan 1797. She died on 15 Sep 1885 at the age of 88 in Provincetown, Mass. She was buried in Hamilton Cemetery, Provincetown, Mass.

James Cook and Anna Hinks had the following children:

7.141

i.  James Cook was born on 17 Jan 1829 in Provincetown, Mass. He died on 27 Feb 1829 in Provincetown, Mass. He was buried in Hamilton Cemetery, Provincetown, Mass.

ii.  James F. Cook was born on 20 Oct 1830 in Provincetown, Mass. He died on 16 Sep 1846 at the age of 15 at sea. He was buried in Hamilton Cemetery, Provincetown, Mass.

iii.  Reuben Cook was born on 9 Oct 1832 in Provincetown, Mass.

iv.  Sally P. Cook was born on 14 Oct 1835 in Provincetown, Mass.

3087  v.  Elisha Hinks Cook, born 28 May 1838, Provincetown, Mass.; married Eliza S. SWIFT, 17 Dec 1863, Provincetown, Mass.; died 1909, Provincetown, Mass.

1490.Elisha Cook II (Solomon-6, Solomon-5, Solomon-4, Josiah-3, Josiah-2, Josias-1) was born on 11 Jul 1799 in Provincetown, Mass. He died on 23 Mar 1874 at the age of 74 in Provincetown, Mass. He was buried in Hamilton Cemetery, Provincetown, Mass.

Elisha Cook II and Almira JONES were married on 23 Nov 1820 in Provincetown, Mass. Almira Jones was born on 27 Jun 1804 in Provincetown, Mass. She died of consumption on 9 Mar 1848 at the age of 43 in Provincetown, Mass.

Elisha Cook and Almira Jones had the following children:

3088  i.  Laura Ann Cook, born 24 Sep 1822, Provincetown, Mass.; married Joshua DYER, 10 Mar 1840, Provincetown, Mass.; died 25 Sep 1843, Provincetown, Mass.

ii.  Thomas Stall Cook was born on 1 Oct 1824 in Provincetown, Mass. He died on 22 Jul 1825. He was buried in Hamilton Cemetery, Provincetown, Mass.

3089  iii.  Belinda N. Cook (Twin), born 24 Sep 1826, Provincetown, Mass.; married John PETTINGILL, 3 Dec 1843, Provincetown, Mass.; died Sep 1857 at sea.

iv.  Adeline Cook (Twin) was born on 24 Sep 1826 in Provincetown, Mass. She died on 23 Jul 1828 in Provincetown, Mass. She was buried in Cemetery Number Two, Old Section, Provincetown, Mass.

3090  v.  Susan F. Cook, born 27 Dec 1833, Provincetown, Mass.; married John W. IVERSON, 2 Dec 1849, Provincetown, Mass.

Elisha Cook II and Ann UNKNOWN were married after 1838 in Provincetown, Mass. Ann was born on 1 Sep 1808 in Truro, Mass. She died on 25 Sep 1886 at the age of 78 in Provincetown, Mass. She was buried in Hamilton Cemetery, Provincetown, Mass.

Elisha Cook and Ann Unknown had the following children:

i.  Sarah (Sally) Ann Cook was born in Oct 1843 in Provincetown, Mass. She died of dysentary on 4 Sep 1845 in Provincetown, Mass. She was buried in Hamilton Cemetery, Provincetown, Mass.

ii. Adiline Cook was born in 1852 in Provincetown, Mass. She died in 1929 at the age of 77 in Provincetown, Mass. She was buried in Cemetery Number Two, Old Section, Provincetown, Mass.

iii. Ephraim Cook was born on 23 Aug 1855 in Provincetown, Mass.

1491. Hannah Cook (Solomon-6, Solomon-5, Solomon-4, Josiah-3, Josiah-2, Josias-1) was born on 30 Jul 1801 in Provincetown, Mass.

Hannah Cook and John ATKINS were married on 12 Mar 1819 in Provincetown, Mass. John Atkins, son of Silas Atkins and Bethiah Nickerson, was born on 2 Sep 1797 in Truro, Mass. He died on 15 Sep 1857 at the age of 60 in Provincetown, Mass.

John Atkins and Hannah Cook had the following children:

i. Lavina Atkins was born on 25 Aug 1819 in Provincetown, Mass.

ii. Susan Cook Atkins, born 25 Aug 1822, Provincetown, Mass.; married Nehemiah NICKERSON.

iii. Hannah Cook Atkins, born 30 Jun 1825, Provincetown, Mass.; married Paul WHEELER; died 30 Aug 1878, Provincetown, Mass.

iv. Rawlins Thomas Atkins was born on 12 May 1827 in Provincetown, Mass. He died on 14 Apr 1832 at the age of 4 in Provincetown, Mass.

v. Sally Ann Atkins was born on 25 Nov 1829 in Provincetown, Mass. She died on 29 Apr 1832 at the age of 2 in Provincetown, Mass.

vi. Rawlins Thomas Atkins was born on 23 Feb 1833 in Provincetown, Mass. He died on 21 Sep 1834 at the age of 1 in Provincetown, Mass.

vii. Lt. Rawlins Thomas Atkins was born in Apr 1835 in Provincetown, Mass. He served in the military as a corporal in Company G, 1st Infantry Regiment during the civil war on 23 May 1861 in State of Massachusetts. He appeared in the census in 1920 in Chelsea Town, Me. He died after 1920 at the age of 85.

viii. Lucena Wilder Atkins was born on 3 Sep 1837 in Provincetown, Mass. She died on 15 Jun 1851 at the age of 13 in Provincetown, Mass.

ix. John Edwin Atkins was born on 22 Jan 1842 in Provincetown, Mass. He died on 18 Feb 1843 in Provincetown, Mass.

x. Lucy (Twin) Atkins was born on 17 Jun 1844 in Provincetown, Mass. She died on 27 Jun 1844.

xi. John (Twin) Atkins was born on 17 Jun 1844 in Provincetown, Mass. He died on 28 Sep 1844.

1492. Coleman Cook (Solomon-6, Solomon-5, Solomon-4, Josiah-3, Josiah-2, Josias-1) was born in 1803 in Provincetown, Mass.

7.143

Coleman Cook and Susan ELDRIDGE were married in 1825.

1493. Susanna Cook (Solomon-6, Solomon-5, Solomon-4, Josiah-3, Josiah-2, Josias-1) was born on 6 Jun 1805 in Provincetown, Mass.

Susanna Cook and James WHORF were married on 19 Sep 1825 in Provincetown, Mass. James Whorf, son of John Whorf and Rebecca Rider, was born on 26 Aug 1804 in Provincetown, Mass. He died on 13 Feb 1871 at the age of 66 in Boston, Mass.

James Whorf and Susanna Cook had the following children:

i. Aurilla Whorf was born on 10 Aug 1826. She died on 3 Sep 1826.
ii. Sarah D. Whorf was born on 12 Sep 1827. She died on 9 Sep 1838 at the age of 10.
iii. Caleb Francis Whorf, born 28 Feb 1830, Provincetown, Mass.; married Aurilla RUSSELL; died 12 Jan 1855, Provincetown, Mass.
iv. John Abbott Whorf, born 16 Sep 1832, Provincetown, Mass.; married Susan BROOKS. They had 7 children.
v. Tilton Whorf was born on 14 Sep 1834. He died on 2 Nov 1834.
vi. Mary (Polly) Whorf, born 8 May 1836, Provincetown, Mass.; married William SLACK.
vii. Sarah F. Whorf, born 16 Mar 1840, Provincetown, Mass.; married William H. LAWRENCE, bef 1858; died 4 Apr 1891, Fitchburg, Mass. They had 4 children.
viii. Susan Whorf was born on 24 Aug 1842 in Provincetown, Mass. She died in about 1842.
ix. Susan Whorf was born on 30 Jun 1844.
x. James A. Whorf was born on 30 Jul 1847 in Provincetown, Mass.

1494. Capt. Jacob Cook (Joshua-6, Solomon-5, Solomon-4, Josiah-3, Josiah-2, Josias-1) was born on 9 Sep 1797 in Provincetown, Mass. He died on 25 Dec 1871 at the age of 74 in Provincetown, Mass. He was buried in Hamilton Cemetery, Provincetown, Mass.

Capt. Jacob Cook and Mary Atkins were married on 12 Feb 1820 in Truro, Mass. They appeared in the census in 1830 in Provincetown, Mass. Mary Atkins was born in Truro, Mass.

Jacob Cook and Mary Atkins had the following children:

i. Mary G. Cook was born on 8 Aug 1834 in Provincetown, Mass. She died on 22 Jul 1836 in Provincetown, Mass. She was buried in Hamilton Cemetery, Provincetown, Mass.
3095 ii. Melville W. Cook, born 1835; married Ellen Selina NICKERSON, 22 Jun 1862, Provincetown, Mass.; died 27 Jan 1867, Provincetown, Mass.
iii. Virginia Cook was born in Jan 1840 in Provincetown, Mass. She died on 3 Aug 1851 at the age of 11 in Provincetown, Mass. She was buried in Hamilton Cemetery,

Provincetown, Mass.

1495.Joshua Cook II (Joshua-6, Solomon-5, Solomon-4, Josiah-3, Josiah-2, Josias-1) was born on
25 Aug 1799 in Provincetown, Mass. He died of paralysis (6 years), on 10 Mar 1867 at the
age of 67 in Provincetown, Mass.

Joshua Cook II and Joanna HIGGINS were married on 2 Jan 1823 in Provincetown, Mass.
Joanna Higgins was born on 12 Sep 1803 in Provincetown, Mass. She died of cancer on 30
Aug 1865 at the age of 61 in Provincetown, Mass.

Joshua Cook and Joanna Higgins had the following children:

    3096   i.    Apphia D. Cook, born 12 Jan 1825, Provincetown, Mass.; married Hatsuld
              FREEMAN Jr., 31 Dec 1848, Provincetown, Mass.
          ii.   Eliza Paine Cook was born on 13 Oct 1828 in Provincetown, Mass. She died on 4 Aug
              1830 in Provincetown, Mass. She was buried in Cemetery Number Two, Old Section,
              Provincetown, Mass.
        iii. Joshua Cook was born on 7 Jan 1834 in Provincetown, Mass. He died on 20 Feb 1836.
    3097   iv. James Bradford Cook, born 14 May 1840, Provincetown, Mass.; married Almena
              Ellen HOPKINS, 7 Jul 1868, Provincetown, Mass.; died 17 May 1901,
              Provincetown, Mass.
    3098   v.   Joshua Cook U.S.N., born 7 Jan 1843, Provincetown, Mass.; married Effie L.
              HOPKINS, 2 Sep 1867, Provincetown, Mass.; died 1920.

1496.Elizabeth Cook (Joshua-6, Solomon-5, Solomon-4, Josiah-3, Josiah-2, Josias-1) was born on
15 Sep 1801 in Provincetown, Mass. She died on 17 Sep 1828 at the age of 27 in
Provincetown, Mass.  She was buried in Provincetown Cemetery Number Two.

Elizabeth Cook and Lemuel PAINE had marriage banns published on 29 Jan 1820 in Truro,
Mass. They were married on 9 Mar 1820 in Provincetown, Mass. Lemuel Paine, son of
Elkanah Paine and Esther Harding, was born on 12 Jan 1797 in Truro, Mass. He died on 1
Sep 1876 at the age of 79 in Provincetown, Mass.

Lemuel Paine and Elizabeth Cook had the following children:

        i.   Harvy Cook Paine was born in 1822 in Provincetown, Mass. He died on 27 Sep 1826. He
            was buried in Provincetown Cemetery Number Two.
        ii.  A son was born in Sep 1828. He died in Sep 1828.

1497.Richard Atkins Cook (Joshua-6, Solomon-5, Solomon-4, Josiah-3, Josiah-2, Josias-1) was born
on 30 Jun 1804 in Provincetown, Mass. He died of "Palsy"on 25 Jun 1862 at the age of 57 in

Provincetown, Mass. He was buried in Hamilton Cemetery, Provincetown, Mass.

Richard Atkins Cook and Martha ATKINS were married on 10 Jan 1828 in Provincetown, Mass. Martha Atkins was born on 21 Dec 1805. She died of childbirth on 16 Jul 1845 at the age of 39 in Provincetown, Mass. She was buried in Hamilton Cemetery, Provincetown, Mass.

Richard Atkins Cook and Martha Atkins had the following children:

     i.   Franklin Willis Cook was born on 22 Oct 1828 in Provincetown, Mass. He died on 8 Mar 1830. He was buried in Hamilton Cemetery, Provincetown, Mass.

3099  ii.  Martha Willis Cook, born 10 Jul 1830, Provincetown, Mass.; married Joseph R. ATKINS, 4 Nov 1849, Provincetown, Mass.; died 1903, Provincetown, Mass.

3100  iii.  Franklin W. "Francis" Cook, born 10 Oct 1831, Provincetown, Mass.; married Ellen S. HOPKINS, 2 Oct 1854, Provincetown, Mass.; died 10 Apr 1856, Truro, Mass.

    iv.  Lauretta A. Cook was born on 23 Nov 1832 in Provincetown, Mass. She died on 28 Aug 1834. She was buried in Hamilton Cemetery, Provincetown, Mass.

    v.  Lauretta A. Cook was born on 18 Oct 1834 in Provincetown, Mass. She died on 14 Mar 1875 at the age of 40 in Boston, Mass. She was buried in Hamilton Cemetery, Provincetown, Mass.

    vi.  Eliza W. Cook was born on 28 Jan 1836 in Provincetown, Mass. She died in 1920 at the age of 84 in Provincetown, Mass. She was buried in Gifford Cemetery, Provincetown, Mass.

    vii.  Lemuel P. Cook was born on 18 Aug 1838 in Provincetown, Mass.

3101  viii.  Roxanna A. "Anna" Cook, born 8 May 1842, Provincetown, Mass.; married Rufus EMERY, 20 Dec 1866, Provincetown, Mass.

    ix.  Phebe C. W. Cook was born on 9 Jul 1845 in Provincetown, Mass. She died of dysentary on 11 Sep 1845. She was buried in Cemetery Number Two, Old Section, Provincetown, Mass.

Richard Atkins Cook and Betsy (Collins) LOMBARD were married on 13 Sep 1846. Betsy (Collins) Lombard, daughter of Thomas and Elizabeth Lombard, was born in 1816 in Provincetown, Mass.

Richard Atkins Cook and Betsy (Collins) Lombard had the following child:

    i.  Phebe A. Cook was born on 4 Mar 1849 in Provincetown, Mass.

1498.Harvey Cook (Joshua-6, Solomon-5, Solomon-4, Josiah-3, Josiah-2, Josias-1) was born on 11 Sep 1806 in Provincetown, Mass.

Harvey Cook and Jedediah A. SMITH were married on 13 Jul 1839 in Provincetown, Mass. Jedediah A. Smith, daughter of Richard and Phebe Smith, was born in 1817 in Provincetown, Mass. She died on 23 Mar 1840 at the age of 23 in Provincetown, Mass. She was buried in Hamilton Cemetery, Provincetown, Mass.

Harvey Cook and Hannah G. ELLINGOOD were married. Hannah G. Ellingood, daughter of Ebenezer Ellingood, was born in 1825 in Beverly, Mass. She died of disease of the bowels on 29 Mar 1850 at the age of 25 in Provincetown, Mass. She was buried in Beverly, Mass.

Harvey Cook and Hannah G. Ellingood had the following child:

    i.   Hannah G. Cook was born in 1850 in Provincetown, Mass.

Harvey Cook and Susan P. UNKNOWN were married. Susan P. Unknown was born in Saco, York, Me.

Harvey Cook and Susan P. Unknown had the following children:

    i.   A daughter Cook was born on 3 Nov 1853 in Provincetown, Mass.
    ii.  Susan C. Cook was born in 1855 in Provincetown, Mass.

1499. Roxana Cook (Joshua-6, Solomon-5, Solomon-4, Josiah-3, Josiah-2, Josias-1) was born on 12 Dec 1808 in Provincetown, Mass. She died on 20 Sep 1888 at the age of 79 in Provincetown, Mass.  She was buried in Gifford Cemetery, Provincetown, Mass.

Roxana Cook and Reuben ATKINS were married on 18 Dec 1826 in Provincetown, Mass. Reuben Atkins, son of Joseph Atkins and Ruth Nickerson, was born on 24 Nov 1808 in Provincetown, Mass. He died on 24 Sep 1883 at the age of 74 in Provincetown, Mass.

Reuben Atkins and Roxana Cook had the following children:

  2965   i.   Maria F. Atkins, born 1829, Provincetown, Mass.; married James FULLER.
  2966   ii.  Eliza Cook Atkins, born 1831, Provincetown, Mass.; married Richard BAXTER; died 1909.
  2967   iii. Mary Gray Atkins, born 1837, Provincetown, Mass.; married Malcolm RAMSEY.

1500. Maria Cook (Joshua-6, Solomon-5, Solomon-4, Josiah-3, Josiah-2, Josias-1) was born on 13 Apr 1812 or 30 Apr 1812 in Provincetown, Mass. She died on 23 Dec 1888 at the age of 76 in Provincetown, Mass.

Maria Cook and Samuel COOK Jr. were married on 19 Jan 1832 in Provincetown, Mass.

Samuel Cook Jr., son of Samuel Cook and Tamsey (Tamsin) Brown, was born on 21 Aug 1806 in Provincetown, Mass. He died on 14 Feb 1841 at the age of 34 in Provincetown, Mass. In 1847 Samuel was a ship owner.

Samuel Cook and Maria Cook had the following children:

    3102   i.   Harvey Cook, born 28 Oct 1832, Provincetown, Mass.; married Susan UNKNOWN; died 27 May 1872, Provincetown, Mass.

            ii.  Helen Maria Cook was born on 12 Feb 1835 in Provincetown, Mass.

            iii. Jedidah A. Cook was born on 3 Aug 1840 in Provincetown, Mass.

            iv. Jedediah Cook was born in 1842 in Provincetown, Mass.

            v.  Alfred Cook died in 1840 in Provincetown, Mass.

1509. Sally A. Cook (Barnabas-6, Barnabas-5, Solomon-4, Josiah-3, Josiah-2, Josias-1) was born on 14 Jun 1820 in Truro, Mass. She died before 1850 at the age of 30.

Sally A. Cook and Isaac R. AYDELOT were married on 29 Nov 1837 in Truro, Mass. Isaac R. Aydelot appeared in the census in 1850 in Truro, Mass. In 1850 he was a mariner. He was born in Truro, Mass.

Isaac R. Aydelot and Sally A. Cook had the following children:

            i.   Sally A. Aydelot was born about 1840.

            ii.  Sarah Aydelot was born in 1842. She died before 1850 at the age of 8.

            iii. Isaac Aydelot was born about 1844.

1510. Dorcas B. Cook (Barnabas-6, Barnabas-5, Solomon-4, Josiah-3, Josiah-2, Josias-1) was born on 21 Nov 1823 in Truro, Mass.

Dorcas B. Cook and John DOROTHY were married on 5 Jan 1841 in Truro, Mass. John Dorothy was born in Truro, Mass.

1511. Anna Cook (Barnabas-6, Barnabas-5, Solomon-4, Josiah-3, Josiah-2, Josias-1) was born on 6 Apr 1825 in Truro, Mass.

Anna Cook and Joshua RICH were married on 26 Oct 1844 in Truro, Mass. They moved to Salem, Mass. before 1860. Joshua Rich, son of Mulford Rich, was born on 6 Apr 1825 in Truro, Mass.

Joshua Rich and Anna Cook had the following children:

i.  John D. Rich was born in 1847 in Provincetown, Mass.
ii.  Joshua A. Rich was born in 1848 in Provincetown, Mass.
iii.  James P. Rich was born in 1851.
iv.  Nathan K. Rich was born in 1854.
v.  Adam Rich was born in 1856. He died before 1870 at the age of 14.

1512.Harriet G. Cook (Barnabas-6, Barnabas-5, Solomon-4, Josiah-3, Josiah-2, Josias-1) was born
on 22 Oct 1828 in Truro, Mass.

Harriet G. Cook and Daniel LOMBARD were married on 6 Jun 1847 in Truro, Mass. Daniel
Lombard was born in 1825 in Truro, Mass.

Daniel Lombard and Harriet G. Cook had the following child:

i.  A.D. Lombard was born in May 1850 in Truro, Mass.

1513.Barnabas Cook (Barnabas-6, Barnabas-5, Solomon-4, Josiah-3, Josiah-2, Josias-1) was born
on 31 Dec 1830 in Truro, Mass. In 1850 he was a mariner.

Barnabas Cook and Rebecca (Pierce) COOK were married on 2 Dec 1851 in Wellfleet,
Mass.   Rebecca (Pierce) Cook was the daughter of Thomas Cook.

1514.Sally Cook (Elisha-6, Elisha-5, Solomon-4, Josiah-3, Josiah-2, Josias-1) was born on 4 May
1794 in Provincetown, Mass. She died on 12 Oct 1871 at the age of 77 in Provincetown,
Mass.  gravestone

Sally Cook and Solomon D. COOK III were married on 12 Dec 1813 in Provincetown,
Mass. Solomon D. Cook III, son of Solomon Cook and Susanna Bates, was born on 10 Sep
1790 in Provincetown, Mass. He died of typhoid fever on 24 Jul 1868 at the age of 77 in
Provincetown, Mass. See #1486 for children.

1515.Elisha Cook 2nd (Elisha-6, Elisha-5, Solomon-4, Josiah-3, Josiah-2, Josias-1) was born on 1
Aug 1797 in Provincetown, Mass..

Elisha Cook 2nd and Sally HILLYARD were married on 30 Dec 1824 in Provincetown,
Mass. Sally Hillyard, daughter of Thomas and Sally Hilliard, was born in 1806 in
Provincetown, Mass. She died on 7 Jul 1838 at the age of 32 in Provincetown, Mass.

Elisha Cook and Sally Hillyard had the following children:

i.  Adeline Cook was born in 1826 in Provincetown, Mass. She died on 23 Jul 1828. She was buried in Cemetery Number Two, Old Section, Provincetown, Mass.

ii. Solomon Thomas Cook was born on 11 Jan 1830 in Provincetown, Mass. He died by drowning on 29 Sep 1858 at the age of 28 in Provincetown, Mass. He was buried in Hamilton Cemetery, Provincctown, Mass.

Elisha Cook 2nd and Rebecca COOK were married on 24 Mar 1850 in Provincetown, Mass. Rebecca Cook, daughter of Isaac Cook and Tabitha Smith, was born on 29 Aug 1805 in Provincetown, Mass. She died on 5 Sep 1896 at the age of 91 in Provincetown, Mass. She was buried in Winthrop Street Cemetery, Provincetown, Mass.

1516.Abigail Cook (Elisha-6, Elisha-5, Solomon-4, Josiah-3, Josiah-2, Josias-1) was born on 2 Jul 1806 in Provincetown, Mass.

Abigail Cook and Taylor SMALL were married.

1517.Polly Cook (Elisha-6, Elisha-5, Solomon-4, Josiah-3, Josiah-2, Josias-1) was born on 8 Jun 1815 in Provincetown, Mass. She died on 14 Jun 1842 at the age of 27 in Provincetown, Mass. She was buried in Cemetery Number Two, Provincetown, Mass.

Polly Cook and Hon. Joseph Proper JOHNSON were married. Hon. Joseph Proper Johnson was born in 1814 in Essex, Conn. He died in 1891 at the age of 77.

Joseph Proper Johnson and Polly Cook had the following children:

i. Isaac Thomas Johnson (Twin) was born in 1835 in Provincetown, Mass. He died in 1836.
ii. Timothy Parker Johnson (Twin) was born in 1835 in Provincetown, Mass. He died in 1836.
iii. Isaac Thomas Johnson was born in 1837 in Provincetown, Mass. He died in 1837.
iv. Lemuel Cook Johnson was born in 1840 in Provincetown, Mass. He died in 1841.
v. Polly Cook Johnson was born in 1843 in Provincetown, Mass. She died in 1843.

1518.Capt. Lemuel "Captain Lem" Cook (David A.-6, Elisha-5, Solomon-4, Josiah-3, Josiah-2, Josias-1) was born on 21 Sep 1804 in Provincetown, Mass. In 1845 he was a ship owner in Provincetown, Mass. He died on 7 May 1869 at the age of 64 in Provincetown, Mass. Captain Lem was buried in Hamilton Cemetery, Provincetown, Mass.

Capt. Lemuel "Captain Lem" Cook and Belinda NICKERSON were married on 11 Apr 1827 in Provincetown, Mass. Belinda Nickerson, daughter of Nathaniel Nickerson and Linda Young, was born on 2 Feb 1806 in Provincetown, Mass. She died of "disability" on 31 May 1889 at the age of 83 in Provincetown, Mass. She was buried in Hamilton Cemetery, Provincetown, Mass.

Lemuel Cook and Belinda Nickerson had the following children:

    3112   i.   Reuben Francis Cook, born 18 Sep 1828, Provincetown, Mass.; married Louisa TYLER, 27 Nov 1855, Boston, Suffolk, Mass.; married Anna B. DAVIS, 20 Mar 1876, Norwich, Conn.; died 21 Apr 1896, Cleveland, Oh.

           ii.  Lemuel F. Cook was born on 4 Aug 1830 in Provincetown, Mass. He died on 24 Aug 1830. He was buried in Cemetery Number Two, Old Section, Provincetown, Mass.

          iii.  Apphia L. Cook was born on 17 Sep 1831 in Provincetown, Mass. She died on 21 Jun 1835. She was buried in Hamilton Cemetery, Provincetown, Mass.

          iv.  Lemuel F. Cook was born on 30 Mar 1834 in Provincetown, Mass. He died on 2 Jan 1836. He was buried in Hamilton Cemetery, Provincetown, Mass.

          v.  Eliza A. Cook was born on 9 Mar 1839 in Provincetown, Mass. She died on 23 Oct 1927 at the age of 88 in Provincetown, Mass. Eliza was a schoolteacher. She was buried in Winthrop Street Cemetery, Provincetown, Mass.

          vi.  Apphia L. Cook was born on 4 May 1840 in Provincetown, Mass. She died on 7 Jul 1842.

    3113   vii. Lucia N. Cook, born 8 Dec 1844, Provincetown, Mass.; married John Henry LOVERING, 20 Jan 1875, Provincetown, Mass.

1519.David Cook, Jr. (David A.-6, Elisha-5, Solomon-4, Josiah-3, Josiah-2, Josias-1) was born on 15 Nov 1808 in Provincetown, Mass. He died in 1839 at the age of 31 at sea.

David Cook, Jr. and Louisa ATKINS were married on 4 Apr 1831 in Provincetown, Mass. Louisa Atkins, daughter of Joseph Atkins and Ruth Nickerson, was born on 27 Oct 1804 in Provincetown, Mass.

David Cook and Louisa Atkins had the following children:

    2964   i.   Louisa R. Cook, born 9 Aug 1831, Provincetown, Mass.; married Benjamin Fessenden FREEMAN, 5 Jun 1854, Provincetown, Mass.; died 12 Jan 1859, Provincetown, Mass.

          ii.  A son was born and died in 1833.

          iii.  Salome A. Cook was born on 16 Jul 1835 in Provincetown, Mass. Salome died of consumption on 1 Nov 1856 at the age of 21 in Provincetown, Mass. She was buried in Hamilton Cemetery, Provincetown, Mass.

1520.Elizabeth Paine Cook (David A.-6, Elisha-5, Solomon-4, Josiah-3, Josiah-2, Josias-1) was born on 27 Nov 1806 in Provincetown, Mass. She died on 8 Mar 1893 at the age of 86 in Barnstable County, Mass. She was buried in Hamilton Cemetery, Provincetown, Mass.

Elizabeth Paine Cook and Enoch "Enos" NICKERSON were married on 19 Dec 1827 in

Provincetown, Mass. Enoch "Enos" Nickerson, son of Allen Nickerson and Polly Collins, was born on 11 Aug 1805 in Provincetown, Mass. He was buried in Hamilton Cemetery, Provincetown, Mass. He was a mariner.

Enoch Nickerson and Elizabeth Paine Cook had the following children:

    i.   Lydia Susan Nickerson, born 4 Jul 1828, Provincetown, Mass.; married Frances B. TUCK, 13 Nov 1849, Provincetown, Mass.; died 30 Apr 1905, Provincetown, Mass.

    ii.  Elvira G. Nickerson, born 21 Sep 1832, Provincetown, Mass.; married Charles D. HALLETT, 5 Feb 1852, Provincetown, Mass.; died 1915, Barnstable County, Mass.

    iii. Richard Franklin Nickerson was born on 4 Jun 1836 in Provincetown, Mass. He died on 21 Sep 1839. He was buried in Hamilton Cemetery, Provincetown, Mass.

    iv. Rebecca Allen Nickerson, born 22 Jun 1838, Provincetown, Mass.; married John T. SMALL, 7 Apr 1870, Provincetown, Mass. They had 2 children.

1521. Mary "Polly" Cook (James-6, John-5, Solomon-4, Josiah-3, Josiah-2, Josias-1) was born in 1801 in Provincetown, Mass. She died in 1880 at the age of 79 in State of Maine.

Mary "Polly" Cook and Henry PARTRIDGE were married about 1817. Henry Partridge was the son of Daniel Partridge and Sarah Ames.

1522. Rebecca Cook (Isaac-6, John-5, Solomon-4, Josiah-3, Josiah-2, Josias-1) was born on 29 Aug 1805 in Provincetown, Mass. She died on 5 Sep 1896 at the age of 91 in Provincetown, Mass. She was buried in Winthrop Street Cemetery, Provincetown, Mass.

Rebecca Cook and Samuel Parker BROOKS were married. Samuel Parker Brooks died in 1834 in Provincetown, Mass.

Samuel Parker Brooks and Rebecca Cook had the following child:

    i.   Samuel Parker Brooks was born in 1833 in Provincetown, Mass.

Rebecca Cook and Charles REED were married on 15 Mar 1836 in Provincetown, Mass. Charles Reed died in Apr 1832 at sea.

Charles Reed and Rebecca Cook had the following child:

    i.   Lyria R. Reed was born in 1837 in Provincetown, Mass.

Rebecca Cook and Elisha COOK 2nd were married on 24 Mar 1850 in Provincetown, Mass. Elisha Cook 2nd, son of Elisha Cook and Abigail UNKNOWN, was born on 1 Aug 1797 in

Provincetown, Mass.  Rebecca and Elisha were second cousins.

1523. Capt. Isaac Cook Jr. (Isaac-6, John-5, Solomon-4, Josiah-3, Josiah-2, Josias-1) was born on 7
Oct 1809 in Provincetown, Mass. He died of fever on 30 Apr 1851 at the age of 41 in
Provincetown, Mass. Isaac was buried in Winthrop Street Cemetery, Provincetown, Mass.

Capt. Isaac Cook Jr. and Phebe NICKERSON were married on 10 Oct 1831 in
Provincetown, Mass. Phebe Nickerson, daughter of Elisha Nickerson and Bethia Atkins, was
born on 16 Dec 1811 in Provincetown, Mass. She died on 9 Jul 1868 at the age of 56 in
Somerville, Mass.   Phebe was buried in Winthrop Street Cemetery, Provincetown, Mass.

Isaac Cook and Phebe Nickerson had the following children:

   i.   Isaac A. Cook was born on 16 Sep 1831 in Provincetown, Mass. He died on 31 Mar
        1832. He was buried in Winthrop Street Cemetery, Provincetown, Mass.
   ii.  Phebe L. N. Cook was born on 29 Aug 1834 in Provincetown, Mass. She died on 17 Feb
        1836.  She was buried in Winthrop Street Cemetery, Provincetown, Mass.
3117 iii. Isaac F. Cook, born 18 Aug 1838, Provincetown, Mass.; married Jane DELANO,
        1864, Provincetown, Mass.
   iv.  A child was born in 1840 in Provincetown, Mass. It died on 11 Aug. and was buried in
        Winthrop Street Cemetery, Provincetown, Mass.
   v.   Atkins N. Cook was born on 11 Mar 1842 in Provincetown, Mass. He died on 9 Jul 1936
        at the age of 94 in Provincetown, Mass.  He was buried in Winthrop Street Cemetery,
        Provincetown, Mass.
   vi.  Augustus D. Cook was born on 4 Nov 1844 in Provincetown, Mass.
   vii. Frances E. Cook was born on 14 Oct 1846 in Provincetown, Mass.
   viii.   Frances E Cook was born in 1847 in Provincetown, Mass. She died on 14 Apr 1849
        at the age of 2 in Provincetown, Mass. She was buried in Winthrop Street
        Cemetery, Provincetown, Mass.

1524. Myrick S. Cook (Isaac-6, John-5, Solomon-4, Josiah-3, Josiah-2, Josias-1) was born on 15
Dec 1813 in Provincetown, Mass. He died on 11 Jun 1877 at the age of 63 in Provincetown,
Mass. He was a mariner.

Myrick S. Cook and Elizabeth E. BURT were married on 26 Apr 1840 in Provincetown,
Mass. Elizabeth E. Burt, daughter of John C. Burt and Elizabeth S. Unknown, was born on 1
May 1817 in Boston, Suffolk, Mass. She died of apoplexy on 11 Sep 1889 at the age of 72 in
Provincetown, Mass.

Myrick S. Cook and Elizabeth E. Burt had the following children:

i.   John C. Cook was born on 31 May 1841 in Provincetown, Mass. He died on 23 Jun 1842 in Provincetown, Mass.
ii.  Edward Burt Cook was born on 9 Oct 1844 in Provincetown, Mass. He died on 11 Jul 1868 at the age of 23 at sea.  He was buried in Cemetery Number Two, Old Section, Provincetown, Mass.
iii. A son was born in 1853 in Provincetown, Mass.
iv.  Charles A. Cook was born on 31 Dec 1854 in Provincetown, Mass. He died of a bowel inflammation on 3 Oct 1861 at the age of 6 in Provincetown, Mass.
v.   A son was born on 26 Nov 1856 in Provincetown, Mass.

1534.Josiah Cook (John-6, John-5, Solomon-4, Josiah-3, Josiah-2, Josias-1) was born on 31 Jul 1809 in Provincetown, Mass. He died of diabetes on 6 Apr 1874 at the age of 64 in Provincetown, Mass.

Josiah Cook and Caroline KENT were married on 10 Jul 1842 in Provincetown, Mass. Caroline Kent, daughter of William Kent and Sarah , was born in Feb 1814 in Marshfield, Mass. She died of liver disease on 8 Jul 1869 at the age of 55 in Provincetown, Mass.

Josiah Cook and Caroline Kent had the following children:

3119   i.   James E. Cook, born 1840, Provincetown, Mass.; married Abigail C. CASE, 21 Sep 1863, Provincetown, Mass.; died bef 1876, Provincetown, Mass.
       ii.  Caroline W. Cook was born on 10 Apr 1843 in Provincetown, Mass. She died of palsy on 25 Aug 1857 at the age of 14 in Provincetown, Mass. She was buried in Hamilton Cemetery, Provincetown, Mass.
       iii. Josiah W. Cook was born on 11 Sep 1844 in Provincetown, Mass.
       iv.  A daughter Cook was born on 20 Mar 1846 in Provincetown, Mass. She died on 25 Mar 1846.
       v.   A boy Cook was born on 15 May 1848 in Provincetown, Mass. He died on 27 May 1848.
       vi.  Miles H. Cook was born on 1 Jan 1850 in Provincetown, Mass. He died of consumption on 11 Sep 1850.
3120   vii. Wallace J. Cook, born 3 Nov 1851, Provincetown, Mass.; married Susie T. MAYO, 27 Sep 1872, Provincetown, Mass.
3121   viii. William W. Cook, born 1852, Provincetown, Mass.; married Annie F. SNOW, 30 Nov 1876, Provincetown, Mass.
       ix.  Clarissa Cook was born on 1 Jul 1853 in Provincetown, Mass. She died of dropsy on the brain on 20 May 1854.

1535.Desire B. Cook (John-6, John-5, Solomon-4, Josiah-3, Josiah-2, Josias-1) was born on 1 Dec 1811 in Provincetown, Mass.

Desire B. Cook and John Young JACOBS were married. John Young Jacobs was the son of Justin Bradford Jacobs and Lydia Young.

John Young Jacobs and Desire B. Cook had the following children:

  3122   i.   Everett Sargent Jacobs, born 7 May 1845, w; married Annette Eliza NEWCOMB, 4 Oct 1899, w; died 7 Dec 1915, w.
  3123   ii.  Lydia Young Jacobs, married John BARNARD.

1536.Capt. John J. Cook (John-6, John-5, Solomon-4, Josiah-3, Josiah-2, Josias-1) was born on 22 Mar 1818 in Provincetown, Mass. He died in 1907 at the age of 89 in Provincetown, Mass. He was buried in Hamilton Cemetery, Provincetown, Mass.

   Capt. John J. Cook and Elizabeth S. TAYLOR were married before 1849. Elizabeth S. Taylor, daughter of William Taylor and Eliza S. Kent, was born in 1826 in Marshfield, Mass. She died in 1911 at the age of 85.

John J. Cook and Elizabeth S. Taylor had the following children:

      i.    Richard W. Cook was born in 1849. He died in 1924 at the age of 75.
      ii.   Martha E. Cook was born on 15 Jan 1853 in Provincetown, Mass. She died of scarlet fever on 19 Apr 1857 at the age of 4 in Provincetown, Mass.   She was buried in Marshfield, Mass.
  3124  iii.  Emma B. "Emmie" Cook, born 12 Jul 1856, Provincetown, Mass.; married Charles Henry HOLBROOK, 7 May 1884, Provincetown, Mass.
  3125  iv.   Frederick Willis Cook, born 24 Oct 1858, Provincetown, Mass.; married Addie UNKNOWN; died 1906.
      v.    John J. Cook was born on 23 May 1863 in Provincetown, Mass. He died of Scarlet Fever on 18 Mar 1864 in Provincetown, Mass.
      vi.   Elizabeth K. "Lizzie" Cook was born on 3 Sep 1866 in Provincetown, Mass. She died in 1948 at the age of 82.

1537.James E. Cook (Josiah-6, John-5, Solomon-4, Josiah-3, Josiah-2, Josias-1) was born on 27 Jul 1839 in Provincetown, Mass.

   James E. Cook and Abigail C. CASE were married in Provincetown, Mass. Abigail C. Case, daughter of Washington Case and Elizabeth T. Higgins, was born in 1841 in Chatham, Mass.

1542.Martha "Patty" Cook (David Newcomb-6, Jonathan-5, Solomon-4, Josiah-3, Josiah-2, Josias-1) was born on 9 Jan 1804 in Provincetown, Mass. She died of dropsy on 12 May 1857 at the age of 53 in Provincetown, Mass. She was buried in Hamilton Cemetery,

Provincetown, Mass.

Martha "Patty" Cook and James STANFORD were married on 15 Jun 1823 in Provincetown, Mass. James Stanford was born about 1800 in Provincetown, Mass. He died in 1825 at the age of 25 in Boston, Mass. He was buried in Cemetery Number Two, Old Section, Provincetown, Mass.

James Stanford and Martha Cook had the following children:

 3131  i.  Thomas D. Stanford, born 3 Aug 1823, Provincetown, Mass.; married Nabby Nickerson CHAPMAN, 24 Oct 1847; married Emily BASS.
     ii.  David C. Stanford was born on 6 Mar 1826 in Provincetown, Mass.

1543.Rebecca Cook (David Newcomb-6, Jonathan-5, Solomon-4, Josiah-3, Josiah-2, Josias-1) was born on 9 Jul 1806 in Provincetown, Mass. She died on 3 Nov 1892 at the age of 86 in Provincetown, Mass.  She was buried in Hamilton Cemetery, Provincetown, Mass.

Rebecca Cook and Thomas LOTHROP were married on 30 Apr 1826 in Provincetown, Mass. Thomas Lothrop, son of Ebenezer Lothrop and Temperance Lewis, was a yeoman.

Thomas Lothrop and Rebecca Cook had the following children:

  i.  Salome C. Lothrop was born in 1828 in Provincetown, Mass. She died in 1900 at the age of 72.
  ii.  Eben Lothrop was born in 1830 in Provincetown, Mass. He died in 1914 at the age of 84.
  iii.  Adeline Lothrop was born in 1832 in Provincetown, Mass. She died in 1909 at the age of 77.
  iv.  Thomas Lothrop was born in 1836 in Provincetown, Mass.
  v.  Sarah F. Lothrop was born in 1839 in Provincetown, Mass. She died in 1914 at the age of 75.
  vi.  Rozetta C. Lothrop was born in 1842 in Provincetown, Mass. She died in 1933 at the age of 91.
  vii.  Rebecca Lothrop, born 1845, Provincetown, Mass.; married Warren Fielding; died 1913.
  viii.  Marcus M. Lothrop was born in 1847 in Provincetown, Mass. He died in 1847 at the age of 0 in Provincetown, Mass.
  ix.  Benjamin L. Lothrop was born in 1848 in Provincetown, Mass.

1544.Lemuel Cook 2nd (David Newcomb-6, Jonathan-5, Solomon-4, Josiah-3, Josiah-2, Josias-1) was born on 2 Nov 1811 in Provincetown, Mass. In 1852 he was a lighthouse keeper in Provincetown, Mass. Lemuel died of heart disease on 15 Jan 1888 at the age of 76 in Provincetown, Mass. He was buried in Cemetery Number Two, Old Section, Provincetown,

Mass.

Lemuel Cook 2nd and Mary Jones WEEKS were married on 4 Feb 1841 in Provincetown, Mass. Mary Jones Weeks, daughter of Edward Quinzey Weeks and Judah Unknown, was born on 29 Aug 1821. She died of dropsy on 20 Aug 1859 at the age of 37 in Provincetown, Mass. She was buried in Hamilton Cemetery, Provincetown, Mass.

Lemuel Cook and Mary Jones Weeks had the following children:

    i.   Martha L. Cook was born on 24 Dec 1846 in Provincetown, Mass. She died of lung fever on 15 Mar 1848 in Provincetown, Mass.

3133  ii.   Capt. Emerson D. Cook, born 9 Apr 1850, Provincetown, Mass.; married Kathleen O. LYNCH; died 1904, Provincetown, Mass.

    iii.  Albert W. Cook was born on 17 Jun 1852 in Provincetown, Mass. He died of consumption on 27 Mar 1853 in Provincetown, Mass.

    iv.  A son was born on 30 Dec 1855 in Provincetown, Mass. He died in 1856.

    v.   A son was born on 15 Jan 1856 in Provincetown, Mass. He died of "fits" on 15 Jan 1857 in Provincetown, Mass.

Lemuel Cook 2nd and Ann (Atwood) LEWIS were married on 17 Apr 1861 in Provincetown, Mass. Ann (Atwood) Lewis was born in 1821 in Bucksport, Me.

1545.Rosetta Cook (David Newcomb-6, Jonathan-5, Solomon-4, Josiah-3, Josiah-2, Josias-1) was born on 31 May 1814 in Provincetown, Mass. She died on 29 Mar 1849 at the age of 34 in Provincetown, Mass. She was buried in Hamilton Cemetery, Provincetown, Mass. Rosetta was also known as Rozetta Cook.

Rosetta Cook and Capt. Enoch HALL were married on 29 Dec 1840 in Provincetown, Mass. Capt. Enoch Hall died on 23 Oct 1843 at sea.

Enoch Hall and Rosetta Cook had the following child:

    i.   Eliza Emerson Hall was born in Nov 1841 in Provincetown, Mass. She died on 23 Mar 1843 in Provincetown, Mass. She was buried in Hamilton Cemetery, Provincetown, Mass.

1546.Benjamin Lombard Cook (David Newcomb-6, Jonathan-5, Solomon-4, Josiah-3, Josiah-2, Josias-1) was born on 5 Oct 1819 in Provincetown, Mass. He was a mariner.

Benjamin Lombard Cook and Anne E. HAMMERSLEY were married on 23 Mar 1845 in Provincetown, Mass. Anne E. Hammersley, daughter of Hugh Hammersley and Mary

UNKNOWN, was born in 1826 in Provincetown, Mass. She was a dressmaker.

1547.Eliza Bryant Cook (David Newcomb-6, Jonathan-5, Solomon-4, Josiah-3, Josiah-2, Josias-1) was born on 26 Feb 1822 in Provincetown, Mass.

Eliza Bryant Cook and Peter E. DOLLIVER were married on 24 Jan 1841 in Provincetown, Mass. Peter E. Dolliver was born in 1816. He died in 1887 at the age of 71.

Peter E. Dolliver and Eliza Bryant Cook had the following child:

 i. Catherine S. Dolliver was born in 1851 in Provincetown, Mass.

1548.Edward Cook (Jonathan-6, Jonathan-5, Solomon-4, Josiah-3, Josiah-2, Josias-1) was born on 30 Nov 1804 in Provincetown, Mass. He died on 2 Oct 1825 at the age of 20 in Provincetown, Mass.   He was buried in Hamilton Cemetery, Provincetown, Mass.

Edward Cook and Servina LEWIS were married on 14 Jul 1826 in Provincetown, Mass.

Edward Cook and Servina Lewis had the following child:

 i. Survina E. Cook was born on 21 May 1826 in Provincetown, Mass.

1549.Capt. William Cook (Jonathan-6, Jonathan-5, Solomon-4, Josiah-3, Josiah-2, Josias-1) was born on 1 Oct 1808 in Provincetown, Mass. He appeared in the census in 1830 in Provincetown, Mass. He died on 5 Jul 1868 at the age of 59 in Provincetown, Mass.

Capt. William Cook and Rebecca RYDER were married before 1832 in Provincetown, Mass. Rebecca Ryder, daughter of Reuben Ryder and Susanna Swift, was born on 15 Jul 1810 in Provincetown, Mass. She died on 25 May 1840 at the age of 29 in Provincetown, Mass.

William Cook and Rebecca Ryder had the following children:

 i. A female child was born on 2 Mar 1831 in Provincetown, Mass. She died on 23 Mar 1831. She was buried in Cemetery Number Two, Provincetown, Mass.
3134 ii. Elizabeth C. "Betsey" Cook, born 1 Sep 1832, Provincetown, Mass.; married James COBB, 30 Oct 1853, Provincetown, Mass.; died 1914, Provincetown, Mass.
 iii. Edward Cook was born in Feb 1835 in Provincetown, Mass. He died on 2 Apr 1836. He was buried in Cemetery Number Two, Old Section, Provincetown, Mass.
3135 iv. Rebecca Cook, born 10 Sep 1836, Provincetown, Mass.; married Richard A. STEVENS, 21 Jan 1860, Provincetown, Mass.
 v. Reuben Ryder Cook was born on 9 May 1840 in Provincetown, Mass. He died on 7 Jun

1840. He was buried in Gifford Cemetery, Provincetown, Mass.

Capt. William Cook and Joanna R. HIGGINS were married on 24 Feb 1841 in Provincetown, Mass. Joanna R. Higgins was born in 1816. She died in 1893 at the age of 77 in Provincetown, Mass.

William Cook and Joanna R. Higgins had the following children:

i.   William A. Cook was born on 12 Jul 1842 in Provincetown, Mass.
ii.  Caroline F. Cook was born on 8 Jul 1844 in Provincetown, Mass. She died in 1924 at the age of 80 in Provincetown, Mass.
iii. Edward Cook was born on 9 Dec 1846 in Provincetown, Mass.
iv.  Cadelia Cook was born in 1849 in Provincetown, Mass.
v.   Horace W. Cook was born on 12 May 1851 in Provincetown, Mass. He died in 1896 at the age of 45 in Provincetown, Mass.   He was buried in Gifford Cemetery, Provincetown, Mass.

1550. Philip Cook II (Jonathan-6, Jonathan-5, Solomon-4, Josiah-3, Josiah-2, Josias-1) was born on 28 Apr 1810 in Provincetown, Mass. He died on 9 Mar 1893 at the age of 82 in Provincetown, Mass. He was buried in Hamilton Cemetery, Provincetown, Mass. Philip was a port master in Provincetown, Mass.

Philip Cook II and Eliza A. WHORF were married on 9 Feb 1832 in Provincetown, Mass. Eliza A. Whorf, daughter of Thomas Ryder Whorf and Elizabeth Atkins Snow, was born on 6 Jul 1813 in Provincetown, Mass. She died before 1838 at the age of 25.

Philip Cook II and Betsy N. FREEMAN were married on 18 Nov 1838 in Provincetown, Mass. Betsy N. Freeman, daughter of Elisha Freeman and Phebe Nickerson, was born on 24 Sep 1818 in Provincetown, Mass. She died of "softening of the brain" on 30 Jan 1885 at the age of 66 in Provincetown, Mass. She was buried in Hamilton Cemetery, Provincetown, Mass.

Philip Cook and Betsy N. Freeman had the following children:

3136  i.   Eliza W. Cook, born Feb 1844, Provincetown, Mass.; married Amasa SMITH, 3 Jan 1881, Provincetown, Mass.
3137  ii.  Elisha Freeman Cook, born 25 Mar 1846, Provincetown, Mass.; married Hannah R. UNKNOWN.

1551. Sally Cook (Jonathan-6, Jonathan-5, Solomon-4, Josiah-3, Josiah-2, Josias-1) was born on 23 Feb 1812 in Provincetown, Mass. She died on 11 Oct 1892 at the age of 80.   She was buried in Cemetery Number Two, Old Section, Provincetown, Mass.

Sally Cook and Stephen HILLIARD were married on 4 Mar 1830 in Provincetown, Mass. Stephen Hilliard, son of Thomas and Sally Hilliard, was born on 7 Aug 1808.

Stephen Hilliard and Sally Cook had the following children:

    i.   Cordelia Holmes Hilliard was born in 1832 in Provincetown, Mass. She died in 1832.

    ii.  Edward Cook Hilliard was born in 1823 in Provincetown, Mass. He died in 1834 at the age of 11 in Provincetown, Mass.

3138   iii.  Stephen A. Hilliard, born 1836, Provincetown, Mass.; married Sarah G. UNKNOWN; died 1869.

1552.Cordelia Cook (Jonathan-6, Jonathan-5, Solomon-4, Josiah-3, Josiah-2, Josias-1) was born on 25 Feb 1814 in Provincetown, Mass.

    Cordelia Cook and Paron C. HOLMES were married on 9 Nov 1829 in Provincetown, Mass.

    Cordelia Cook and John BELCHER were married on 23 Jun 1839 in Provincetown, Mass.

1553.Olive Wadsworth Cook (Jonathan-6, Jonathan-5, Solomon-4, Josiah-3, Josiah-2, Josias-1) was born on 15 Apr 1818 in Provincetown, Mass. She died in 1907 at the age of 89 in Provincetown, Mass. She was buried in Gifford Cemetery, Provincetown, Mass.

    Olive Wadsworth Cook and Capt. Russell Knox ELLIOT were married on 18 Nov 1838 in Provincetown, Mass. Capt. Russell Knox Elliot was born in 1817 in Provincetown, Mass. He died of fever in 1857 at the age of 40 off the "coast of Africa." He was buried in Gifford Cemetery, Provincetown, Mass.

Russell Knox Elliot and Olive Wadsworth Cook had the following children:

    i.   Russell Dunson Elliot, born 1849; married Elizabeth Hannum KENNEY; died 1933. They had 1 child.

    ii.  A son was born in 1851 in Provincetown, Mass. He died in 1851 in Provincetown, Mass.

    iii. A daughter was born in 1854 in Provincetown, Mass. She died in 1854 in Provincetown, Mass.

1554.James Munroe Cook (Jonathan-6, Jonathan-5, Solomon-4, Josiah-3, Josiah-2, Josias-1) was born on 9 Apr 1820 in Provincetown, Mass. He died in 1898 at the age of 78 in Provincetown, Mass.

James Munroe Cook and Levina HOWES were married on 5 Mar 1843 in Provincetown, Mass. Levina Howes was born in Bucksport, Me.

James Munroe Cook and Levina Howes had the following children:

i.   Louisa B. Cook was born in Mar 1844 in Provincetown, Mass. She died of consumption on 18 Nov 1858 at the age of 14 in Provincetown, Mass.
ii.  Wales H. Cook was born on 15 Sep 1850 in Provincetown, Mass.
iii. Edward L. Cook was born on 25 Aug 1858 in Provincetown, Mass. He died of dropsy on 5 Feb 1859.
iv.  A son was born on 18 Oct 1861 in Provincetown, Mass. He was premature and died on 18 Oct 1861.

James Munroe Cook and Louisa Unknown were married.

1555.Capt. Charles Augustus Cook (Jonathan-6, Jonathan-5, Solomon-4, Josiah-3, Josiah-2, Josias-1) was born on 14 Jul 1822 in Provincetown, Mass. He died on 8 Oct 1891 at the age of 69 in Provincetown, Mass. He was buried in Hamilton Cemetery, Provincetown, Mass.

Capt. Charles Augustus Cook and Sarah Higgins "Sally" DUNHAM were married on 8 Nov 1843 in Provincetown, Mass. Sarah Higgins "Sally" Dunham, daughter of Nathan Dunham and Sally Higgins, was born on 20 Oct 1825. She died of consumption on 9 Feb 1848 at the age of 22 in Provincetown, Mass. She was buried in Hamilton Cemetery, Provincetown, Mass.

Charles Augustus Cook and Sarah Higgins Dunham had the following child:

i.   Jonathan Y. Cook was born on 4 Oct 1847 in Provincetown, Mass. He died on 1 Jan 1929 at the age of 81 in Provincetown, Mass.  He was buried in Hamilton Cemetery, Provincetown, Mass.

Capt. Charles Augustus Cook and Olive ATKINS were married on 19 Dec 1848 in Provincetown, Mass. Olive Atkins, daughter of Isaiah Atkins and Rebecca Cowell Cook, was born on 23 Nov 1828. She died on 12 Aug 1917 at the age of 88 in Provincetown, Mass.

Charles Augustus Cook and Olive Atkins had the following children:

3140  i.   Charles Augustus Cook Jr., born 12 Jul 1850, Provincetown, Mass.; married Minnie F. PAINE, bef 1872, Provincetown, Mass.
3141  ii.  Sarah D. "Sadie" Cook, born 21 Sep 1854, Provincetown, Mass.; married Harlan J. HIGGINS, 27 May 1875.
3142  iii. Louisa F. Cook, born 20 Feb 1859, Provincetown, Mass.; married W. WILLIAMS;

died 1912.

3143   iv.  Angie Young Cook, born 26 Jul 1866, Provincetown, Mass.; married James Wallace FULLER, 19 Apr 1886, Provincetown, Mass.; died 1944.

     v.  George P. Cook was born on 9 Apr 1874 in Provincetown, Mass. He died on 7 Dec 1893 at the age of 19 in Provincetown, Mass. He was buried in Hamilton Cemetery, Provincetown, Mass.

1556. Salome Cook (Jonathan-6, Jonathan-5, Solomon-4, Josiah-3, Josiah-2, Josias-1) was born on 27 Sep 1824 in Provincetown, Mass.

Salome Cook and Jonathan N. YOUNG were married on 1 Dec 1844 in Provincetown, Mass. Jonathan N. Young, son of Bangs Young and Hannah, was born about 1819 in Provincetown, Mass.

1557. Almira Cook (Philip-6, Jonathan-5, Solomon-4, Josiah-3, Josiah-2, Josias-1) was born in 1809 in Provincetown, Mass. She died of consumption on 20 Mar 1851 at the age of 42 in Provincetown, Mass.

Almira Cook and Anthony BROWN were married on 17 May 1829 in Provincetown, Mass.

1558. Abigail "Nabby" Cook (Philip-6, Jonathan-5, Solomon-4, Josiah-3, Josiah-2, Josias-1) was born on 3 Jul 1812 in Provincetown, Mass. She died on 27 Feb 1896 at the age of 83 in Provincetown, Mass.

Abigail "Nabby" Cook and Benjamin LANCY were married. Benjamin Lancy, son of Benjamin Lancy and Jane Nickerson, was born on 21 Sep 1810 in Provincetown, Mass. He died of a fall in 1859 at the age of 49 in Provincetown, Mass.

Benjamin Lancy and Abigail Cook had the following children:

3144   i.  Anna Cook Lancy, born 1836, Provincetown, Mass.; married Charles Baxter SNOW; died 1913, Provincetown, Mass.

    ii.  Abigail Cook Lancy was born in 1838 in Provincetown, Mass.

   iii.  Maria Smith Lancy was born in 1841 in Provincetown, Mass.

   iv.  Benjamin Lancy Jr. was born in 1843 in Provincetown, Mass. He died in 1843.

    v.  Benjamin Lancy Jr. was born in 1846 in Provincetown, Mass.

   vi.  Almira Brown Lancy was born in 1848 in Provincetown, Mass.

1559. Rebecca Cook Sparks (Bethia Cook-6, Jonathan-5, Solomon-4, Josiah-3, Josiah-2, Josias-1) was born on 14 Aug 1803 in Provincetown, Mass.

Rebecca Cook Sparks and Oliver BOWLEY were married.

1563. David Cook (Lemuel-6, Jonathan-5, Solomon-4, Josiah-3, Josiah-2, Josias-1) was born on 15 Oct 1808 in Provincetown, Mass. He died on 7 Dec 1849 at the age of 41 at sea. He was also known as Winthrop David Cook.

David Cook and Sally WATKINS were married on 24 Oct 1830 in Provincetown, Mass. Sally Watkins was born in 1812. She died in 1886 at the age of 74 in Provincetown, Mass.

David Cook and Sally Watkins had the following children:

     i.   Emily Cook was born on 18 Nov 1830 in Provincetown, Mass. She died on 10 Mar 1831.
     ii.  Joseph Watkins Cook was born on 10 Jul 1832 in Provincetown, Mass. He died in 1849 at the age of 17 in Provincetown, Mass. He was buried in Hamilton Cemetery, Provincetown, Mass.
3148  iii. Emily Tilton Cook, born 14 Oct 1834, Provincetown, Mass.; died 1922.
     iv. David Cook was born on 11 Aug 1836 in Provincetown, Mass.
     v.  Ephraim Henry Cook was born on 22 Sep 1838 in Provincetown, Mass. He died on 4 May 1840.

1564. Capt. Tilton Cook (Lemuel-6, Jonathan-5, Solomon-4, Josiah-3, Josiah-2, Josias-1) was born on 10 Jul 1810 in Provincetown, Mass. He died in 1893 at the age of 83 in Provincetown, Mass.

Capt. Tilton Cook and Clarinda COOK were married on 15 Dec 1835 in Provincetown, Mass. Clarinda Cook was born in 1818. She died in 1889 at the age of 71.

Tilton Cook and Clarinda Cook had the following children:

3149  i.   Rebecca A. Cook, born 4 Dec 1838, Provincetown, Mass.; married George H. HOLMES, 26 Jul 1858, Provincetown, Mass.; died 1928, Provincetown, Mass.
     ii.  A child was born on 15 Feb 1843 in Provincetown, Mass. He/she died on 15 Feb 1843.
     iii. Clarinda Tilton Cook was born on 14 May 1846 in Provincetown, Mass. She died of "inflammation" on 31 Aug 1854 at the age of 8 in Provincetown, Mass.
     iv. Clara T. Cook was born in 1859 in Provincetown, Mass. She died in 1864 at the age of 5 in Provincetown, Mass.
     v.  Caroline B. Cook was born in 1860. She died in 1907 at the age of 47.
     vi. Lottie E. Cook was born in 1861. She died in 1864 at the age of 3.
     vii. Blanche A. Cook was born in 1871. She died in 1956 at the age of 85.

1565. Charles Dyer Cook (Lemuel-6, Jonathan-5, Solomon-4, Josiah-3, Josiah-2, Josias-1) was born on 12 Jun 1813 in Provincetown, Mass. Between 1840 and 1880 he was a sail maker in Provincetown, Mass. He died of paralysis on 13 Feb 1888 at the age of 74 in Provincetown, Mass. Charles was buried in Gifford Cemetery, Provincetown, Mass.

Charles Dyer Cook and Ellen B. UNKNOWN were married before 1846 in Provincetown, Mass. Ellen B. Unknown was born on 9 May 1820 in Provincetown, Mass. She died on 22 May 1873 at the age of 53 in Provincetown, Mass. She was buried in Gifford Cemetery, Provincetown, Mass.

Charles Dyer Cook and Ellen B. Unknown had the following children:

    i.   Charles E. Cook was born on 13 Nov 1845 in Provincetown, Mass. He died of dropsy on the brain on 1 Sep 1846. He was buried in Gifford Cemetery, Provincetown, Mass.

    iii.  Ellen B. Cook was born on 9 May 1820 in Provincetown, Mass. She died on 22 May 1873 at the age of 53 in Provincetown, Mass.

1566.Emily Cook (Lemuel-6, Jonathan-5, Solomon-4, Josiah-3, Josiah-2, Josias-1) was born on 12 Oct 1815 in Provincetown, Mass. She died on 29 Mar 1886 at the age of 70 in Provincetown, Mass.  She was buried in Hamilton Cemetery, Provincetown, Mass.

Emily Cook and Jarius H. HILLIARD were married on 20 Feb 1833 in Provincetown, Mass. Jarius H. Hilliard was the son of Thomas Hilliard and Sally.

Jarius H. Hilliard and Emily Cook had the following children:

    i.   John D. Hilliard, born 1836, Provincetown, Mass.; married Rebecca HILL; married Lizzie H. Paine; died 1906. With Rebecca he had 3 children. With Lizzie he had 1 child.
    ii.  A son was born in 1839 in Provincetown, Mass. He died in 1839.
    iii.  Emily Cook Hilliard was born in Apr 1840 in Provincetown, Mass. She died on 3 Jul 1840 in Provincetown, Mass.
    iv.  Almeda Ann Hilliard was born in 1842 in Provincetown, Mass. She died in 1842.
    v.  A son was born in 1845 in Provincetown, Mass. He died in 1845.
    vi.  Jarius Howard Hilliard was born in 1849 in Provincetown, Mass. He died in 1856 at the age of 7.

1567.Ephraim Ryder Cook (Lemuel-6, Jonathan-5, Solomon-4, Josiah-3, Josiah-2, Josias-1) was born on 16 Jul 1818 in Provincetown, Mass. He was a merchant.

Ephraim Ryder Cook and Abbie H. CONNANT were married on 29 Oct 1847 in Provincetown, Mass. Abbie H. Connant was born in 1823 in Provincetown, Mass.

Ephraim Ryder Cook and Abbie H. Connant had the following children:

i.   Mary Cook.
ii.  Benjamin C. Cook was born on 1 Aug 1850 in Provincetown, Mass.
iii. Sadie Cook was born on 29 Mar 1852 in Provincetown, Mass. She died in 1852.

1568.Lemuel Cook 3rd (Lemuel-6, Jonathan-5, Solomon-4, Josiah-3, Josiah-2, Josias-1) was born on 30 Mar 1828 in Provincetown, Mass. In 1852 he was a sailmaker in Provincetown, Mass. He died of liver disease on 11 Nov 1885 at the age of 57 in Provincetown, Mass. Lemuel was buried on 30 Nov 1885 in Gifford Cemetery, Provincetown, Mass.

Lemuel Cook 3rd and Rebecca A. Morgan were married on 15 Nov 1852 in Provincetown, Mass. They appeared in the census in 1860 in Provincetown, Mass. They appeared in the census in 1870 in Provincetown, Mass. Rebecca A. Morgan, daughter of Lewis P. Morgan and Rebecca Atkins, was born on 30 Jun 1838. She died on 14 Jun 1898 at the age of 59 in Provincetown, Mass.  gravestone

Lemuel Cook and Rebecca A. Morgan had the following children:

3151   i.   Walter Shelton Cook, born 15 Nov 1852, Provincetown, Mass.; married Annie King WHORF, 18 Dec 1890, Provincetown, Mass.; died 1922, Provincetown, Mass.
3152   ii.  Joseph W. Cook, born 5 Jul 1854, Provincetown, Mass.; married Mary Abbie SMITH, 29 Sep 1875, Provincetown, Mass.
       iii. Adilot L. Cook was born on 24 Mar 1857 in Provincetown, Mass.
       iv.  A son was born on 13 Apr 1859 in Provincetown, Mass.
3153   v.   Cassandra C. "Cassie" Cook, born 1861, Provincetown, Mass.; married Clarence A. COOK, 26 Sep 1877, Provincetown, Mass.
3154   vi.  Frederick F. "Freddie" Cook, born 22 Dec 1861, Provincetown, Mass.; married Emma P. PIERCE, 1 Jan 1885, Provincetown, Mass.; died 1906, Provincetown, Mass.
       vii. Henry Ryder Cook was born on 10 Sep 1866 in Provincetown, Mass.
       viii.    Harriet R. Cook was born in 1867 in Provincetown, Mass.
       ix.  Atwood Sears "Eldwood" Cook was born on 19 Oct 1868 in Provincetown, Mass. He died in 1897 at the age of 29 in Provincetown, Mass.

1569.Parker Cook (Ephraim-6, Samuel-5, Solomon-4, Josiah-3, Josiah-2, Josias-1) was born on 18 Aug 1804 in Provincetown, Mass. In 1845 he was a ship owner in Provincetown, Mass. He died of Bilious colic on 12 Sep 1849 at the age of 45 in Provincetown, Mass. Parker was buried in Hamilton Cemetery, Provincetown, Mass. He was a merchant.

Parker Cook and Hannah HINKS were married on 14 Sep 1834 in Provincetown, Mass.

Hannah Hinks, daughter of Elisha Hinks and Temperance Unknown, was born about 1815 in Bucksport, Me.

Parker Cook and Hannah Hinks had the following children:

    i.   Naomi H. Cook was born on 29 Sep 1835 in Provincetown, Mass.

    ii.  Atkins D. Cook was born in Jul 1849 in Provincetown, Mass.

1570.Capt. Ephraim Cook (Ephraim-6, Samuel-5, Solomon-4, Josiah-3, Josiah-2, Josias-1) was born on 3 Nov 1806 in Provincetown, Mass. He died on 22 Feb 1891 at the age of 84 in Provincetown, Mass. He was buried in Gifford Cemetery, Provincetown, Mass.

Capt. Ephraim Cook and Rebecca E. WILEY were married about 1834. Rebecca E. Wiley, daughter of Ephraim Wiley and Rebecca E., was born in 1816 in Provincetown, Mass. She died of childbirth on 26 Dec 1850 at the age of 34 in Provincetown, Mass.

Ephraim Cook and Rebecca E. Wiley had the following children:

3155  i.   Phebe W. Cook, born 7 Aug 1838, Provincetown, Mass.; married William E. MORGAN, 28 Nov 1867, Provincetown, Mass.

3156  ii.  Ephraim Parker "Parker" Cook, born 24 Sep 1841, Provincetown, Mass.; married Alemeda H. CASE, 26 Jan 1866, Provincetown, Mass.

3157  iii. George S. Cook, born 4 Jun 1843, Provincetown, Mass.; married Julia N. SMITH, 5 Dec 1866, Provincetown, Mass.

    iv.  Cornelius Cook was born on 5 Dec 1850 in Provincetown, Mass. He died on 5 Feb 1851.

Capt. Ephraim Cook and Hannah CHENEY were married before 1860 in Provincetown, Mass. Hannah Cheney, daughter of Ebenezer Cheney and Hannah Unknown, was born in 1816 in Provincetown, Mass. She died of Typhoid Fever on 15 Sep 1864 at the age of 48 in Provincetown, Mass.

Capt. Ephraim Cook and Betsy L. COOK were married on 25 Oct 1870 in Provincetown, Mass. Betsy L. Cook, daughter of Thomas Cook and Elizabeth Unknown, was born in 1816 in Truro, Mass. She died in 1891 at the age of 75 in Provincetown, Mass.

1571.Anna Cook (Ephraim-6, Samuel-5, Solomon-4, Josiah-3, Josiah-2, Josias-1) was born on 23 Dec 1808 in Provincetown, Mass. She signed a will on 15 May 1879 in Provincetown, Mass. She died on 17 Nov 1887 at the age of 78 in Provincetown, Mass. Anna was buried in Provincetown Cemetery Number Two.

Anna Cook and Harvey NICKERSON were married on 11 Jan 1831 in Provincetown, Mass.

Harvey Nickerson, son of Enos Nickerson and Lucy Nickerson, was born on 24 Aug 1805 in Provincetown, Mass. He died on 4 Mar 1875 at the age of 69. He was a sea captain.

1572. Ebenezer Cook (Ephraim-6, Samuel-5, Solomon-4, Josiah-3, Josiah-2, Josias-1) was born on 2 Feb 1811 in Provincetown, Mass. In 1845 he was a ship owner in Provincetown, Mass. He died on 10 Oct 1898 at the age of 87 in Provincetown, Mass. Ebenezer was buried in Hamilton Cemetery, Provincetown, Mass.

Ebenezer Cook and Sarah R. NICKERSON were married on 9 Oct 1839 in Provincetown, Mass. Sarah R. Nickerson, daughter of Isaac Nickerson and Bethia Ryder, was born on 15 Jul 1819 in Provincetown, Mass. She died of carcinoma on 24 Mar 1887 at the age of 67 in Provincetown, Mass. She was buried in Hamilton Cemetery, Provincetown, Mass.

Ebenezer Cook and Sarah R. Nickerson had the following child:

i.    Eben A. Cook was born on 22 Feb 1841 in Provincetown, Mass. He died of paralysis on 4 Feb 1873 at the age of 31 in Provincetown, Mass. He was buried in Hamilton Cemetery, Provincetown, Mass.

1573. Rebecca (Nickerson) Cook (Ephraim-6, Samuel-5, Solomon-4, Josiah-3, Josiah-2, Josias-1) was born on 29 Aug 1813 in Provincetown, Mass. She died in 1901 at the age of 88.  She was buried in Provincetown Cemetery Number Two.

Rebecca (Nickerson) Cook and Thomas HILLIARD were married on 4 Aug 1850 in Provincetown, Mass. Thomas Hilliard, son of Thomas Hilliard and Sally, was born on 23 Nov 1802 in Provincetown, Mass. He died on 9 Apr 1879 at the age of 76 in Provincetown, Mass. He was buried in Provincetown Cemetery Number Two.

Rebecca (Nickerson) Cook and Nathaniel Lewis NICKERSON were married on 27 Feb 1834 in Provincetown, Mass. Nathaniel Lewis Nickerson, son of Enos Nickerson and Lucy Nickerson, was born on 30 Aug 1810 in Provincetown, Mass. He died on 5 Dec 1839 at the age of 29 in At sea.

Nathaniel Lewis Nickerson and Rebecca (Nickerson) Cook had the following children:

3158  i.    Apphia Cook Nickerson, born 23 Dec 1834, Provincetown, Mass.; married Nathan D. FREEMAN, 23 Dec 1834, Provincetown, Mass.; died 20 Jul 1884, Provincetown, Mass.
ii.   Rebecca Lewis Nickerson was born on 2 Aug 1837 in Provincetown, Mass. She died on 21 Jan 1915 at the age of 77. She was buried in Provincetown Cemetery Number Two.

1574. Cornelius Cook (Ephraim-6, Samuel-5, Solomon-4, Josiah-3, Josiah-2, Josias-1) was born on 15 Nov 1819 in Provincetown, Mass. He died of consumption on 16 Nov 1849 at the age of 30 in Provincetown, Mass. He was buried in Gifford Cemetery, Provincetown, Mass.

Cornelius Cook and Mary Brown HILLIARD were married on 24 Nov 1846 in Provincetown, Mass. Mary Brown Hilliard, daughter of Thomas Hilliard and Paulina Brown, was born in 1827 in Provincetown, Mass. She died of myolitis on 29 Mar 1874 at the age of 47 in Provincetown, Mass. She was buried in Gifford Cemetery, Provincetown, Mass.

1575. Capt. Daniel Cross Cook (Ephraim-6, Samuel-5, Solomon-4, Josiah-3, Josiah-2, Josias-1) was born on 30 Jan 1822 in Provincetown, Mass. He died of apoplexy on 18 Dec 1888 at the age of 66 in Provincetown, Mass. He was buried in Gifford Cemetery, Provincetown, Mass.

Capt. Daniel Cross Cook and Mary Brown HILLIARD were married on 22 Jan 1851 in Provincetown, Mass. Mary Brown Hilliard, daughter of Thomas Hilliard and Paulina Brown, was born in 1827 in Provincetown, Mass. She died of myelitis on 29 Mar 1874 at the age of 47 in Provincetown, Mass. She was buried in Gifford Cemetery, Provincetown, Mass.

1576. Capt. Epephras Kibby Cook (Ephraim-6, Samuel-5, Solomon-4, Josiah-3, Josiah-2, Josias-1) was born on 14 Jun 1824 in Provincetown, Mass. He died on 25 Jul 1905 at the age of 81 in Provincetown, Mass. He was buried in Hamilton Cemetery, Provincetown, Mass.

Capt. Epephras Kibby Cook and Sarah G. UNKNOWN were married. Sarah G. was born on 2 Sep 1826. She died on 6 Apr 1883 at the age of 56 in Provincetown, Mass.

1577. Betsy Cook (Samuel-6, Samuel-5, Solomon-4, Josiah-3, Josiah-2, Josias-1) was born on 8 Jul 1804 in Provincetown, Mass. She died of pleurisy fever on 15 Apr 1847 at the age of 42 in Provincetown, Mass.

Betsy Cook and James SMALLEY were married on 4 Jan 1825 in Provincetown, Mass. James Smalley, son of Abraham Smalley and Polly , was born in 1801 in Provincetown, Mass. He died on 16 Sep 1846 at the age of 45 at sea.

James Smalley and Betsy Cook had the following children:

    i.   Joshua Dyer Parker Smalley was born on 13 Aug 1825 in Provincetown, Mass. He died on 16 Sep 1846 at the age of 21 in At sea. death
    ii.   Betsey Cook Small, born 31 Aug 1828, Provincetown, Mass.; married Benjamin B. Handy.
    iii.   James Henry Small was born on 19 Nov 1831 in Provincetown, Mass. He died on 16 Sep 1846 at the age of 14 in At sea. death

iv. Mary Tamsin Small was born on 8 May 1833 in Provincetown, Mass.
v. Benjamin Franklin Small was born on 28 Oct 1835 in Provincetown, Mass.
vi. Samuel C. Small was born on 13 Sep 1837 in Provincetown, Mass.
vii. Harriet N. Smalley was born in 1839 in Provincetown, Mass.
viii. James H. Small (Twin) was born on 16 Jul 1841. He died on 2 Feb 1914 at the age of 72 in Provincetown, Mass. He was buried in Gifford Cemetery, Provincetown, Mass.
ix. Frederick U. Smalley (Twin) was born on 16 Jul 1841 in Provincetown, Mass.
x. Emma Virginia Smalley was born in 1846 in Provincetown, Mass.

1578. Samuel Cook Jr. (Samuel-6, Samuel-5, Solomon-4, Josiah-3, Josiah-2, Josias-1) was born on 21 Aug 1806 in Provincetown, Mass. He appeared in the census in 1830 in Provincetown, Mass. He died on 14 Feb 1841 at the age of 34 in Provincetown, Mass. In 1847 Samuel was a ship owner in Provincetown, Mass.

Samuel Cook Jr. and Maria COOK were married on 19 Jan 1832 in Provincetown, Mass. Maria Cook, daughter of Joshua Cook and Elizabeth Atkins, was born on 13 Apr 1812 or 30 Apr 1812 in Provincetown, Mass. She appeared in the census in 1860 in Provincetown, Mass. She died on 23 Dec 1888 at the age of 76 in Provincetown, Mass. Samuel and Maria were second cousins.

Samuel Cook and Maria Cook had the following children:

3102 i. Harvey Cook, born 28 Oct 1832, Provincetown, Mass.; married Susan ; died 27 May 1872, Provincetown, Mass.
ii. Helen Maria Cook was born on 12 Feb 1835 in Provincetown, Mass.
iii. Jedidah A. Cook was born on 3 Aug 1840 in Provincetown, Mass.
iv. Jedediah Cook was born in 1842 in Provincetown, Mass.
v. Alfred Cook died in 1840 in Provincetown, Mass.

1579. Tamsin "Tamsey" Cook (Samuel-6, Samuel-5, Solomon-4, Josiah-3, Josiah-2, Josias-1) was born on 22 Jun 1810 in Provincetown, Mass.

Tamsin "Tamsey" Cook and Elisha TILLSON were married on 21 Dec 1831 in Provincetown, Mass.

Elisha Tillson and Tamsin Cook had the following child:

i. Apphia Cook Tillson was born about 1833 in Provincetown, Mass.

1580. Sylvanus Cook (Samuel-6, Samuel-5, Solomon-4, Josiah-3, Josiah-2, Josias-1) was born on 19

Apr 1812 in Provincetown, Mass. He died in 1892 at the age of 80 in Provincetown, Mass.

Sylvanus Cook and Louisa YOUNG were married on 17 Nov 1844 in Provincetown, Mass. Louisa Young, daughter of Eleazor Young and Rebecca Smalley, was born in 1822 in Provincetown, Mass.

Sylvanus Cook and Louisa Young had the following children:

    3160   i.   Hannah L. Cook, born 23 Oct 1845, Provincetown, Mass.; married Joseph B. DYER, 19 Oct 1864, Provincetown, Mass.

           ii.  Laura Cook was born on 26 Oct 1847 in Provincetown, Mass. She died of encephalitis on 30 Oct 1849 at the age of 2 in Provincetown, Mass.

1581.Capt. Henry Cook (Samuel-6, Samuel-5, Solomon-4, Josiah-3, Josiah-2, Josias-1) was born on 29 Nov 1813 in Provincetown, Mass. He died on 26 May 1893 at the age of 79 in Provincetown, Mass.

Capt. Henry Cook and Abigail Rich DYER were married on 14 Dec 1837 in Provincetown, Mass. Abigail Rich Dyer, daughter of Elijah Dyer and Rebecca Rich, was born on 10 Apr 1819 in Provincetown, Mass. She died on 16 Oct 1902 at the age of 83 in Provincetown, Mass.

Henry Cook and Abigail Rich Dyer had the following children:

           i.   A Daughter "Nellie" Cook (Twin) was born on 8 Sep 1838 in Provincetown, Mass. She died on 12 Sep 1838.

    3161   ii.  Adelaide Osborne Cook (Twin), born 8 Sep 1838, Provincetown, Mass.; married A. Lewis PUTNAM, 1860, Provincetown, Mass.; died Provincetown, Mass.

           iii. James H. Cook was born in 1839.

           iv. Alded O. Cook was born on 4 Jan 1840 in Provincetown, Mass.

1582.Capt. Alfred Cook (Samuel-6, Samuel-5, Solomon-4, Josiah-3, Josiah-2, Josias-1) was born on 12 Aug 1816 in Provincetown, Mass. In 1845 he was a ship owner in Provincetown, Mass. He died on 16 May 1897 at the age of 80 in Provincetown, Mass. Alfred was buried in Hamilton Cemetery, Provincetown, Mass.

Capt. Alfred Cook and Rebecca Macomber BOWLEY were married on 27 Sep 1842 in Provincetown, Mass. Rebecca Macomber Bowley, daughter of Gideon Bowley and Mary W. , was born on 6 Sep 1819 in Provincetown, Mass. She died of gall stones on 17 Dec 1869 at the age of 50 in Provincetown, Mass. She was buried in Hamilton Cemetery, Provincetown, Mass.

Alfred Cook and Rebecca Macomber Bowley had the following children:

      i.   Edwin E. Cook was born on 12 Sep 1843 in Provincetown, Mass. He died of scrofula (lymph node infection due to Tuberculosis) on 23 Oct 1852 at the age of 9 in Provincetown, Mass.

3162  ii.   Clarence A. Cook, born 1855, Provincetown, Mass.; married Cassandra C. COOK, 26 Sep 1877, Provincetown, Mass.; died 1916, Provincetown, Mass.

Capt. Alfred Cook and Caroline E. (Howard) SMITH were married on 16 Mar 1871 in Provincetown, Mass. Caroline E. (Howard) Smith, daughter of Roderick Smith and Flora Unknown, was born on 19 Jun 1833. She died on 17 Sep 1879 at the age of 46 in Provincetown, Mass.

Capt. Alfred Cook and Emily S. CHAPEL were married on 21 Nov 1888 in Provincetown, Mass. Emily S. Chapel, daughter of Manuel Chapel and Mary, was born in 1835 in Provincetown, Mass.

1583.Mary A. Cook (Samuel-6, Samuel-5, Solomon-4, Josiah-3, Josiah-2, Josias-1) was born on 19 Aug 1819 in Provincetown, Mass.

Mary A. Cook and John ADAMS were married. John Adams was the son of John Adams and Sally Atkins.

Mary A. Cook and Solomon N. ADAMS were married on 24 Jul 1867 in Provincetown, Mass. Solomon N. Adams, the son of George M. And Abbie, was born on 21 Sep 1823 in Provincetown, Mass.

1584.Dorinda Cook (Samuel-6, Samuel-5, Solomon-4, Josiah-3, Josiah-2, Josias-1) was born on 30 Aug 1820 in Provincetown, Mass. She died of bilious fever on 2 Oct 1851 at the age of 31 in Provincetown, Mass. She was buried in Hamilton Cemetery, Provincetown, Mass.

Dorinda Cook and Silas Small YOUNG were married on 31 Dec 1837 in Provincetown, Mass. Silas Small Young, son of Eleazor Young and Rebecca Smalley, was born on 5 Nov 1814 in Provincetown, Mass. He was a sailor. Silas died on 23 Sep 1887 at the age of 72 in Provincetown, Mass. He was buried in Hamilton Cemetery, Provincetown, Mass.

Silas Small Young and Dorinda Cook had the following children:

      i.   Hannah L Young was born in May 1839 in Provincetown, Mass. She died on 2 Oct 1839. She was buried in Hamilton Cemetery, Provincetown, Mass.

     ii.   Dorinda C. Young was born on 6 Sep 1851 in Provincetown, Mass. She died on 21 Jun

1852. She was buried in Hamilton Cemetery, Provincetown, Mass.

1585. Louisa Cook (Samuel-6, Samuel-5, Solomon-4, Josiah-3, Josiah-2, Josias-1) was born on 20 Sep 1823 in Provincetown, Mass. She died on 18 Dec 1890 at the age of 67 in Provincetown, Mass. She was buried in Hamilton Cemetery, Provincetown, Mass.

Louisa Cook and Nathaniel N. COOK were married on 8 Oct 1843 in Provincetown, Mass. They appeared in the census in 1860 in Provincetown, Mass. Nathaniel N. Cook, son of Joshua Cook and Rebecca Atkins, was born on 17 Nov 1821 in Provincetown, Mass. He died of heart disease on 12 Jul 1888 at the age of 66 in Provincetown, Mass. He was buried in Hamilton Cemetery, Provincetown, Mass. Louisa and Nathaniel were third cousins.

Nathaniel N. Cook and Louisa Cook had the following children:

      i.   Rebecca D. Cook was born on 4 Nov 1846 in Provincetown, Mass.

3163  ii.  Albertina Frances "Tenie" Cook, born abt 1848, Provincetown, Mass.; married Josiah Frances KNOWLES, 19 Jun 1871, Provincetown, Mass.; died 27 Oct 1874, Provincetown, Mass.

3164  iii.  Jennie Cook, born abt 1848, Provincetown, Mass.; married Josiah F. KNOWLES, 19 Jun 1871, Provincetown, Mass.

     iv.  Nathaniel "Nattie" Cook was born on 3 Dec 1850 in Provincetown, Mass. He died of croup on 12 Jun 1852. He was buried in Hamilton Cemetery, Provincetown, Mass.

1586. Phebe A. Cook (Samuel-6, Samuel-5, Solomon-4, Josiah-3, Josiah-2, Josias-1) was born on 23 Sep 1828 in Provincetown, Mass. She died in 1914 at the age of 86 in Provincetown, Mass. She was buried in Hamilton Cemetery, Provincetown, Mass.

Phebe A. Cook and Eleazor YOUNG were married on 1 Nov 1846 in Provincetown, Mass. Eleazor Young, son of Eleazor Young and Rebecca Smalley, was born in 1820 in Provincetown, Mass.  He was a mariner.

Eleazor Young and Phebe A. Cook had the following children:

      i.   Alpheus Waldo Young, born 1851, Provincetown, Mass.; married Mercy H. UNKNOWN; died 1920.

     ii.  Dorinda C. Young, born 1854, Provincetown, Mass.; married Prince I. FREEMAN; died 1899.

1587. Eleanor Cook (Jesse-6, Samuel-5, Solomon-4, Josiah-3, Josiah-2, Josias-1) was born on 23 Aug 1809 in Provincetown, Mass. She died on 30 Mar 1893 at the age of 83 in Provincetown, Mass. She was buried in Hamilton Cemetery, Provincetown, Mass.

Eleanor Cook and Charles NICKERSON were married on 8 Jan 1835 in Provincetown, Mass. Charles Nickerson, son of Enos Nickerson and Lucy Nickerson, was born on 5 Aug 1807 in Provincetown, Mass. He died on 29 May 1887 at the age of 79 in Provincetown, Mass. He was buried in Hamilton Cemetery, Provincetown, Mass.

Charles Nickerson and Eleanor Cook had the following children:

    i.   Lucy Maria Nickerson, born 15 Feb 1836, Provincetown, Mass.; married Joseph A. HANNUM, 5 Aug 1856, Provincetown, Mass.; died 8 Apr 1857, Provincetown, Mass.

   ii.   Ellen C. Nickerson was born on 6 Jul 1840 in Provincetown, Mass. She died of pneumonia on 12 Oct 1886 at the age of 46 in Provincetown, Mass. She was buried in Hamilton Cemetery, Provincetown, Mass.

  iii.   Emeline C. Nickerson was born on 24 Oct 1843 in Provincetown, Mass. She died on 11 Oct 1907 at the age of 63 in Provincetown, Mass. She was buried in Hamilton Cemetery, Provincetown, Mass.

1588.Jesse Cook Jr. (Jesse-6, Samuel-5, Solomon-4, Josiah-3, Josiah-2, Josias-1) was born on 16 Oct 1814 in Provincetown, Mass. He appeared in the census in 1850 in Provincetown, Mass. He died of heart disease and dropsy on 2 Nov 1876 at the age of 62 in Provincetown, Mass. Jesse was buried in Gifford Cemetery, Provincetown, Mass.

Jesse Cook Jr. and Adeline ADAMS were married on 14 Jan 1838 in Provincetown, Mass. They appeared in the census in 1840 in Provincetown, Mass. Adeline Adams, daughter of John Adams and Sally Atkins, was born in 1818 in Provincetown, Mass. She died of consumption on 5 Sep 1843 at the age of 25 in Provincetown, Mass.

Jesse Cook and Adeline Adams had the following child:

    i.   Capt. John Atkins "Parker" Cook was born on 15 Feb 1841 in Provincetown, Mass. He died of "Congestion of the Brain" on 13 Jun 1864 at the age of 23 in Provincetown, Mass. Parker was buried in Gifford Cemetery, Provincetown, Mass.

1589.Capt. Leonard Cook (Stephen-6, Samuel-5, Solomon-4, Josiah-3, Josiah-2, Josias-1) was born on 5 Sep 1809 in Provincetown, Mass. He appeared in the census in 1840 in Provincetown, Mass. He appeared in the census in 1860 in Provincetown, Mass. Leonard died of paralysis on 25 Dec 1882 at the age of 73 in Provincetown, Mass.   He was buried in Hamilton Cemetery, Provincetown, Mass.

Capt. Leonard Cook and Calista NICKERSON were married on 2 May 1836 in Provincetown, Mass. Calista Nickerson, daughter of Seth Nickerson and Ruth Atkins, was born on 15 May 1817 in Provincetown, Mass. She died before 1860 at the age of 43.

Leonard Cook and Calista Nickerson had the following children:

3168   i.   Delia L. Cook, born 7 May 1841, Provincetown, Mass.; married Josiah SWIFT, 23 Aug 1863, Provincetown, Mass.; died 1930, Provincetown, Mass.
3169   ii.  George E. Cook, born 23 Jun 1845, Provincetown, Mass.; married Desire SNOW, 31 Oct 1869, Provincetown, Mass.

1590.Jane C. Cook (Stephen-6, Samuel-5, Solomon-4, Josiah-3, Josiah-2, Josias-1) was born on 22 Nov 1814 in Provincetown, Mass. She died on 14 Apr 1883 at the age of 68 in Provincetown, Mass.

Jane C. Cook and Joshua Elsbery BOWLEY were married on 21 Feb 1837 in Provincetown, Mass. Joshua Elsbery Bowley, son of Gideon and Mary W. Bowley, was born on 3 Oct 1812 in Provincetown, Mass. He was a merchant.

Joshua Elsbery Bowley and Jane C. Cook had the following children:

i.    Betsy K. Bowley, born 1838, Provincetown, Mass.; married Amos F. Whorf, ef 1870; died 1905. They had 1 child.
ii.   Joshua E. Bowley Jr. was born in 1848 in Provincetown, Mass. In 1870 he was a clerk. In 1880 he was a painter in Provincetown, Mass. Joshua died in 1885 at the age of 37.
iii.  William W. Bowley was born in 1852 in Provincetown, Mass. In 1870 he was a clerk. He was a sailor.
iv.   Rebecca E. Bowley was born in 1854 in Provincetown, Mass. She died in 1911 at the age of 57.

1591.Stephen Cook Jr. (Stephen-6, Samuel-5, Solomon-4, Josiah-3, Josiah-2, Josias-1) was born on 20 May 1817 in Provincetown, Mass. He appeared in the census in 1850 in Provincetown, Mass. In 1870 he was a ship chandler in Provincetown, Mass. Stephen died of bronchitis on 3 Sep 1888 at the age of 71 in Provincetown, Mass,

Stephen Cook Jr. and Lucy Ann WILEY were married before 1847. Lucy Ann Wiley, daughter of Ephraim Wiley and Rebecca E. , was born on 11 Sep 1822 in Provincetown, Mass. She died of childbirth on 27 May 1847 at the age of 24 in Provincetown, Mass.

Stephen Cook and Lucy Ann Wiley had the following child:

i.    Lucy Ann Cook was born on 19 May 1847 in Provincetown, Mass. She died on 25 Aug 1847 in Provincetown, Mass.

Stephen Cook Jr. and Mary A. HIGGINS were married after 1848. Mary A. Higgins, daughter of Josiah and Sarah Higgins, was born on 15 Sep 1830 in Provincetown, Mass. She died of "Phohysis" on 31 Jan 1864 at the age of 33 in Provincetown, Mass. She was buried in Hamilton Cemetery, Provincetown, Mass.

Stephen Cook and Mary A. Higgins had the following child:

    i.   Charles H. Cook was born on 16 Feb 1858 in Provincetown, Mass. He died of "Scarlitinia" (prob. Scarlet Fever) on 6 Apr 1864 at the age of 6 in Provincetown, Mass.

Stephen Cook Jr. and Julia F. HIGGINS were married on 26 Jan 1865 in Provincetown, Mass. Julia F. Higgins, daughter of Ebenezer and Ruth Higgins, was born on 15 Jan 1828 in Provincetown, Mass. She died on 8 Sep 1865 at the age of 37 in Provincetown, Mass. She was buried in Hamilton Cemetery, Provincetown, Mass.

Stephen Cook Jr. and Jane Eliza "Jennie" CHURCHILL were married on 17 Oct 1871 in Provincetown, Mass. Jane Eliza "Jennie" Churchill, daughter of John and Eliza Churchill, was born on 14 Jun 1840 in Nashua, N.H. She died on 15 Feb 1912 at the age of 71 in Provincetown, Mass. She was buried in Hamilton Cemetery, Provincetown, Mass.

1592.Dilliah "Dilley" Cook (Stephen-6, Samuel-5, Solomon-4, Josiah-3, Josiah-2, Josias-1) was born on 1 Aug 1822 in Provincetown, Mass. She appeared in the census in 1860 in Provincetown, Mass. She died on 9 Jul 1899 at the age of 76 in Provincetown, Mass. She was buried in Cemetery Number Two, Old Section, Provincetown, Mass.

Dilliah "Dilley" Cook and Joseph P. KNOWLES were married on 25 Nov 1841 in Provincetown, Mass. Joseph P. Knowles, son of Samuel and Hannah Knowles and Hannah, was born in 1817. In 1850 he was a shoe salesman in Provincetown, Mass.

Joseph P. Knowles and Dilliah COOK had the following children:

    i.   George O. Knowles, born 1842, Provincetown, Mass.; married Georgia M. DYER, abt 1875. They had 2 children.

    ii.   Lovisa Kibby Knowles was born in 1844 in Provincetown, Mass. She died in 1845 at the age of 1 in Provincetown, Mass.

    iii.   Joseph W. Knowles, born 1846, Provincetown, Mass.; married Anna B. UNKNOWN. They had 1 child.

    iv.   Lovisa Kibby Knowles was born in 1849 in Provincetown, Mass. She died in 1855 at the age of 6 in Provincetown, Mass.

    v.   Lucy A. Knowles was born in 1851 in Provincetown, Mass. She died in 1936 at the age of

85. She was a tailor in Provincetown, Mass.

vi.  Hannah Kidder Knowles was born in 1854 in Provincetown, Mass. She died in 1855 at the age of 1 in Provincetown, Mass.

vii. Lizzie B. Knowles (Twin) was born in 1861 in Provincetown, Mass. She died in 1863 at the age of 2 in Provincetown, Mass.

viii.    Willy B. Knowles (Twin) was born in 1861 in Provincetown, Mass. He died in 1861.

ix.  Julia C. Knowles, born 1865, Provincetown, Mass.; married Howard F. HOPKINS; died 1948, Provincetown, Mass.


1593. Sarah Cook (Stephen-6, Samuel-5, Solomon-4, Josiah-3, Josiah-2, Josias-1) was born on 25 Apr 1826 in Provincetown, Mass. She appeared in the census in 1850 in Provincetown, Mass. She died on 5 Jun 1872 at the age of 46 in Provincetown, Mass. Sarah was buried in Hamilton Cemetery, Provincetown, Mass.

Sarah Cook and Silas Small YOUNG were married after 1851. Silas Small Young, son of Eleazor Young and Rebecca Smalley, was born on 5 Nov 1814 in Provincetown, Mass. He was a sailor. Silas died on 23 Sep 1887 at the age of 72 in Provincetown, Mass. He was buried in Hamilton Cemetery, Provincetown, Mass.


1594. James Tilton Cook (James Tilton-6, Samuel-5, Solomon-4, Josiah-3, Josiah-2, Josias-1) was born on 17 Oct 1820 in Provincetown, Mass. In 1850 he was a mariner in Provincetown, Mass. He died of Bright's Disease on 7 Dec 1889 at the age of 69 in Provincetown, Mass.

James Tilton Cook and Emily ATKINS were married on 13 Dec 1846 in Provincetown, Mass. Emily Atkins, daughter of John Atkins and Bethiah Sparks, was born in 1827 in Provincetown, Mass. She died in 1906 at the age of 79 in Provincetown, Mass.

James Tilton Cook and Emily Atkins had the following child:

3174   i.   Capt. John Atkins Cook, born 26 Mar 1859, Provincetown, Mass.; married Viola Delphine FISH, 29 Apr 1877, Provincetown, Mass.; married Ethel Maria MACK; died Jul 1938, Coral Gables, Fla.


1595. Harvey S. Cook (James Tilton-6, Samuel-5, Solomon-4, Josiah-3, Josiah-2, Josias-1) was born on 9 Dec 1835 in Provincetown, Mass. He died on 22 Feb 1905 at the age of 69 in Provincetown, Mass.

Harvey S. Cook and Charlotte HOOTON were married on 20 Nov 1856. Charlotte Hooton, daughter of Robert Hooton and Margaret Pincknew, was born on 1 Jan 1841 in Boston, Suffolk, Mass. She died on 26 Jun 1912 at the age of 71 in Tisbury, Dukes, Mass. She was buried in Gifford Cemetery, Provincetown, Mass.

Harvey S. Cook and Charlotte Hooton had the following children:

3175   i.   Harvey A. Cook, born 1857, Provincetown, Mass.; married Susan M. RICH, 30 Dec
            1886, Provincetown, Mass.; died 1892, Provincetown, Mass.
       ii.  Bethia W. Cook was born on 6 Jun 1862 in Provincetown, Mass.
       iii. Clara H. Cook was born on 10 Jul 1880 in Provincetown, Mass.
       iv.  Bertha Cook was born in 1881 in Provincetown, Mass.

1596.Phebe A. Cook (James Tilton-6, Samuel-5, Solomon-4, Josiah-3, Josiah-2, Josias-1) was born
        on 13 Apr 1836 in Provincetown, Mass. She died on 11 Feb 1923 at the age of 86 in
        Provincetown, Mass. Phebe was buried in Hamilton Cemetery, Provincetown, Mass.

        Phebe A. Cook and James Collins Nickerson PAINE were married on 16 Nov 1857 in
        Provincetown, Mass. James Collins Nickerson Paine, son of Lot Paine and Olive Nickerson,
        was born on 22 Sep 1818 in Provincetown, Mass. In 1857 he was a master. He died in 1905
        at the age of 87 in Provincetown, Mass. James was buried in Hamilton Cemetery,
        Provincetown, Mass.

James Collins Nickerson Paine and Phebe A. Cook had the following children:

       i.   Louisa C. Paine was born in 1860 in Provincetown, Mass. She died in 1951 at the age of
            91.
       ii.  Clara H. Paine was born in 1864 in Provincetown, Mass.

1597.Heman S. Cook (James Tilton-6, Samuel-5, Solomon-4, Josiah-3, Josiah-2, Josias-1) was born
        on 26 May 1840 in Provincetown, Mass. He died on 4 Nov 1927 at the age of 87 in
        Provincetown, Mass. He was buried in Hamilton Cemetery, Provincetown, Mass.

        Heman S. Cook and Hannah C. FREEMAN were married on 26 May 1840. Hannah C.
        Freeman, daughter of Franklin Freeman and Lucy Cummings, was born in 1837 in Orleans,
        Barnstable, Mass. She died in 1923 at the age of 86. She was buried in Hamilton Cemetery,
        Provincetown, Mass.

1607.Benjamin Cook (Miles-6, Thomas-5, Thomas-4, Richard-3, Josiah-2, Josias-1) was born in
        1791.He died on 13 Jun 1880 at the age of 89 in Jefferson County, NY. Benjamin was buried
        in Foster-Kinne Cemetery, Antwerp, NY. He was a farmer.

        Benjamin Cook and Lucinda FOSTER were married before 1832. Lucinda Foster was born in
        1809. She died on 18 Dec 1852 at the age of 43 in Jefferson County, NY. She was buried in
        Foster-Kinne Cemetery, Antwerp, Jefferson, NY.

Benjamin Cook and Lucinda Foster had the following children:

       i.   Roley Cooke was born in 1832.
3185  ii.  Omar Cook, born 1834.
3186  iii. Miles E. Cook, born 1836, New York; married Jennie L. UNKNOWN.
      iv. James Cooke was born in 1843.
      v.  Sarah Cooke was born in 1837.
      vi. Louisa Cooke was born in 1846.

1608. Samuel Cook (Miles-6, Thomas-5, Thomas-4, Richard-3, Josiah-2, Josias-1) was born in 1795 in NY. He died on 27 Jun 1874 at the age of 79 in Wilma, Jefferson, NY.

Samuel Cook and Elizabeth HATFIELD were married. Elizabeth Hatfield was born in 1795 in Antwerp, NY.

Samuel Cook and Elizabeth Hatfield had the following children:

3187  i.   Alfred Clark Cook, born Mar 1816, Jefferson County, NY.; married Sarah Jane HOLLAND, 19 Dec 1850, Logan County, Ky.; died 1 Jul 1902, Whiteville, N.C.
      ii.  Alvin Cook was born in Oct 1820 in Antwerp, Jefferson, NY. He died on 19 Jan 1823 at the age of 2 in Jefferson County, NY. He was buried on 19 Jan 1823 in Foster-Kinne Cemetery, Antwerp, Jefferson, NY.
3188  iii. Eliza Cook, born 1822, NY.
3189  iv. Samuel Cook ,Jr., born 1824; died 1874.
3190  v.  David J. Cook, born 1827, NY; died Iowa.
3191  vi. Mary J. Cook, born 1830, Jefferson County, NY.; married James H. MORROW, 1849, Jefferson County, NY.
      vii. Seth Cook was born on 24 Jul 1835 in Jefferson County, NY. He died on 2 Nov 1855 at the age of 20 in Jefferson County, NY.

1609. Miles Cook Jr. (Miles-6, Thomas-5, Thomas-4, Richard-3, Josiah-2, Josias-1) was born in 1797.

Miles Cook Jr. and Hannah UNKNOWN were married.

1610. Mary Griffin Cook (Miles-6, Thomas-5, Thomas-4, Richard-3, Josiah-2, Josias-1) was born in 1800 in New York. She lived in Van Buren County, Mich. after 1 Jun 1840. She signed a will on 19 Jul 1845 in Van Buren County, Mich. Mary died between 20 Jul 1845 and 18 Jun 1847 at the age of 45 in Lawrence, Mich.

Mary Griffin Cook and John RAVEN were married (poss.) in 1825 in Antwerp, Jefferson,

NY. John Raven was born between 1790 and 1801 in New York. He died on 1 Feb 1842 at the age of 52 in Lawrence, Van Buren, Mich. He was buried in Lawrence Hill Cemetery, Lawrence, Van Buren, Mich.

John Raven and Mary Griffin Cook had the following children:

    i.  Lucien John Raven, born 17 Aug 1826, Antwerp, Jefferson, NY.; married Elenoria M. Pitcher, 23 Apr 1850, Lawrence, Van Buren, Mich.; died 17 Jul 1920, Bangor, Van Buren, Mich. They had 9 children.

    ii.  Julia Raven, born bet 1828 and 1829, Antwerp, Jefferson, NY.; married Thomas Kemp, 1848, Van Buren County, Mich.; died 5 Dec 1886, Bangor, Van Buren, Mich. They had 8 children.

    iii.  Adah Lucinda Raven, born bet 1830 and 1832, Antwerp, Jefferson, NY.; married Horatio Joy Hendryx, 1852. They had 3 children.

    iv.  Mary Raven, born abt 1834, Antwerp, Jefferson, NY.; married James Stiles, 22 Nov 1859, Ceresco, Calhoun, Mich.

    v.  Hamilton Samuel Raven, born 17 Apr 1839, Antwerp, Jefferson, NY.; married Almira Jane Baker, 15 Sep 1870, Contra Costa, Cal.; married Martha N. Smith, 14 Dec 1897, Tice Valley, Contra Costa, Cal.; died 27 Dec 1904, Alamo, Contra Costa, Cal. They had 6 children.

    vi.  Charles Hamilton Raven, born Aug 1842, Lawrence, Van Buren, Mich.; married Mary C. Donel, 8 Oct 1867, Calhoun County, Mich.; died 16 Mar 1907, Marshall, Calhoun, Mich. They had 1 child.

1611.Gideon Cook (Miles-6, Thomas-5, Thomas-4, Richard-3, Josiah-2, Josias-1) was born in 1803 in New York. He was a laborer.

Gideon Cook and Ruth NELSON were married before 1836. Ruth Nelson was born in 1807 in State of Vermont.

Gideon Cook and Ruth Nelson had the following children:

    i.  Teressa Cook was born in 1836.

    ii.  Jerome Cook was born in 1837.

3198   iii.  George Cook, born 1839, New York; married Olive UNKNOWN.

    iv.  Ann "Celia" Cook was born in 1841 in New York.

    v.  Mary Wood Cook was born in 1843 in York.

    vi.  William Cook was born in 1846 in New York.

1612.Rhoda Cook (Miles-6, Thomas-5, Thomas-4, Richard-3, Josiah-2, Josias-1) was born in 1810.

Rhoda Cook and Horace GRAVES were married. Horace Graves was born in 1806.

Horace Graves and Rhoda Cook had the following child:

  i.   Celia Graves was born in 1837.

1613. Thomas Bishop Cook (Elisha-6, Thomas-5, Thomas-4, Richard-3, Josiah-2, Josias-1) was born on 31 Jul 1796 in Schoharie County, NY. He was a farmer. He was a minister.

Thomas Bishop Cook and Leah JOHNSON were married in 1835. They appeared in the census in 1860 and 1870 in Morrow, Mo. Leah Johnson was born in 1810 in the Indiana.

Thomas Bishop Cook and Leah Johnson had the following children:

3199   i.   Jacob Ransom Cook, born Apr 1838, Indiana; married Catherine RIDER; died 31 Dec 1924, Wilson, Adair, Mo.
       ii.   Rachel J. Cook was born estimated 1839 in Indiana.
      iii.   Wealthy Content Cook was born estimated 1841 in Indiana. She appeared in the census in 1860 in Morrow, Adair, Mo.
3200  iv.   Esther Ann "Hester" Cook, born 5 Aug 1843, Indiana; married William Henry Harrison SHIBLEY, 10 Aug 1866, Dearborn, Ind.; died 18 Aug 1912, Van Buren, Ark.
       v.   Phoebe Mariah Cook was born estimated 1847 in Indiana.

1614. Seth Cook (Elisha-6, Thomas-5, Thomas-4, Richard-3, Josiah-2, Josias-1) was born on 22 Feb 1798 in Schoharie County, NY. He was buried in 1873 in Myrick Cemetery, Chilicothe, Ia. He died on 21 Jul 1873 at the age of 75 in Chilicothe, Ia.

Seth Cook and Lucy UNKNOWN were married on 1 Jan 1824. Lucy Unknown was born on 9 Dec 1793 in Vermont. She died on 12 Jan 1835 at the age of 41 in Ohio.

Seth Cook and Lucy Unknown had the following children:

  i.   Daniel Cook was born on 10 May 1825. He died on 10 May 1825.
3201   ii.   James W. Cook, born 23 Sep 1826, Indiana; married Mary McCREW, 28 Dec 1877; married Mary HARRIS, 28 Dec 1877; died 18 Feb 1913.
      iii.   Letty Cook was born on 17 Nov 1828.
3202  iv.   Elisha Cook, born 3 Dec 1830; died 10 May 1906, Weaver, Ia.
3203   v.   Miles Cook, born 27 Jan 1833, Ohio; married Susan KUHNS, 4 Sep 1859; married Frances COFFLAND, 1882; died 29 Dec 1922, Horton, Kans.

Seth Cook and Nancy Ann MILAM were married in 1844. They appeared in the census in

1850 in Washington, Ripley, Ind. They appeared in the census in 1860 in Polk, Wapello, Ia. Nancy Ann Milam, daughter of Zachariah Milam and Rhoda Blankenship, was born on 17 Nov 1824 in Bedford County, Va. She died on 27 Jan 1877 at the age of 52 in Myrick Cemetery, Chilicothe, Ia.

Seth Cook and Nancy Ann Milam had the following children:

3204   i.   Mary Jane Cook, born 30 Jan 1845, Wapello County, Ia.; married Lot CONWELL, 28 Nov 1868; died 22 Feb 1901.

3205   ii.   Lucy Laura Cook, born 1848, Wapello County, Ia.; married E. L. BYRAM, 19 Mar 1868, Wapello, Ind.

       iii.   Rhoda Wealthy Cook was born on 22 Jun 1851 in Wapello County, Ia. She died on 21 Sep 1870 at the age of 19 in Wapello County, Ia.

3206   iv.   Harriet Malvina Cook, born 1855, Wapello County, Ia.; married Charles GILLENS, 9 May 1872, Ottumwa, Wapello, Ia.

3207   v.   Seth Benjamin Tryon Cook, born 3 Nov 1859, Christiansburg, Ia.; married Emma CANFIELD, 2 Mar 1882, Ottumwa, Wapello, Ia.; died 14 Jul 1952, Pueblo, Pueblo, Col.

1615. Wealthy Cook (Elisha-6, Thomas-5, Thomas-4, Richard-3, Josiah-2, Josias-1) was born on 5 Aug 1806 in Schoharie County, NY.

Wealthy Cook and Enoch Major TERRILL were married in 1824. They appeared in the census in 1850 in Manchester, Dearborn, Ind. They appeared in the census in 1860 in Polk, Wapello, Ia. Enoch Major Terrill was born on 18 Jul 1805 in Connecticut.

Enoch Major Terrill and Wealthy Cook had the following children:

3208   i.   Asahel Terrill, born abt 1830, Indiana; married Marilla UNKNOWN.

       ii.   Benjamin Terrill was born in 1832 in Indiana.

       iii.   Rosetta Terrill was born in 1835 in Indiana.

       iv.   Sewel Terrill was born in 1842 in Indiana.

       v.   Content Terrill was born in 1845 in Indiana.

       vi.   Wealthy Terrill was born in 1846 in Indiana.

       vii.   Satah E. Terrill was born in 1851 in Iowa.

1616. Elisha Cook (Elisha-6, Thomas-5, Thomas-4, Richard-3, Josiah-2, Josias-1) was born on 18 Mar 1811 in Schoharie County, NY. He died on 15 Dec 1880 at the age of 69 in Ottumwa, Ia. He was buried in Ottumwa Cemetary, Ottumwa, Ia.

Elisha Cook and Charlotte M. UNKNOWN were married on 5 Sep 1833. They appeared in the census in 1850 in Washington, Marion, Ind. Elisha and Charlotte moved to Polk, Ia. after 1854 They appeared in the census in 1860 in Polk, Wapello, Ia. Charlotte M. Unknown was born abt 1813 in Maryland. She died on 28 Feb 1889 at the age of 76 in Ottumwa, Wapello, Ia. She was buried in Ottumwa Cemetary, Ottumwa, Ia.

Elisha Cook and Charlotte M. Unknown had the following children:

    i.   Eunice Cook was born in 1833 in Marrion, Ind.
    ii.  Jonathon Cook was born in 1834 in Marrion, Ind.
    iii. Davis Cook was born in 1835 in Marrion, Ind.
3209  iv. Andrew Nelson Cook, born 1836, Marrion, Ind.
    v.  Elizabeth Cook was born in 1838 in Marrion, Ind.
3210  vi. John C Cook, born 29 Oct 1838, Marrion, Ind.; married Josephine CALVIN, 28 Dec 1865.
    vii. Samuel Cook was born in 1840 in Marrion, Ind.
    viii.   Wealthy A Cook was born in 1841 in Marrion, Ind.
    ix. Hiram P Cook was born in 1846 in Marrion, Ind.
    x.  Nancy J Cook (Twin) was born in 1851 in Marrion, Ind.
    xi. Sarah E Cook (Twin) was born in 1851 in Marrion, Ind.
    xii. Mary Etta Cook was born in 1854 in Lee, Ia.

1617.David Cook (Elisha-6, Thomas-5, Thomas-4, Richard-3, Josiah-2, Josias-1) was born on 3 Sep 1813 in Schoharie County, NY. He died on 16 Jan 1891 at the age of 77 in Ottumwa, Wapello, Ia. He was buried in Chisman Cemetery Number One (David Cook and Harriet Vinson).

David Cook and Harriet VINSON were married. Harriet Vinson was born on 10 Jul 1820. She died on 31 Jan 1879 at the age of 58 in Wapello, Ia. She was buried in Chisman Cemetery Number One.

David Cook and Harriet Vinson had the following children:

3211  i.   John F Cook, born 21 Oct 1838, Indiana; died 16 Nov 1892.
3212  ii.  William R Cook, born 1842, Indiana; married Lydia Unknown; died 1924.
3213  iii. Elias Nelson Cook, born 1843, Iowa; died 1928.
3214  iv. Wealthy Ann Cook, born 1845, Kentucky.
3215  v.  Richard C. Cook, born 1847, Iowa.
    vi. Albert O Cook was born in 1849 in Iowa.
    vii. Mary A Cook was born in 1851 in Iowa.
    viii.   Andrew L Cook was born on 23 Apr 1852 in Wapello, Ia. He died on 24 Sep 1853.
    ix. Alfred Cook was born on 29 May 1854 in Iowa. He died on 29 May 1854.

x.   Harriet E Cook was born on 29 May 1854 in Wapello, Ia. She died on 20 Aug 1855.

3216   xi.  Cyrus H Cook, born 1856, Iowa; married Lucy Nannie CONE, 30 May 1882, Iowa.

xii. Seth C Cook was born in 1858 in Wapello, Ia.

3217   xiii.   Elisha David Cook, born 6 Apr 1861, Iowa; married Mary Ellen MCMULLIN, 1 Apr 1897; died 9 Feb 1939 in Iowa.


1618.Hannah Ann Cook (Elisha-6, Thomas-5, Thomas-4, Richard-3, Josiah-2, Josias-1) was born on 28 Mar 1816.


Hannah Ann Cook and David P. FERRIS were married.


1628.Don Pedro Aquilla Cook (Bela-6, Jesse-5, Thomas-4, Richard-3, Josiah-2, Josias-1) was born on 16 Sep 1803 in Hancock County, Ga. He died on 18 Jul 1873 at the age of 69 in Union Parish, Louisiana.


Don Pedro Aquilla Cook and Mary Jane TURNER were married on 18 Aug 1826 in Mississippi. Mary Jane Turner was born on 19 Jan 1809 in Wilkinson County, Miss. She died on 21 May 1837 at the age of 28 in Quachita Parish, La.


Don Pedro Aquilla Cook and Mary Jane Turner had the following children:

3241   i.   John Bela Cook, born 10 Jul 1827, Wilkinson County, Miss.; married Martha Ann KELLY, 17 Dec 1857, Walker County, Tex.; died 11 Dec 1911, Jasper, Texas.

3242   ii.  Abigail Elizabeth Cook, born 2 Jan 1830, Wilkinson County, Miss.; married Joseph Hamilton GREEN, Union Parish, Louisiana; died 19 Mar 1895, Union Parish, Louisiana.

iii. Eliza Ann Cook was born on 1 Feb 1832 in Wilkinson County, Miss. She died on 18 Aug 1833 in Wilkinson County, Miss.

3243   iv.  Benjamin Parker Cook, born 24 Aug 1834, Wilkinson County, Miss.; married Mary Ann GOODYEAR, 21 Jan 1857, Union Parish, Louisiana; died 27 Jan 1892, Union Parish, Louisiana.

v.   Mary Jane Cook was born on 4 Mar 1837 in Union Parish, Louisiana. She died on 11 Aug 1842 at the age of 5 in Union Parish, Louisiana.

vi.  Artemisia "Ann" Cook was born on 19 Aug 1839 in Union Parish, Louisiana.


Don Pedro Aquilla Cook and Susan Amanda BEATY were married on 19 Jul 1842 in Union Parish, Louisiana. Susan Amanda Beaty was born in 1819. She died on 24 Sep 1879 at the age of 60.


Don Pedro Aquilla Cook and Susan Amanda Beaty had the following children:

i. James Quine Cook was born on 9 Sep 1843 in State of Mississippi. He died in Sep 1851 at the age of 8 in Union Parish, Louisiana.

ii. Don Pedro Aquilla Cook was born on 12 Jul 1845 in Union Parish, Louisiana. He died on 9 Oct 1846 in Union Parish, Louisiana.

iii. David Cook was born in 1848 in Union, La.

1629. Alonzo Talcott Cook (Talcott Fairchild Smithson-6, Jesse-5, Thomas-4, Richard-3, Josiah-2, Josias-1) was born on 11 Dec 1821 in Afton, Chenango, NY. He died on 6 Sep 1893 at the age of 71.

Alonzo Talcott Cook and Susan WELLS were married on 18 Feb 1847 in Adams, Ill. They appeared in the census in 1860 in Payson, Ill. Susan Wells was born (date unknown).

Alonzo Talcott Cook and Susan Wells had the following children:

i. Homer Cook was born on 28 Feb 1847 in Payson Township, Ill. He died on 28 Aug 1851 at the age of 4.

3244 ii. Jesse Fairchild Cook, born 19 Jan 1849, Payson Township, Ill.; married Ella HARTSHORN, 20 Apr 1871; died 8 Feb 1903.

3245 iii. Chauncey E. Cook, born 20 Jul 1850, Payson Township, Ill.; married Orena E. TYLER, 6 Sep 1871, Richfield, Adams, Ill.; died 3 May 1900, Quincy, Ill.

3246 iv. William K. Cook, born 16 Nov 1853, Payson Township, Ill.; died Aug 1921.

v. Albert Cook was born in Nov 1854 in Payson Township, Ill. He died on 14 Jan 1856 at the age of 1.

vi. Olive Cook was born on 2 Jul 1857 in Payson Township, Ill. She died on 14 Feb 1932 at the age of 74.

3247 vii. Talcott Cook, born 1859, Payson Township, Ill.; married Nellie EASTON, 22 Jun 1891; died 23 Apr 1925.

3248 viii. Abner Wells Cook, born 23 Aug 1861, Payson Township, Ill.; married Lydia Francis GRUBB, 91 jan 1884; died 16 Mar 1946.

3249 ix. Joy Ann Cook, born 7 Oct 1866, Payson Township, Ill.; married Benjamin Franklin STRATTON, 10 Oct 1889; died 1940.

3250 x. Henry S. Cook, born 5 Aug 1868, Payson Township, Ill.; married Josephine E. GETZ, 24 Dec 1893; died 26 Apr 1922.

2041. Jacob Cook (Isaiah-6, Joshua-5, Joshua-4, Joshua-3, Josiah-2, Josias-1) was born about 1800 in Ondoga County, NY.

Jacob Cook and Candice UNKNOWN were married. Candice Unknown was born about 1806.

Jacob Cook and Candice Unknown had the following children:

      i.   Louisa Cook was born about 1825.
     ii.   Maria Cook was born about 1828.
4223  iii.   Mahlan Cook, born Aug 1831; married Elizabeth UNKNOWN.
4224  iv.   Guy Cook, born Aug 1833; married Lucretia UNKNOWN.

2052. William W. Cook (William Walker-6, Ebenezer-5, Ebenezer-4, Joshua-3, Josiah-2, Josias-1) was born on 22 Oct 1803 in Broome County, NY. In 1850 he was a sheriff and tailor. He lived in Conklin, NY. in 1852. William appeared in the census in 1855 in New York. In 1870 he was a postmaster. He died on 7 Mar 1889 at the age of 85 in Whitney Point, NY., poss. Falling from a ladder. He was buried in Riverside Cemetery in Whitney Point, NY.

William W. Cook and Frances Maria Whitney (Twin) were married on 2 Mar 1825 in Whitney Point, NY. Frances Maria Whitney (Twin), daughter of Thomas Whitney and Polly Gilbert, was born on 20 Oct 1807 in Broome County, NY. She died on 22 May 1872 at the age of 64 in Whitney Point, NY. She was buried on 23 May 1872 at Riverside Cemetery in Whitney Point, NY.

2053. Charles Abby Cook (William Walker-6, Ebenezer-5, Ebenezer-4, Joshua-3, Josiah-2, Josias-1) was born on 11 Dec 1805 in Killawog, NY. He lived moved to Triangle, Broome, NY. in 1836/7. He died on 23 Jan 1881 at the age of 75 in Whitney Point, NY. Charles was buried in Lisle Cemetery, Lisle, Broome, NY. Copies of relevant pages of his bible can be found in some libraries.

Charles Abby Cook and Phebe Odell FORD were married on 3 Feb 1831 in Lisle, NY. Phebe Odell Ford, daughter of Henry Ford and Elizabeth Darcy, was born on 21 Mar 1811. She died on 29 Sep 1863 at the age of 52 in Whitney Point, NY. Phebe was buried in Lisle Cemetery, Lisle, Broome, NY.

Charles Abby Cook and Phebe Odell Ford had the following children:

      i.   Henry William Cook was born on 5 Feb 1832 in Broome County, NY. He died on 7 Feb 1849 at the age of 17. He was buried in Lisle Cemetery, Lisle, NY.
4243  ii.   Charles Mason Cook, born 15 Nov 1833, Killawog, New York; married Susan Augusta SEYMOUR, 22 May 1866, Whitney Point, NY.; died 17 Aug 1917, Whitney Point, NY. Family legend is that Susan was a descendant of Sir Edward Seymour, Lord High Protector of England during the reign of Henry VIII through her father John Belden Seymour. Susan Seymour was also a descendant of William Bradford of the *Mayflower*, through her mother. Her Bradford lineage is (*Elizabeth Thompson-8, Sophronia Manning-7, David-6, David-5, Irene*

7.185

*Ripley-4, Hannah Bradford-3, William Jr,-2, William Bradford-1.*) Susan was also a descendant of one of the oldest families known: The Beldon Family of Baildon, England, which can trace itself to before the Battle of Hastings in 1066. The name was spelled Baylden until 1641, in Wethersford Records as Beldon from 1641-1643; Belding from 1643 to 1736; Beldon from 1736 to 1753; Belding from 1753 to 1825; Belden from 1825 to the present time. There were as many variations of the name before 1641. The reason it's possible to trace this family is that the surname is a place-surname and there is only one Bailden in England. She is also descended from the Daniel Baylden family of Wethersfield, 4 of whom were slaughtered by American Indians and others taken as slaves during the French and Indian War.

4244 iii. William West Cook, born 4 Dec 1835, Broome County, NY.; married Adeline HALL, 3 Sep 1868; died 28 Feb 1878.

4245 iv. Elizabeth Ford Cook, born 1 Jun 1838, Broome County, NY.; married Richard G. PARDEE, 15 Oct 1876; died 23 Sep 1917. The letters that make up the other half of this book were mostly written, and presumably saved, by Elizabeth.

 v. Edward Gray Cook was born on 14 Feb 1841 in Broome County, NY. Edward served in the military on 9 Aug 1862 in the Civil War from New York. He died on 12 Feb 1879 at the age of 37 in Santa Barbara, Cal. He never married.

 vi. Alexander Ford Cook was born on 9 Jan 1843 in Broome County, NY. He drafted or enlisted in 1863 in Triangle, Broome, New York. Alexander died in the Battle of Spotsylvania Courthouse on 12 May 1864 at the age of 21. He is memorialized in Lisle Cemetery.

4246 vii. Charlotte Ford Cook, born 23 Jan 1846, Broome County, NY.; married Donald Macrae STEWART, 10 Apr 1872; died 16 Apr 1909.

4247 viii. Hon. Lyman Cook, born 4 Feb 1848, Broome County, NY.; married Harriet Melissa ARNAR, 28 Dec 1876; died 1929.

4248 ix. Henry Ford Cook, born 5 Feb 1850; married Emma Harriet RODEHAVER, Jun 1881; died 3 Dec 1928.

 x. John Leighton Wilson Cook was born on 11 Aug 1852 in Broome County, NY. He appeared in the census on 7 Jul 1860 in Triangle, Broome, NY. He died on 3 Apr 1873 at the age of 20 in Santa Barbara, Cal.


Charles Abby Cook and Hannah OSBORNE were married on 3 Feb 1871. Hannah Osborne was born in 1831. They appeared in the census in 1880 in Whitney Point, NY.


Charles Abby Cook and Hannah Osborne had the following children:

 i. Mary Augusta Cook was born on 19 Mar 1872 in Whitney Point, NY. She appeared in the census in 1880 in Whitney Point, NY.

4249 ii. George Lewis Cook, born 30 Jan 1875, Whitney Point, NY.; married Jane BAKER.

2054.Mary West Cook (William Walker-6, Ebenezer-5, Ebenezer-4, Joshua-3, Josiah-2, Josias-1) was born on 17 Jul 1808.

Mary West Cook and George O. WILLS were married on 31 Aug 1829. George O. Wills was born (date unknown).

George O. Wills and Mary West Cook had the following children:

 i. George Ashbel Wills.
 ii. Mary Ann Wills.
 iii. William Cook Wills.
 iv. Edward Lyman Wills.

2055.Harriet Cook (Ebenezer-6, Ebenezer-5, Ebenezer-4, Joshua-3, Josiah-2, Josias-1) was born on 22 Oct 1793. Harriet died in 1870 at the age of 77.

Harriet Cook and William BALL were married in 1818. William Ball was born (date unknown).

William Ball and Harriet Cook had the following children:

 i. Rodney Ball.
 ii. Elizabeth Ball.

2056.Aurilla Cook (Ebenezer-6, Ebenezer-5, Ebenezer-4, Joshua-3, Josiah-2, Josias-1) was born in Oct 1795. Aurilla died in 1817 at the age of 22.

Aurilla Cook and Dennis CORSAW were married in 1813.

Dennis Corsaw and Aurilla Cook had the following children:

 i. Charles Corsaw.
 ii. Clarissa Corsaw.

2057.Charles West Cook (Ebenezer-6, Ebenezer-5, Ebenezer-4, Joshua-3, Josiah-2, Josias-1) was born on 1 Feb 1800. He appeared in the census in 1810 in Berkshire, Tioga, NY. He died on 19 May 1845 at the age of 45.

Charles West Cook and Amy ROYCE were married in 1823. They moved in Chicago, Ill. after 1823. Amy Royce was born on 10 Jan 1803. She died on 24 Aug 1835 at the age of 32.

Charles West Cook and Amy Royce had the following children:

    i.   Aurilla B. Cook.
    ii.  Asahel Royce Cook died in 1827.
    iii. Charles Henry Cook.
    iv. Franklin Cook.
    v.  Ebenezer Cook.

Charles West Cook and Amanda NEWTON were married in 1836.

Charles West Cook and Amanda Newton had the following children:

    i.   George Develson Cook.
    ii.  Harriet Elizabeth Cook.
    iii. Josephine Cook died in Jan 1845.
    iv. Frederic Cook died in Jan 1841.

2058.Abigail West Cook (Ebenezer-6, Ebenezer-5, Ebenezer-4, Joshua-3, Josiah-2, Josias-1) was born on 26 Apr 1804. She moved to Chicago, Ill. between 1845 and 1874. She died on 24 Nov 1874 at the age of 70. Abigail was buried in Berkshire, Tioga, NY.

Abigail West Cook and James Hobart FORD were married on 29 Apr 1835. James Hobart Ford, son of Nathaniel Ford and Caroline Rees, was born on 26 Sep 1807 in Berkshire, Tioga, NY. He died on 29 May 1854 at the age of 46.

2059.George Churchill Cook (Ebenezer-6, Ebenezer-5, Ebenezer-4, Joshua-3, Josiah-2, Josias-1) was born on 10 Mar 1811.

George Churchill Cook and Lucy Maria MCWILLIAMS were married on 10 Nov 1834. They moved to Chicago, Cook, Ill. in 1844.

George Churchill Cook and Lucy Maria McWilliams had the following children:

    i.   Henry W. Cook was born on 10 Jul 1836.
    ii.  William W. Cook was born on 30 Nov 1838. He died on 23 Sep 1847 at the age of 8.

2066.Ebenezer Cook (Ira-6, Ebenezer-5, Ebenezer-4, Joshua-3, Josiah-2, Josias-1) was born on 14 Feb 1810 in Whitestown, NY. He moved to Davenport, Ia. in 1836. He was admitted to the bar in 1839.

Between 1840 and 1857 Ebenezer was an owner of a chain of banks called Cook & Sargent with his brother John in Iowa. In 1858/9 he was the mayor of Davenport, Ia. He died on 7 Oct 1871 at the age of 61 in Davenport, Ia. Photograph is from his time as mayor.

Ebenezer Cook and Clarissa Bryan were married on 6 Feb 1833. Clarissa Bryan, daughter of Fowler P. Bryan and Lucretia Wattles, was born on 4 Aug 1811 in Sydney, Delaware County, NY. She died on 19 Feb 1879 at the age of 67 in Davenport, Ia.

2067.Patience Ells Cook (Ira-6, Ebenezer-5, Ebenezer-4, Joshua-3, Josiah-2, Josias-1) was born on 18 Oct 1811 in Whitestown, NY. She moved to Davenport, Ia. in 1836.

Patience Ells Cook and William Van Tuyl were married on 7 Oct 1835. William Van Tuyl, son of John Van Tuyl and Jane White, was born on 23 Jul 1810 in Otsego County, NY. In 1850 he was a land agent for the CRI and PRR in Davenport, Ia. He died on 19 Jun 1887 at the age of 76 in Iowa. William was buried in Oakdale Cemetery, Iowa. [See Appendix A for more information.]

William Van Tuyl and Patience Ells Cook had the following children:

   i.   Cornelia Van Tuyl was born in 1838 in Iowa.
   ii.  Ira C. Van Tuyl was born in 1840 in Iowa.
   iii. Amanda Van Tuyl was born in 1842 in Iowa.
   iv.  Caroline C. Van Tuyl was born in 1845 in Iowa.
   v.   Ebenezer C. Van Tuyl was born in 1848 in Iowa.

2068.Mary Curtis Cook (Ira-6, Ebenezer-5, Ebenezer-4, Joshua-3, Josiah-2, Josias-1) was born on 17 Nov 1815 in Whitestown, NY.

Mary Curtis Cook and John Wright BROWN were married on 11 Sep 1833. John Wright Brown was born on 11 Mar 1811 in Green River, NY. In 1840 he was a farmer in Shiloh County, Ia.

2069.John Parsons Cook (Ira-6, Ebenezer-5, Ebenezer-4, Joshua-3, Josiah-2, Josias-1) was born on 31 Aug 1817 in Whitestown, NY. He moved to Davenport, Ia. in 1836. He was admitted to the bar in Iowa in 1841. In 1845 John was a lawyer in Davenport, Ia. He appeared in the census in 1850 in Center Township, Cedar, Ia. He appeared in the census in 1860 in Scott County, Ia. John died on 16 Apr 1872 at the age of 54 in Davenport, Ia. He was buried in Oakdale Cemetery, Iowa. He was a the representative of his congressional district in the 33rd Congress of the United States. John was a fire insurance agent.

John Parsons Cook and Eliza Ann ROWE were married on 26 Oct 1842. Eliza Ann Rowe, daughter of Christopher Rowe and Elizabeth Look, was born on 3 Dec 1822 in Steuben County, NY.

John Parsons Cook and Eliza Ann Rowe had the following children:

4259   i.   Edward E. Cook, born 13 Aug 1843; married Ellen Katherine DODGE, 20 Dec 1866; died 16 Jun 1914.  Their second son was George Cram "Jig" Cook, who discovered and supported Eugene O'Neill for the first decade of his career. George was one of the founders of the Provincetown Theatre in Provincetown, and later New York. He has been largely forgotten in the shadow of many great people, including his wife Susan Glaspell, but he is was a very important figure in American theatre.

ii.   Lowe P. Cook was born about 1846.

iii.   Ebenezer Cook was born in 1856 in Iowa.

iv.   John F. Cook was born about 1857 in Iowa.

2070.Ira S. Cook (Ira-6, Ebenezer-5, Ebenezer-4, Joshua-3, Josiah-2, Josias-1) was born on 26 Oct 1821 in Whitestown, NY. He appeared in the census in 1850 in Scott County, Ia. In 1855 he was an insurance agent in Des Moines, Ia.

Ira S. Cook and Mary Crane OWENS were married on 26 Apr 1854 in Center Lisle, Broome, NY. Mary Crane Owens, daughter of John Owens and Eunice Meeker, was born on 6 Nov 1831 in Cincinnati, O. [See Appendixes A and B for his narratives of life as a pioneer in Iowa.]

Ira S. Cook and Mary Crane Owens had the following children:

i.   Carrie Cook was born in 1853.

ii.   Rachel Cook was born in 1859 in Iowa.

iii.   Matt Dazelle was born in 1878 in Iowa. He was adopted.

2071.Olive Martha Cook (John-6, Gideon-5, Ebenezer-4, Joshua-3, Josiah-2, Josias-1) was born before Jul 1816. She was baptized in Jul 1816.

Olive Martha Cook and Charles CRUTTENDEN were married on 8 Apr 1840. Charles Cruttenden was born in Chatham, Mass.

2072.David Brainerd Cook (William-6, Gideon-5, Ebenezer-4, Joshua-3, Josiah-2, Josias-1) was born on 23 Jul 1808 in East Haddam, Conn.

David Brainerd Cook and Esther Ann AUGER were married. Esther Ann Auger was born in

Saybrook, Conn.

2073.Lucinda Cook (Azel-6, Gideon-5, Ebenezer-4, Joshua-3, Josiah-2, Josias-1) was born on 19
Sep 1829 in Kingston, Ont., Canada. She died on 31 Dec 1912 at the age of 83 in Wolfe
Island, Ontario, Canada.

Lucinda Cook and Nelson DEAN were married. Nelson Dean was born on 13 Jul 1825 in
Watson, NY. He died on 3 May 1888 at the age of 62 in Wolfe Island, Ontario, Canada.

Nelson Dean and Lucinda Cook had the following child:

i.   Emma Dean, born 9 Dec 1856, Wolfe Island, Ontario, Canada; died 27 Feb 1935,
     Kingston, Ont., Canada.

2074.James Cook (Ebenezer-6, Gideon-5, Ebenezer-4, Joshua-3, Josiah-2, Josias-1) was born on 24
Apr 1834. He died on 10 Jun 1903 at the age of 69 in Meriden, New Haven, Conn. He was a
printer and real estate salesman.

James Cook and Emma L. FAY were married on 10 Jun 1903. Emma L. Fay, daughter of
Lorenzo Fay and Elizabeth Unknown, was born in Jul 1850.

James Cook and Emma L. Fay had the following children:

4261   i.   Arthur E. Cook, born Mar 1879, Meriden, New Haven, Conn.; married Edna
            UNKNOWN.
       ii.  Unknown Cook.

2075.Henry Cook (Ebenezer-6, Gideon-5, Ebenezer-4, Joshua-3, Josiah-2, Josias-1) was born on 4
Dec 1835. He died on 17 Feb 1909 at the age of 73.

Henry Cook and Alice GLADWIN were married on 25 Mar 1870 in Episcopal Church,
Middletown, Mass.

2076.Susan Louisa Cook (Ebenezer-6, Gideon-5, Ebenezer-4, Joshua-3, Josiah-2, Josias-1) was
born in 1838. She died on 4 Oct 1916 at the age of 78. She was buried in Farm Hill,
Middletown, Conn.

Susan Louisa Cook and Joseph HUBBARD were married. Joseph Hubbard was an overseer
of a wet mill.

Joseph Hubbard and Susan Louisa Cook had the following children:

7.191

i.   Henry W. Hubbard, born 1863, Connecticut; married Addie Unknown.
ii.  Franklin G. Hubbard, born Oct 1864, Connecticut; married Cora Unknown.
iii. Joseph P. Hubbard was born in Jan 1870 in Connecticut. He appeared in the census in
      1870 in Middletown, Conn.

2077. Elizabeth Cook (Moses Bassett-6, Moses-5, Ephraim-4, Joshua-3, Josiah-2, Josias-1) was born
       on 25 Nov 1794 in Connecticut. She died on 18 Jun 1866 at the age of 71 in Lenawee
       County, Mich.

       Elizabeth Cook and John Hawthorne CARPENTER were married on 2 Nov 1815 in Elmira,
       NY. They moved in Fairfield, Lenawee, Mich. between 1827 and 1832. John Hawthorne
       Carpenter was born on 2 May 1790 in Elmira, NY. He died on 3 Jul 1874 at the age of 84 in
       Lenawee County, Mich.

John Hawthorne Carpenter and Elizabeth Cook had the following children:

       i.   Daniel Carpenter was born in 1827 in New York.
       ii.  Elsa A. Carpenter was born in 1832 in Michigan.
       iii. Martha Carpenter was born in 1836 in Michigan.

2078. Lydia Cook (Moses Bassett-6, Moses-5, Ephraim-4, Joshua-3, Josiah-2, Josias-1) was born
       about 1798.

       Lydia Cook and William C. LOWE were married. William C. Lowe was born in 1800. He
       died in 1886 at the age of 86.

William C. Lowe and Lydia Cook had the following children:

       i.   William C. Lowe was born in 1827 in New York.
       ii.  Phebe E. Lowe was born in 1831 in New York.
       iii. Judson Lowe was born in 1834 in Michigan.
       iv.  George W. Lowe was born in 1836 in Michigan.
       v.   Nathan C. Lowe was born in 1838 in Michigan.

2079. Zachariah Cook (James-6, Moses-5, Ephraim-4, Joshua-3, Josiah-2, Josias-1) was born on 10
       Sep 1786. He lived in Locke, Cayuga, NY. in 1820. He died on 23 Feb 1827 at the age of 40
       in Locke, Cayuga, NY.

       Zachariah Cook and Polly LOOMIS were married. Polly Loomis was born on 8 Jun 1794.

Zachariah Cook and Polly Loomis had the following children:

4264   i.   Reuben Cook, born 6 Mar 1816, Locke, Cayuga, NY.; married Hannah DANN, bef
            1842; died 12 Aug 1892, Locke, Cayuga, NY.
4265   ii.  Simon James Cook, born 16 Oct 1818, Locke, Cayuga, NY.; married Caroline
            ROWLEY; died 31 Jan 1906, Locke, Cayuga, NY.


2080.Deacon John Cook (James-6, Moses-5, Ephraim-4, Joshua-3, Josiah-2, Josias-1) was born on
    10 Sep 1786 in Freehold, Cayuga, NY. He served in the military in the War of 1812 between
    1812 and 1814. He died on 5 Aug 1857 at the age of 70 in Mecca, Oh. John was buried in
    East Mecca Cemetery, Mecca, Oh.

    Deacon John Cook and Ruth CURTIS were married before 1820. Ruth Curtis was born on 19
    Jun 1786. She was born on 19 Jun 1786 in Caanan, Litchfield, Conn. She died on 13 Feb
    1850 at the age of 63 in Mecca, Oh. Ruth was buried in Feb 1850 in East Mecca Cemetery,
    Mecca, Oh.

John Cook and Ruth Curtis had the following children:

4266   i.    Huldah Cook, born 20 Apr 1806, Locke, Cayuga, NY.; married Henry SMITH.
       ii.   Sally Cook was born on 19 May 1807 in Locke, Cayuga, NY. She died on 27 May 1818
             at the age of 11 in Locke, Cayuga, NY.
       iii.  Reuben Cook was born on 15 Jul 1809 in Groton, NY. He died on 22 Nov 1809 in
             Groton, NY.
4267   iv.   Zachariah Amos Cook, born 11 Sep 1810, Freehold, Cayuga, NY.; married Eunice
             BENNETT, abt 1829; died aft 1857, Iowa.
4268   v.    Lois Ann Cook, born 20 Sep 1812, Bath, NY.; married George OATMAN, 21 Dec
             1838, Trumbull County, O.; died 14 Apr 1847, Laharp, Hancock, Ill.
4269   vi.   Ruth Cook, born 26 Sep 1814, Bath, NY.; married Elisha James BENNETT, 20 Dec
             1829; died 29 Jul 1851, Mecca, Oh.
4270   vii.  Polly Cook, born abt 1815, New York; married Aaron HALL, 10 Oct 1839, Trumbull
             County, O.
4271   viii. Eunice L. Cook, born 10 Aug 1816, Bath, NY.; married Alford S. SPERRY, 25
             Sep 1832, Trumbull County, O.; died 11 May 1840, Trumbull County, O.
4272   ix.   James Edward Cook, born 25 Jun 1819, Locke, Cayuga, NY.; married Sarah
             SHANNON; married Mary Madeline CHAFFEE, 13 Dec 1838, Mecca, Oh.;
             died 1891, Henderson, Knox, Ill.
4273   x.    Wealthy Cook, born 15 Mar 1821, Locke, Cayuga, NY.; married Joseph G.
             CHAFFEE, 24 Dec 1838; died 1 Sep 1892, Mecca, Oh.
4274   xi.   Aaron Cook, born 22 Dec 1826, New York; married E. CLARK, 21 Dec 1846.
       xii.  William Henry Cook was born on 18 Mar 1829 in Locke, Cayuga, NY. He died on 15
             May 1829 in Locke, Cayuga, NY.

Deacon John Cook and Elizabeth GRAY were married on 1 Apr 1851 in Concord, Erie, NY. Elizabeth Gray was born on 11 Oct 1790 in Kinderhook, NY.

2081.Nathan Cook (James-6, Moses-5, Ephraim-4, Joshua-3, Josiah-2, Josias-1) was born about 1800 in Locke, Cayuga, NY. He moved to Mosquito Creek, Mecca, Oh. after 1832. He died on 24 Nov 1887 at the age of 87 in Mecca, Oh. Nathan was buried after 24 Nov 1887 in East Mecca Cemetery, Mecca, Oh.

Nathan Cook and Permilia HADLOCK were married in 1819. Permilia Hadlock was born about 1817 in New York. She died in Apr 1846 at the age of 29 in Trumbull County, O.

Nathan Cook and Permilia Hadlock had the following children:

4275   i.   Asa Jane Cook, born 1820; married Manley MCCAULY; died aft 1900.
4276   ii.  James Cook, born 21 Jul 1821, New York; married Permilia COLE, 2 Sep 1844, Ashtabula, Ashtabula, O.; married Mary POOLE, 10 Nov 1858, Trumbull County, O.; died aft 1904, Warren, Trumbull, O.
4277   iii. Nathan Cook, born 1822, New York; married Delia KIESECKER, 14 Jul 1842, Trumbull County, O.; died 1867, Cerro Gordo, Ia.
4278   iv.  Lois Cook, born bet 1825 and 1830; married Ezra SCOVILLE, 10 Sep 1843, Trumbull County, O.; died aft 1893.
4279   v.   Elizabeth Cook, born 1827; married Unknown SPITLER, 1866, Michigan; married Samuel HELSEL; died aft 1896.
4280   vi.  Joseph William Cook, born 14 Jan 1831, Locke, Cayuga, NY.; married Zelia Emily FOLSOM, 28 Nov 1857, Ostego, Wisc.; died 23 Nov 1890, Grant Township, Cerro Gorde, Ia.
4281   vii. Euphemia L. Cook, born 1837, Mosquito Creek, Mecca, Oh.; married Henry B. OGRAM, 7 Oct 1860, Trumbull County, O.; died 1 Mar 1917, Trumbull County, O.

2082.Samuel Cook (James-6, Moses-5, Ephraim-4, Joshua-3, Josiah-2, Josias-1) was born before 1791. He died on 4 Mar 1825 at the age of 34 in Groton, NY.

Samuel Cook and Philinda UNKNOWN were married.

Samuel Cook and Philinda Unknown had the following child:

i.   Clarissa Eleanor Cook was born about 1817.

2083.Lovina Cook (James-6, Moses-5, Ephraim-4, Joshua-3, Josiah-2, Josias-1) was born about 1827 in Locke, Cayuga, NY.

Lovina Cook and Silas N. JONES were married. Silas N. Jones was born in 1830 in Ohio.

Silas N. Jones and Lovina Cook had the following children:

    i.   Elmer Jones was born in 1845.
    ii.  Laurena Jones was born in 1848.
    iii. Theodocia Jones was born in 1853.

2084.Reuben C. Cook (Ivory-6, Reuben-5, Ephraim-4, Joshua-3, Josiah-2, Josias-1) was born in Aug 1792 in Orwell, Vt. He died on 3 Feb 1885 at the age of 92 in Shoreham, Vt.

Reuben C. Cook and Roxalana WILSON were married on 9 Oct 1817. Roxalana Wilson was born about 1796. She died in 1875 at the age of 79 in Shoreham, Vt.

Reuben C. Cook and Roxalana Wilson had the following children:

    i.   James Cook was born about 1822.
    ii.  ?Luaph Cook was born about 1827.
    iii. Edmund Cook was born about 1829.

2085.Ivory Cook Jr. (Ivory-6, Reuben-5, Ephraim-4, Joshua-3, Josiah-2, Josias-1) was born on 11 Oct 1793 in Orwell, Vt. He died on 22 Oct 1879 at the age of 86 in West Haven, Rutland, Vt. He was a farmer.

Ivory Cook Jr. and Calista COOK were married. Calista Cook, daughter of Oliver Cook and Mercy Harris, was born about 1799 in Coventry, Conn. She died on 3 Jan 1872 at the age of 73 in West Haven, Rutland, Vt. Ivory and Calista were cousins.

Ivory Cook and Calista Cook had the following children:

    i.   Louisa A. Cook was born about 1827.
 4282  ii.  Ivory Cook, born abt 1831; married Olive RIVETT, bef 1860.

2086.Phebe Cook (Ivory-6, Reuben-5, Ephraim-4, Joshua-3, Josiah-2, Josias-1) was born (date unknown).

Phebe Cook and Harry CULVER were married.

2087.Truman Cook (Ivory-6, Reuben-5, Ephraim-4, Joshua-3, Josiah-2, Josias-1) was born (date unknown).

Truman Cook and Dolly UNKNOWN were married in 1790 in Orwell, Vt.

Truman Cook and Dolly Unknown had the following children:

 4283 i. Nelson Cook, born 1811, Connecticut; married Lucretia UNKNOWN.
   ii. John W. Cook was born in 1821 in New York.
   iii. George J. Cook was born in 1827 in New York.
   iv. Henry Cook was born in 1828.
   v. William Cook was born in 1833.

2088.Omira Cook (Ivory-6, Reuben-5, Ephraim-4, Joshua-3, Josiah-2, Josias-1) was born on 11 Sep 1798 in Orwell, Vt. She died on 8 Jun 1875 at the age of 76 in Shoreham, Vt.

Omira Cook and James WILSON were married on 19 Oct 1821. James Wilson was born on 10 Mar 1791.

James Wilson and Omira Cook had the following children:

   i. Emily Wilson was born in 1830.
   ii. Delia Wilson was born in 1834.

2089.Oliver Cook (Ivory-6, Reuben-5, Ephraim-4, Joshua-3, Josiah-2, Josias-1) was born (date unknown).

Oliver Cook married.

Oliver Cook had the following children:

   i. Benjamin Cook.
   ii. Ivory Cook.
   iii. Emily Cook.
   iv. Mary Cook.
   v. Amanda Cook.
   vi. Oliver Cook Jr..

2090.Marie Cook (Ivory-6, Reuben-5, Ephraim-4, Joshua-3, Josiah-2, Josias-1) was born (date unknown).

Marie Cook and Ezra GOODENOW were married. He was also known as Goodenough Ezra.

2091.Melista Cook (Ivory-6, Reuben-5, Ephraim-4, Joshua-3, Josiah-2, Josias-1) was born (date
        unknown).

        Melista Cook and Atwood MARSH were married.

2092.Chauncey Cook (Ivory-6, Reuben-5, Ephraim-4, Joshua-3, Josiah-2, Josias-1) was born in
        1808 in Orwell, Vt.

        Chauncey Cook and Salina CONVERSE were married. Salina Converse was born about
        1810.

Chauncey Cook and Salina Converse had the following children:

   i.   Sarah M. Cook was born about 1835.
   ii.  Charlotte Cook was born in 1837.

2093.Emily Cook (Ivory-6, Reuben-5, Ephraim-4, Joshua-3, Josiah-2, Josias-1) was born (date
        unknown).

        Emily Cook and William SPOONER were married.

2094.Daniel Mason Cook (David-6, Reuben-5, Ephraim-4, Joshua-3, Josiah-2, Josias-1) was born on
        9 Dec 1790 in Canaan, NY.He died on 22 Dec 1873 at the age of 83 in Orwell, Vt.

        Daniel Mason Cook and Elizabeth BREWER were married on 30 Nov 1814 in Orwell, Vt.
        Elizabeth Brewer, daughter of Archibald Brewer and Miriam Grant, was born on 17 May 1791
        in Orwell, Vt. She died on 19 Jul 1868 at the age of 77.

Daniel Mason Cook and Elizabeth Brewer had the following children:

        i.   Sally Maryette Cook was born on 10 Nov 1815 in Orwell, Vt. She died on 5 Apr 1818 at
                the age of 2 in Orwell, Vt.
   4284 ii.  James Brewer Cook, born 3 Feb 1818, Orwell, Vt.; married Lucretia Palmer
                CAULKINS, 6 Oct 1841, Connecticut; died 6 Aug 1879, Orwell, Vt.
        iii. William Mason Cook was born on 1 Feb 1820 in Orwell, Vt. He died on 27 Oct 2837 at
                the age of 17 in Orwell, Vt.
        iv.  Lucinda Grant Cook was born in Feb 1822 in Vermont.
   4285  v.  Samuel Riley Cook, born 7 Jan 1825, Orwell, Vt.; married Thirza MEACHAM; died
                16 Jan 1866, Orwell, Vt.
   4286  vi. Henry Gordon Cook, born 18 Mar 1827, Orwell, Vt.; married Jane UNKNOWN.
   4287  vii. Eliza Ann Cook, born 7 Jul 1829, Orwell, Vt.; married William Edson ROYCE, 1 Oct

1856.
4288   viii.     Charles Archibald Cook, born 18 Dec 1832, Orwell, Vt.; married Ida Emogene
            MATHER.

2095.Cynthia Cook (David-6, Reuben-5, Ephraim-4, Joshua-3, Josiah-2, Josias-1) was born on 5
      Apr 1792 in Orwell, Vt. She died on 9 Apr 1853 at the age of 61 in Orwell, Vt.

Cynthia Cook and William FULLER were married in 1810.

William Fuller and Cynthia Cook had the following children:

   i.    William Pride Fuller, born 8 Mar 1811, Orwell, Vt.; married Lovina P. BROWN; married
         Unknown CAMPBELL; died 7 Apr 1882, Clymer, Chautauqua, NY. With Lovina he
         had 1 child. With his 2nd wife he had 3 children.
   ii.   David C. Fuller was born in 1813. He d.y.
   iii.  Mary Ella Fuller, born 14 May 1815, Buffalo, Erie, NY.; married Nehemiah Royce.
   iv.   David Manning Fuller was born in 1816.

Cynthia Cook and William FISHER were married in 1821.

\

William Fisher and Cynthia Cook had the following children:

   i.    Caroline Cynthia Fisher, born 11 Apr 1822; married Albert G. WHITE, 28 Jan 1845.
         They had 2 children.
   ii.   Angeline Elizabeth Fisher, born 25 Feb 1824; married Horatio A. GRISWOLD, 4 May
         1843, Orwell, Vt. They had 4 children.
   iii.  William Darwin Fisher, born 11 Mar 1826; married Miranda MURRAY, Jan 1849. They
         had 4 children.
   iv.   Abigail Eveline Fisher was born on 8 Apr 1828. She died on 26 Nov 1857 at the age of 29
         in New York, NY.

Cynthia Cook and John BROWN were married.

2096.Nancy Cook (David-6, Reuben-5, Ephraim-4, Joshua-3, Josiah-2, Josias-1) was born on 23
      Apr 1795 in Orwell, Vt.

Nancy Cook and Levi WILKINSON were married about 1816 in Vermont. Levi Wilkinson
was born on 21 Sep 1789 in New York. He appeared in the census in 1850 in Victory,
Cayuga, NY.

Levi Wilkinson and Nancy Cook had the following children:

i.   Jane Wilkinson was born about 1820.
ii.  Wallace Wilkinson was born about 1820.
iii. Harriet Wilkinson was born about 1827.
iv.  Cynthia Wilkinson was born about 1828.

2097. Henry Gordon Cook (Twin) (David-6, Reuben-5, Ephraim-4, Joshua-3, Josiah-2, Josias-1) was born on 9 Dec 1798 in Orwell, Vt. He died on 6 Jan 1879 at the age of 80 in Malone, Franklin, NY.

Henry Gordon Cook (Twin) and Marina DOANE were married.

Henry Gordon Cook and Marina Doane had the following children:

i.   Jane Doane Cook was born in 1826 in Shoreham, Vt. She died in 1844 at the age of 18.
ii.  Ellen Cook was born in 1835. She lived in Malone, Franklin, NY.

2098. Harriet Cook (Twin) (David-6, Reuben-5, Ephraim-4, Joshua-3, Josiah-2, Josias-1) was born on 9 Dec 1798 in Orwell, Vt. She died in 1832 at the age of 34.

Harriet Cook (Twin) and Dr. Russell HUMPHREY were married in 1816 in Bainbridge, Chenango, NY. Dr. Russell Humphrey was the son of Abner Humphrey and Abigail Bennett.

Russell Humphrey and Harriet Cook had the following children:

i.    Abner D. Humphrey was born on 12 Jul 1817.
ii.   Elizabeth G. Humphrey was born on 19 Jul 1819.
4294  iii.  Mariette Humphrey, born 1821; married Unknown NICKERSON.
4295  iv.   Edward A. Humphrey.
v.    Ira M. Humphrey.
vi.   George C. Humphrey.
vii.  Cynthia Humphrey.

2099. Maria Cook (David-6, Reuben-5, Ephraim-4, Joshua-3, Josiah-2, Josias-1) was born on 29 Apr 1801.

Maria Cook and Unknown BROOKS were married.

2100. Russell Humphrey Cook (David-6, Reuben-5, Ephraim-4, Joshua-3, Josiah-2, Josias-1) was born on 5 Jul 1803 in Benson, Vt. He died on 21 Oct 1837 at the age of 34 in Salt Lick, O.

Russell Humphrey Cook and Peninnah BAKER were married in Feb 1832 in Little Sandusky,

Ohio. Peninnah Baker was born on 4 Feb 1806 in Massachusetts.

Russell Humphrey Cook and Peninnah Baker had the following children:

4296   i.   Lefee Amanda Cook, born 22 Feb 1833, Little Sciota, O.; married William Walden BRADY, 9 Jan 1850, Marion, O.
      ii.   Olive Sidney Cook was born on 4 Oct 1835 in Little Sciota, O. She died in Oct 1837 at the age of 2.

2101.Elizabeth Cook (David-6, Reuben-5, Ephraim-4, Joshua-3, Josiah-2, Josias-1) was born on 30 May 1805 in Orwell, Vt. She died in Cedar Rapids, Linn, Ia.

Elizabeth Cook and Zuriel FOWLER were married.

2102.Lorenzo Hopkins Cook (David-6, Reuben-5, Ephraim-4, Joshua-3, Josiah-2, Josias-1) was born on 2 Apr 1810 in Orwell, Vt. He died on 10 Apr 1874 at the age of 64 in Ohio.

Lorenzo Hopkins Cook and Eliza CUDWITH were married. Eliza Cudwith was born in Shoreham, Vt.

Lorenzo Hopkins Cook and Sabina ADAMS were married.

Lorenzo Hopkins Cook and Sabina Adams had the following child:

      i.   George Cook was born in 1853.

2103.Clarissa Cook (Oliver-6, Reuben-5, Ephraim-4, Joshua-3, Josiah-2, Josias-1) was born about 1788 in Coventry, Conn. She was baptized in Oct 1793. She died on 1 Mar 1846 at the age of 58 in Benson, Vt. Clarissa was buried in Orwell Village Cemetery, Vt.

Clarissa Cook and Elisha ADAMS were married on 16 Mar 1806 in Coventry First Church, Coventry, Conn. Elisha Adams, son of James Adams and Jerusha Knight, was born on 1 Jun 1782 in Canterbury, Conn. He died on 12 Nov 1863 at the age of 81 in Benson, Vt.

Elisha Adams and Clarissa Cook had the following child:

      i.   Gordon Cook Adams.

2104.Millie Cook (Oliver-6, Reuben-5, Ephraim-4, Joshua-3, Josiah-2, Josias-1) was born (date unknown).

Millie Cook and Samuel SWETLAND were married on 31 Aug 1806 in Coventry, Conn. Samuel Swetland was the son of Ebenezer Sweatland.

2105.Benajah Cook (Oliver-6, Reuben-5, Ephraim-4, Joshua-3, Josiah-2, Josias-1) was born about 1794 in Connecticut. He died on 26 Oct 1865 at the age of 71 in Middletown, Vt.

Benajah Cook and Nancy COLEMAN were married about 1824. Nancy Coleman was born in 1795. She died on 8 Dec 1854 at the age of 59.

Benajah Cook and Ruth JENNISON were married on 17 Mar 1819 in Shoreham, Vt. Ruth Jennison was born in 1779 in Vermont. She died on 18 May 1821 at the age of 42 in Shoreham, Vt.

Benajah Cook and Eliza PERRY were married on 27 Mar 1857 in Middletown, Conn.

2106.Calista Cook (Oliver-6, Reuben-5, Ephraim-4, Joshua-3, Josiah-2, Josias-1) was born about 1799 in Coventry, Conn. She died on 3 Jan 1872 at the age of 73 in West Haven, Rutland, Vt. Calista Cook and Ivory Cook Jr. (#2085) were married.

For children of this marriage see #2085.

2107.Gordon Cook (Oliver-6, Reuben-5, Ephraim-4, Joshua-3, Josiah-2, Josias-1) was born about 1804 in Coventry, Conn.

Gordon Cook and Adeline WARREN were married on 9 Jan 1827 in Orwell, Vt. Adeline Warren was born about 1816 in Vermont.

Gordon Cook and Adeline Warren had the following children:

   i.   Harris L. Cook was born in 1828 in Vermont.
   ii.  Montgomery Cook was born in 1832 in Vermont.
   iii. Marcia O. Cook was born in 1834 in Vermont.
   iv. Imus R. Cook was born in 1836 in Vermont.
   v.  Edwin Cook was born in 1843 in Vermont.
   vi. Margette Cook was born in 1847 in Vermont.

2108.Herman S. Cook (John-6, Ephraim-5, Ephraim-4, Joshua-3, Josiah-2, Josias-1) was born (date unknown).

Herman S. Cook and Philena M. WEDGE were married on 24 Jul 1846. Philena M. Wedge was born in Warren, Conn.

2109.Melissa Cook (John-6, Ephraim-5, Ephraim-4, Joshua-3, Josiah-2, Josias-1) was born (date unknown).

Melissa Cook and Sheldon CLARK were married. Sheldon Clark was born in Cornwall, Conn.

2110.Ephraim Cook (Silas-6, Ephraim-5, Ephraim-4, Joshua-3, Josiah-2, Josias-1) was born on 23 Apr 1804 in Canaan, Conn. He died on 9 Dec 1861 at the age of 57 in Bedford, Cuyahoga, Oh.

Ephraim Cook and Eliza CURTIS were married on 13 Nov 1830 in Portage, Portage, O. Eliza CURTIS was born on 10 Mar 1810 in Sheffield, Berkshire, Mass. She died in 1889 at the age of 79 in Bedford, Oh.

Ephraim Cook and Eliza CURTIS had the following children:

4297   i.   Daniel Cook, born 10 Oct 1831, Hudson, Oh.; married Roxey A., abt 1855; died 1910, Bedford, Oh.
4298   ii.  George B. Cook, born 20 Oct 1833, Summit County, Oh.; married Minerva IVES; died 4 Apr 1909, New Lyme, Oh.
       iii. Silas Cook was born on 3 Jun 1835 in Summit County, Oh.
       iv.  Amasa B. Cook was born on 27 Apr 1838 in Summit County, Oh. Amasa appeared in the census on 26 Jul 1860 in Independence, Oh. He served in the military in the Civil War as a Private in Co. A, 42d OH Infantry Regiment between 20 Sep 1861 and 1865 in Ohio. He died mortally wounded in the civil war on 5 Jun 1863 at the age of 25 in Chickasaw Bayou, Warren County, Miss.
       v.   Ephraim Cook was born on 28 May 1842 in Solon, Oh. Ephraim served in the military in the civil war as a Private in Co. A, 42d Ohio Infantry Regiment between 20 Sep 1861 in Ohio.
       vi.  Samuel Cook was born on 23 Feb 1845 in Solon, Cuyahoga, O. He died in Mar 1926 at the age of 81 in New Lyme, Ashtabula, Oh. Samuel was buried in New Lyme, Ashtabula, Oh.
4299   vii. Orris Crosby Cook, born 26 Mar 1847, Independence, Cuyahoga, O.; married Alice Mahala EVANS, 2 Feb 1875, New Lyme, Ashtabula, Oh.; died 18 Feb 1929, Rome, Oh.
4300   viii. Romeo R. Cook, born 29 Jan 1849, Solon, Cuyahoga, Oh.; married Sarah ; died 28 Apr 1928.
       ix.  Julia Harriet Cook was born on 30 Jan 1854 in Independence, Oh.

2111.Sidney R. Cook (John Young-6, Nathan-5, Ephraim-4, Joshua-3, Josiah-2, Josias-1) was born on 1 Feb 1807 in Coventry, Conn. He died on 12 May 1869 at the age of 62 in Springfield,

Mass.

Sidney R. Cook and Pamelia R. PORTER were married on 16 Nov 1829 in Coventry, Conn. Pamelia R. Porter was born (date unknown).

Sidney R. Cook and Pamelia R. Porter had the following child:

  i.   Clarissa C. Cook, born Aug 1831; married Horace Gilbert DAVIS, 30 Nov 1848.

2112.Mary Cook (David-6, Nathan-5, Ephraim-4, Joshua-3, Josiah-2, Josias-1) died before 1885.

  Mary Cook and Unknown POTZER were married.

2113.Nathan Moore Cook (David-6, Nathan-5, Ephraim-4, Joshua-3, Josiah-2, Josias-1) was born on 9 Apr 1816 in Suffield, Oh. He died on 2 Feb 1875 at the age of 58 in Suffield, Oh.

  Nathan Moore Cook and Clarinda HULBERT were married on 14 Jan 1842.

2114.Lee Cook (David-6, Nathan-5, Ephraim-4, Joshua-3, Josiah-2, Josias-1) was born on 11 Nov 1821. He lived in Suffield, Oh. in 1885.

  Lee Cook and Phebe BUCKMAN were married.

  Lee Cook and Margaret EBEL were married.

2115.Galvin Cook (David-6, Nathan-5, Ephraim-4, Joshua-3, Josiah-2, Josias-1) was born about 1827 in Suffield, Oh. He died after 1885 at the age of 58.

  Galvin Cook and Mary Ann STOUT were married.

2116.Rachel Cook (David-6, Nathan-5, Ephraim-4, Joshua-3, Josiah-2, Josias-1) died after 1885.

  Rachel Cook and Stahl SMITH were married.

2117.William P Cook (Bela Reynolds-6, Nathan-5, Ephraim-4, Joshua-3, Josiah-2, Josias-1) was born in 1821 in Andover, Conn. He died on 16 Jun 1867 at the age of 46 in Andover, Conn. He was buried in 1867 in Andover Congregational Church, Andover, Conn.

  William P Cook and Martha E. A. HENDEE were married on 26 Dec 1852 in Andover, Conn. Martha E. A. Hendee was born in 1830. She died in 1894 at the age of 64.

William P Cook and Martha E. A. Hendee had the following children:

4302   i.   (Minnie)Julia E  Cook, born 23 Aug 1867, Andover, Tolland, Conn.; married Edwin Andrew STANDISH, Andover Congregational Church, Andover, Conn.; died 28 Dec 1927, Andover, Conn.

4303   ii.   Edwin H Cook, born 1858; married Nellie A BASS; died 1953.

2118.DeLance Cook (Bela Reynolds-6, Nathan-5, Ephraim-4, Joshua-3, Josiah-2, Josias-1) was born in Jul 1827 in Andover, Conn. He died in 1902 at the age of 75 in Hampton, Ill. He was buried in 1902 in Hampton, Ill.

DeLance Cook and Mary Lucinda LEE were married on 28 Mar 1852 in Hebron, Conn. Mary Lucinda Lee was born on 26 Jul 1837 in Hebron, Conn.

DeLance Cook and Mary Lucinda Lee had the following children:

4304   i.   Herbert E Cook, born 16 Oct 1854; died 1918.

      ii.   Walter Cook.

4305   iii.   Francis Marie Cook, married William Albert BEAL; died aft 1880.

      iv.   Ella L Cook was born in Mar 1858. She died on 19 Sep 1858.

      v.   Lester Cook was born in May 1868. He died on 6 Oct 1868.

2119.Oliver Cook (Bela Reynolds-6, Nathan-5, Ephraim-4, Joshua-3, Josiah-2, Josias-1) was born in 1829 in Connecticut, U.S. He died on 13 May 1906 at the age of 77 in Hampton, Rock Island, Ill. He was buried on 15 May 1906 in Hampton, Rock Island, Ill.

Oliver Cook and Sarah Elizabeth LEE were married on 12 Sep 1852 in Hebron, Conn. Sarah Elizabeth Lee was born on 29 Oct 1830 in Connecticut. She died on 12 Sep 1905 at the age of 74.

Oliver Cook and Sarah Elizabeth Lee had the following children:

4306   i.   Orin Beale Cook, born 11 Jul 1854, Connecticut, U.S.; married Mary Caroline BENSON, 15 Dec 1877 in Illinois; died 4 Mar 1939, East Moline, Ill.

4307   ii.   David A Cook, born 1859; married Lona GUCKERT, 25 Nov 1883; died 1933.

      iii.   Belle Cook.

      iv.   Fred Cook.

2140.Noah Cook (Lemuel-6, Moses-5, Simeon-4, Joshua-3, Josiah-2, Josias-1) was born in 1804 in Dutchess County, NY. He died in Jun 1896 at the age of 92 in Chattaraugus County, NY.

Noah Cook and Annie WARES were married. Annie Wares, daughter of Rufus Wares, was born on 14 Jan 1806 in Saratoga, NY. She died on 30 Apr 1882 at the age of 76 in Perrysburg, NY.

Noah Cook and Annie Wares had the following children:

4324  i.  Phebe Cook, born 1822; married Jesse JOHNSON.
4325  ii. Joel G. Cook, born 3 Dec 1825; married Caroline DAVIS, 12 Sep 1849.
4326  iii. Elisha H. Cook, born 1829; married Emerilla UNKNOWN; married Althea BROWN.
      iv. Eloda Cook was born in 1835.
4327  v.  Myron J. Cook, born 10 Dec 1840, Perrysburg, NY.; married Melissa BIERCE, 9 Mar 1870, Perrysburg, NY.; married Ann E. KIMBLE; died 1910, North Collins, NY.
4328  vi. Marvin W. Cook, born 7 Oct 1849; married Laura J. HARRINGTON, 8 May 1872; died 1930, Versailles, NY.

2256. Ansel Cook (Willard-6, Nathaniel-5, Jonathan-4, Joshua-3, Josiah-2, Josias-1) was born on 18 Aug 1823 in Haddam, Conn. He appeared in the census in 1850 in Fremont, Lake, Ill.

Ansel Cook and Helen M. FOSTER were married on 2 Dec 1849. They appeared in the census in 1870 in Libertyville, Ill. Helen M. Foster, daughter of Jessie Foster, died on 19 Jan 1881.

Ansel Cook and Helen M. Foster had the following child:

i.  Ida F. Cook was born on 20 Jan 1850. She died on 16 Sep 1850.

Ansel Cook and Annie B. BARROWS were married on 2 Feb 1882.

2257. Abby Florilla Cook (Willard-6, Nathaniel-5, Jonathan-4, Joshua-3, Josiah-2, Josias-1) was born on 27 Nov 1827 in Haddam, Conn.

Abby Florilla Cook and John F. MENDSEN were married on 21 Nov 1859. John F. Mendsen, son of F.W. Mendsen, was born in Lehigh, Pa.

2258. Charles Willard Cook (Willard-6, Nathaniel-5, Jonathan-4, Joshua-3, Josiah-2, Josias-1) was born on 13 Jul 1832 in Haddam, Conn.

Charles Willard Cook and Sarah A. COONLEY were married in 1857. Sarah A. Coonley was born in 1840 in Albany, NY. She died in 1872 at the age of 32.

Charles Willard Cook and Sarah A. Coonley had the following children:

    i.   Charles Ira Cook was born in 1863.He lived in Menominie, Mich. Charles was a wholesale merchant.

4354  ii.  Albert Eugene Cook, born 1865, Illinois.

4355  iii. Emma Cook, born 1866, Geneva, Lake, Ill.; married Frederick Ives CARPENTER.

    iv. ?Willard Cook.

    v.  ?A child.

Charles Willard Cook and Jennie W. (Sterges) WADE were married on 18 Jun 1874. They appeared in the census in 1880 in Chicago, Cook, Ill. Jennie W. (Sterges) Wade, daughter of John Wade and Sofronia Unknown, was born in Texas.

2259.Ellen Sophia Cook (Willard-6, Nathaniel-5, Jonathan-4, Joshua-3, Josiah-2, Josias-1) was born on 6 Aug 1840 in Haddam, Conn.

Ellen Sophia Cook and Rev Edwin Luther JAGGER were married on 29 Apr 1861. Rev Edwin Luther Jagger was born on 6 Dec 1835 in Millhall, Pa. He died on 28 Nov 1899 at the age of 63 in Springfield, Mass.

Edwin Luther Jagger and Ellen Sophia Cook had the following children:

    i.   Edwin Brainerd Jagger was born on 7 Sep 1863 in Warren, Mass. He died on 23 Apr 1875 at the age of 11 in Auburndale, Mass.

    ii.  Charles Henry Jagger was born on 14 Mar 1865 in Auburndale, Mass.

    iii. Walter Cook Jagger was born on 11 Jul 1869 in South Deerfield, Mass. He died on 3 Dec 1873 at the age of 4 in Medford, Mass.

    iv. Clarence Ernest Jagger was born on 26 Mar 1874 in West Medford, Mass.

2261.Jerusha "Rue" Cook (Ichabod-6, Amos-5, Jonathan-4, Joshua-3, Josiah-2, Josias-1) was born in 1815 in Greene County, NY. She died on 3 Mar 1877 at the age of 62 in Mayville, Chautauqua, NY.

Jerusha "Rue" Cook and Charles Peter BEAUJEAN were married. Charles Peter Beaujean was born on 6 Jul 1806 in Greene County, NY.

Charles Peter Beaujean and Jerusha Cook had the following child:

    i.   Michael Beaujean, born Jamestown, Chatauqua, NY.; married Unknown .

2262.Henry S. Cook (Ichabod-6, Amos-5, Jonathan-4, Joshua-3, Josiah-2, Josias-1) was born on 8

Jun 1820 in Windham, NY. In 1875 he was a farmer. He died on 19 Mar 1887 at the age of 66. Henry signed a will on 16 Apr 1887 in Greene County, NY. He was buried in Mountain Valley Cemetery, Ashland, Green, NY.

Henry S. Cook and Elizabeth BEERS were married on 10 May 1843 in West Settlement, Ashland, Green, NY. Elizabeth Beers, daughter of Seth Beers and Rachel Conine, was born on 24 Feb 1823 in Windham, NY. She died on 23 Feb 1900 at the age of 76 in Ashland, NY.

Henry S. Cook and Elizabeth Beers had the following children:

4359 i. Rachel B. Cook, born 22 Oct 1844, Ashland, NY.; married John B. YOUNG, 20 Dec 1870; died 26 Dec 1912.

4360 ii. Ichabod "Ick" Cook, born 29 Dec 1846, W. Settlement, Ashland, Green, NY.; married Sarah Elizabeth WEST, 21 Nov 1872, Windham, NY.; died 4 May 1923, Cornwallville, Greene, NY.

4361 iii. Clarrissa B. "Clara" Cook, born 12 Feb 1849, Ashland, NY.; married Oscar A. TOMPKINS, 28 Feb 1888; died 26 Feb 1889.

 iv. Sally M. Cook was born on 15 Oct 1851 in Ashland, NY. She died on 28 Dec 1874 at the age of 23. She was buried in Mountain Valley Cemetery, Ashland, Green, NY.

4362 v. Cornelius B. Cook, born 19 Apr 1854, Ashland, NY.; married Cora E. HINMAN, 8 Jan 1878, Conesville, Schoharie, NY.; died 4 Mar 1919, West Conesville, Schoharie, NY.

4363 vi. Amos "Bailey" Cook, born 11 Aug 1856; married Eva E. TRAVER, 11 Oct 1880; died 15 Dec 1917.

4364 vii. Minetta Elizabeth "Minnie" Cook, born 28 Apr 1859, Ashland, NY.; married Charles Sabra KISSOCK, 17 Jan 1882, Windham, NY.; died 28 Apr 1931, Windham, NY.

 viii. Henry Seth Cook was born on 6 Dec 1861. He died on 5 Sep 1917 at the age of 55 in Ashland, NY.

4365 ix. Lambert Brandow Cook, born 20 May 1864, Ashland, NY.; married Emma TUTTLE, 18 Feb 1885.

2263.Margaret B. Cook (Twin) (Ichabod-6, Amos-5, Jonathan-4, Joshua-3, Josiah-2, Josias-1) was born on 16 Jan 1827 in Ashland, NY. She died on 5 Feb 1903 at the age of 76 in Ashland, NY. She was buried in Mountain Valley Cemetery, Ashland, Green, NY.

Margaret B. Cook (Twin) and Calvin Luther SUTTON were married on 4 Jun 1846 in Windham, NY. Calvin Luther Sutton was born on 11 Aug 1822 in Schoharie County, NY. It might be interesting to find out more about the connection between these siblings and the Suttons. Calvin's brother married both Clarissa and Teressa, and his sister married Thomas.

Calvin Luther Sutton and Margaret B. Cook had the following children:

      i.   Thomas Ichabod Sutton was born about 1848 in Greene County, NY.
     ii.  Elizabeth Sutton was born about 1850 in Ashland, NY. She died after 1903 at the age of 53.
    iii.  Lovina Sutton was born about 1851 in Ashland, NY. She died after 1903 at the age of 52.
    iv.  Phebe A. Sutton was born about 1852 in Ashland, NY. She died after 1903 at the age of 51.
     v.  Henry C. Sutton, born 1854, Ashland, NY.; married Polly F. ; died 11 Feb 1902, Ashland, NY. They had 1 child.
    vi.  Lillian "Lillie" Sutton, born abt 1860, Ashland, NY.; married Hiram James DAVIS, 2 Dec 1885, Conesville, Schoharie, NY.; died aft 1903.
   vii.  Flora A. Sutton, born 12 Aug 1861; married Alonzo JOHNSON; died 27 Feb 1928, Ashland, NY. They had 3 children.

2264. Clarissa B. "Clarry" Cook (Twin) (Ichabod-6, Amos-5, Jonathan-4, Joshua-3, Josiah-2, Josias-1) was born on 16 Jan 1827 in Ashland, NY. She died on 28 Mar 1906 at the age of 79. She was buried in Huttersfield Cemetery, Prattsville, Greene, NY.

Clarissa B. "Clarry" Cook (Twin) and Stephen W. TRUESDELL were married. Stephen W. Truesdell was born on 15 Sep 1815 in Delaware Co., NY. He died on 16 Jan 1886 at the age of 70 in Prattsville, Greene, NY. He was buried in Huttersfield Cemetery, Prattsville, Greene, NY.

2265. Elizabeth "Betsy" Cook (Ichabod-6, Amos-5, Jonathan-4, Joshua-3, Josiah-2, Josias-1) was born on 14 Jul 1830 in Ashland, NY. She died on 14 Jan 1863 at the age of 32 in Windham, NY.

Elizabeth "Betsy" Cook and Addison "Adin" SUTTON were married before 1855. Addison "Adin" Sutton was born about 1826 in Schoharie County, NY.

Addison Sutton and Elizabeth Cook had the following children:

      i.   Elizabeth Sutton was born about 1854 in Ashland, NY.
     ii.  Polly Sutton was born in 1855 in Ashland, NY.
    iii.  Ella J. Sutton was born in 1857 in Ashland, NY.
    iv.  Ichabod Sutton was born in 1863 in Ashland, NY.

2266. Terressa H. Cook (Ichabod-6, Amos-5, Jonathan-4, Joshua-3, Josiah-2, Josias-1) was born about Mar 1834. She died on 25 Jan 1871 at the age of 36. She was buried in Mountain Valley Cemetery, Ashland, Green, NY.

Terressa H. Cook and Addison "Adin" SUTTON were married after 1863. Addison "Adin" Sutton was born about 1826 in Schoharie County, NY. Addison first married Terressa's sister Elizabeth #2265. His brother Calvin married their sister Margaret #2263. And Terressa, Elizabeth and Margaret's brother Thomas Bradley Cook #2268 married Mary Sutton.

Addison Sutton and Terressa H. Cook had the following child:

    i.   Ursula A. Sutton was born in 1865 in Ashland, NY.

2267.Polly S. Cook (Ichabod-6, Amos-5, Jonathan-4, Joshua-3, Josiah-2, Josias-1) was born about 1836 in Ashland, NY. She died in 1903 at the age of 67 in Ashland, NY. She was buried in Mountain Valley Cemetery, Ashland, Green, NY.

Polly S. Cook and Rev. George W. FERRIS were married in 1861.Rev. George W. Ferris was born in 1839 in Prattsville, Greene, NY. He was a minister of the gospel.

George W. Ferris and Polly S. Cook had the following children:

    i.   Seymour H. Ferris was born in 1854. He died in 1860 at the age of 6.
    ii.   Seymour B. Ferris was born on 5 Oct 1862 in Ashland, NY. He died on 30 Jun 1869 at the age of 6 in Ashland, NY. He was buried in Mountain Valley Cemetery, Ashland, Green, NY.
  4369   iii.  George Fletcher Ferris, born 31 Aug 1864; married Nancy Avery BEACH, 10 Jun 1891, Beach's Corner, NY.
  4370   iv.  Rose Ferris, born 1 Apr 1866, Livingstonville, Schoharie, NY; married Archie JACKSON, 22 Aug 1885, Bloomville, Delaware, NY.
  4371   v.  Lincoln Abraham Ferris, born 10 Oct 1867, North Blenheim, Schoharie, NY; married Lillian O'DONNEL.
    vi.  Elizabeth E. Ferris was born on 23 Nov 1876 in Manorkill, Conesville, Schoharie, NY.

2268.Thomas Bradley Cook (Ichabod-6, Amos-5, Jonathan-4, Joshua-3, Josiah-2, Josias-1) was born in 1839 in New York. He died in 1903 at the age of 64 in Ashland, NY. He was buried in Mountain Valley Cemetery, Ashland, Green, NY.

Thomas Bradley Cook and Mary SUTTON appeared in the census in 1880 in Ashland, NY. They were married.

Thomas Bradley Cook and Mary Sutton had the following children:

  4372   i.  William "Willie" Cook, born 1865, Ashland, NY.; married Rosa May COVEL, 21 Oct 1891, Prattsville, Greene, NY.

ii.   Manley B. Cook was born in 1868 in Ashland, NY.
iii.  Rutherford H. Cook was born in 1872 in Ashland, NY.

2269. Ichabod Cook Jr. (Ichabod-6, Amos-5, Jonathan-4, Joshua-3, Josiah-2, Josias-1) was born on 13 Sep 1842 in Ashland, NY. He died on 9 Jul 1894 at the age of 51 in Ashland, NY.

Ichabod Cook Jr. and Electa CHRISTIAN were married on 30 Oct 1865 in Ashland, NY. Electa Christian, daughter of James Christian and Cynthia Unknown, was born on 6 Mar 1842.

Ichabod Cook and Electa Christian had the following children:

i.   Hiram Cook was born in 1868 in Ashland, NY.
ii.  Cora B. Cook was born in 1872 in Ashland, NY.
iii. Anna Cook was born in Jan 1880.

2270. Ashbel Cook (Amos-6, Amos-5, Jonathan-4, Joshua-3, Josiah-2, Josias-1) was born in 1794 in Connecticut.

Ashbel Cook and Julia A. UNKNOWN were married. Julia A. Unknown was born about 1801 in Greene County, NY.

Ashbel Cook and Julia A. Unknown had the following children:

      i.   Nancy Cook was born in 1822.
4373  ii.  Amos Cook, born 1824, Greene County, NY.; married Jane C. BULL, 10 Oct 1850, Windham, NY.
      iii. Nancy Cook was born about 1828.
      iv.  Jane Cook was born about 1831 in Ashland, NY.
      v.   Ruah Cook was born in 1833.
      vi.  Cynthia Cook was born abg 1835.
      vii. Hannah Cook was born about 1837.
      viii.   Frances Cook was born about 1845.

2280. Alanson Cook (Lewis-6, Solomon-5, Hezekiah-4, Joshua-3, Josiah-2, Josias-1) was born on 17 Dec 1804 in New Marlborough, Mass.

Alanson Cook and Emily PALMER were married on 29 Sep 1830 in New Marlborough, Mass. Emily Palmer was born about 1803. She died on 8 Apr 1844 at the age of 41 in New Marlborough, Mass.

Alanson Cook and Emily Palmer had the following child:

i. Isabella Cook.

2281.Levi Cook (Lewis-6, Solomon-5, Hezekiah-4, Joshua-3, Josiah-2, Josias-1) was born on 7 Jun 1807 in New Marlborough, Mass. He died in May 1871 at the age of 63 in Colebrook, Litchfield, Conn.

Levi Cook and Amelia TODD were married on 21 Sep 1829 in Sandisfield, Mass. Amelia Todd was born in 1802 in Connecticut.

Levi Cook and Amelia Todd had the following child:

☞ 4381    i.   Hon. Lorrin Alanson Cooke, born 6 Apr 1831, New Marlborough, Mass.; married Matilda E. WEBSTER, 1858; married Josephine WARD, 1870; died 12 Aug 1902, Winsted, Conn.

*(Taken from an article prepared by the Connecticut State Library.)*

Lorrin Alanson Cooke was the governor of the State of Connecticut from 1897 to 1899. He also held the following offices:

    Representative, Connecticut General Assembly, 1856-1857
    First Selectman of Colebrook, Connecticut, 1865-1869
    Postmaster for Riverton, Connecticut, 1877-1881
    Senator, Connecticut General Assembly, 1882-1885
    President Pro Tempore of the Connecticut Senate, 1884-1885
    President of the Connecticut Senate, 1885-1887
    Delegate to the Republican National Convention in Minneapolis, 1892
    Lieutenant Governor of Connecticut, 1885-1887 and 1895-1897
    Governor of Connecticut, 1897-1899

7.211

Governor Lorrin A. Cooke used his considerable organizational and financial management talents to stabilize the finances of the State of Connecticut in the 1890s. His work as governor pulled Connecticut out of debt and saved the fiscal future of the then-struggling state.

Lorrin Alanson Cooke was born on April 6, 1831 in New Marlborough, Massachusetts, a small village on a stagecoach line in the Berkshires, less than ten miles from the Connecticut state line. He was the son and only child of Levi and Amelia (Todd) Cooke. The family descended from early colonial inhabitants of western Massachusetts, as well as from some of the first settlers of the New Haven Colony and the Mayflower passengers.

Young Lorrin began his schooling in New Marlborough, but in 1837, Levi Cooke moved his family to Norfolk, Connecticut, southeast of New Marlborough. There, Lorrin finished elementary school and continued his education at the Norfolk Academy. For several years after high school, he taught school in the Norfolk area in the winter and worked on his father's farm in the summer. He had a talent for teaching, but it did not appeal to him as a career.

By 1850, when Lorrin was nineteen, the Cooke family had moved once again, this time to Colebrook, Connecticut, where Levi Cooke rented a farm. As time progressed, Lorrin Cooke became a young farmer who wanted to learn about and use the latest developments in agriculture. He joined the local agricultural society and was eventually elected its president.

With this election, Lorrin Cooke's real talent - leadership -- began to develop. His fellow farmers had no way to get their produce to New York, so Lorrin worked with railroad officials to route a train through the remote Colebrook area. Sales of Colebrook agricultural products rose dramatically as produce was freighted to the big city, and the town prospered. People began to see Lorrin Cooke as a man who could do things for Colebrook. Cooke's election to the Connecticut General Assembly as the representative from the Town of Colebrook took place in 1856, when he was only 25 years old. This one-year term in the Connecticut General Assembly gave him his first experiences in state politics.

In 1858, Cooke married Matilda E. Webster of Sandisfield, Massachusetts. She was the daughter of Abner S. and Mary (Alford) Webster. Lorrin and Matilda had no children, and Matilda Webster Cooke died in 1868. Two years later, Lorrin married Josephine Ward of Riverton, Connecticut, daughter of Michael and Sarah Ward. The couple had three children, Edward L., Ward, and Edna, though only Edna survived into adulthood.

After his term in the General Assembly ended in 1857, Cooke held various public offices at the town level. He was appointed as first selectman of Colebrook in 1865. That appointment was an honor, and he might have remained in Colebrook, serving the town as selectman for years to come, but in 1869, his life took a new direction. It was then that he was persuaded to take the job of manager of the Eagle Scythe Company in the village of Riverton in the town of

Barkhamsted. The company was in bad financial condition, but Cooke, with shrewd business insights and sound financial practices, pulled it out of the red. The company ran smoothly with Cooke as its manager, until it closed its doors in 1889.

Prominent people in Riverton soon noticed Cooke's business talents and his success with Eagle Scythe. In time, he overcame political opposition in the heavily Democratic town and was appointed postmaster while he was still working at Eagle Scythe. He served as postmaster for Riverton until November of 1881.

Working as postmaster and running Eagle Scythe gave Lorrin Cooke further training in leadership and administration. He ran for the Connecticut Senate in 1882 in the 18th District, and won in every town except his strongly Democratic hometown, Colebrook. The new senator served well, being appointed to the committee on education, and impressing his colleagues with his efforts in that cause. Cooke's senate work during his first term was so good that he was re-elected in 1883 against a strong Democratic opponent.

Cooke's second term in the Connecticut Senate found him advancing politically. He was elected President Pro Tempore of the Connecticut Senate in 1884 and was said to preside with "fairness and dignity." His increased responsibilities included the chairmanship of the committee on engrossed bills, which made sure that bills originating from the Senate had fulfilled all legal and technical requirements. He also served on a committee that investigated certain aspects of the Connecticut Agricultural College.

His outstanding work in the Connecticut Senate earned Cooke a Republican nomination for lieutenant governor in 1885, running with Henry B. Harrison for Governor. The team won, and had a successful two-year term. Further honors came to Cooke in 1892, when he was appointed a delegate to the Republican National Convention in Minneapolis, Minnesota. In 1895, he was elected a second time as lieutenant governor of Connecticut.

Lorrin Cooke's four years as lieutenant governor, his talents, and his background of previous service led to his nomination as the Republican candidate for governor of Connecticut in 1897. He was elected by an overwhelming majority, earning 108,807 votes compared to 56, 524 votes for his Democratic opponent, James Sargent. This was the most votes any candidate had received before, or would receive until 1916. He was also the first Connecticut governor since Charles Pond (elected in 1853, over 40 years earlier) to move directly from the position of lieutenant governor to the governorship.

Cooke brought to the governorship a background in business and agriculture. His business experience in making the Eagle Scythe Company fiscally solvent especially proved useful. When Cooke began his term as governor, the state's financial condition was not good. Reducing the budget was one of Cooke's primary goals. He soon persuaded lawmakers to cut

7.213

expenses in areas where spending was extravagant. Connecticut's finances did well under his guidance, even though the Spanish-American War required the state government to share the costs of that conflict with the federal government. Under Cooke, Connecticut sent two regiments of troops to the Spanish-American War.

Lorrin Cooke moved to Winsted, Connecticut, while he was governor. When his term ended, he returned there. He was active in religious and social causes the rest of his life. He was a member of the Society of Sons of the American Revolution.

Lorrin Cooke died on August 12, 1902, at age 71. He is buried near the family members that preceded him in Colebrook's Center Cemetery. His second wife, Josephine, and his daughter Edna survived him.

The house that Cooke built in Riverton stands next to the Post Office there and has a marker next to its front steps. His Winsted house also still exists. Both homes are privately owned.

2282.Isaac Rhodes Cook (Lewis-6, Solomon-5, Hezekiah-4, Joshua-3, Josiah-2, Josias-1) was born on 10 Oct 1809 in New Marlborough, Mass.

Isaac Rhodes Cook and Eliza UNKNOWN were married on 15 Oct 1836 in Charlestown, Middlesex, Mass.

Isaac Rhodes Cook and Eliza Unknown had the following children:

    i.   Thomas A. Cook was born in 1838.
    ii.  Isaac L. Cook was born in 1844.
    iii. Anna J. Cook was born in Jan 1850.

2283.Lydia Perna Cook (Lewis-6, Solomon-5, Hezekiah-4, Joshua-3, Josiah-2, Josias-1) was born on 29 Jul 1812 in New Marlborough, Mass.

Lydia Perna Cook and Reuben FREEMAN were married on 16 Oct 1829 in New Marlborough, Mass.

2284.Alvin Cook (Lorrin-6, Solomon-5, Hezekiah-4, Joshua-3, Josiah-2, Josias-1) was born in 1820 in New York.

Alvin Cook and Adeline UNKNOWN were married. Adeline Unknown was born about 1820 in New York.

Alvin Cook and Adeline Unknown had the following child:

    i.   Ann Eliza Cook was born in 1845 in New York.

**2285.Ledyard Cook** (Lorrin-6, Solomon-5, Hezekiah-4, Joshua-3, Josiah-2, Josias-1) was born about 1823 in New York.

Ledyard Cook and Esther UNKNOWN were married.

# Wars

This list isn't meant to be exhaustive. I've done no research on military matters, except for a little about the civil war. Most of this comes from Wikipedia. This list includes military service that I've discovered more or less by accident. I've included the husbands of Cook women. I've put a star symbol next to anyone who died in the particular war, otherwise, all survived — although some never fully recovered. Though there were other wars, such as the Beaver Wars which involved the Great Lakes, the Utah War (sometimes called the Mormon War), and the U.S.-Mexican war, these five were the wars in which Cook descendants served.

**King Philip's War (1675–78)**

This war was not the first war in America, but it marked a decisive end to the peace that "the Pilgrims" (and William Bradford in particular) had managed to achieve with Massassoit. After Massassoit's death, his sons became sachem. King Philip was Massassoit's second son — his real name was Metacomet — and he became sachem in 1662 after his older sibling Wamsutta died suspiciously. Metacomet felt threatened that the British colonists refused to stop acquiring land and creating settlements. In 1675, the triggering event of the war was the arrest and execution of three Wampanoag by Plymouth Colony for the murder of a American Indian Christian convert named John Sassamon. In retaliation, a band of Pokanoket men attacked several homesteads in Swansea and then destroyed the settlement. From there the war spread outward. There were about 110 settlements at the time. The war was fought on two fronts: a northern one along the border with Acadia (Maine), and a southern one, in Massachusetts, Rhode Island and Connecticut.

The result of the war was bloodshed and a continuation of the English expansion. It was the worst (but not the only) conflict the region had seen since English settlers had landed fifty years earlier. As far as casualties, there were about 3,000 dead American Indians and 600 dead colonists. Several hundred American Indians had been captured and were sold into slavery in Bermuda.

Cook descendants who served:

4. Josiah Cooke (Josias-1) was the only descendant who was alive at the time of King Philip's War and he is recorded as having served. As all men were part of the local militia, his service would probably have been automatic and he would have brought his own weapon if any men from his town were mustered out. Their service was for England and it's unlikely they were starting to think of themselves as Americans.

**French and Indian War (1754–1763)**

This war is sometimes called The Seven Year's war or The War of Conquest. It was a war between New France and New England. It was an important war in that many of the men who served in it, served a few years later during the American Revolution, including General Washington. The earliest authenticated portrait of Washington was made during this war. The French were badly outnumbered and recruited American Indians to increase their numbers. The border between the two colonies ran from present day Pittsburgh (Ft. Duquesne), up to Fort Niagra, Fort Owego, and along the St. Lawrence Seaway to present day Nova Scotia (named Acadia at the time).

The result of the war was a huge increase of land for England and Spain; a near total loss for France. (France, it should be said, was not as interested in the colonies as England and Spain.) England won all the land east of the Mississippi: at that point the inhabited borders of the 13 colonies extended to about halfway through New York and Pennsylvania, southward to the western boundary of Georgia. Land between the border of the 13 colonies and the Mississippi River became American Indian Reservation. (The American Indians were later driven off this land.)

Spain already controlled the land in Mexico up to about the panhandle of Texas and the southern border of present day Oklahoma. It won Louisiana which was all the unexplored land north of this line and west of the Mississippi. This land was later reclaimed from Spain by Napoleon in 1800 and almost immediately resold to the new United States government in the Louisiana Purchase which everyone learns about in school.

In the north, the 80,000 French settlers of Acadia were expelled. The land was given to British settlers from Massachusetts and Connecticut, including many Cook descendants who migrated there. There were about 1500 French who refused to leave, and they were forcibly expelled. Finding no refuge anywhere on the Atlantic coast, they eventually found a home in New Orleans. These are the people that became Cajun. Nova Scotia is Latin for New Scotland.

I have not been able to tell from casual reading whether the men who served did so for the sake of England or for themselves as Americans. The American revolution was only about a decade away and there were a large number of people who still felt loyal to the King, even when the revolution began.

Cook descendants who served:

93. iv.  Isaiah Cook (Joshua-4, Joshua-3, Josiah-2, Josias-1) was born on 13 Jul 1737 in Chatham, Mass. He served and died in the French and Indian War on 6 Sep 1758 at the age of 21.

101.  Hezekiah Cook (Joshua-3, Josiah-2, Josias-1) was born about 1728 in Eastham, Mass. He served in the military in the French and Indian war about 1762.

323.  Josiah Cook (Josiah-4, Joshua-3, Josiah-2, Josias-1) was born on 3 Dec 1735 in Eastham, Mass. He served in the French and Indian war under Captain Eleazor Fitch, 4th Regiment, 3rd Company in 1759.

8.217

324.   Capt. Elijah Cook (Josiah-4, Joshua-3, Josiah-2, Josias-1) was born on 8 Jun 1737 in
       Eastham, Mass. He served in the French and Indian war in 1758.

325.   Joshua Cook (Josiah-4, Joshua-3, Josiah-2, Josias-1) was born on 12 Apr 1740 in Eastham,
       Mass. He served in the French and Indian war in 1758.

331.   ★James Cook (Joshua-4, Joshua-3, Josiah-2, Josias-1) was born on 7 Jun 1731 in Eastham,
       Mass. He served in the French and Indian war in 1759. He was killed in the war on 7 Dec
       1759 at the age of 28.

338.   Moses Cook (Ephraim-4, Joshua-3, Josiah-2, Josias-1) was born in 1738 in Coventry, Conn.
       He served in the French and Indian War in the 8th Company in 1757 in Connecticut.

339.   Reuben Cook (Ephraim-4, Joshua-3, Josiah-2, Josias-1) was born on 20 Aug 1741 in
       Eastham, Mass. He served in the French and Indian War as a private in the 12th Co. under
       Hebron, CT officers between 25 May 1759 and 14 Dec 1759. He later served in as a
       Sergeant in the 11th Co. under a Plainfield Captain between 16 Mar 1763 and 3 Dec 1763.

**The American Revolutionary War (1775 - 1783)**

After the French and Indian war, England was heavily in debt and imposed, for the first time, a tax to pay for the cost of British troops stationed in the Colonies. The Stamp Act of 1765 applied a tax to all printed materials, such as playing cards, newspapers, court documents, deeds and licenses. The most expensive tax of £10 was, oddly, for the license to be a lawyer. Taxes are never popular, but some are more tolerated than others. This tax was especially hated. Some argued that it was a violation of their right not to be taxed without representation in Parliament. The English believed that the colonies were simply corporate entities or properties of England and had no rights of representation. The act was repealed in 1766, but it was an important event of several events that led to a desire for independence.

Taxation continued in other ways, but eventually the British only retained a single tax, which was the tax on tea. The Tea Act of 1773 allowed the East India Company to sell tea directly to selected merchants in the colonies. This cut out the middle merchants who were in the business of bidding on tea in London and importing that tea to the colonies. It effectively created a corporate monopoly for the East India Company. In 1773 the company sent 600,000 pounds of tea in 3 ships to Charleston, New York, Philadelphia and 4 ships to Boston. Charleston, New York and Philadelphia refused to allow the ships to unload their tea. In Boston, however, the royal governor Thomas Hutchinson refused to send them away. The "Boston Tea Party," as it's now called, took place after a meeting run by Samuel Adams got out of hand. About 100 men, some dressed as Mohawk warriors (presumably to stress their Americanism and to look more fierce), boarded the ships anchored in Boston and dumped all 342 chests into the bay. (People also stopped drinking tea in a loose ad-hoc boycott. They switched to coffee, and tea never regained a solid place in the American diet.)

Parliament ordered Boston harbor closed in 1774 until the tea was paid for. It then passed an act which gave the crown the right to appoint the upper house of Massachusetts, and the governor the right to appoint and remove judges, sheriffs and other officials. Jurors would be selected by those appointees. All of these actions were called the "Intolerable Acts." That same year, the First Continental Congress was convened with representatives from 12 of the 13 colonies' legislative bodies: this was probably the seed of the first federal government or what was eventually called the United States, even though the congress rejected a "plan of union."

In February, 1775 Parliament declared Massachusetts to be in a state of rebellion. On April 18, 1775, 700 soldiers were sent to Concord to retrieve munitions. Riders (including Paul Revere) raced ahead to alert the countryside that the British were on the move. At Lexington, on April 19, the first shots were exchanged with Minutemen. They moved on to Concord and were met by another 500 Minutemen. The British retreated to Boston. In July, 1775, George Washington took charge of the colonial army. A standoff lasted until March 17, 1776, at which point the British fled to their base in Nova Scotia. This day is celebrated in Massachusetts as Evacuation Day. Washington then took his troops to New York City which only occupied the very southern tip of the island: everything north of the city was farmland or untouched woodland, and ultimately became important to Washington and his troops' movement. In June, 1776, drafting was begun on the Declaration of Independence, the Articles of Confederation (which led to the Constitution) and A Model Treaty (which was a guide on how to conduct foreign relations). As we all know, the Declaration of Independence was ratified on July 4, 1776.

After the war, the peace treaty with Britain was signed in 1783. It is known as The Treaty of Paris. It gave the United States all the land east of the Mississippi and South of the Great Lakes, with the exception of Florida, which was given to Spain under the Treaty of Versailles. The United States Constitution was drafted in 1787 and went into effect in 1789. George Washington was elected president a few months later and re-elected in 1792.

In the new country, Maine was part of Massachusetts. Vermont was extra legal and not part of United States. Virginia was made up of Virginia, West Virginia and Kentucky. What would become Ohio, Indiana, Illinois, Michigan, Wisconsin and a tiny piece of Minnesota was one large territory called the Northwest Territory. Tennessee, Mississippi and Alabama made up a second territory. Florida and all the land west of the Mississippi belonged to Spain and the two pieces were connected by the Florida panhandle which extended all the way to the Mississippi River. Vermont joined in the Union in 1791 and Kentucky was created from Virginia in 1792. Tennessee was formed from a part of the southern territory in 1796 — the first "new land" state. A piece of Ohio had been given to Connecticut as reparations for those whose homes were burned by the British during the revolution. (It was called The Western Reserve.) The state, which included the western reserve, was created from the Northwest territory in 1803 although because of oversight it was never officially declared the 17th State by the United States congress until the 1950s. In 1953, President Eisenhower signed a joint proclamation by Congress declaring March 1, 1803 to be the date of Ohio's admission to the union. No other states entered the Union until after the next war (although the Louisiana Purchase in 1803 had effectively doubled the size of the country.) It's thought by some that it wasn't until after the next war with Britain (the War of 1812) that America developed its very strong sense of national identity and patriotism.

Cook descendants who served:

94.     Ebenezer Cook (Joshua-3, Josiah-2, Josias-1) was born on 25 Nov 1711 in Eastham, Mass. He served in the military in the American Revolution as a private in Captain Long's company

99. i.  ★Jonathan Cook (Jonathan-4, Joshua-3, Josiah-2, Josias-1) was born in Apr 1752 in Haddam, Conn. He died as a prisoner of war in Aug 1777 at the age of 25 in New York, NY. (What is today called the Brooklyn Navy Yards was, during the revolution, the place where the British kept their prison ships anchored. Prisoners were not given much thought and many were poisoned simply to get rid of them. Jonathan Cook was probably one of those who was poisoned.)

101.    Hezekiah Cook (Joshua-3, Josiah-2, Josias-1) was born about 1728 in Eastham, Mass. He served in the military in the French and Indian war about 1762 and in the American Revolution from Berkshire County, Mass.

211.    Solomon Cook Sr. (Solomon-4, Josiah-3, Josiah-2, Josias-1) was born on 12 Sep 1737 in Provincetown, Mass. He served in the American Revolution from Massachusetts.

217.    Jonathan Cook Sr. (Solomon-4, Josiah-3, Josiah-2, Josias-1) was born on 22 Jul 1753 in Provincetown, Mass. He served in the military in the American Revolution from Massachusetts.

223.    Thomas Cook Jr. (Thomas-4, Richard-3, Josiah-2, Josias-1) was born in 1728 in Durham, Conn. He served in the American Revolution from Connecticut.

234.    John Mayo, husband of Lydia Cook (Caleb-4, Richard-3, Josiah-2, Josias-1) was born on 19 Apr 1733 in Eastham, Mass. He served in the American Revolution from Massachusetts.

325.    Joshua Cook (Josiah-4, Joshua-3, Josiah-2, Josias-1) was born on 12 Apr 1740 in Eastham, Mass. He served in the military in the French and Indian war in 1758. He served in the military as an Ensign in the American Revolution from Connecticut.

325. i.    ★Elihu Cook (Joshua-5, Josiah-4, Joshua-3, Josiah-2, Josias-1) was born in Mar 1765 in East Haddam, Conn. He served in the American Revolution from Connecticut under Col. Butler. He died (probably in the war) on 4 Jun 1782 at the age of 17 in New York.

326.    Deacon Moses Cook (Josiah-4, Joshua-3, Josiah-2, Josias-1) was born on 23 Oct 1742 in Middletown, Conn. He served in the military doing public service for the American Revolution for Connecticut.

327.    Lieut. Titus Carrier, husband of Mercy Cook (Josiah-4, Joshua-3, Josiah-2, Josias-1) was born on 23 Aug 1733. He served as an ensign in the American Revolution, probably from Connecticut.

329.    Simeon Wright, husband of Roda Cook (Josiah-4, Joshua-3, Josiah-2, Josias-1) was born abt. 1736. He served as a private in the American Revolution from Connecticut.

330.    Richard Cook (Josiah-4, Joshua-3, Josiah-2, Josias-1) was born on 17 Mar 1753 in Middletown, Conn. He served in the American Revolution from Connecticut.

333.    Joshua Cook (Joshua-4, Joshua-3, Josiah-2, Josias-1) was born before 1745. He served as an Ensign in the American Revolution from Connecticut.


8.221

335.  Ebenezer Cook Jr. (Ebenezer-4, Joshua-3, Josiah-2, Josias-1) was born before 12 Oct 1746. He served in American Revolution under Col. John Brown as a Minute Man Captain in Massachusetts.

336.  Gideon Cook (Ebenezer-4, Joshua-3, Josiah-2, Josias-1) was born on 10 Jan 1750 in East Haddam, Conn. He served in the American Revolution from Connecticut.

338.  Moses Cook (Ephraim-4, Joshua-3, Josiah-2, Josias-1) was born in 1738 in Coventry, Conn. He served in the French and Indian War in the 8th Company in 1757 in Connecticut. He served in the American Revolution with sons Moses #(918), James (#919) and Aaron between 1776 and 1784 in Dutchess, NY.

338. iv.  Aaron Cook (Moses-5, Ephraim-4, Joshua-3, Josiah-2, Josiah-1) was born between 1765 and 1770. He served in the American Revolution between 1776 and 1784 in Freehold, NY.

340.  Ephraim Cook (Ephraim-4, Joshua-3, Josiah-2, Josias-1) was born about 1743 in Mansfield or Coventry, Connecticut. He served in the American Revolution in the 10th Company, Connecticut's First Regiment between 18 Mar 1762 and 3 Dec 1762.

349.  Joseph Cook (Simeon-4, Joshua-3, Josiah-2, Josias-1) was born on 27 Sep 1751 in New Marlborough, Mass. He served in the American Revolution in New Marlborough, Mass.

353.  William Thomas, husband of Huldah Cook (Zaccheus-4, Joshua-3, Josiah-2, Josias-1) served in the military as a marine in the American Revolution from Connecticut. Note: The Marine Corp uses November 10, 1775 as the date of their foundation, but between 1783 and 1798 there was no Marine corp in existence. The Marine Corp of the revolution was very small, with only about 2,000 enlisted men. Their duty was primarily to serve as guards to captains and crew.

366.  Sgt. Nathaniel Cook (Jonathan-4, Joshua-3, Josiah-2, Josias-1) was born about Feb 1756 in Haddam, Conn. He served in the military as a Corporal and then Sergeant in the American Revolution from Connecticut.

380.  Solomon Cook (Hezekiah-4, Joshua-3, Josiah-2, Josias-1) was born on 21 Dec 1761 in New Marlborough, Mass. He served in the military in the American Revolution, including a period as a substitute for his father about 1778 in Massachusetts.

684.  Miles Cook (Thomas-5, Thomas-4, Richard-3, Josiah-2, Josias-1) was baptized on 16 Jun 1765 in Durham, Conn. He served as a drummer in the American Revolution. (He was somewhere between the age of 10 and 18)

693.    Uriah Nickerson, husband of Deborah Cook (Samuel-5, Caleb-4, Richard-3, Josiah-2, Josias-1) was born in 1763 in Eastham, Mass. He served in the military in the American Revolution under Capt. Joseph Brown on 18 Jul 1780.

918.    Moses Bassett Cook (Moses-5, Ephraim-4, Joshua-3, Josiah-2, Josias-1) was born on 6 Apr 1762 in New Marlborough, Mass. He served in the military for three years in the American Revolution about 1779 in Fishkill, NY.

919.    James Cook (Moses-5, Ephraim-4, Joshua-3, Josiah-2, Josias-1) was born in 1763 in New Marlborough, Mass. He served in the military in the American Revolution for three months in 1780. He served in the military for an additional 3 months in the American Revolution in 1781. He also served in the war of 1812.

## War of 1812.

This was another war with the United Kingdom that is seen by some as a part of the Napoleonic wars. In the United States and Canada it is usually described as a separate war. One of the main fronts of the war was the border with Canada and the Great Lakes. War was declared by the United States and it lasted for 2-½ years. The war was sometimes seen as the second war of independence and after it was won, American nationalism soared. Borders did not change, but it cemented United States suppression of the American Indians and the western borders of the country.

Cook descendants who served:

901. Henry Haugton, husband of Levina Cook (Joshua-5, Joshua-4, Joshua-3, Josiah-2, Josias-1) was was the son of Samuel and Lois Haughton , was born in Dec 1766 in Haddam, Conn. He died in 1845 at the age of 79. Henry served in the military in the War of 1812.

906. Col William Walker Cook (Ebenezer-5, Ebenezer-4, Joshua-3, Josiah-2, Josias-1) was born on 31 Aug 1773 in Stockbridge, Mass. He served in the military in the war of 1812. He died on 23 Feb 1830 at the age of 56 in Killawog, NY and is buried in Killawog Cemetery.

919. James Cook (Moses-5, Ephraim-4, Joshua-3, Josiah-2, Josias-1) was born in 1763 in New Marlborough, Mass. He served in the military in the American Revolution for three months in 1780. He served in the military for an additional 3 months in the American Revolution in 1781. He later served in the war of 1812.

929. David Cook (Nathan-5, Ephraim-4, Joshua-3, Josiah-2, Josias-1) was born before Feb 1787 in Coventry, Conn. He served in the military served in the War of 1812. David died in 1859 at the age of 72 in Suffield, Oh.

8.223

1012.Ichabod Cook (Amos-5, Jonathan-4, Joshua-3, Josiah-2, Josias-1) was born on 3 Jun 1792 in
       Connecticut. He served in the military as a private under Capt. Van Dalsen in the War of 1812
       in New York. He died on 23 Oct 1866 at the age of 74 in Ashland, NY.

2080.Deacon John Cook (James-6, Moses-5, Ephraim-4, Joshua-3, Josiah-2, Josias-1) was born on
       10 Sep 1786 in Freehold, Cayuga, NY. He served in the military in the War of 1812 between
       1812 and 1814. He died on 5 Aug 1857 at the age of 70 in Mecca, Oh. John was buried in
       East Mecca Cemetery, Mecca, Oh.

**American Civil War (1861 - 1865)**

Of the many causes of the civil war, it might have been slavery in the new states that contributed the
most, as the debate about slavery itself had been running since the founding of the country. The
Northwest ordinance of 1787 had made Ohio, Indiana, Illinois, Michigan and Wisconsin free states. In
order to prevent slave holding states being outnumbered by free states, the Missouri Compromise of
1820 allowed states to be admitted only in pairs: so that for every free state there was a slave holding
state. (In the case of Missouri, it was balanced by the admission of Maine.) Additionally, it was
decided that slavery in the new territories would be allowed only below the 36°30′ parallel, which was
Missouri's southern border. It was thought that this would balance the expansion, and it did until
California joined the union in 1850 and made it 16-15. In exchange for admitting California, Congress
ruled that no restrictions on slavery would be allowed in Utah and New Mexico. All of this was
declared unconstitutional by the Supreme Court in the 1857 Dred Scott case, which also stated that
people with "African blood" had no right to U.S. citizenship. The decision basically allowed slavery to
exist in any state that wanted it. Abolition in the north was a very strong force, as was the novel *Uncle
Tom's Cabin,* the abolitionist John Brown and the raid on Harper's Ferry. Abraham Lincoln's election
caused further stress, though he stated he would not interfere with slavery where it already existed, but
was against any expansion of slavery.

After Lincoln's election, South Carolina voted to secede in 1860. Urged to join them by South
Carolinian ambassadors, Mississippi, Florida, Alabama, Georgia, Louisiana, and Texas also seceded.
The war began when the Confederates fired on Fort Sumpter in Charleston Harbor, South Carolina,
April 12, 1861. Lincoln called up a volunteer force of 75,000. Virginia, Arkansas, North Carolina and
Tennessee joined the Confederate States. Part of Virginia split off and became West Virginia and
stayed with the Union. Kansas and Nevada became Union states.

Cook descendants who served (all on the Union side):

1446.  i.    ★Leonard Elder, son of Harriet Eliza Cook (Alva-6, Elisha-5, Jacob-4, Josiah-3, Josiah-2,
             Josias-1) and James Elder, was born in Sep 1839. He died in the civil war about 1863 at
             the age of 24.

1491.vii.   Lt. Rawlins Thomas Atkins, son of Hannah Cook and John Atkins, was born in Apr 1835 in Provincetown, Mass. He served as a corporal in Company G, 1st Infantry Regiment during the civil war on 23 May 1861 for Massachusetts.

2053. v.   Edward Gray Cook (Charles-7, William Walker-6, Ebenezer-5, Ebenezer-4, Joshua-3, Josiah-2, Josias-1) was born on 14 Feb 1841 in Broome County, NY. He served in the Civil War on 9 Aug 1862 in New York. He was injured in the war.

vi.   ★Alexander Ford Cook (Charles-7, William Walker-6, Ebenezer-5, Ebenezer-4, Joshua-3, Josiah-2, Josias-1) was born on 9 Jan 1843 in Broome County, NY. He was drafted in 1863 in Triangle, Broome County, New York and made part of the 109th Regiment. Alexander died in the battle of Spottsylvania Court House, fought May 12, 1864. He was 21. From the notation in Charles Abby Cook's bible record, he (Charles) did not entirely believe this. But as the company entered with 1200 and left with 400, chances are very high that Alexander was killed there.

2110.iv.   ★Amasa B. Cook (Ephraim-7, Silas-6, Ephraim-5, Ephraim-4, Joshua-3, Josiah-2, Josias-1) was born on 27 Apr 1838 in Summit County, Oh. He served in the military in the Civil War as a Private in Co. A, 42d OH Infantry Regiment between 20 Sep 1861 and 1865 in Ohio. He died mortally wounded in the civil war on 5 Jun 1863 at the age of 25 in Chickasaw Bayou, Warren, Miss.

2110.v.   ★Ephraim Cook (Ephraim-7, Silas-6, Ephraim-5, Ephraim-4, Joshua-3, Josiah-2, Josias-1) was born on 28 May 1842 in Solon, Oh. Ephraim served in the military in the civil war as a Private in Co. A, 42d Ohio Infantry Regiment after 20 Sep 1861 in Ohio. He is presumed to have died in the war.

Appendix A

The following are copies of facsimile pages of an article that Ira S. Cook (son of Ira Cook and Rachel Faxon) wrote in the Annals of Iowa, about his family, their westward migration in 1835 and 1836, and subsequent founding of the city of Davenport, IA.

# REMINISCENCES.



Sixty-four years ago this day I came to Iowa, landing where now stands the city of Davenport, and although nearly two-thirds of a century have passed since that day, and I am fast nearing my four score years; I cannot forget the impression then produced on my mind, boy as I was, that it was the most beautiful land on God's green earth, and the richness of the soil, the wondrous profusion and fragrance of the wild flowers, the green hills, and pleasant valleys, still remain with me after all these long years.

A journey in those days from our home in western New York to the new land, was a very different affair from that of the same trip to-day. My father, one sister and her husband came out in October, 1835. They came to Buffalo by the Erie canal, thence to Cleveland by steamboat, down the Portsmouth Canal to the Ohio River, then down the Ohio and up the Mississippi Rivers by steamboat to Rock Island. The trip consumed just one month.

In the spring of 1836 the remainder of the family, consisting of twelve people, including the children of my brothers and sisters, left home on the 25th day of March. Our route was one-hundred miles by wagon to "Olean Point," on the Alleghany River. There we built cabins on a lumber raft and floated down to Pittsburgh, from there to Cincinnati by steamboat, thence by way of Ohio and Mississippi river boats to Rock Island. We were two months, less two days, making the trip.

In those days three to four weeks were required to bring from, or send a letter to New York, and the postage was twenty-five cents for a half ounce. Then Iowa was attached to Michigan for judicial purposes, and my father held a commission from the Governor of Michigan as a justice of the peace. Only what was called the "Black Hawk Purchase" then belonged to the government, and the settlements were mostly confined to a narrow strip along the Mississippi River; all of the rest of this great State, now the home of 2,000,000 people, belonged to the Indian tribes.

During the years 1836 and 1837 the influx of people into the new territory was great and the country was full of "land hunters." My father had a hewed log house with a *shingle roof,* which in those early days was considered "quite swell;" and although there were fourteen all told in the family, still in a way that cabin was a hotel, for there was scarcely a night that some one did not apply for something to eat and a place to sleep, and my father was a man with so kind a heart that no man was ever turned away hungry or tired, so long as there was any thing to eat in the house, or a place to stow away another body, and that would generally be on the soft side of a hard wood (oak) "puncheon." The Indians called him Nish-i-shin Che-mo-ka-man (good white man). I should say here that, in addition to the log cabin described, which was 16 x 18, it had a loft reached by a ladder, where people could be stowed away, and another very small cabin made of rough logs and roofed with "shakes," which, by the way, make a very good "fair weather roof," excellent so far as ventilation is concerned.

As I have before said, we arrived on the 23d of May, 1836. My father and William Van Tuyl, my brother-in-law, had prepared and had ready for planting about twenty acres, broken up the previous year, and on the 24th all hands turned in to planting this ground to corn. We had then none of the modern farm implements and so that crop was planted in the old-fashioned way. The ground was furrowed with a horse, the corn dropped by hand and covered with a hoe. We had a very good crop, and I believe it was the first crop of corn raised in the vicinity of Davenport. I know we had no neighbors within several miles who raised any corn that year.

In connection with this crop of corn, I must tell of a boyish prank of mine. Our field was only about one-half fenced, and as soon as the corn was planted all hands went to the timber making rails to complete the fencing. One evening on returning from the timber we found that a drove of hogs belonging to a neighbor, a man by the name of Faulkner, had been in the field and had made sad havoc with the newly planted corn, so the next day I was left at home to guard the field and replant the corn. Well, if that drove of hogs did not make it lively for me that hot summer day, then I lose my guess! I was a small boy for my age, with very short legs; that drove of hogs was very large, with very long legs (the "razor-back breed"), and they could go around the field and get in their work sooner than I could go across and head them off. The day came to an end, and it came near making an end of me, too. That night I told my brother, John P., of the awful time I had and then he said: "See here, Bub, I tell you what to do. After we go out in the morning you take 'Old Betsey' ('Old Betsey' was a single-barrel shot gun about six feet long), fill your pocket with peas (we had a barrel, brought out for seed) and I think you can keep them off." This looked like a large-sized picnic for me and I acted upon his advice promptly. I did not have to wait long for the enemy, and I was ready for them. As soon as they were in range "Old Betsey" spoke in her loudest voice. That shot took effect, because the individual hog which received the charge "squealed," but it had no more effect on that drove than if I had thrown a stone among them. I kept up that "cannonade" for a half hour. The confounded drove would retreat, but immediately make a charge on another part of the field. At last hot, mad, tired out, the devil thought it a good time to make his appearance, and I have noticed that when "Auld Cloutie" has work for his subjects to do, he takes particular care to provide the means. I happened just then to put my hand in my pocket and there I found a dozen or more buckshot that a man had given me. Without any hesitation I rolled six or eight of them down

"Betsey's" throat, and as the enemy was then just within fair range, I blazed away. The result—yes, sir, all that his satanic majesty could desire! Two of the largest fell to rise no more; others, how many I do not know, went limping and squealing home. One, I know, only succeeded in going a few rods to an Indian trail, where it lay down and became "pork," making a total "bag" of *three!* The enemy were effectually routed and I saw no more of them that day.

The Indians were plenty with us. They were not reconciled to give up their hunting and fishing ground on Rock Island and vicinity. Black Hawk says in his life, dictated by himself: "This was our garden spot, our fruit orchard, and was very dear to us." And so they lingered in the vicinity and made frequent visits to their loved and lost old homes. They were, as a rule, peaceable and well behaved, glad to exchange game and fish for the products of the white man's fields. Occasionally, when under the influence of whiskey, they became troublesome. One such incident happened to my sister, Mrs. Van Tuyl. She was alone in the house when two Indians came in. They had a bottle of whiskey and were already under its influence. It was a cold day, and after warming themselves they made signs that they wanted a drinking cup. My sister gave them a tea cup, which they managed to drop on the floor and, of course, it went to pieces. Then they asked for another, but she said "no," and shook her head. At once one of them drew a knife and threatened her. She stepped to a corner of the room, seized a broom, pointed to the door and said "puckochee!" (go), and sure enough they went, and in a hurry, too. It seems to be a fact that a "brave" fears nothing so much on earth as to be struck by a woman. He is disgraced forever.

Those pioneer days were days of toil, interspersed with frequent attacks of ague, and, as I have somewhere said before, "when we were not at work we were shaking." I well remember that in the fall of 1836, 1837 and 1838, and especially in 1837, there were not enough well people in all the country to care for the sick.

Where the flourishing city of Davenport now stands there was not a single house, on what was the original town site, only a cabin on the bank of the river, in which lived the ferryman. Further up the river and about opposite the Rock Island bridge lived Mr. Antoine Le Claire, and that was the sum total of the inhabitants in May, 1836. During that year and the succeeding ones the influx of settlers was great and we soon had plenty of neighbors. The town of Davenport began to grow and was soon a thriving village, with churches, schools, stores and mechanical trades in full operation.

The country around Rock Island in those days was a paradise for sportsmen. Game was plenty and the river fairly swarmed with fish. To those who had the leisure to take advantage of this condition of affairs, there was lots of sport every day in the week; but to those of us who were compelled by necessity to labor from dawn to dark, and then do the "chores," the fun was not so apparent. However, even we, the unfortunates, occasionally got a "half day off," and on days when it rained so hard and steadily that we could not work, even in the barn, we were allowed to "go a fishin'."

Of public men and public measures in those early days I can say but little. I was but a boy of 15 or 16 years, and that boy was confined closely on a farm and worked from fourteen to sixteen hours each day. I remember one morning seeing Gov. Henry Dodge of Wisconsin pass our farm on his way to Burlington to attend the annual session of the legislature. He was on horseback and attended by other state officers. They had ridden the entire distance from the then capital of Wisconsin, which I believe was at Mineral Point, and still had a ride of one hundred and twenty miles before them.

I once met and was introduced to Gen. Robert Lucas, our first territorial governor. I believe this occurred in the spring of 1841. I was then living in Tipton, Cedar county. Some of "us boys" one day borrowed an old horse and wagon and started over to Rock Creek for the purpose of fishing. As we were driving through the timber we saw coming toward us two men on horseback. We soon recognized one as Mr. Harmon Van Antwerp, the then member of the territorial legislature from Cedar county. When we met we stopped and Mr. Van Antwerp introduced his companion as "Gov. Lucas." After a little chat and a kindly inquiry by the governor as to where we boys were bound, we said "Good morning" and went on our way. I mention this interview to give me an opportunity to tell how one, at least, of our early governors was dressed. First, he had on a complete suit of blue linsey woolsey, evidently of home manufacture, and the cut and fit showed the handiwork of an amateur. His shirt was of unbleached cotton cloth, with turn down collar, and shirt front of the same material; a pair of coarse cowhide boots and a soft wool hat completed his attire. A sturdy figure of a pioneer was he, but under that soft felt hat was a brain large enough for a ruler of nations, and we of this day (as those of that day could not) can see how much that plain old man contributed to the solid foundations of this great commonwealth.

A notable person in those very early days was Antoine Le Claire. He lived in a very comfortable house, about opposite the lower end of Rock Island, on a section (640 acres) reserved for him by the Indians when they made their first sale to the United States of their Iowa lands.

Mr. Le Claire was of French and Indian blood. He was well educated and exercised a powerful influence over the Indians. He was for very many years in the employ of the United States as an interpreter. He officiated in that capacity in making the treaty at the time (September 21, 1832) the government made the first purchase of the Indians, called locally the "Black Hawk Purchase." And again in 1836 when General Scott made a treaty with the Sacs and

Foxes, at which time a further large purchase of land was made. That treaty was made on the reservation belonging to Mr. Le Claire and was attended by the entire tribe, many thousands in numbers. I remember distinctly the hundreds and hundreds of Indians, squaws, pappooses, ponies and dogs, that for days prior to that of the treaty swarmed past our cabin. The main trail from the Indian villages on the Iowa river to the agency on Rock Island passed within twenty or thirty rods of our cabin and right across our land. So, as I was confined at home with the "shakes" (ague) and could not go to the treaty grounds some two or three miles away, I used to sit day after day and watch the moving procession.

Mr. Le Claire was a man of immense proportions, weighing from 350 to 400 pounds, yet he could mount a horse or dance a cotillion with more ease and grace than many a man of half his weight.

He was a good citizen, liberal, public-spirited, benevolent, and always ready to help the deserving. The city of Davenport owes much to him. He accumulated large wealth for those days, and made good use of it. He died September 21, 1861.

Col. George Davenport was another man who figured in the local affairs of Iowa and Davenport, although his residence was on Rock Island, where he had lived since 1816 or 1817, coming there, I believe, with the soldiers who built Fort Armstrong. He had been for many years, and was still as late as 1836, an Indian trader. He was one of the original proprietors of the town of Davenport, and it bears his name. For years he had been again and again placed in deadly peril in his dealings with hostile tribes, yet he lived to meet death at the hands of cowardly robbers, who first shot him, and then so abused and maltreated him to force him to tell where his money was that he died that night.

The pursuit and capture of his murderers was one of the most thrilling chapters of western history. My brother,

233

Ebenezer, was of the counsel for the prosecution, and his story of the pursuit and capture of Birch, Fox, the two Longs and Young, was most interesting. Birch and Fox escaped in some mysterious way, but John and Aaron Long and Young were tried and condemned, and I had the satisfaction, together with some thousands of other spectators, of seeing them hung! Maybe that sounds rather sanguinary, but the whole country was aroused by the brutal murder of an unoffending peaceable old gentleman, who was known to every citizen, old and young, in the country, and there were not many but who would have been glad to pull upon a rope to one end of which dangled the murderers.

There were many other men who came to Davenport and Scott county in 1836 and 1837 and later who deserve and are entitled to honorable mention and praise for their efforts in building up the new country, but space forbids the record of their names here.

On the 22d day of February, 1858, (Washington's birthday) the Pioneer Settlers' Association of Scott County held their first re-union at the Burtis House. J. A. Birchard, Esq., of Pleasant Valley, in responding to the toast, "The History of Scott County," closed as follows: "We have made the new homes; raised the new altars; built the new school houses and churches. To do this required men; men of iron nerve, of strong arms and large hearts, and such men were the pioneers of Scott county, and I may justly add, and so of all Iowa."

My sister, Mrs. William Van Tuyl, of Davenport, is to-day the oldest living settler of Davenport, and, I believe, with the exception of Capt. Lewis Clark, of Buffalo, of Scott county.

But there were others who aided in laying the foundations of Iowa strong and deep and who contributed largely to the final result. The pioneers of Iowa were a strong and sturdy set of men and of the very best blood of this nation. It took a man of more than ordinary courage and determination, sixty and more years ago, to decide to pack up his worldly possessions and leave the comforts of the east and come to what was then the very far west; and so it was, that those that did come were of the best, and the best equipped for the work before them.

Last winter, at the biennial meeting of the "Pioneer Law Makers" in the city of Des Moines, on the occasion of the reception of that body by the legislature, then in session, the Hon. S. P. Yeomans, of Lucas county, one of the pioneer legislators, in reply to an address made by the presiding officer of one branch of the legislature, tells the story of the work of the pioneers far better than I can. He said:

> I could not keep you on the mountain top if I would. I ask you to step down to the level plain of facts. The profound compliments we receive may turn our heads. Our work was not so marvelous after all. The truth is that the Lord Almighty made Iowa. When we came here we found in Iowa a veritable cornucopia of wealth. We found it in soil, climate, sky and woods. Our civilization was crude. The men who laid the foundations of the state were not pioneer law makers, but for the most part pioneer farmers. They planted trees, they tilled the land, they raised the crops. Prosperity came apace. The iron horse came to carry away to the east the products of the farm. It is true that laws had to be established. A judiciary system was devised, schools were organized and were made free to all. If we did our work well, we have received our reward.

Des Moines, Iowa, May 23, 1900.

---

Go to the West.—We say, as we have ever said, to young men or young women of light purse, but willing hand; to the farmer or mechanic of increasing family, slender means or dubious prospects, your true home is in the West! Seek it, rear your children there to larger opportunities than await them on the rugged hill-side or in the crowded streets of the East.—*Horace Greeley, Oct. 15, 1857.*

This is an article that the same Ira S. Cook wrote about being a surveyor in Iowa in the first days of settlement. It was published before the article about his family and includes two photos of Ira, one dressed fine and one in his frontier or surveying outfit.

IRA COOK.
From a recent photograph.

237

## GOVERNMENT SURVEYING IN EARLY IOWA.

### BY IRA COOK.

It has occurred to me that it would be well to preserve in THE ANNALS some facts and incidents connnected with the Government surveys in our State, and with this end in view I propose to relate some of my own experiences.

Except immediately along the Mississippi and in a few localities on some of the larger streams, these surveys preceded the settlement of the country, so that the deputy surveyor who had a contract to survey a given district generally found himself beyond any settlement, and, as a consequence, must carry with him his house (tent) and his supplies of provisions and complete outfit for a trip extending, in some cases, over many months. It followed, of course, that he was obliged to restrict himself and his men to the simplest necessities of food and clothing. A barrel or two of salt pork, flour in barrels, navy beans, with sugar, coffee, salt and pepper, made up the sum of our larder. For bedding we had rubber blankets, buffalo robes and heavy woolen blankets. With these we could keep both warm and dry.

A surveying party would consist of either six or eleven men, depending upon whether it was intended to use one or two instruments. First, the surveyor, then two chainmen and an axeman or mound-builder, made up the field party; a cook and teamster completed the party. This would allow us one extra man in case of sickness of any of the party, or we could use him as a flagman when needed.

My first experience was in the fall and winter of 1849 and 1850. By purchase I became the half owner of a contract to sub-divide ten townships, our district being within it is to-day. It took time and patience and sturdy manhood to do what was necessary to bring about subsequent results. Many times we were confronted by a broad, deep river, some of the numerous branches of the Grand or Missouri Platte, no bridge, no ford, and but very limited means at our command to overcome the obstacle. All the same the job was there and we must cross, with horses, wagon and camp equipage, provisions, etc. Sometimes we would look for two large cottonwood trees on opposite sides of the stream. These we would cut down, so that they would meet and overlap each other in mid-stream, thus forming a foot bridge. Over this we would transport our movables; then we would swim the horses over; then with chains and ropes so fasten the axles and wheels of our wagon to the box that they would float; then when that was floated to the other shore hitch the horses to the end of the wagon tongue and, with the aid of the strong arms of the men, land the same on the bank, load up and go on our way rejoicing.

I remember one occasion of this kind where we had hardly accomplished the crossing when night settled down upon us. Too tired to put up our tent, we ate a cold bite, maybe had a cup of coffee with it, and then every man seized his blanket and, picking out the softest spot that he could find, lay down for the night. My own bed was at the foot of an oak tree, using the root for a pillow. As this was my first experience of this kind, I remember I thought it rather tough, but I soon got used to that sort of thing.

The time covered by my service as a government surveyor was from 1849 to 1853, and of all the men then engaged as brother surveyors with whom I was acquainted and more or less intimate, I can not now recall a half dozen that are living. Our work was hard, our days long; in winter or summer we were at work in the morning as soon as we could see, worked as long as we could see at night, and then tramped to camp by moonlight or starlight, often for many miles. We lived on bread, salt pork, beans and coffee. Occasionally we would vary it by the capture of wild game. On this trip I remember one of the boys shot a deer, and once we found a "bee-tree" containing several gallons of honey; and once, with the aid of a big dog, a jack staff and a convenient snow bank, we captured a two hundred and fifty pound wild hog. Incidents of this kind helped not only our larder, but also broke the monotony of our lives.

We completed our work in January, 1850, broke camp and started for home. In order to have the benefit of the settlements in Missouri we travelled directly south, and on the first night of our homeward journey occurred an incident which I will relate as showing what men can endure in the way of cold, when inured to it by long exposure. We reached Platte river at nightfall, but found no timber in which to camp, only some scattering trees for firewood, and the ground frozen so hard that we could not put up our tent. We built a good, big fire, got supper, drew the wagon up so as to form a wind-break and camped down between it and the fire. We were painfully aware that it was cold, very cold, but just how cold we could not tell. Next day before noon we reached a settlement in Gentry county, Missouri, and, making inquiry as to the temperature that morning, were informed that the thermometer registered 31 degrees below zero!

I spent seven months of 1851, and January, 1852, in Wisconsin. For some months I worked in the heavy timber and swamps between Wisconsin river and Wolf river. This was really on the divide between the waters of the Mississippi and the Great Lakes, as the Wisconsin runs to the Mississippi and the Wolf river into Green Bay. The timber, both on the high lands and in the swamp, was so dense that a good square look at the face of the sun was a rare sight. As we progressed with our work the country become impassable for a wagon.   We left that, and being provided with pack-saddles, loaded our camp equipage on the horses, but not for long, and soon we left the horses and only carried what we could on our backs.   Necessarily our rations shrank more and more, until on one occasion I remember we were reduced for a day and a half to *salt pork and coffee*.   During this time there happened one of the saddest incidents in my experience in this work.

In the district adjoining mine on the east, a brother of the late Hon. Platt Smith, of Dubuque, was at work. One night we had a terrible thunder storm and hurricane, Mr. Smith had been over to my camp the Sunday before and I knew about where he was at work.   The second day after the storm I found his camp, or, rather, where it had been the night of the storm, and right across the spot where his tent stood lay an immense basswood tree, uprooted by the storm.   In looking around for some evidence of what had happened, we found a large beech tree, on the smooth bark of which the men had cut with a marking iron a brief history of what had happened.   The particulars I learned afterward.   They had camped early, got their supper and the men had all lain down for the night but Mr. Smith.   He was tying his cravat to the tent pole when the storm struck them blowing the large tree directly across their tent, killing instantly Mr. Smith and one of his men and crippling another for life.   My party were so shocked and overcome by the tragedy that I doubt if a laugh was heard in my camp for a week afterwards.

Later that year I was at work further south on Fox River in the vicinity of the town of Berlin.   We were now in a settled country and had more of a variety for our table.   In January, 1852, I closed my work there and started home by the way of Dubuque.   From Buffalo Lake, the head of Fox River, where we closed our work, to Dubuque was a good three hundred miles.   People who know me now would hardly give me credit as a "sprinter;" still I walked every mile of that three hundred except six.

Early in 1852 the United States commenced the location of the boundary line between Iowa and Minnesota. As soon as the commission was well under way, I was sent up there to close up and sub-divide Township 100. I think my district included five ranges in Allamakee and Winneshiek Counties. My work was partly in that portion of those counties which a writer in a recent number of the "Midland Monthly" calls the "Switzerland of Iowa." Here among swiftly running streams, deep canons, mountainous hills and rocky precipices, I worked for two months and really here I had the most pleasant and enjoyable time of all my different trips. I found that the brooks and creeks were pretty well stocked with speckled trout. I had not seen one since a boy of ten years, and I could not resist the temptation to go after them. And go I did. For one whole week a cousin and myself whipped the streams, large and small. How many we captured I do not say, as I am not writing "Fish Stories," but it is enough to say that *we* were satisfied.

One incident that happened on this survey I must relate as a curiosity. The most of the land that was available had been taken up by squatters, and so there were a good many settlers in my district. This township 100 consists of five full sections north and south, but the sixth section was only about two or three chains wide, say eight to twelve rods. One day in running up one of my range lines I struck a man's farm. It was partly in Iowa and partly in Minnesota. When I was through with running my lines, his cultivated land was situated in two States, four townships and six sections! I thought he was pretty well scattered.

My work completed, we came down to Lansing, expecting soon to get a steamboat for Dubuque. We were, however, informed that there would not be a boat down

IRA COOK.
U. S. Government Surveyor, from an old Daguerreotype.

243

for five days.   This was a good while to wait, with the wages and board of five or six men going steadily onward; so I decided to build a boat of my own.   I bought two Indian canoes about twelve feet long, some two-by-fours and enough lumber to deck my craft.   We lashed the canoes firmly side by side, decked them over, loaded our traps, and we *seven* men stepped on board.   When we were all on board, we had not more than four inches between the surface of the water and the top of the canoes, but the craft was as steady as a seventy-four gun ship and we pulled out and made the trip to Davenport in safety.

In September, 1852, the Surveyor General, Hon. George B. Sargent, sent me to sub-divide a district comprising ten townships, pretty well up on the head waters of the Raccoon river, now comprised in the counties of Carroll and Sac.   At that time this district was many miles beyond the limits of white settlements and was the home of the elk, the deer and the wolf.   My home was then in Davenport, and, with my company of ten men, I made the trip to Des Moines on foot, my one pair of horses being sufficiently loaded with our supplies, camp equipage, etc.   Here at Des Moines we spent a day replenishing our stock of provisions and necessaries for the long months we expected to spend on the prairies.   Down on Second street, well toward the lower end, I found B. F. Allen with a general stock of merchandise, of whom I made my purchases.

Having now more "plunder" than my team could haul, I procured the services of our genial fellow-citizen, Ed. R. Clapp, to aid me in getting my "traps," including corn for my horses, up to my district.   Ed. was not the millionaire then that he is now, but he was the same wholehearted, good fellow that the citizens of Des Moines have known all these years.   At the crossing of Walnut Creek, he suggested that a farmer at that point was famous for the "watermelons" he raised, and, of course, we all wanted some. We could find no one about the premises, but Ed. said we must have the melons, and, as he knew the way to the "patch," we soon increased the weight of our wagon-load. Ed. said something about stopping on his return and settling the bill, but I guess it is pretty safe to say that he came back by the other road.

About two miles beyond the present town of Panora, which had then just been surveyed and platted, there lived a squatter by the name of Van Order. His cabin of rough logs was occupied by himself, wife and a half-grown son. I mention this man and his little cabin because we had to do with them later. Here we left a barrel of pork and a barrel of flour, to be sent for when needed. From this point we would have no traveled roads, portions of the way were rough, and it became necessary to lighten our loads. On the third day after leaving Des Moines we reached our destination and found on the prairie a "Township Corner" that marked the beginning of my district. Here we camped, unloaded Clapp's wagon and the next morning, bright and early, he started on his lonely ride home.

For the next three or four months we worked early and late, in sunshine and storm; amid rain, sleet and snow we toiled on, but we had glorious appetites and our rations of bread, beans, salt pork and coffee never went begging, but were eaten with a hearty relish; and although we slept in a tent without other fire than that out of doors, and with the mercury often down below zero, yet we did sleep, and sleep well.

I will here relate a discovery we made, and to us it was wonderful as showing the instinct, sagacity and almost human intelligence of an animal. This was a beaver dam across the main branch of the Raccoon river. This dam was by measurement one and one-half chains (six rods) in length. Built with the skill of an engineer, diagonally across the stream from one high point to another, the breast of this dam was *four feet high*, constructed of trees from two to five inches in diameter, built as children build cob houses, a course up and down the stream, then a course crosswise, and so on until the required height was reached. These were filled in with smaller limbs and with clay until it became sufficiently tight to retain the water. We used this dam as a bridge for a week and never crossed it, that we did not wonder at, and admire the almost human sagacity of this little animal.

After New Year's, 1853, the cold became too intense even for us, hardened to cold as we were. Then our provisions were getting very low, and only that we found a camp of beaver trappers in a large grove on the river, from whom we were able to purchase venison, we would have been out entirely. Then, I should not wonder if we were getting "homesick." Think of it. For four months we had not heard one word from the outside world. A presidential election had been held and we had no word of the result. We decided to break up camp, go home and come back in the spring and finish up. We were about two and a half day's fair travel from Van Order's cabin, and, taking an inventory of stock, found we had just three days' rations. The first day we made good progress, after packing up, fully one-third of the way. The second morning the weather looked threatening, but we made an early start, following down the "divide" between the middle and south forks of the 'Coon river. About nine o'clock it began to snow and in a very short time the air was so full that we could no longer see our course. As a matter of safety, we turned down into the timber and camped on "Middle 'Coon." This was on Saturday. It snowed all day, and the most of that night, and Sunday morning we awoke to find two feet of snow covering woodland and prairie. I saw trouble ahead and directed the cook to boil the remainder of our slender stock of beans, and make up what flour we had left into biscuits. When we had done this, I put the whole into the "camp chest," locked it and put the key in my pocket, gravely informing the boys that I was commissary-general for the rest of that campaign.

Monday morning we dug our way out of the snow, crossed the river on the ice, and started on our weary, weary way home. The men were formed in two lines and broke a path for the horses and wagon. When the leaders were exhausted, (remember the snow was knee-deep) they would step outside and the next two men take their places as "breakers," the former leaders falling in behind. And so for three days we worked steadily, but our progress was slow. The days were short and much time (nearly one-half) was consumed going back and forth to the timber for camping purposes. On the morning of the seventh day we decided to leave our wagon. The horses had nothing but hazel brush to eat and were getting weak. The seventh day was warm and pleasant and the sun melted the snow considerably. That night we camped at the mouth of Willow Creek, in Guthrie county. We had no tent or shelter, but at dark the weather was not cold, and with a good fire we were fairly comfortable. We made coffee, ate a biscuit apiece and congratulated each other that we were doing so well. However, about nine o'clock the wind shifted suddenly into the northwest and blew almost a gale, growing colder each minute, and for the rest of that night we were not very comfortable, but we had enough fire to keep us from freezing. At four o'clock next morning the cook made a pot of strong coffee and distributed the very last of our food, which consisted of one small biscuit (then five days old) and one very small spoonful of cold boiled beans to each, and long before daylight we were tramping over the prairie by moonlight, nine men in a string, breaking the frozen crust of the snow to make a path for the horses and the two other men, (one sick, the other the cook, a cripple) who rode the horses. In this way we traveled until about eleven o'clock, when, ascending a high divide, we saw, several miles to the south of us, a house on the prairie and knew that our troubles were nearly over.   We stopped that night with the settler and the next day before noon were at the cabin of Van Order.

We opened that barrel of flour and that barrel of pork in a hurry and set Mrs. Van Order to work, and for six days, and I may say nights, that blessed woman worked incessantly trying to fill up eleven empty men!   The old man was a "mighty hunter" and deer, turkeys, prairie chickens and other game hung dangling from every ridge-pole of his cabin.   We were able very shortly to reduce the stock on hand, while our flour and pork were as greatly enjoyed by these good people, who had seen nothing but corn bread and wild game for months.

Here I hired a man with an ox team to go after my wagon, and when he returned, having pretty well recruited our horses, we started on our homeward journey and arrived safely, without any further incident of note.

This trip closed my career as a government surveyor.

DES MOINES, November, 1896.

---

THE Board of Trustees of the Iowa Lunatic Asylum met at Mt. Pleasant last week and made arrangements for the speedy building of the institution for the reception and care of patients.   H. Winslow, who has been superintendent of the building, was appointed steward, over Judge Wayne of Keosauqua.—*Ottumwa Courier, January 2, 1861.*

---

D. C. BLOOMER, Esq., of Council Bluffs, has been elected a member of the State Board of Education by a large majority, in a district opposed to him in politics—a fine compliment to his abilities and most worthily bestowed.—*Ottumwa Courier, January 2, 1861.*

**Sources**

I've put the most useful at the top of this list. None are internet sources. Internet sources can be correct, but are usually the result of copying or importing someone else's work (especially the Roots Web's "World Connect" database) and almost always lack sources. Other databases, like the database of the LDS (Mormon Church) have too much unreliable information. The U.S. census before 1850 only listed head of house (usually male) surnames and used tick marks to indicate wives and children (and slaves), but the earlier censuses can be useful in gleaning family movement. The 1890 census was mostly destroyed in a fire.

1.  General Society of Mayflower Descendants, *Mayflower Families through 5 generations, 3rd Edition;* Plymouth, Massachusetts, 2001.

2.  Laura(McGaffey) Clarenbach of Maidson, Wis. and Loretta (Broadwell) Ford, of Wethersfield, Conn, *"Joshua Cook (Josiah, Josiah) of Eastham, Mass. ";* New England Historical and Genealogical Register - Vol. 126, No. 2, Apr 1972, pgs. 81-92 and continued in July 1972 at pg. 171.

3.  Vital Records of: Antwerp, Chatham, Eastham, Granville, Harwich, Lee, Middletown, Monroe, Nova Scotia, Otis, Plymouth, Provincetown, Rhode Island, Sandisfield, Springfield, Stockbridge, Truro, and Wellfleet.

4.  United States Census: 1790, 1800, 1810, 1820, 1830, 1840, 1850, 1860, 1870, 1880, 1900.

5.  New York State Census: 1855, 1875.

6.  Michigan State Census: 1894

7.  Iowa State Census: 1885.

8.  Maude N. Stockberger, assisted by A. Bohmer Rudd, *Alva Cook and Lydia Cooper Their Ancestors and Descendants*, Washington D.C., 1958

9.  Mary E. Harding Baird, *Our Harding Family, A Record of the Family and Descendants of Samuel Harding Whose Ancestor Was Joseph Harding, Son of John of England, and of Love Mayhew Harding, Wife of Samuel Harding, Whose Ancestor Was Thomas Mayhew, Son of Joseph of England : With Historical Sketches;* 1867-1937. [This record of almost 2,000 people contains no places and almost no sources.]

10. *Genealogical Memoir of Nathaniel Slosson of Kent, Connecticut and His Descendants, 1696 - 1872;* The Marigold Printing Company, 1896.

11. The Provincetown Advocate.

12. Mary Heaton Vorse, *Time and The Town, a Provincetown Chronicle*, Cape Cod Pilgrim Memorial Assn., July 1990.

13. E.F. and L.W. Ferguson, *Register of Provincetown & Truro residents during the 18th and 19th Centuries*; 5 volumes.

14. Frank Warren, *T he Descendants of John Ball of Watertown, Mass*, 1932.

15. Paul C. Reed, *The English Ancestry of Richard Belden of Wethersfield, Connecticut, With the Probable Ancestry of William Belden of Westherfield*; The American Genealogist (76:1-2, Jan and Apr 2001).

16. *Biographical History of Northeastern Ohio*; Lewis Publishing Company, Chicago, 1893.

17. Milton E. Terry and Anne Borden Harding, *Notebook on The Descendants of Elder William Brewster of Plymouth Colony*; 1985.

18. *Death Notices Published In The Broome County Republican, A Weekly Newspaper of Binghamton, From 1831-1870*, compiled by Ray C. Sawyer, New York, 1942.

19. Cook, Junius Ford, *Genealogical records of certain families residing in Central New York States, circa 1800, including the Thompson-Manning, Seymour-Stoddard, Ford-Darcy & Cook-Whittlesey families of Killawog, Lisle & Whitney's Point in Northern Broome County, N.Y.,* Chicago, Ill., 1961.

20. *Three centuries of the Cape Cod county, Barnstable, Massachusetts 1685 to 1985 / written by its people for the three hundredth anniversary year.* Barnstable County, 1985.

21. *Genealogical notes of Cape Cod families*, compiled by Lydia B. Brownson, Grace W. Held [and] Doris V. Norton.; Wilmington, Del., 1972.

22. George S. May, editor. *Some Descendants of Thomas Carrier of Andover and Billerica, Massachusetts Who Died in Colchester, Connecticut May 16, 1735 and his wife Martha (Allen) Carrier Who as a result of the infamous with trials, was hung at Salem, Massachusetts on August 19, 1692* ; Fair Oaks, Calif.; 1978.

23. *History of Chenango and Madison Counties*, N.Y., Syracuse, N.Y., 1880.

24. *Dawes-Gates ancestral lines*, compiled by Mary Walton Ferris, [Milwaukee, Wis. : Wisconsin Cuneo Press, Inc..], 1931-1943.

25. Elizabeth Cobb Stewart, *Descendants of Andrew Ford of Weymouth, Ma.* (Capital City Press, Montpelier, VT, 1968)

26. James Savage, *A genealogical dictionary of the first settlers of New England : showing three generations of those who came before May, 1692, on the basis of Farmer's Register*, Baltimore: Genealogical Pub. Co., 1990.

27. Alfred Adler Doane. *The Doane Family*. Alfred Doane, 136 1st St, Boston, Mass, 1902.

28. Josiah Paine, *Early Settlers of Eastham*, Harwich, Fiske Center Collection, Seattle.

29. *The Records of East Hampton Congregational Church published on their anniversary in 1898.* [These records were kept by Reverend John Norton starting in about 1764. The original manuscript was possessed by Edward E. Cornwell, of Brooklyn. He stated he had given the manuscript to the Long Island Historical Society, but when queried, the LIHS could not find the manuscript, so these records are now only found in the published book. This book has not been microfiched by the New York Public Library, but it's held in 10 other libraries. There is a gap in these records between 1772 and 1779.]

30. Edward Leodore Smith, *Ancient Eastham, Massachusetts. Two Lists of Those Proprietors There in Seventeen Hundred and Fifteen, from the originals in Town Books Lands and Ways. 1711-1747*, 1913.

31. *Descendants of Joseph Easton, Hartford Conn., 1636-1899,* compiled by William Starr Easton, St. Paul, Minn., 1899

32. *The History of the Faxon Family*: the descendants of Thomas Faxon of Braintree, Mass, by George L. Faxon, Sprinfield Print Co., 1880, 394 pp.

33. *Ferguson Manuscript* in Provincetown Library, Provincetown, Mass.

34. Folsom, Elizabeth Knowles, *Genealogy of the Folsom Family : a revised and extended edition including English records*, Rutland, Vt.: Tuttle Pub. Co., 1938-1980.

35. Elizabeth Pearson White, C.G. of Winnetka, Ill., *The Godfreys of Chatham, Mass.* Mayflower Families, p. 60 -83.

36. Greene Genes Quarterly, 1988 - 1999.

251

37. Maurice Hitt, *Genealogical Gleanings from Early Broome County Newspapers 1806-1882*, 1996 and other items on file at the Broome County Historian's Office.

38. Jane Grozier Anspach, *The Grozier Family*, Columbus, Ohio.

39. *Historical Gazetteer of Tioga County, 1785-1888. Early Households of Berkshire*, by W.B. Gay, Syracuse, N.Y.; W.B.Gay & Co

40. Simeon L. Deyo, *History of Barnstable County Massachusetts, 1620-1890. Chapter 24: Wellfleet* (1890. New York: H. W. Blake & Co.)

41. Pierce, Josiah, *A History of the town of Gorham, Maine. Prepared at the request of the town,* Portland, Foster & Cushing, 1862.

42. Bates, Samuel P., *History of Greene County,* (J.B. Beers, 1884)

43. Whitehead, Henry, *History of Middlesex County, Connecticut,* (J.B. Beers, 1884)

44. Harriet Taylor Upton, *History of The Western Reserve*, Chicago, New York, The Lewis publishing company, 1910.

45. Leroy W. Kingman*, Our People and Its People, A Memorial History of Tioga County, New York.* (Elmira, N.Y., W. A. Fergusson & Co. [189-?]-97)

46. Humphreys, Frederick, *The Humphreys family in America*, assisted by Otis M. Humphreys, Henry R. Stiles, Mrs. Sarah M. Churchill; New York, 1883.

47. *A Narrative History of the People of Iowa*, by Edgar Ruben Harlan, Vol. IV. The American Historical Society, Inc., Chicago and New York 1931

48. www.kinghiramslodge.org/history_part1.htm

49. *Descendants of Richard Knowles, 1673-1973*, compiled by Virginia Knowles Hufbauer, (Ventures International, San Diego, Cal., 1974.)

50. Hearn, Daniel Allen, *Legal Executions in New England, 1623 - 1960*, Jefferson, N.C. : McFarland, 1997.

51. Merrick, Barbara Lambert, *Brewster of the Mayflower, and the Fifth Generation Descendants of His Daughter Patience*, [Plymouth, Mass.] : General Society of Mayflower Descendants,

2001.

52. Susan E. Roser, *Mayflower Increasings*, Genealogical Publ, Baltimore, 2nd ed. 1995.

53. Leon Clark Hills, *"History and Genealogy of the Mayflower Planters and First Comers to Ye Olde Colonie"* reprint, Clearfield Company; Baltimore, 1990.

54. *Andrew Newcomb, 1618-1686, and his descendants; a revised edition of "Genealogical memoir" of the Newcomb family, published 1874 by John Bearse Newcomb, compiled and revised by Bethuel Merritt Newcomb, New Haven, Conn.,* Priv. print. for the author by the Tuttle, Morehouse & Taylor co., 1923.

55. *The Nickerson Family, Descendants of William Nickerson*, Chatham, Mass., Nickerson Family Association, 1973-76, 3 vols.

56. Katharine Elizabeth Chapin Higgins, *Richard Higgins, a resident and pioneer settler at Plymouth and Eastham, Massachusetts, and at Piscataway, New Jersey, and his descendants.* Worcester, Mass.: Higgins, 1918.

57. Brainard, Homer W., *"Henry Rowley and Some of His Descendants."*

58. *Family Bible of Samuel Cook, 1805,* printed by Mathew Carey, 122 Market Street, Philadelphia, P.A., published in The Mayflower Descendant.

59. *A History Of The Seymour Family,* Under the direction of George Dudley Seymour, by Donald Lines Jacobus, The Tuttle, Morehouse and Taylor Company, New Haven, CT, 1939.

60. *A Genealogical Memoir of Nathaniel Slosson of Kent & His Descendants, 1696-1872*

61. Slawson George Clark, *The Slason - Slauson - Slawson - Slosson Family*, Waverly, New York: The Waverly Sun, Inc., 1946.

62. *Sparrow Genealogy, 1623-1871,* by Sarah Sparrow, printed by Lane Brothers, Norton, Mass., 1888.

63. Starbuck, Alexander, *History of the American Whale Fishery, From Its Earliest Inception to the Year 1876*, New York, Argosy-Antiquarian, 1964.

64. *John Stoddard of Wethersfield, Conn., and his descendants,* 1642-1872, by Patterson D. Williams, Authors Edition, 1873.

65. Katherine Chapin Higgins, *Supplement to Richard Higgins and his descendants*, Worcester, Mass: K Higgins, 1924.

66. Robert Charles Anderson, *The Great Migration Begins: immigrants to New England 1620-1633,* New England Historic Genealogical Society, Boston, 1995, Three volumes.

67. Glaspell, Susan, *The Road To The Temple*, *A biography of George Cram Cook,* New York, 1927. Reissued 1941 and 2005.

68. Lincoln, *History of the Town of Hingham, Massachusetts,* Town of Hingham, 1893.

69. Members of the Trumbull County Chapter of the Ohio Genealogical Society, *Trumbull County Ohio Cemetery Inscriptions 1800-1930* (Copied by Mrs. Winnagle in 1927, and by Tom Kachur and Mr & Mrs Arthur LIst in 1979.)

70. Truro, Mass Church Records, published in The Mayflower Descendant, Vol. IX: 53-58, 74-77, 175-178, 242-246; Vol x: 41-43, 149-152, 238 -241; XI: 19 - 21.

71. *Genealogy of the Whittlesey-Whittelsey Family*, by Charles Barney Whittelsey, 1941, published by Whittlesey House, a Division of McGraw-Hill

72. Cook, Ira. "Reminiscences." *The Annals of Iowa* (1900), 522-530.
Available at: http://ir.uiowa.edu/annals-of-iowa/vol4/iss7/6.

73. Cook, Ira. "Government Surveying in Early Iowa." *The Annals of Iowa* (1897), 603-613.
Available at: http://ir.uiowa.edu/annals-of-iowa/vol2/iss8/3.

83. The Berg Collection, New York Public Library Research Division, The papers of George Cram Cook (1873 - 1924).